"An impressive account of how 'dialogue therapy' helps couples achieve new intimacy. . . . Young-Eisendrath sees the process as a transformation from disillusionment into trust . . . Scholarly and thoughtful yet totally accessible and quite practical."

—Kirkus Reviews

"A guide to help spouses from the he-said-she-said breakdowns, and along the way to discover a new level of intimacy."

—Frazier Moore, AP

"A marvelous book. A creative, dynamic mind has clarified the complexity of intimate partnership."

—Harville Hendrix, author of *Getting the Love You Want* and *Keeping the Love You Find*

"A stunning complement to Deborah Tannen's *You Just Don't Understand* because it helps us to see in our own psyches the 'dream lovers' that all too often turn love relations into a battleground."

—Peggy Reeves Sandy, author of *Female Power and Male Dominance*

"Fosters profound relationships between men and women as equals, enabling men and women to transcend the gender roles assigned by society. Provocative and enriching!"

—June Singer, Ph.D., author of *Boundaries of the Soul*

"An extraordinary and far-reaching work . . . that provides a template of revolutionary change in male-female relationships."

—David Rosen, M.D.

"For everyone who struggles with a relationship—and who does not?—this is a book of wise counsel."

—Murray Stein, Ph.D., author of *In Midlife: A Jungian Perspective*

"Polly Young-Eisendrath's ideas are impressive for their clarity and wisdom."

—Daniel Gottlieb, Ph.D., host of National Public Radio's *Voices in the Family*

"In accessible language, she demonstrates that culture, not biology, promotes gender-biased stereotypes that, along with shattered dreams, often prevent couples from establishing true intimacy."

—*Publishers Weekly*

"This book is absolutely required reading."

—Andrew Samuels, author of *The Political Psyche*

you're not what I expected

learning to love the opposite sex

Polly Young-Eisendrath, Ph.D.

A TOUCHSTONE BOOK
Published by Simon & Schuster
New York London Toronto
Sydney Tokyo Singapore

TOUCHSTONE
Rockefeller Center
1230 Avenue of the Americas
New York, New York 10020

First Touchstone Edition 1994
Published by arrangement with William Morrow & Company, Inc.

TOUCHSTONE and colophon are registered trademarks
of Simon & Schuster Inc.

Manufactured in the United States of America

1 3 5 7 9 10 8 6 4 2

Library of Congress Cataloging-in-Publication Data

Young-Eisendrath, Polly, date.
You're not what I expected: learning to love the opposite sex/
Polly Young-Eisendrath.—1st Touchstone ed.
p. cm.
"A Touchstone book."
Includes bibliographical references and index.
1.Intimacy (Psychology) 2. Man—woman relationships.
3. Marital psychotherapy. I. Title.
[BF575.I5Y68 1994]
158'.2—dc20 93-44772 CIP
ISBN 0-671-89119-7

For those individuals and couples who have revealed themselves to me in psychotherapy. I have learned a great deal from you, and am very grateful.

table of contents

This book is about a radical new topic: intimacy between the sexes. Radical? New? Hasn't it been overworked in all forms of media? Therapists and other professionals constantly offer "cures" for the disappointments of heterosexuality, while they admit that the research on marital happiness doesn't look promising. You've probably read the statistics showing that marriage is detrimental to women. Certainly you've heard about men's avoidance and fear of commitment.

But consider the possibility that heterosexual intimacy has never before been tried. Only in the last two decades have married people sought intimacy. Previously they viewed marriage as a contract and the relationship mostly as a form of business. If it was enjoyable, that was lucky, but generally it was not expected to be. Think of your parents' marriage. Were they concerned about their "relationship"? Did they feel they were "best friends"? Probably not. My parents found friendships among their acquaintances, not as part of their marriage, and most other parents I knew did the same.

Long-term intimate friendship is based on equality, and equality between the sexes is only now barely imaginable. Intimacy is rooted in trust, shared interest, and conversational exchange. Dialogue, as an exchange of points of view, is for the first time in history possible between women and men. Until just recently, women could not be "speakers." Without a culture of their own, often without knowing the formal language in which to write and read, without history and records of their experiences, women could not speak for themselves. They could only be spoken for (as in the marriage ceremony, when a father "gives away" his daughter to her husband) or borrow words and concepts from men. In a sense, we can see now that men were often speaking for all of us in a voice or viewpoint that was considered to be universal, but actually was not.

Over the past twenty years things have changed and women have gone on record. Feminist scholars have been laboring to rescue the contributions of women from the past to literature, the arts, and science. Contemporary women writers, speakers, and artists have been expressing their concerns and perspectives on everything from child abuse to the philosophy of science. Women are now contributors in all the major professions, increasingly speaking in their own voices, from their hearts. Women have accounts from other women of how things are. All of this has led to this moment when both sexes have viewpoints and the possibility to listen to and understand each other.

Preparing to write this book and wanting to know about *dialogue* as a method of learning and development (originating with the Greek philosophers and moving through the centuries into the present), I searched the human sciences for models. Philosophy, theology, pedagogy, psychology, sociology, and the history of mind. I found models of dialogue between men, between man and God, between man and nature, between the soul and the body, between the heart and the mind, but not between a man and a woman. Obviously there had been no need for such a model—until now. If women weren't legitimate speakers, men didn't have to think about how to learn from them or have exchanges of viewpoints.

I believe we have unintentionally arrived at a turning point in history, chiefly through two means—a massive planetary crisis and the recent wave of feminism. At the brink of an emergency of overpopulation and depletion of resources, we members of the human species need new stories and a new way of life. Many, if not most, of the old stories involve conquest, mastery, and dominion over others, the earth, ourselves. The old stories get us into trouble now. We're looking for new ones. Sometimes I play with the analogy between the search for extraterrestrial intelligence and the search for heterosexual intimacy. Stories about the former carry us past the barriers of gravity or time and space, and stories about the latter carry us past the barriers of trust, envy, and power between the sexes.

The stories I tell in this book, related to me by innumerable couples, weave a new narrative of *limitation, cooperation*, and *equality of influence*. If our planetary crisis is forcing an end to the old stories of dominance-submission, as I believe it is, then the search for heterosexual intimacy is providing a means to a new adaptation. Knowing something about the ingenuity of human adaptation, I believe we are unintentionally protecting our survival through this new broad search for intimacy between the sexes. Sneaking up on the most entrenched sexists among us is the necessity to convert the desire for intimacy and companionship with a mate into a respect for equality and shared power.

American psychiatrist Harry Stack Sullivan was the first theorist to offer a clear definition of intimacy. He defined it as a special kind of relationship based on reciprocity, trust, and equality. After working with psychiatrically disturbed adolescents for much of his career, Sullivan concluded that many people are unprepared for intimacy because they have never experienced trust based on reciprocity. Trust based on reciprocity is found first and foremost in the love for an equal. It cannot happen between parent and child; they are not equals. This kind of trust comes from loving another as much as oneself, not more and not less. If we are lucky, we first encounter intimacy in our early peer relationships, with our chums. We learn about ourselves through a balanced give-and-take, spontaneously discovering the worth of equality.

Although this book is grounded in everyday matters such as fighting, sex, and parenting as part of an intimate relationship, it has a much broader scope and meaning. This book is about the possibilities of and barriers to sexual equality, experienced by men and women who want more intimate and pleasurable contact with each other. In my view, heterosexual intimacy rests on sexual equality on the personal and public levels. Personally it requires a couple to respond to the inequity in power, status, and income that exists now between the sexes. Male privilege is a barrier to intimacy. Female silence is a barrier to intimacy. Equality in a heterosexual friendship or marriage is not a fifty-fifty split of tasks and income (the onerous chit list of what each partner owes), but the rhythm of equal influence in conversation through dialogue. This is a rhythm of give-and-take that requires speaking one's mind and understanding another's. Dialogue, as a particular form of conversation, is a practice of the rhythm of equal influence. As we will see, dialogue leads a couple into an ongoing adult form of dependence on each other—something I have dubbed "mature dependence," using a term from psychoanalyst W. Ronald Fairbairn.

On a public level too the mutual alignment of women and men on the themes of intimacy (such as trust, reciprocity, equal voices) leads to new awareness and action in favor of sexual equality. Especially in the area of sexual pleasure and desire, heterosexual couples stand to gain much through political and social actions that protect women against a tyranny of insult and assault. Men's respect for female sexuality leads to an awakening of desire in both.

I believe that the search for heterosexual intimacy is an outgrowth of contemporary feminism, a hopeful one in contrast to disappointingly slow and small changes in social and political institutions. My feminism led me to appreciate trust based on reciprocity between the sexes. Here is my own definition of feminism as I have given it in many public lectures and publications:

> . . . a discipline of thought and action that aims to enhance mutuality and trust among all people; to reveal the meanings of gender differences, especially as these might interfere with reciprocity and trust . . . and to oppose all models and methods

> of dominance-submission for relationships among people. What feminism has revealed, in its many forms from theology to literary criticism to psychology and philosophy, is that the silencing and trivializing of women and their ideas affect all of us all of the time in the way that we expect the world and ourselves to be.

Intimacy depends on equality. Equality between the sexes is not possible until women enter the culture as fully privileged speakers, something that is only now beginning to be accomplished.

Feminism has made us all conscious of the meanings of gender, and this new consciousness has awakened men as well as women. We have all been altered by ceasing to speak in generalizations about "mankind" that now so clearly seem to be distortions of people of both sexes. We see the effects of gender stereotypes as inhibiting and limiting for everyone, not just women. The invulnerable man who fears dependence is severely limited in his relationships. The nurturant woman who thinks of others' needs as primary is sadly limited in her decision-making and personal authority. The stories we have told ourselves about how men and women "should" be and behave are changing every day. In part they are changing because women and men want intimacy and friendship in their relationships. Marriage is no longer merely a social contract. Suddenly it is a commitment to a relationship.

locating myself

Before I go further in tracing the implications of the search for heterosexual intimacy, let me locate myself within it. Because of the stereotypes and expectations about female people, it's hard for me to know what to list first so that you won't immediately say "Aha, she's *this* kind of woman and so this book must be about *that*." It's true that I am a woman, mother, psychologist, feminist, author, and partner in a blended family (a family that blends children from earlier marriages) with a man, father, social worker, lecturer, and associate in business. It's true that my husband and

I have many interests in common, not the least of which is our practice of couple psychotherapy. It's also true that I am dedicated to "family" in whatever form it occurs for anyone—and also to my children and stepchildren, my garden, and my house. There's much more that would introduce me, but I want to focus on one thing especially that characterizes me to myself. I am earnestly, perhaps overearnestly, dedicated to intimate partnerships between people. The two-person relationship, particularly between equals (people of equal influence), is the place where I find the sacred or transcendent in human life. This kind of relationship occurs in friendship, intimate partnership, and psychotherapy. Speaking face-to-face and eye-to-eye with a partner gives anyone the possibility of *mirroring transformations*, my term for the reflections offered and the boundaries clarified of the self in intimate relationship. When an equal and intimate partner offers a view, a criticism, or a compliment, the gesture carries heartfelt (from heart to heart) meaning that helps us transcend the limits of ourselves. Over time these mirroring gestures are invitations to growth and change. We change because we value the mirroring partner as much as the self. I believe this is what Harry Stack Sullivan discovered in the intimacy of peers that seemed so worthwhile and delicious.

I am an advocate of mirroring transformations through intimate relationships. I can also be dubious about *heterosexual* intimacy—which is where this book begins. The irony of the title of the first chapter, "Doing What's Natural," is apparent every time I sit with couples in therapy or on social occasions. Because of the biases of our male-dominated society and the history of heterosexuality itself, we heterosexual people tend to believe that our intimacy is "natural," something like the birds and bees. Nothing could be further from the truth. Not only has intimacy between the sexes just recently become possible, but also it is hampered on every side by envy, power, and gender differences that are in fact very difficult to unearth and claim. Until now heterosexuality has also been clouded by ideals of romance and romantic love that are confusing for couples because these ideals don't work in a long-term relationship. Instead of evolving "just naturally" from the "right" relationship (as many people believe it does and should), intimacy is as unnatural between the sexes as it is between any two groups of people who have been cast as antagonists and opponents of each other over millennia. Our stories about men and women, hence our expectations for their relationships, are based on dominance-submission and power struggle, not on trust and reciprocity. This is true especially in stories about romance in which the woman is powerful or important only because she is sought by a handsome, powerful, or important man. The romance ends "happily ever after" when marriage or commitment begins. At the beginning of the commitment, the woman loses all her legitimate power and importance. She cannot be the hero; she can only be the hag. In the old stories, the married man can still conquer new frontiers, even other women, and stay within the story. The married woman loses her power at the end of the courtship.

This book is about new stories of the adventure of heterosexual trust. It's also about the connection between equality and development through relationship. Working through the differences, conflicts, and stereotypes we bring into relationships with the opposite sex can lead to mirroring transformations of the self. The only method, in my view, that can make this process work is dialogue.

Although dialogue may sound boring or "unsexy" to some, it is the core of mutual respect and empathy. Heterosexual trust is built on a recognition and acceptance of differences between the sexes.

gender and difference

I am a Jungian psychoanalyst and a psychologist who studies human development by doing psychotherapy and research. These avenues of learning and knowledge have led me to my own, perhaps unique understanding of gender. In my view, *gender* is the meaning, role, power, and privilege assigned to each sex by society. Gender is made of *stories* into which each of us is born, stories about how female and male people should be and become. In this period of time, we mostly tell biological stories to justify the differences we expect to see between the sexes, stories about hormones and brain chemistry, for instance. In other periods, people told a theological story about God's limiting men and women in clear, predetermined ways. (Some people still tell this story.) All human communities are divided into two exclusive groups (clubs that we are made to join). Every infant is assigned at birth—or even before, through modern technology—to one of these groups. If the body of the infant is anomalous, the body is changed surgically so that the infant can be assigned as quickly as possible. The *sex* of an infant is the structure (and function) of the body, which is "read" by elders in order to make a gender assignment. Gender limits everyone to particular expectations. In our society, men are expected to be stronger and more intelligent than women, and women are expected to be more emotionally expressive and empathic than men. These limitations differ from society to society. The qualities that are assigned to either sex depend on the environment and the tasks that need to be accomplished for survival and development in that society.

All of what I describe above happens "unconsciously" in the sense that no one "decides" or even becomes aware of the implications of gender. Most people believe that gender is *reality* based on sexual differences. In North American societies, for example, many people would argue that women are better at expressing their feelings and caring for others because they are "biologically programmed" to pay attention to infants since they are the childbearers. In other societies, for example the French, women may be assumed to be more narcissistic and envious than men because they are "naturally" in competition with other women to "possess" a man. Biological explanations are usually given for gender differences in the contemporary world, although these differences vary considerably between cultures.

In the past decade in the United States, many studies have claimed to have "discovered" differences in the hormonal or brain chemistry, or brain structure, of the two sexes that "explain" gender differences. For example, the fact that the connecting fiber between the cerebral hemispheres (the corpus callosum) of the female brain is thicker than that of the male brain is often used to explain the belief that women can synthesize more interpersonal information and hence be more attentive in their relations with others. Although some prominent researchers, like psychologist John Money, long ago concluded that the major part of gender identity is "left by nature" to be accomplished by culture after birth, some scientists are looking to reduce explanations of gender to sex differences in biology.

To be frank, I do not believe that gender or culture is the "product" of biology, any more than I believe that expectations about racial differences refer to biological constraints. Rather I believe that culture has the upper hand in shaping explanations. As psychologist Jerome Bruner says, "To invoke biological devils . . . is to dodge responsibility for what we ourselves have created." Although we are all constrained by our biology and cannot transcend the bodies in which we live, the meanings we create are more the product of experience than biology. This is clear to anyone who reads the history of mind and is exposed to the vastly different explanations for human thought and behavior that have evolved in different cultures over time.

In psychological and popular accounts of gender differences, some people rely heavily on the idea that the two genders are fulfilling two different destinies: Men are more autonomous, independent, and objective while women are more related, dependent, and subjective. My friends and colleagues, psychologists Rachel Hare-Mustin and Jeanne Marecek, call this an "exaggeration" premise about gender differences. It is a premise that because of either biology or human practice (for example, having a female caregiver in the early years), the two sexes are *vastly different* in their assumptions and experiences. Supposedly, they speak different languages. With this premise one can believe that men and women have inherent difficulties with trust because they can barely translate back and forth across the chasm of their differences. Psychiatrist Carl Jung also believed this. He thought that men were biologically and universally the natural "culture makers"—more objective, better leaders, more rational, and more independent. He believed that women were biologically and universally the "relaters," who were better at caring for others, knowing their feelings and emotions, and valuing relationships. Psychiatrist Sigmund Freud believed that women were "inferior men," missing certain aspects of intelligence and morality endowed in the male biological makeup. By contrast, Jung believed that women and men were designed to "specialize" in different but equally valuable contributions. Jung also believed in the possibility of all of us capturing the "other side" of our potential as we encounter our own unconscious in the second half of adult life.

I do not believe in Jung's premise of natural capacities of gender, but I find much that is valuable in his concept of *the opposite within*. This is the term Jung used to name the characteristics, ideals, and fears that each of us connects with the opposite sex. Gradually, in the second half of life, a woman can claim and express what she previously thought was masculine, the property of men. A man can claim and express what he thought was feminine. Jung believed this was a natural, biological progression from an original limited identity with one's own sex to an eventual expanded identity with characteristics from both sexes. In later life, then, women would become more aggressive and authoritative, and men would become more passive and nurturant. I believe that both our initial gender identity and any later development of opposite characteristics are sustained through relationships. These relationships, intimate and otherwise, provide the stories about gender that we may accept or reject. Nurturance, aggression, empathy, and independence are qualities that shift by culture, family, and immediate situation.

In my view, our long-term intimate relationships with the opposite sex provide the *opportunity*, but not the necessity, of developing the characteristics previously thought to belong to the other sex. Intimate partners often refuse to be labeled and characterized in ways that we desperately want to label them. This desperation speaks of our desire to see aspects of ourselves as "opposite" to us, as belonging to the opposite sex. The possibility of broadening, mixing, making more fluid the identity with a particular gender is not guaranteed through the fact of aging, however. It is a developmental accomplishment of the highest order to become aware of and alert to—to integrate—the opposite within while remaining comfortably identified with one's embodied sexuality.

Although I don't believe in fixed characteristics that are male or female, I also don't believe that the sexes are equally capable of the same things. The belief in the sameness of the sexes is a sort of "elimination" premise, as named by Rachel Hare-Mustin and Jeanne Marecek. This claim dismisses or eliminates the power, status, and biological differences that do exist between the sexes.

I believe that we are all powerfully influenced by the division of the human community into two exclusive groups, and by the meaning, role, power, and privilege that are assigned to each group. Not until six or seven years of age do children fully grasp the *exclusive* nature of gender. Although children as young as two years old can name some of the things associated with being a boy or girl, it is only at the beginning of the school years that they come to see that they will *never* (not if they change names, hairstyles, or clothes) be allowed to do what the others do. Girls will never be free to roam the streets and boys will never have babies. This division creates envy of the other gender.

The recognition of the immutability of one's gender sends all of us to our same-sex friends to find out what it's all about. This is where gender is most powerfully shaped, in my opinion: among same-sex peers in childhood and adolescence. From our friends (and the media) we find out about self and Other. Just as each of us comes to identify the self with its assigned meaning, role, power, and privilege, we also come to organize an "Other" within, our subjective experience of an opposite who constrains or inhibits the self. Here is where I find Jung's theory of gender to be helpful. He believes that this opposite, this Other, is crucial to our development in adulthood. In order to know ourselves, our own potentials and fears, we have to claim the Other and integrate it into the self. For each of us, this Other consists of what we hold to be the opposite of the self, parts of our personalities and our experiences that we consciously or unconsciously exclude from ourselves and label as opposite, different, not-me.

The division of the human community results in splits both in the world of interaction with other people and in individual psychological life. When we are with others of the opposite sex, each of us imagines, idealizes, envies, and fears them as outsiders. Within ourselves, each of us has images and beliefs connected to wishes, ideals, and fears that we associate with "them" but that belong to ourselves. Our internal Others, our *dream lovers*, are imagined to be members of the opposite sex, but are aspects of ourselves that we reject because somehow they don't fit the story of what we're supposed to be. Our fantasies of dream lovers are reinforced by peers and the media with collective images of the opposite sex. Many advertising media work specifically to manipulate people by playing with unconscious images, feeding us fantasies and images of ourselves and the opposite sex to promote fashions or products that are supposed to make us sexy and appealing. Complicating the picture further are stereotypes of gender promoted by society. Stereotypes and dream lovers intermingle when we are imagining and fearing the opposite sex. Stereotypes are "data" used to reinforce our subjective impressions, and dream lovers are "gut feelings" that reinforce stereotypes.

Trying to establish an intimate friendship with a person of the other sex requires reclaiming stereotypes and dream lovers back into the self. If we want to understand—and not silence or inhibit—another person in order to befriend that person, we have to allow that person's claims and statements to overtake our prejudices. This is a momentous challenge for heterosexual couples, as we will see.

If the challenge is met, a woman and a man in intimate exchange will come to know themselves through mirroring transformations. They will come to know not only what has been recognized as self all along, but also other personalities within—other voices that intimidate, desire, and inspire in ways that had been imagined to belong to the opposite sex. When a couple can accomplish this kind of transformation together over years, they discover a relationship that is infinitely fascinating.

difficulty at the beginning

Not only do heterosexual couples have difficulty in committing themselves after the romance has faded, but we all have difficulty in pulling apart and understanding the levels at which we entertain the notion of "difference" about "the opposite sex." It is this notion of difference as Other that interferes in a unique way with trust between the sexes.

This book focuses exclusively on heterosexual intimacy, although I also see same-sex couples in psychotherapy. I have chosen to treat heterosexuality exclusively here because of its mystified and suppressed difficulties. Differences of power and privilege between the sexes make heterosexuality an especially difficult place to trust another. The division of the human community and the human psyche into self and Other adds permutations to the problems of power. Mistakes and limitations of understanding are inevitable, the absolute ground of male-female relationships. Dialogue and mirroring transformations are not cures, but methods for proceeding if two people want to form an intimate relationship that continues to be satisfying over time.

Another difficulty at the beginning is writing about these topics before I've begun my story. I hope that I have cast a large net in which to put the issue of heterosexual intimacy. This is not a self-help or a how-to book (as you've probably guessed). Nor is it merely a theory of heterosexual intimacy. Rather this is an account of a method—dialogue—used to pull apart the levels and strands of confusion between the sexes.

In giving my account I will reveal aspects of my own search for heterosexual intimacy and of my experience as a psychoanalyst, psychotherapist, and couple therapist. I will pull out all the stops in telling you *everything* that I have learned, with lots of examples, so that you can get the big picture. Whether you are a woman or a man, I hope you will find yourself in this book. I hope also that you will find a path revealed that will enhance your mirroring transformations through intimacy.

chapter 1

doing what's natural

When I was a little girl playing house with my cousins, I wanted to play the Mommy but I didn't want a husband. I remember my mother drawing me aside once and anxiously explaining, "It's not nice to pretend to have children without having a husband." My small being responded to the fear in her voice by taking note of what she said ("not nice"), but my knowledge of the body and the world was not developed enough to know what she meant. This was probably my first encounter with the strange gender. I must have been four years old.

By *strange gender* I mean the way we imagine the opposite sex. When I was four I had only a vague sense about boys and men: They smelled worse than girls and women, they often caused trouble and were loud—and my father, as a major contributor to my strange gender, brought a great change of mood to our house when he returned at night. Mostly it was negative. Sometimes it was positive. It was always a *big* change in the emotional weather. I preferred the calm and breezy environment my mother and I maintained. In my four-year-old mind, I had created masculinity as "rough, uncomfortable, to be avoided." This category was my own and yet I assumed that it came from boys and my father because they evoked those uncomfortable feelings in me. All of this was entirely unconscious and unknown to me at the time, until that fateful moment when my mother flagged me down to say that my feelings were "not nice." After that, I became somewhat conscious that I had not-nice feelings about husbands, fathers, boys.

Strange gender acquires a sharper focus in childhood when we realize that the two sexes are exclusive clubs and we can belong to only one. Forever we must look in at members of the other club as outsiders. We can never join them. With this realization, the strange gender begins to transform into "dream lovers": the specific images of those Others we fear and desire because we imagine they are *different* from us. (I capitalize Other to indicate a subjective image rather than another person.) They may be angels or demons, seductive or celibate, but they have enormous power because of their imagined difference. As adults, we have a store of dream lovers and project one or several onto people of the opposite sex for a variety of reasons—to defend ourselves, to fall in love, to blame another. No matter what our sexual preference is, these dream lovers prowl through our nights and catch us unawares during the day. They are evoked by others of the opposite sex around us, but they carry no real knowledge about those others.

When I was four, I did not understand much about boys or men. Although I knew a number of boys in the neighborhood and my father took me for cherished outings on Saturday mornings, I had no clear sense of what maleness was about. Like most people who grew up in the 1950s and 1960s, I had a father who was away from home most of the time. (And so I really did not understand what role he had in the family.) All of the authorities in charge of my life were women. Almost all of my friends and all but one of my closest cousins were female. I had no brothers or sisters. We lived in the countryside and my world encompassed only my next-door cousins and the neighbors on our street. I recall vividly my putting everyone, all people, into one category, "person like me." Even though I had seen my male cousin's penis, it made no impression on me. Just another body part, I thought. I had no category such as "opposite of me."

Most kids at four do not understand gender. They can cite what seem to be *differences* between girls and boys (boys have penises; girls wear dresses), but they do not yet understand the "big secret" that will give such power to the strange gender. The secret is that we cannot change into our opposite. With the beginning of elementary school and the mental maturity of five or six years of age, a child will be able to get it. I will be a *girl forever*. You will be a *boy forever*. No matter what clothes we wear and no matter how we cut our hair or how fast we run or what toys we play with, we are stuck in a box, a category.

Many children rebel against this notion, finding it inherently irrational and unjust. Children are often bolder in their protests ("What do you *mean* I can't have a baby? Why not? You did it, Mommy!" or "Why *can't* I go fishing with the boys? My brother goes all the time!") than we adults will ever be. Adults appear polite and contained about all of this envy and hatred. Unfairness? Injustice? We appear to have consciously accepted our lot, but unconsciously it's a different story.

The strange gender in each of us eventually emerges as particular dream lovers that fill us with emotion, often outside of our awareness. By the time we are adults, our dream lovers are powerful aspects of our personalities. We are "driven" by them as we project them onto the opposite sex. This is unavoidable and it makes heterosexual intimacy a hard-to-reach goal. No wonder we feel "different" from opposite-sex friends and less comfortable with them than with same-sex friends. Dream lovers and their cultural counterparts, stereotypes, do not usually disrupt same-sex relating and may even enhance our friendships as we indulge in stories about the Others. In same-sex peer groups, girls and women feel a bond among themselves when they can launch an aggressive attack against those "stupid men!" Similarly boys and men share stories of conquest and sometimes detailed accounts of female body parts to enhance their feelings of dominance. These are dream lover descriptions that are based on fears and fantasies, not on actual relationships with the other sex.

This book is about the difficulty of heterosexual intimacy. Our strange gender—in the form of dream lovers and stereotypes—can interfere with trust of the opposite sex. At the same time, relating to the opposite sex can bring us face-to-face with our own Otherness. Confronting the Others in ourselves and learning to distinguish them from actual others is a task of mature development. Not only fears and fantasies, but also ideals and admiration are the stuff of dream lovers. As we reclaim both our own aggression and our own ideals, we become fuller individuals with expanded identities—often including characteristics that we previously thought to be beyond us. Encountering our dream lovers opens us to truths about ourselves and to empathy with the others.

My views about love relationships certainly extend to gay male and lesbian partnerships, but I will be directing my ideas here only to relationships with the opposite sex, intimate and otherwise. The intricacies of strange gender, projection of dream lovers, and power differences between the sexes are so difficult in themselves that I dare not add more complexity to my topic. Same-sex love relationships can be understood along some of the lines I will follow here, but there are also many differences.

I question the widespread belief that heterosexual couples who are seeking intimate love are "doing what's natural." *Natural* implies instinct or preprogramming. I don't find either of these playing any role in providing a basis for trust between women and men. Intimacy is the product of trust, and trust does not come naturally between people of unequal power, people who are labeled as opposite by the culture in which they live. Intimacy between the sexes is an achievement of hard work and understanding another from that person's point of view, while maintaining one's own. Ultimately this means accepting the other person fully with his or her flaws and doing the same for yourself. In my experience this is "unnatural" between men and women.

Back to my childhood for a moment. Even after I recognized that people were sorted into two clubs in which the membership is exclusive, I thought things would be fair. Most children believe they will be. When I heard about menstruation, for instance, I thought surely the boys have the same sort of thing. I asked other girls about this (I was nine or ten) and they said, "Yes, of course." I felt reassured for a while, knowing that although I had to "keep a secret from the boys" about exactly what happened to girls, they also were keeping secret from us what their form of bleeding was. By the age of twelve the truth of female menstruation was clear to me, but I continued to believe that people's opportunities and freedoms must be equal, regardless of gender. Some children learn earlier than I did that things are going to be inherently unfair, unequal, unjust, and just plain *different* for the sexes in certain fundamental ways. Eventually we all learn. I learned in college.

What I confronted in my freshman year at college was that no matter how "smart" I tried to be, no matter how many honors I might achieve, no professor was going to credit *me* (a girl) with my own ideas in class, no male student was going to recognize my point of view (without seeing his version of it as "more to the point"), and my appearance was the only access to power I had. I figured this out in my first two weeks at college and it was a depressing blow. So I did what other fresh*men* women did—I went after the guys. I began to indulge some new aspects of my strange gender: fantasy, envy, desire. I "fell in love" (as I describe in the next chapter). Unbeknownst to me at the time, I fell in love with an ideal dream lover, but I saw him in the person of a handsome young man. This initial fall gave me a first opportunity to examine my dream lovers in detail, but it took me years to complete the process. It was many years later that I recognized this dream lover clearly as an aspect of myself.

romance and disillusionment

In order for heterosexual intimacy to succeed in adulthood, we eventually have to engage in an "unnatural" examination of ourselves and our dream lovers. Inequality between the sexes, the unconscious complexity of the strange gender, and the ongoing constraints of gender stereotypes give new meaning to "love."

In my view, the search for the right partner has little to do with having a good relationship. Our society is rife with "commitment phobia," especially in regard to marriage. Many people are searching for the "right" partner and are afraid to commit to the current one in case another might be more ideal (ideal in terms of matching an ideal dream lover). Romance is the method we use to find a partner. We call it falling in love. This search may eventually bind us to someone who represents something from our earliest family relationships that we want to match or avoid. Romance itself is a projection, a transference of an aspect of oneself to the would-be partner. It usually ends abruptly when commitment sets in.

The experience of being identified with another person shakes everyone to the foundation. Something as subtle as being called "a couple" or as clear as having a child or getting married will interrupt the romance and throw a couple into disillusionment. Disillusionment is experienced as grave disappointment in the partner or the relationship. Some people flee from a relationship at the first sign of disillusionment. Other people stay and live in a "cold war" atmosphere of unresolved resentments and hurts for many years. Still others are able to develop shared goals and common ground, but they may find that intimacy is always a distant prospect. A few couples are able to develop the trust and shared horizon of meaning of true partnership without going into psychotherapy. It's grace or good luck, but a few do seem to recognize the disillusionment as a stage in a process. On their own, they learn to reclaim dream lovers and stop blaming their partners. Most people, however, do not know that disillusionment is a necessary step in developing heterosexual intimacy. They just know that something is wrong with them, and so they may seek psychotherapy at this point.

As a feminist psychotherapist and a Jungian psychoanalyst, I have the privilege of looking deeply into the private lives of couples and working with them through disillusionment into partnership and intimacy. This process is a transformation of the partners as individuals and the couple as a unit. This book describes the transformation.

I see both individuals and couples in psychotherapy. About a third of my practice is made up of couples. In addition, as a partner in marriage, a parent and stepparent to teenagers and young adults, a public lecturer, and a woman, I know at first hand about the struggle for heterosexual trust and intimacy. The problems that couples bring to therapy are similar to what happens everywhere with couples, in my family and yours. Although some couples in therapy suffer from deep psychological distress, abuse in childhood, or serious betrayals in their relationships, many are simply exhausted by the repetitive fights or emotional wasteland of their everyday encounters. Coming to therapy speaks of their wisdom in getting help. I mention this because the four couples I follow in the book are couples in therapy. Although they are in therapy, their problems are no different from what I witness on social occasions or hear at the local shopping mall. These four couples represent all couples who are striving for greater intimacy. The only difference is that they will be successful in the transformation from disillusionment to partnership. You will witness their journeys. I tell their stories from my knowledge of many couples over fifteen years of doing this kind of therapy.

The stories you will encounter here are not portraits of specific individuals, but are composites drawn from many people who have seen me in therapy. I cannot divulge information about the couples I see, but I can express their truths in a veritable way. In the course of this book, these four couples will develop as they would in therapy. Their stories unfold as the book unfolds, and I invite you to identify with them as "real people" but not to look for them in my consulting room.

Together with my husband, Ed Epstein, I use a method of couple therapy that we originated and developed. We first called it "dyadic-dialogical therapy," but recently shortened that to "dialogue therapy." This method is presented in detail in a book that I published in 1984 called *Hags and Heroes: A Feminist Approach to Jungian Psychotherapy with Couples*. The method is designed to work intensively and quickly (six sessions, one per month over six months, and a seventh session six months later). My husband and I work as a dyadic team in emotionally intense encounters with couples. Each session is two hours long, during which the couple, facing each other, are directed into conversation while we, the therapists, sit slightly behind and out of the view of each partner. I sit behind the right shoulder of the woman, and my husband behind the left shoulder of the man. We are out of their fields of vision but fully attentive to what is going on. While the couple attempt to talk together, we act as "doubles" or "alter egos" and speak out of the feelings and meanings that are implied but not clarified in what is being said. I try to empathize with the felt predicament of the woman, and my husband with the man. This method is designed to teach and encourage dialogue.

Dialogue is a particular form of conversation that involves having and maintaining one's own point of view, while being able to understand another's. On the road from disillusionment to trust, partners need dialogue. They learn how to maintain separateness (of their own thoughts and feelings) and openness (really listening to another). In this way, both partners come to claim and understand their own strange gender, and to disclaim but tolerate the strange gender of the other. By disclaim, I mean refuse to identify with or be labeled by a partner's dream lovers. Increasingly, the two people gain a fundamental acceptance of their own subjective states. With this comes a new respect and curiosity about the partner. They feel confidence in being able to talk about their differences. They come to believe that they can really understand each other even though that understanding sometimes leads to disappointment—the knowledge of limitation in a partner or oneself, a limitation in the capacity to change or grow.

the couples

Each of the four couples you will meet represents a style of relating and a cultural context. Patty and Joe are in early adulthood, have working-class backgrounds, and see themselves as "nontraditional" because they both support Patty's developing a professional career while Joe doesn't want one. A midlife couple, Larry and Louise are struggling with the effects of social changes, the necessity of a dual income, and the promise of autonomy for women, as they move through their forties. Karen and Jonathon are "thirty somethings" and exemplify an urban, accomplished, and upwardly mobile type of feminist couple. By "feminist couple," I mean that they want to be equal as partners, to have roles that are not confined by gender categories, and they consider themselves to be feminists. Finally, Charles and Pamela are in their sixties and bring us a broad range of issues that face the traditional, patriarchal couple in a changing world.

In heterosexual couples over the last decade and a half, women have been asking for greater openness and more access to the inner lives of men. By and large, men have obliged. The irony is how angry and even depressed women are about what they have found. Looking into the hearts of men has produced despair in women. It seems that women had hoped to find the motives of women in the hearts of men. All four women in our couples are angry and disappointed in their partners.

Men feel insulted and alienated when their female partners disparage their ideas and activities. The common theme of the men in these four couples is indignation. Whether they admire and support their wives and lovers in striving for new possibilities, openly defy and deny women's rights and freedoms, or passively accept what their partners tell them, men feel depreciated in the modern couple.

There are also differences in these four couples. The younger couples have fantasies about heroism and possibilities, about dreams for the future and children growing up in a world in which the genders are equal and sex roles are flexible. They believe that erotic excitement should continue over the years, side by side with monogamy. The midlife couple in their forties are struggling with worries about death and depression. They feel limited by the hatred and fears that have developed between them. Their earliest ideals had to do with helping each other get started: he in his career and she in her role as mother. Eventually the women's movement affected them, and the husband dreamed that his wife would develop a satisfying career while she thought he would become a more active father. Now they see these possibilities as illusions and feel entrapped in the cultural and power differences between the sexes. Our oldest couple have fears about death and about declining sexuality. They are full of envy of each other. She envies his power, status, and privilege. He envies her lesser responsibilities and greater closeness to their adult children. Each believes the other has had a better, more meaningful life, and each has little empathy for the other's suffering.

patty and joe

A woman in her late twenties, Patty was strikingly beautiful with translucent skin, delicate Italian features, and wavy black hair pulled back to the nape of her neck. Chic and slender, Patty conveyed the intelligence of artifice and grace that some women seem innately to possess. All of this belied her working-class origin.

Patty stared down at her hands as she nervously addressed her husband, Joe, in the initial session of couple psychotherapy, saying, "You never want to improve, as far as I can see." Like many women I meet in couple therapy, Patty said she was "disappointed in Joe." Partly this was a result of comparing him to herself, in her view. Through her personal therapy and self-help groups, Patty had learned to speak from her feelings and to honor a particular way of responsibly handling her own desires and wishes. She believed that she could express herself and she wanted the same for Joe. Patty was adamant in saying she wanted Joe to tell her how he felt and to share with her his deepest secrets and desires. More significantly, Patty wanted Joe to improve his fathering of their two young children (a girl, five, and a boy, seven) and to make more male friends at church and in the community. (Joe had a group of "guys" he'd hung around with since high school, but Patty didn't approve of them.)

Appearing to be self-assured, Patty described her ideals for a trusting relationship. She wanted openness, sharing, no advice giving to each other—and a good amount of flexibility in their roles. Like many women now, Patty believed that her experience of development through therapy and education had provided her with a formula for emotional relating that would work with Joe, as it had with other friends.

What Patty does not understand is that her relationship with Joe is unique and experimental. She and Joe are "stuck together" in a way she is not stuck with her other friends. She and Joe are trying to do something that has never before been attempted in recorded history: They are trying to have an equal and intimate heterosexual relationship.

There are no models or maps in philosophy, theology, or psychology for heterosexual trust and intimacy. Sharing power and contractual agreements as well as feelings and inner life is a revolutionary agenda for the sexes. And yet somehow we believe that it should be "just natural" for women and men to come together eyeball-to-eyeball (typical female interactive style) or shoulder-to-shoulder (typical male style).

Like many of her contemporaries Patty believed that she and her husband were shamefully out of step because they could not "just share the simplest experiences." Patty gave me another signal in the first interview that alerted me to wishes that I often find in myself and other women. Patty was hoping that Joe would be the hero she wanted him to be, that he would benefit from the search for self-fulfillment she was making. Perhaps more significantly, she assumed that Joe had in him a greater potential for success than he could see. From her point of view, Joe's star could rise farther and faster if he could see the kind of potential he had to be a better friend, lover, worker, father, husband, human being.

As a psychoanalyst and a feminist, I can see how Patty is dreaming up what Joe could be. She is developing Joe in her fantasy and then exhausting herself in trying to convert him to the program. In this process, she is disclaiming the responsibility for her own dream lover. Love relationships provide the opportunity to confront and engage our fantasies and idealizations of the Others. Patty wants to become a lawyer even though she has just begun undergraduate college. She has many courses and examinations to master before she'll know whether her wishes are realistic. Developing Joe in her fantasies takes her mind off anxieties about her own achievements.

In response to Patty's rather long speech about what she wanted from therapy, Joe finally spoke up with his side of the story. "I don't like what's been happening to us either. I go all these places you want me to go, to these therapists and talks and church and all, but none of it ever makes you happy." He said Patty was "obsessed with self-improvement." He said that he did not mind watching the kids and cooking when Patty was out in the evening attending college courses or going to therapy (and I believed him). He was pleased with himself that he "believed in women's liberation and in Patty doing what she wanted with her life." What troubled Joe most was Patty's unhappiness and her criticisms of him. He angrily insisted on one thing: I will do things *my* way and not *yours*. Joe believed that Patty was trying to make him her puppet.

From Joe's point of view, he was offering everything he could to the relationship. He worked and supported the family (making more money than Patty) and he supplied the child care while Patty was out. He was not going to give up the freedom to decide on his own life course. He complained bitterly about the "bitching and moaning" that Patty did at home and how much she wanted to "dominate" his thoughts and feelings. He believed that Patty held nothing of his to be sacred. She criticized his friends, his religion, his way of caring for the kids, his salary, and his family of origin.

Like many men I see in therapy, Joe seemed to admire his wife and her search for meaning and purpose. If anything he seemed to want more credit and admiration from his young, attractive, and independent wife. He saw in Patty a certain ideal of intelligence and self-motivation that he disclaimed in himself. In some ways he seemed to want this ideal for himself, and yet he did not want it on "her" terms. (I put *her* in quotation marks here to indicate that it is Joe's dream lover, not Patty, who is causing the real trouble.) His vision of Patty as a strong, independent woman was a dilemma for him. How could he gain the strengths that he saw in this independent-minded woman and yet be true to himself while he had to support his family?

As a society we are currently in a peculiar situation regarding envy between the sexes. Many men envy the clear and competent identities and the emotional support and closeness that women have found in their searches for something better or more whole in their lives. Because many white men are unconscious of their power advantages, they fail to see that identity searches and liberation movements are pursued by the oppressed, not the powerful. The emotional rewards of oppression (if one can call them such) come in the form of greater solidarity with one's own kind and more access to the mundane tasks of everyday life: caring for the young, the sick, the disabled, and the very old. One comes to know the boundaries and domain of one's personal strengths. These are the rewards that may be denied to the more powerful.

Patty grew up in South Philadelphia as the fourth child in a family with eight children. Her father was a plumber and a drunk. He was full of temper and demands. His fits and rages were unpredictable, and Patty tried to stay out of his way because she found it impossible not to defy him when he faced her down. Repeatedly she was the target of his aggressions: Once he cut her face with a bottle and another time he dislocated her rib. At seventeen she moved out. She worked nights as an office assistant at a legal firm and finished high school on her own. When she graduated, her parents didn't attend the ceremony, and Patty still does not speak to them.

Patty exemplifies yet another difficult issue that affects many heterosexual couples. I call it the "hidden heroism" of female lives, and it can easily fuse with men's envy of women in a particular couple in which both partners implicitly or explicitly assume that the woman is a hero. Women surprise themselves with their achievements, friendships, and self-reliance, especially in midlife. Most of them sorely underestimate their own strengths and abilities coming out of adolescence. What they achieve by midlife is often welcomed with a wondrous feeling of gratitude.

Female people contend with bodies whose emotional and physical landscapes change and fluctuate with menstrual periods, pregnancies, births, infertility, and eventually menopause. These changes require a direct physical courage. Often women are unafraid of blood, guts, vomit, and bodily wastes because they have become familiar with them through the natural events of their own bodies—and through birth, child care, and nursing the ill and dying. Only in times of war or disaster do men regularly have direct contact with such unsavory aspects of embodiment unless they are in medicine or a related profession.

Women see the greater privileges and power afforded men and assume that these should or must connect to heroism or courage in men. We have all been shaped through the educational process to believe and expect men to possess quite naturally the intelligence, objectivity, and courage to run the world. Women tend to look (consciously or unconsciously) to their male partners to show this assumed heroism or intelligence in everyday life. In other words, women may expect men to be the heroes that they are themselves, or at least to equal what they have seen in their mothers, sisters, and friends. Men are often flattered by this expectation (although it may also baffle them) and they may try to meet it because everyone seeks admiration.

Patty met Joe at a South Philly bar and they became friends immediately. Joe was eight years her senior and seemed to her to be a strong, protective figure. Patty said she respected him before she loved him. Joe had initially helped Patty in every way. He bought her a car and taught her to drive. He helped pay for her apartment and finally convinced her to move in with him. When Patty was nineteen she began to live with Joe and at twenty she married him. Although Patty depended on Joe initially to find her way into the world, she quickly became independent and self-supporting. Gradually working her way into the position of administrative assistant to the vice president of a corporate legal firm, Patty earned a stable, increasing income through her years with Joe.

Joe's family was Yugoslavian and tended to look down on Italians like Patty. One of three sons, Joe was proud of his parents and his past. Joe had wanted to "make something of his life" and to succeed. At thirty-six Joe seemed disappointed in himself, although he voiced this in terms of how little respect he got from his wife.

The belief that men are innately or naturally more powerful than women carries a range of consequences for men. Some men, perhaps even most, simply assume this attitude and feel strengthened by it. Especially in adolescence, when athletic and other competitions prepare young men for eventual leadership, they may revel in the presumed opportunities ahead. In adulthood, many men move into positions of being "culture makers" and believe themselves fully capable of meeting their responsibilities. Other men—especially nontraditional (for example, feminist), gay, less educated, or minority men—are unable or unwilling to compete for success. They tend to be burdened by this belief. They may feel allied or similar to women and oppressed by our cultural standards. Their predicament is different from women's, however. Because they are members of the "powerful" gender club, and cannot escape it (even transvestism and so-called sex change operations do not permit actual escape from one's embodiment), men suffer in the male hierarchy *differently* than women suffer.

It is likely, we know from research on boys in childhood and adolescence, that as a boy or young man Joe had expectations that he would succeed (for example, achieve more than his father had) if he applied himself. Most junior high and high school males tend to overestimate their abilities and inflate their dreams of what they will become. They feel a great loss when they are unable to meet these goals. In midlife especially, many men endure a painful parting with the dreams of youth. Whether or not a man consciously identified with male dominance, he is inevitably shaped by the expectation that he should be heroic, successful, or uniquely powerful in some way.

Midlife men are often sadly disappointed in themselves and fear that they are a disappointment to everyone, especially to their wives, lovers, and children. They have not attained the special status, power, money, creativity, courage, or insight that they somehow assumed they were destined to have. (And they are recognizing this at about the same time their wives or partners, if the latter are also in midlife, are beginning to feel good about achievements.) This is a kind of grief over manhood that is, I believe, connected especially with the dreams of heroism and privilege openly promoted in men, who supposedly are free to pursue their own desires in life.

Joe slouched down throughout the first therapy session. His balding head formed an obvious contrast to Patty's vibrant, youthful manner and dress. Joe was a handsome, slight man with an olive complexion and gray-green eyes under thick black brows. His hair was sprinkled with gray, but still mostly black. Joe's pronunciation and manner exuded his working-class origin. He conveyed a feeling of pride about his past and about his work in a food-processing plant.

When Joe talked about his job, he sounded enthusiastic. His disappointment in himself seemed to stem from Patty's reflections of him. He complained about her criticisms and seemed angry and resentful that she "never shows me the respect I get at work." Joe tended to focus on the differences in education between them. He said that Patty might admire him more if he went to college as she was doing, but he knew that college was not for him.

Patty's belief in Joe's greater potential kept her from seeing his vulnerability and his fears. It also kept her from appreciating the resources Joe offered. Patty never openly acknowledged the financial and emotional support that Joe had provided over their years together. She simply said that she had done "plenty in exchange for anything he gave me." Patty envied Joe's greater earning power and what she perceived as "his freedom to come and go as he pleases." When Patty asked Joe to talk about his feelings and to tell her about his inner life, she refused to see how unadmired he felt or how incapable he believed himself to be in meeting the challenges that she had opened up.

strange gender and dream lovers

By the time we get to adulthood, we have developed and defended within ourselves a strong case of strange gender. Our strange gender, the way we imagine the opposite sex and all that goes with it, becomes emotionally powerful only after we know that we cannot escape our own gender. At this point, sometime around the beginning of the school years, fantasies, fears, and envy mix with the strange gender as we become more and more convinced that "they" are different, even "opposite" from us. As we begin to identify more fully with our same-sex peers, we share stories with them about the Others. Cultural stereotypes mix with these stories as we become media consumers. Eventually within each of us the strange gender becomes almost another gender category. By the time we reach puberty, each of us has both a conscious gender identity and a less conscious Otherness. Four gender categories are operative in male-female relating: male and male strange gender; female and female strange gender. The more removed we are from the opposite sex (for example, going to a same-sex school), the more exotic the Others become. Even without such distance, all of us are eventually swept up into beliefs and expectations that derive from our fantasies about the opposite sex.

Dream lovers are the specific meanings and images that are powerful and particular fantasies within each of us. They begin to develop prior to our understanding of gender and its exclusivity. By age five or six, when children master the idea of gender exclusivity, they have already spent a long time relating to parents, siblings, other caregivers, and friends. In the first two or three years of life we are relatively helpless, without language to assist us. During that time, our experiences are sorted into categories or meanings based on repeated interactions with caregivers, the physical environment, and emotional states (sad, angry, joyful, curious, afraid, and so on).

Dream lovers begin as emotion-based images. They develop from the emotional forces that shape our ability to love and trust even before they are associated in any way with the same or the opposite gender. In our years of greatest helplessness, parents and siblings or other caregivers engage us through care. Their voices, faces, ability (or inability) to be tender and available will mark us forever. *Emotional image traces* from early life collect around our needs and how they are met. These are the first building blocks of personality. They eventually become *psychological complexes* organized by core states of emotional arousal. A complex is a set of unconscious impulses that strongly influence our personal style, behavior, and beliefs. Every complex is grounded in a particular set of images and meanings marked by emotion. For example, most of us have a "great mother complex" that is known to us through comfort and ease from nurturance and sustenance connected with the sounds, smells, voice, and handling of a woman. Initially we did not know of "woman," but later, when we understood that category, we assigned the term and perceived Mama as woman. The early emotional image traces of a complex are not rational and fall outside of language. The image traces originated in actual experiences but those experiences were mostly nonverbal. They are hard to reach and understand later in life when they have infused our dream lovers with meanings that seem to "stem from the gut." They escape our ability to explain them. "I just *know* that you *hate* me because I feel it in my body" can be so convincing to the person who feels these emotions and yet so wrong about the partner. A "perception" like this is usually rooted in a negative, critical, aggressive dream lover whose image or meaning has been evoked by a gesture, manner, voice, or other stimulus coming from the partner.

As adults, our dream lovers can come between us and our best efforts to be fair with a spouse or friend of the opposite sex. It is not that dream lovers are specifically negative images of the opposite sex—not at all. Often they are idealized and inflated beliefs in the magical powers of the others. Dream lovers are simply "wrong" categories for understanding actual others because they are are based on our own experiences, sex, and gender. Dream lovers are spoken of and felt through the particular categories of oneself and not another. They are assumptions based on our own subjective states and not on the experiences of the other. It may turn out that aspects of one's own dream lover match very well with characteristics of one's partner or friend, but that is rare.

Dream lovers are reinforced by our same-sex friends in childhood, adolescence, and adulthood. When we get together with friends and talk about the others, to figure them out and bring them under control, we frequently use stereotypes of "us" and "them." Stereotypes are themselves products of dream lovers reinforced by culture and society. The cultural meanings of stereotypes (used to sort people into "in" and "out" groups according to dominance hierarchies) blend into images of dream lovers. Because dream lovers are based on the emotional image traces of early life they are "powerful" and so can be easily drafted into blame—ideas that "women are manipulative" or "men are aggressive."

Ordinary social conversations of adulthood are bathed in stereotypes about the sexes that are hard to oppose because they are used to gauge "normalcy." If you don't go along with them, you're not normal. When I am with male friends or colleagues, I frequently hear stereotypes about women (for example, women just "don't know how to get accurate directions" or "feminists have caused trouble for all of us") that I would like to challenge (and sometimes do). Frequently I back off because breaking up the conversational pattern at each stereotypical comment would seem weird and disruptive. When I am in an all-female group, I often hear stereotypes about men (for example, they're so "developmentally disabled" or "all they want to do is sit around and watch TV"). I try to challenge these on occasion, but hesitate because I don't want to be a social deviant. Stereotypes reinforce dream lovers and dream lovers feed stereotypes.

Dream lovers can be positive or negative figures. We have already met Patty's idealized Hero, whom she tries to find in Joe. Although Joe feels flattered by her, he does not find the qualities of Patty's Hero in himself. Joe, on the other hand, fears a critical Terrible Mother who wants to control and dominate his life—an example of a common dream lover in men. Joe's overly close and demanding mother was extremely watchful, especially of his manners and habits around the house. Although Joe accommodated to his mother's rather excessive cleanliness and prudishness in childhood, he was almost always afraid of displeasing her. Now he complains about Patty's comments as though she were his parent. Patty does not find this Terrible Mother in herself, but she may be tempted to identify with her when Patty is critical of herself.

Joe's Terrible Mother is related to a common image of an emotionally powerful negative woman, the witch. We find her throughout the history of male-dominated societies, in folktales, fantasy, and fiction of the stepmother, mother-in-law, and intrusive wife, and in everyday accounts of the "nagging bitch." We'll learn quite a lot about the Terrible Mother from the men in our couples.

Patty also has a Terrible Father dream lover who is connected with her experiences of physical abuse in childhood. Images of the Terrible Father are also legion. In myths and fairytales, he is well known as the devil, rapist, killer, demon male who intrudes on and captures women and children. Patty's experiences of traumatic abuse make her Terrible Father an especially malignant aspect of her personality. Because she suffered attacks so many times she has countless associations with smells, sights, feelings, and such that can reactivate her fear, dread, and rage.

Even without abuse or trauma in childhood, we are all haunted by negatively powerful images of Mother and Father. Without traumatic abuse, these images are related to the aggressive and enraged feelings that colored our experiences of our caregivers when our own needs went unmet during our early helpless dependence. All of us suffered periods (longer or shorter) when our needs were not met because the caregiver was distracted, unavailable, or providing for someone else. Actual childhood abuse produces a specific kind of malignant and overwhelming Terrible Parent complex that is destructive of basic trust for years to come. Ordinary failures in caregiving produce Terrible Mother and Father dream lovers that are less disruptive and overwhelming, but are alive in our psyches all the same.

Similarly, most of us have powerfully nurturant or positive dream lovers organized around emotional image traces of comfort and satisfaction—fulfillment. These contribute to idealized dream lovers such as the Hero or the Great Mother about which we will learn much more. These idealized dream lovers are filled with emotional meanings of completion and satisfaction that far surpass anything a real person might be able to do. They emanate from experiences of complete care and utter comfort in infancy—or from a magical belief in the power and goodness of our caregivers. "Once upon a time, there was a king and a queen" is the fairytale testimony to these figures.

projections: sending and receiving

A love relationship in adulthood is the ground for *projections* from our earliest attachment relationships. A couple carries all the tendencies of both partners to experience each other as powerful dream lovers. Projection is a defense mechanism that allows me to experience an unlikable, alien, or ideal aspect of myself as though it existed in someone else. Paradoxically, when I'm projecting a feeling or characteristic image, I will feel as though the other person (the target) has control of me and is "making me feel this way." This is the effect of putting a part of oneself—a feeling or image—into another. But wouldn't I *want* to acknowledge my own ideals or ideal aspects? A cartoon I saw recently answers this question well: A fairy godmother is waving her magic wand over a young girl who looks panicked and says "Hey, wait a minute, maybe I don't want the responsibility!" If I see my ideals in someone else, then I don't have the responsibility for them. Similarly, if I see my darker aspects as existing in someone else, I am free of responsibility—and I can even imagine myself as the victim of another's motives.

The *sender* of the projection believes that he or she can see and know another's inner state or deepest motives with or without the other's confirmation. Even confirmation by the other person does not exclude the possibility that a projection is occurring, because people will confirm that they fit others' scripts for them (as Joe might agree with Patty's accusations that he doesn't want to improve himself). In projection, the sender unconsciously wants to get rid of feared or idealized aspects of the self because they seem too overwhelming, more than one could be responsible for. The sender of the projection actually feels as though he or she were *under the control* of the other person. Joe believes he cannot enjoy himself at home because Patty "never stops criticizing." Joe believes his thoughts and feelings are under the control of Patty. Patty believes that Joe will undo her confidence and retreat from her because he appears at moments to be cold and demanding, like her Terrible Father dream lover. She experiences him as "breaking down" her confidence.

Whether the projected dream lover is feared or idealized, the recipient may *identify* with the projection and in some way *confirm* its meaning to the sender. Patty might actually yell at Joe just when he feels afraid of her—usually because he has provoked it by being uncooperative. This sets up a delusional belief system within the couple that is called *projective identification* by therapists. Joe believes that Patty controls his mind, and Patty agrees she *is* infuriated with him and wants to remake him. Usually these meanings are implied, not openly confirmed.

All of us have shameful, aggressive, and idealized dream lovers that are hard to claim because we would have to become either more responsible or more vulnerable. We prefer to see them in other people, the best candidates being those people with whom we feel "stuck." Projection is difficult to pinpoint (outside of therapy) because it happens unconsciously and is a reliving of the emotional image traces that reach back to earliest childhood.

If a partner identifies with a projection and then acts out the expected image or meaning, the couple becomes engaged in a fixed and harmful belief system. The partners are confused about who is causing the pain and lack of trust between them. The next couple, Larry and

Louise, is a poignant illustration of the delusional system of projective identification.

larry and louise

Larry was a youthful-looking forty-eight-year-old man dressed in corduroy trousers and a pastel button-down shirt. He was easy and confident in his manner in this initial therapy session, as he said to Louise, "I am here today because you asked me to come. I realize that you have problems that I cannot help you with and so I am here, hoping these good people can come to our aid." His thinning brown hair and wire-framed glasses, coupled with a slightly eccentric charm, gave me the impression that Larry was a professor or a social-activist lawyer. He was reasonable, intelligent, and warm. However, his statement of facts and mission (to help Louise) gave quite another impression, that he had come to preach to us.

Larry was convinced that he knew what was wrong with their relationship: It was Louise. She was unhappy and he suspected she was depressed, perhaps overwhelmed. Larry stated early on (in an official-sounding speech) that the two of them "had been through this therapy thing before" and that he did not "really believe that couple counseling amounts to much," but he wanted to help Louise. Larry told us a well-organized story about his distress with Louise. She was, in his view, "a fine mother and a person that I have always admired." Larry's story was not unlike Joe's. He felt overwhelmed by Louise's complaints and "grievances." He saw Louise as a negative, intrusive, and demanding influence in the family, complaining about others' pleasures and enjoyment. Larry's diagnosis was that Louise was stressed and unhappy in her job.

Although Larry looked directly at Louise throughout his presentation, she remained perched uncomfortably on the edge of her seat staring either at the floor or out the window. Now she peered directly into his eyes with a wincing look. There was an immediate and direct contrast between this apparently smooth and confident man with a professorial manner and his anxious, subdued wife whom he was analyzing. Louise, at forty-six, appeared to be the prototype of a middle-aged woman in a drably colored cotton shirt hanging out over navy-blue polyester trousers, practical walking shoes under them. She fingered her hair and her bifocals while Larry talked. Her face, untended with cosmetics, was stiff and rigid except for an occasional tear.

Louise looked back down at the floor and in a tearful voice said, "I think my kids hate me and I can understand why." She described herself as bitter and demanding. She was afraid that we would see Larry as such a contrast to her that we might think she was "crazy." Her demeanor shifted as she clued us in to Larry's aggressions. With a sudden liveliness, Louise attacked Larry for "being so nice here with the therapists" while he was such a "shit" at home. She described a recent incident in which Larry had slammed doors, thrown his car keys at the wall, and finally punched out a door, leaving a hole where his fist penetrated the wood. She was almost gleeful with the triumph of exposing Larry in this way. Otherwise she complained at being ignored by her sons and her husband and finished up pitifully bemoaning Larry's greater attraction to their pet dog than to her.

A dangerous conversational style that I frequently see in an initial therapy session is monologue. Monologue is a conversation in which both people seem to agree that only one person is right and has all the answers to the couple's problems. Usually it means that they are caught in projective identification, with one person blaming and the other one enacting the problem.

In this case, Louise is playing out the depressed Terrible Mother of Larry. Over the years of Larry's childhood, and especially in his adolescence, he was often alone with his complaining and depressed mother. As the oldest child (with two younger sisters), Larry felt intrinsically responsible for his mother's moods. In his adolescence she took him into her confidence and told him how very disappointing her sexual relationship with his father had been. Larry felt sorry and guilty about his mother, but he also felt proud that his successes comforted her.

Larry's mother told him that his accomplishments were her "only hope for the future" because she knew that his sisters could never match his brilliance.

This kind of guilt-inducing relationship with a child will produce a very powerful dream lover. Larry's emotional image traces of the Terrible Mother are filled with the enormously powerful responsibility that children feel toward their parents. All children feel intrinsically responsible for their parents' moods. Larry now believes that Louise is the Terrible Mother he has under his control and that he *must* fix her in order to feel good enough about himself.

Why does Louise so readily identify with Larry's insistent, depressed Terrible Mother? She has a demanding Terrible Father whom she internalized from feeling ambivalently loved by her seemingly powerful father who was a Methodist minister. Her father told Louise that if she did things "in the right way," then she would be rewarded by God. If she failed she would be punished. Louise learned how to please her judgmental father/God and did well in school and at church, usually managing to gather praise for her virtues. When Larry did not praise Louise now, nor seem impressed by her dedicated hard work at home, she was haunted by a critical and judgmental Terrible Father. She would turn this critical Father on herself and hate anything that fell below her standards: her body or her achievements. Together Larry and Louise submerged themselves into an unconscious swamp of projections and identifications so that it was not possible to clarify anything that could help the two of them move into dialogue. There was no psychic "space" between them when they engaged in their monologue.

Louise and Larry had been married for almost twenty years, and they recalled a blissful romance during the first three years when they had both been working and freely relating to each other without the burden of caring for children. Initially, Louise was a daughterly sort of companion for Larry.

Larry identified with Louise's early projection of a protective Great Father. He enjoyed Louise's dependent reliance on him for guidance and inspiration. Larry had admired his father, an important advertising executive who had amassed quite a fortune for himself and his family.

Larry's father was away from home a lot, and so Larry had "replaced" his father as his mother's companion, but Larry had not faulted his father for this.

Larry projected onto Louise his Maiden Lover, the retiring or shy daughter who needs fostering and bringing out. The fantasied Maiden Lover could be an "equal" to a man, a strong woman in her own right, if she had the right mentoring from a man. In exchange for the man's playing the Guide or Mentor, the woman onto whom this is projected should be obedient and admiring, even a little worshipful. The early projective identification between Larry and Louise prevented any real dialogue or differentiation in their first three years together.

After they had children, Louise found Larry to be a generally absent father who was competitive with the children. She could no longer idealize him, and the couple slipped into the second projective identification in which Louise was represented as the depressed Terrible Mother and Larry was the critical, punitive Terrible Father who clearly saw what a hopelessly failed (unlovable) creature Louise really was.

The beginning of disillusionment is experienced as feared, devaluing, and aggressive feelings about the partner or the relationship. This is the first opportunity for the individuals to encounter their strange gender. Most people have a hard time sorting out what is self from what is other, and only successful dialogue can help them develop a reflective attitude of self-awareness. Many midlife couples, lacking the capacity for dialogue, have lived for years in disillusionment, blaming each other for their unhappiness. Louise and Larry had been in disillusionment for sixteen years and the relationship seemed to have died.

In the initial couple session, it was hard to empathize with Louise because she made attacks on all of her family members and appeared to blame others for her own self-hatred. At the same time it was hard to commiserate with Larry because he held himself to be above the mess and seemed to judge everyone, even the therapists from whom he had sought help.

When I asked Louise what she would like to accomplish in our therapy, she said she wanted Larry to change. She wanted Larry "to be more of a man." She complained of feeling like Larry's mother around the house, especially because he frequently asked her where his clothes were and was irritated at her if something wasn't cleaned and pressed. Larry felt like a child with Louise because he projected the Terrible Mother and believed that Louise was somehow "in charge" when he walked through the door of the house. At the same time, Louise expected Larry to know all of the answers to bigger problems and was disappointed when he seemed vulnerable or confused. When he was critical of her, she turned on her self-hatred and blamed herself for all of the suffering in their family.

Louise and Larry, and Patty and Joe, share a common vulnerability in their relational patterns. They are ripe for stereotyping, with Patty and Louise as the nags or "bitches," and Joe and Larry as little boys, wimps, or "pansies." These stereotypes are built on socialized expectations of what a man or woman should or must be, and they are reinforced by dream lovers. Many of us eagerly latch onto stereotypes because they keep what is dreaded or idealized away from the self.

When women are attempting to trust men (in order to sustain dialogue that would permit intimacy), they have to learn to differentiate between dream lovers or stereotypes and their actual partners. They must come to see and know what is truly self and truly other. In some cases, this means claiming the strengths and resources in themselves (in Patty's case) and no longer just looking for them in men. In other cases, this means becoming responsible for the dreaded and alien inner states that are parts of one's personality (in Louise's case), especially when they are the products of an abusive childhood. To recognize fear as arising in oneself when there is little to fear in one's partner (except perhaps an ordinary complaint or expression of anger) is enormously liberating to the self. Concurrently it frees one's partner of blame.

For most men, a central dream lover at the beginning of adulthood is the Terrible Mother who is imagined as demanding and controlling, or the Great Mother who is seen as generous with life-sustaining love. Men must resist using dream lovers and stereotypes to describe women—especially as the nag, hag, bitch, or witch, the controlling deadly power broker. Such projections prevent men from feeling their own emotional power (as in the case of Joe) and their capacity to induce fear, intimidation, or admiration in their loved ones. When men imagine that women are powerful bitches, the men feel like wimps or victims. Larry is the type of man who could be called passive aggressive because he does not express his vulnerabilities or his needs directly. Larry seems to be aware only of his rational influences on people. He acts as though his judgments of others have no emotional effect. If Larry felt the effects of his own hostile and aggressive feelings, implied in his judgments and his withholding of feelings, he would be surprised at the power he wields in his relationships with others.

Many men assume they have little emotional power. Instead they experience themselves as "trying to offer a solution" or just expressing their thoughts. They may feel adrift in a sea of feelings they believe are being generated by women. Taking back the power of the Mother complex, recognizing that its effects are being generated by oneself (and that other people feel them), can return to men a recognition of their powerful emotional statements, usually ignored when women are assumed to be "the emotional ones."

karen and jonathon

Karen smiled pleasantly in Jonathon's direction and said, "I think we should separate." Karen appeared composed and perhaps hopeful about her decision, although she was sitting in a first session of couple therapy. Why had she come for couple therapy, even initiated the appointment, if she wanted a divorce from her husband of three years? As her story unfolded, it seemed to me that Karen was making a "last stand" in order to get Jonathon's attention. Her voice was mellow and honeyed as she said in a resentful sort of way, "As you know, I have had an affair." Karen described her situation as finding "absolutely irresistible" the offer of a professional colleague to give her pleasure in sex. Although he had told her from the beginning that he would not leave his wife and three children, Karen had been attracted to her colleague because "for the first time in my life I knew what it was like to be *wanted*." Complaining of Jonathon's "sexual problem," Karen said that her husband had shown little sexual interest in her since they got married. Although things had been somewhat better during the six months they lived together before marriage, Karen described Jonathon as "never able to keep his erection or hold back or whatever." She ended abruptly, saying, "He comes too soon."

The greatest challenge in establishing the basis for intimacy between the sexes is relating with respect, acceptance, and empathy. When Karen rather impersonally described her husband in terms of his erections, I felt sure that this marriage had ended. She had no empathy for him. Accepting and honoring a partner's self (that is, not wanting primarily to change it) certainly means honoring a partner's sexuality and erotic connections. When we are faced with someone whose eroticism is profoundly different from our own, we may feel confronted with our darkest fears, such as Karen's feeling that she was unwanted by Jonathon. How can we come to embrace a partner if we don't feel wanted by him? What Karen had unintentionally done, of course, was to communicate to Jonathon that he was unwanted by her, that only another man could fulfill her erotic desires.

Jonathon was blushing and looking down throughout his wife's apparently easy announcement of his sexual difficulties. He seemed somehow eager (although ashamed) to hear more, as though he was interested in knowing the details of the affair. "What did you like so much about him?" he inquired a bit forcefully.

Most painful perhaps is the "separation threat" that is aroused when things go wrong with a couple. Most of us fault our partners when we begin to feel disillusionment. Karen had begun to question whether Jonathon was the "right" man for her and now she had undermined the trust between them. Jonathon's "curiosity" about Karen's affair led me to believe two things: Jonathon had a persecuting, negatively powerful dream lover, and he was quietly letting Karen "hang herself" because he was going to "prove" that she was less of a person than he was. The desire to know what she liked about her lover was self-punitive of Jonathon, but his straightforward gaze into Karen's face at the moment he said this gave a hint of moral superiority.

Karen proceeded to describe the sexual contacts she had had with a friend, Jerry, from her real-estate firm. They had started having lunches together two years ago and gradually came to realize that they were sexually attracted to each other. Jerry had mentioned it first, saying he did not want to act on it, but that he found Karen "to be an erotic woman." Karen "fell in love with that idea" because it was something she held to be deeply true about herself. She had had several passionate love affairs before marrying Jonathon when she was twenty-six. She viewed herself as "a deeply passionate woman who requires a lot of sensual pleasure and stimulation, a lot of body contact, skin to skin."

She eventually confessed this to Jerry. Now she told Jonathon (and us) about her early love affairs, prior to marrying Jonathon: Her orgasms had been deep and reliable, and her body alive with excitement. Jerry had felt "challenged" by Karen's stories and finally "gave in" to his "passion" for her. They began meeting once a week at a local hotel for "lunch in bed." This arrangement was eventually expanded into taking a small apartment where they would meet whenever they could. Finally Karen had called it off because she could tell that "the magic was ending."

Karen's dream lover, the one she had sought in Jonathon and thought she had found in Jerry, is a common type, especially among women who grew up in the 1960s, 1970s, and 1980s. He is erotic, sensitive, creative, and driven—epitomized by the male artist, writer, or musician. I call him the Underground Genius. By "Underground" here I am referring at once to the underground of the culture (marginalized or alternative) and to the unconscious, unknown darkness of a woman's own creativity. A dream lover of this type often belongs to an intelligent, erotic woman. I have also found this type of dream lover associated with a highly intelligent and potentially creative, but often frustrated, mother in the daughter's background. The mother may have been quite depressed (as Karen's mother had been) and felt that her own creative potentials had been wasted, that she had given them up in her marriage. Her daughter is now searching for the lost romantic-creative ideal of the mother.

Unfortunately the Underground Genius dream lover is often projected onto men who merely appear to be sensitive, erotic, or artistic. Jerry is a good example. For years, Jerry had been dabbling in writing fiction and often described himself as "a writer who sells real estate to make a living." He dressed in dark earthy colors and was slender and good-looking. He had perfected a certain seductive, apparently emotionally open manner with women. In contemporary life such men may be passively aggressive and sometimes contemptuous of women, or of committed relationships with women. In essence, they imply or express a disregard for a fully committed relationship of trust and intimacy with a woman. It seemed that Jerry was this type. He was, after all, being dishonest with his wife while claiming to be "up front and honest" about wanting only sex with Karen.

Her husband, Jonathon, was very different (for example, he was scrupulously honest and modest), although it was possible for Karen to see him as an Underground Genius because he was rather quiet and interpersonally remote. Jonathon, a handsome thirtyish man with thick shining dark hair, slight with a wiry build, looked panicked at first, but then gathered his forces to say, "I am furious with you, Karen. You've destroyed everything we worked to put together—trust, our future, the idea of raising a family. I don't think I can go on from here. I don't even know why we're here if you want a separation. It was *your* idea to come here! The only reason I can even talk to you is that *I* still put some faith in basic human values and honesty. I think my sexual problems are mostly related to the way you treat me, which is less than human sometimes."

Jonathon and Karen had both grown up in Jewish families in the Chicago area. Jonathon's was an upwardly mobile middle-class family of educated professionals. Jonathon's doting mother had always wanted a career in law for him, with the hope that he would eventually enter political life. His ideal was to establish himself in the legal profession and then to rear a family in a quiet suburban setting. (He'd just finished law school and joined a legal firm in Philadelphia.) Karen grew up in a religiously observant lower-middle-class family. Jewish customs were stressed in Karen's household and she struggled to set herself "free" when she went away to college.

Karen thought she was choosing a sensitive Underground Genius in Jonathon, someone who would encourage her to feel and see the world colorfully and erotically. Jonathon complied well enough with the projection during the courtship (when people frequently imply "I'll do anything for you") because Karen seemed to him to be a strong, responsible Great Mother figure. Jonathon believed that his own mother had provided the "right kind" of home environment for rearing children, and he was looking to reproduce it. Jonathon liked Karen's reliability and initiative taking, seeing her as competent and complete. Jonathon thought Karen would make a "great mother" and he assumed that the rest of their relationship would just come along.

Near the end of their first therapy session, Jonathon confronted Karen with his own separation threat: "I've had it and I want a divorce."

Surprisingly, Karen said, "I'm willing to try to make this work, if you are willing to change." Karen stressed the fact that sex was important to her and that she did not want to "set it aside like my mother did." She believed that Jonathon had been reluctant to pursue a more satisfying sex life because he thought Karen "should settle for whatever he could do." Karen said she "felt some remorse" about her affair with Jerry, but she felt that only such a stark challenge to Jonathon would "ever move you off your old ways."

Karen had experienced her conversations with Jonathon on the topic of sexuality to be dead and meaningless. Either they had been fights or repetitive exchanges. In fights, often the first symptom of disillusionment, the partners exchange emotionally charged speeches. Each person either makes actively aggressive statements or does passively aggressive things—leaves the room, makes a distracting or sarcastic comment, stops talking. In a fight both partners get hurt. Hurt may turn into bitterness and resentment with repeated fights, and the partners soon tire of "trying to communicate." Each person wants to be right and feels deeply offended by any disagreement. Karen and Jonathon had fought a lot about frequency of sexual contact (she wanted to make love five or six times a week and Jonathon wanted two or three times).

More difficult for Karen and Jonathon, however, had been a series of repetitive conversational exchanges that typify couples in disillusionment. Repetitive exchanges create a merry-go-round effect in which the partners each try to convince the other, but both somehow recognize they are engaged in a deeply entrenched scenario that will always turn out in the same way. Here's a sample.

Karen: I have finally come to appreciate my own sexual desires and I am not going to conform to what you want. All you want is intercourse, no talk, no real foreplay. You seem to have trouble even with me liking sex. I think it turns you off. I can't see why you don't just admit that you have a sexual problem and get some help.

Jonathon: Admit that something's wrong with me when *you* criticize me day and night for what I'm not providing for you sexually? The problem's *your* critical nature. Anyone would be blown away by your criticism. Before you and I got together I had plenty of sexual relationships with women who appreciated my lovemaking and so I *know* there's nothing wrong with me. I've just never known anyone—except maybe your mother—who is so critical and judgmental all the time.

Karen: Leave my mother out of this! I've told you that I won't give up my gut feelings, what I *know* about myself, and I know that *I* love sex and that you have sexual problems! You always think you're *such a wonderful guy* that you're probably just afraid to admit that it's hard for you to really *welcome* a woman's sexual feelings. I know I'm critical of you, but I can't help it when I feel you don't want a part of me that is so central to who I am.

Jonathon: I just don't believe that you're that well adjusted either. I know you like sex, but I think something must be wrong with you because you are always so judgmental. I don't want to admit that I have sexual problems because I don't think that will get us anywhere until you see that you play a role in this too.

This is the kind of conversational exchange that we will stop in a therapy session. It is not dialogue, but a frozen deadening repetition of themes that are based on either ideal or dreaded dream lovers. The depressive emptiness that accompanies this kind of interchange had already led to Karen's fleeing the relationship for an affair.

In this first session, we hoped that Karen was listening to Jonathon's fears and feelings when he claimed Karen had never been attracted to him sexually. He assumed that Karen had been negatively judging his body and build from the way she looked at him. Jonathon had been blocked by these fantasies, but he had never before shared them with Karen. Jonathon's major dream lover was an intrusive (and somewhat seductive) Great Mother. Jonathon's internal Mother generally admired his achievements but was critical of his mistakes. Jonathon had been the favorite child of his intelligent stay-at-home mother, who had always assumed that he would carry her aspirations (to be a political leader) into the world. Super-nurturant and often overly confiding to Jonathon, his mother also expected excellent performance in school from her son. When Jonathon believed that Karen was his internal Mother, he could not hear her advice or suggestions as anything other than an indication of his failure to please her. He lost his faith in himself and then looked to Karen to tell him what to do. With his dream lover in such a powerful role, Jonathon had tended to believe that if he just "sacrificed" enough of his own desires and resources for his partner, Karen would eventually see what a "jewel" he was. Rather than listen to Karen's concerns, Jonathon tried to anticipate them and give in before she had actually described what she wanted.

Karen and Jonathon were operating out of a lot of stereotypes about gender and sexuality. Karen was looking for a "real man" who could provide the excitement and challenge of a sensual encounter. Karen did not believe she could direct this excitement herself, that she could be the initiator or the more sexual partner with her husband. Jonathon thought that a slight build carried the meaning of "unmasculine" and he was looking for a woman to convince him otherwise. Jonathon was afraid of sharing his insecurities with Karen because he feared she would reveal her contempt for him. Karen seemed to have confirmed this in her recent affair with Jerry, but in fact she also wanted to repair her relationship with Jonathon and might actually warm up to his confiding in her. What Jonathon and Karen needed to develop was the basis for dialogue, for talking about their differences instead of acting them out on each other or with outsiders.

Dialogue is fundamentally different from monologue, fighting, and repetitive exchange. All of these dangerous conversational styles are based on the assumption that each partner "already knows" what is going on with the other one. Both have typed each other with dream lovers and are using conversation to demonstrate the "truth" of their typing. Many disillusioned heterosexual couples dread "trying to talk" because they come away from these attempts hurt, resentful, afraid, and hopeless. Many older couples have secretly declared a cold war and they don't attempt to talk at all.

charles and pamela

Pamela insisted that Charles appear with her in our office to make a "last effort" to talk with him. At sixty-four, Charles still cut a dashing figure with his trim, athletic body and his casual, sophisticated dress. Smooth-shaven, with thick graying eyebrows and steely gray eyes, Charles conveyed a patriarchal ease in his every gesture and movement. Charles was always in charge. In the therapy session, he leaned comfortably back on the sofa, staring at his wife of thirty-six years, saying, "You surely don't believe that we could be friends after all this time, do you? I simply don't know why you can't be satisfied with what we have and why you continue to drag me out to see therapists. We have four lovely children and six grandchildren, two beautiful and comfortable homes, the freedom to travel where we want, and a common interest in the theater. What in all the world is *wrong* with that?"

Pamela trembled visibly as she gathered herself to respond. Even the nervous rubbing of her fingers against the wrinkled backs of her hands was painful to watch. Eyes filled with tears, Pamela spit out her words: "I'm so afraid that we'll be miserable in our declining years. I don't know how I'll ever take care of you. Maybe I'm even more afraid of what you'll do to me."

Slender and stylish herself, Pamela's aging had taken a greater toll on her self-confidence than Charles's had on his. Charles had the easy confidence of a man who has improved with the years and expects the admiration of his colleagues. Pamela had the self-consciousness of a woman who had stayed at home too much. Pamela showed the stark, strong face of female aging without much makeup or any cosmetic surgery. Her features had once been stunning but now they were faded: high cheekbones, a sharply pointed nose, clear blue eyes, and thin graceful lips. Her sophisticated, tailored clothes were colorful and in the latest fashion, and her white hair was cut softly around her face in a flattering style. The simple gold jewelry that decorated her neck and wrist seemed stable, strong, and a part of a long history, but it formed a poignant contrast with the quiver in her voice and her nervous manner, making me wonder whether she could endure even the initial therapy session. Pamela was shaking with rage at Charles.

Charles refused to see Pamela as someone who needed him. Instead he insisted on seeing her as a critical, demanding, and rejecting Terrible Mother, a residue of his own mother's narcissism. Although his mother had been openly admiring of him (and Charles glowed with the memory even now), she had also demanded obedience. If he did not fit in with her ideals and her notion of how things should be, then Charles ceased to exist in her regard. Naturally, Charles had complied and become the ideal hero of whom his mother had dreamed. Avuncular though he was, Charles inspired a certain fear with his haughty and assuming manner. Somehow he implied he would protect us (primarily from his judgment) *only* if we went along with his program. Unrevealing of his own emotional needs, Charles seemed content to react to Pamela, although his reactions were thinly disguised, hostile attacks. It was possible to imagine that Charles also held on to a Maiden Lover whom he would find in the younger women at his office, those who looked to him for guidance and protection.

Pamela had ceased looking to him for anything. For too many years Pamela had imagined Charles to be the aggressive, attacking, and imperial Terrible Father for whom the only right way was his way. Pamela assumed that Charles had all the resources and power that any human being could manage. She assumed that he withheld these from her because he thought her ugly, worn, and stupid. She had no idea that Charles himself harbored secret feelings of inferiority and very much wanted her admiration.

Having been sexually estranged for the past twelve years, Pamela and Charles had agreed to live in the same house, to be parents and grandparents together, to sleep in the same bed, but not to call on one another for any intimate contact or comfort. Charles was almost jovial in describing this arrangement, saying it was "the best deal we could come up with after Pamela gave up sex." He reported that Pamela had "just refused to have sex ever again" when they'd been traveling together in France twelve years before. Now Charles regarded their arrangement as "a blessing in some ways" because he felt they had the best of both worlds: a shared history, family, and the fruits of their labors, together with a lot of personal freedom. Pamela was distressed by the arrangement. Although she "had no use for sex" and seemed proud to have finally made that clear to Charles, she wanted "some kind of intimacy" and "some basis for growing old together."

Charles had grown up in an extended family at his maternal grandparents' house in the wealthiest section of Providence, Rhode Island. Having been his mother's favorite and having only one younger sibling, a sister, Charles had grown so accustomed to admiration and the confident expectations of others that he was wholly puzzled when his wife and children complained that he "didn't listen" or "didn't understand their feelings." The president of his own small investment company and a connoisseur of painting and theater, Charles had been respected for years by his friends and colleagues. It seemed that everyone (outside of Pamela and his children) thought he was kind, generous, brilliant, and elegant. According to Charles, he had "made the rounds" of therapists, whom he considered to be "perfectly friendly people" but completely unable to help him and Pamela.

Charles and Pamela appear in this book especially because they represent types of people who were strongly socialized into traditional gender roles. I have seen many like Charles and Pamela in both couple therapy and individual analysis. I want to stress that stereotypes do not capture these people's psyches any better than they capture yours or mine. Still, gender role specializations for women and men were less flexible before the 1970s and the recent wave of feminism. Charles and Pamela exemplify difficulties associated with inflexible gender expectations: the typically powerful man and the typically dependent woman.

Charles and Pamela represent the consequences of narrow gender assignments based on powerful assumptions—that women should be more concerned about the welfare of others, more nurturant, more interpersonally sensitive, more emotionally expressive and dependent. Men are expected to be more assertive and controlling, more independent, more self-sufficient and self-confident, and more objective. Particularly destructive is the *expectation* (from a traditional patriarchal viewpoint) that women are more dependent and less competent than healthy adults. From such a perspective, women are expected to be childlike, and so to prefer the company of children to that of adults.

Pamela was the second daughter of a Philadelphia banking family and had grown up in the conservative Main Line neighborhood outside the city. Her father was a strict disciplinarian and refused to compliment her except on the rarest occasions when she achieved some kind of special recognition. She idealized him, and thought he was "brilliant and wise" in the way he ran his business. She was properly schooled, attended an eastern women's college to study French literature, and had wanted to teach in a university one day. Instead, she married Charles and accepted the roles of mother and housewife with four children and two house servants through most of her adult life. Pamela openly feared she had become "an old frump like my mother," whom Pamela remembered to be kind but ineffectual. A "periodic drinking problem" had originally brought Pamela to therapy and she had succeeded in recovering from it and in exploring her own inner life. This exploration had not led to any career path, however, and Pamela still stayed at home (with one servant now), although the children had been gone for years.

Many women in Pamela's generation have followed a similar life course. By and large, the research on women's lives is now showing that staying at home (with or without children) throughout adulthood does not lead to a healthy outcome over a lifetime. In our modern era, vital involvement with the world takes place away from home. For both men and women, the combination of family and work seems to fare better than either one separately.

The greater privilege and power associated with being male in a male-dominated society contributes importantly to the dreams men have for themselves and the dream lovers women seek through marriage. Although men's greater privileges tend to result in early overestimation of themselves, women's lesser privileges have usually resulted in underestimation. Women like Pamela, educated and cultured, have too often feared the risk of claiming their own authority and taking on paid work. Vicarious authority or creativity does not substitute for one's own contribution to society or culture. Although mothering contributes to society and culture, it cannot be connected with personal identity and control in the way work is, or it will be harmful to children. Pamela had tried to "make her mark on the world" through her children's and husband's achievements. She was now furious with Charles because she felt that he neither valued her nor was faithful to her. Often she compared him unfavorably to her own father, insisting that Charles was not as successful in business as he claimed to be.

Pamela said that she had "refused to comply" with sexual relations while she and Charles were traveling in France. She had never really enjoyed sex with Charles, who "did not bother himself with my pleasures," *and* she suspected that he had been having casual sexual encounters with barmaids and others throughout their trip. Although Charles had denied this accusation, Pamela felt "convinced" that she was right. Pamela believed that she had not been much of a "turn-on" for Charles. She could see him "light up when any half good-looking middle-aged woman comes into view. I've just learned to swallow my pride because it's so obvious to *everyone* that Charles *loves* women, but not his wife."

Pamela could not see that Charles was disappointed in himself, especially because he felt devalued by her. She was too busy feeling devalued by him to understand his feelings. Many midlife and older men are disappointed in what they feel to be a lack of respect from their spouses—and sometimes their children. They frequently feel ashamed that they cannot seem to satisfy their spouses' requests for greater intimacy and vulnerability. Even men who have developed the ability to relate to women and children often feel envious of the emotional support networks that their wives or lovers have set up for themselves.

The problem of envy between the sexes was a lifetime barrier for Pamela and Charles. She envied his greater power, rights, and privileges. He envied her greater closeness to friends and their children and what he assumed was greater protectedness (in terms of income, for instance) and smaller worldly responsibility.

Envy, as I will use the term throughout this book, is the desire to *destroy* another's resources and strengths, to spoil and devalue them. Believing that one cannot possess them for oneself, one can only diminish the worth of another's strengths, contributions, or resources. Envy eats away at respect and destroys gratitude and appreciation. When one is envious of another, one cannot be appreciative. Instead, one becomes intent on "cutting down" the value of the other.

Jealousy, again as I use it here, is less destructive than envy. Jealousy is the desire to *possess* what the other has. In jealousy, one feels capable of possessing the strengths, resources, or talents of the other, so one can concentrate on developing oneself (competing, for instance) instead of diminishing the other. When people are competitive with each other, they will tend to feel jealous if they feel able to compete and envious if they do not.

Dream lovers contribute enormously to envy between the sexes. The fantasies I sustain about the other sex—what powers and privileges and possibilities I see men as having exclusively—will strongly color my dream lovers. Pamela's dream lover, her powerful Terrible Father, had all the brilliance, power, and wit to do whatever he wanted. He was full of possibilities. When Pamela saw Charles in this way, she completely eliminated his vulnerability. She could not sense his need for her or his shame. She wanted only to attack.

sex, gender, and difference

Our four couples, struggling as they are to renew their relationships, are suffering in large measure because they are women and men trying to live together and be intimate. Their problems do not primarily arise from psychopathology, although some of the partners might be classified as having pathological symptoms. They are similar to most other heterosexual couples who sit in my consulting room in one way: Their problems arise primarily from the projection of dream lovers, misunderstanding of gender differences, and unequal power between the sexes.

The "sex" we are born as and the "gender" we are assigned at birth are not the same thing, although one flows from the other. Sex is the difference of embodiment, the structural and functional properties of the human body, which includes both possibilities and constraints on who we can be. Sex is definite and inflexible in most cases. It provides for certain biological possibilities in male and female bodies. Breasts, a vagina, a vulva, smaller body size, menstruation, pregnancy, lactation, menopause, and greater longevity are expected of the female body. A penis, greater body size, greater physical strength, impregnation, and lesser longevity are expected of the male body. These and other biological differences (such as brain structure and chemistry) limit us in terms of both our biological-sexual-reproductive life *and* the gender club to which we belong. Although we may struggle with these differences (for example, by dressing like the other sex or attempting to change the body surgically) we cannot escape our embodiment. It will limit us forever.

Gender is the identity club to which our biological sex assigns us at birth. When sex is anomalous, doctors and parents work quickly to change the body or make a decision about it, so that gender can be assigned. Gender serves many purposes in the way societies organize power and work so that the tasks of life can be coordinated. Most people are anxious to get it assigned.

Gender meanings are flexible in the sense that they vary by context, family, and society. In some societies, for example, men are expected to be more nurturant and home oriented, taking care of the young. In others, like our North American societies, women are expected to be the primary caregivers. Most societies offer biological explanations for their gender meanings.

In all male-dominated societies—all large industrialized societies that now exist—women have less power than men. This a fact. No matter what work women do or what characteristics are expected of them, they have less voice in decision making and fewer privileges and rewards than their male counterparts. I must take this fact into account in understanding dream lovers and the envy between the sexes. In my work with couples, I know that the desire for intimacy means building a foundation of equality and mutuality between the sexes.

Each of our couples has come to therapy through the powerful intuition of an angry woman. Women are insisting on being respected and being treated with dignity. Perhaps ironically, these angry women opened the door to intimacy between men and women for the first time in recorded history. They want to be equals with their male partners. Intimacy depends on trust and trust depends on equality and mutuality. The women of our couples want mutual respect and open exchange between the sexes.

Having asked for this, these women are painfully disappointed with what they have found. All four of them disdain what they see in their male partners. When they ask their partners to open up, the women are unable to accept what they are shown. They state or imply that their partners show primitive development, bullying, stupidity, or just plain "little-boyness." I believe that women must look again and listen better. We need to become conscious of our own ideal and dreaded dream lovers and distinguish them (as aspects of ourselves) from the men we are trying to reach.

Men must do the same. If we speak only to a dream lover and silence a partner, then we will fail to have a dialogue. It is not enough to ask for openness, from either men or women; we must be able to understand, respect, and ultimately accept the person we find. I find this is possible through understanding the larger perspective of gender, power, envy, and the world of dream lovers.

staying together versus getting together

This book is about staying together and turning disillusionment and power struggles into acceptance and deeper commitment. I believe that heterosexual intimacy can become the ideal foundation for development in adulthood if we can reclaim our dream lovers.

The darkness of disillusionment follows the joys of early friendship or romance. Now, one is bonded with another. This is the beginning of a power struggle in which both members of the couple will blame the self or each other (usually the latter) for the miseries that have emerged.

Dream lovers provide the scripts for the dramas that will ensue. Partners previously thought they had found something that would work, but now they encounter the fears, resentments, reexperienced traumas, shame, and rage they had thought to escape. Instead of anticipating this swamp of confusion and mixed identities, most people are horrified by it. They believe that intimacy should naturally follow from finding a suitable partner.

When couples become disillusioned, they become either actively aggressive or passively aggressive. They feel they are fighting for their identities and essential truths, and so they cannot avoid aggression at first. Partners experience a loss of trust when they lose the initial glow of romance or the promise of the early relationship. In this state, conversations become deadly.

The alternative to embattlement or separation is to learn how to make a deeper commitment through dialogue. Much of this book is filled with illustrations of how dialogue works. Dialogue can be used to discuss matters of conflict or agreement. Even when partners agree in a general way, dialogue leads to discovery of individual viewpoints. Dialogue is full of discovery and surprises because it is an exchange of points of view that were not fully known previously.

For example, Patty discovered through dialogue with Joe that he really did want to change and develop. He saw change differently than she did, though. Patty wanted Joe to go to therapy and self-help groups to learn self-discovery and the language of feeling. Joe saw changes as promises to himself. Patty was thrilled to hear about Joe's promise to himself not to use obscenity around the house and not to spend Friday nights out with the guys. These were changes that she had hoped for, but that she had actually failed to recognize when they happened, because she was looking for her Hero dream lover. Now she could see that his goals actually matched hers, but that his means were different.

When partnerships are deeply committed, adult love relationships provide the "mirrors," the reflections of ourselves, that challenge us to accept the most dreaded and ideal aspects of our being. In order to accept ourselves, we must also accept our partners. Intimacy is the product of trust, and trust depends on acceptance. Heterosexual intimacy could bring new meaning to love as women and men seek to resolve their conflicts in an atmosphere of trust rather than power struggles and stereotypes. This book is dedicated to couples who are engaged in this experiment with the deepest hope that we will succeed.

Most of all, this book is dedicated to those couples who have lost their romance. These pages say more about staying together than getting together. Staying together can bring a state of *mature dependence* with an intimate partner, the psychological condition for development in adult life. The psychiatrist Carl Jung believed that a committed love relationship in adulthood could promote *individuation* for both partners. By this term he meant the gradual unpacking of the mysteries of our own beings, coming to see both conscious and unconscious meanings and motives. Reclaiming our dream lovers is the first step in this process.

chapter 2

The metaphor of "falling" in love expresses a tripping up, a downward motion, and a movement into the metaphorical deep space of the unconscious. Most of us assume that what we have fallen into has more to do with another person than with ourselves, but I think otherwise. My first experience of falling in love was my first fall into my own creativity, and yet at the time all I could think of was "him." I put quotation marks around "him" because I want you to know that "he" had little to do with the young man who was the object of my desire. "He" was a brilliant speaker, writer, and artist who had the depth of Goethe and the raw edgy passion of Bob Dylan. I was (in my view) a country bumpkin, a plump, innocent, and uninitiated girl who felt herself to be "his" subordinate, "his" student, "his" follower. The late 1960s supported this way of thinking as I took on the label of "hippy chick," which seemed both insulting and cool.

Having spent most of my early girlhood as a serious, introverted, anxious child, I had gradually transformed in high school into a student leader who appeared to be cheery and ambitious, full of ideals and dreams. In college in the late 1960s I struggled with these two sides of myself, increasingly aware that I was not a unitary self, a solid known quantity. Most of the time I was in a panic, a vague sort of emergency state in which I knew that I had to "figure out" what was happening to me and at the same time continue to be an excellent student to maintain the scholarship that permitted me the luxury of college. Since reading had always been my saving grace and since I had learned that I liked to own books whenever possible (so that I could scribble in the margins and underline everything that seemed important, often at least half of what I read), I spent a lot of my free time searching the college bookstore for answers to my problems. This was especially the case after I fell in love. I spent hours in the poetry section.

Fortunately for both him and me, I recognized that I had fallen in love. I knew that I was captured and crazed and that I should not believe my own thoughts and feelings. I knew this, in part at least, because never before had I been so much beside myself. I couldn't even hate myself in the familiar ways. Mostly I would spend my time fantasizing "him" and being irritated by the distraction. My searches through the poetry section of the bookstore were driven by the conviction that poets knew about love. Certainly from them I would find out something about my lovesickness, something that would ease it or explain it. I found many poems that helped, but none that cured me.

One, however, has remained with me over these twenty-some years, the poem that provided my first key to the mystery of heterosexual love. At the time I first read it, I pondered it deeply and knew it was sage although I could barely sense its meaning. The ideas in the poem would eventually lead me to study the psychology of Carl Jung. The poem, called "De Anima," was written by Howard Nemerov. Here I quote two verses from it, describing a girl at night, standing at a window and seeing only her own image in the darkness of the glass, while across the street is a young man who looks at the girl in her brilliant room.

In looking at herself, she tries to look
Beyond herself, and half become another,

Admiring and resenting, maybe dreaming
Her lover might see her so.

The other, the stranger standing in cold and dark,
Looks at the young girl in her crystalline room.
He sees clearly, and hopelessly desires,
A life that is not his.

The poem told me that my love was a "stranger" and that in meeting "him" for the first time I was trying to look beyond myself and half become another. Although I knew even then that I was encountering something disconcerting in myself, I saw only dimly that this might mean I would have to change. Instead I clung to the hope that if I possessed him, I would possess myself. In my mind he was a genius who would initiate me into the world of art and culture and endow me (and my body) with stature and meaning I could neither bring myself nor get from my past.

Fortunately or unfortunately, I have fallen in love several times in my life. Each time I have had the same distinctly unpleasant feeling of losing my old familiar self in favor of an intoxicating and destabilizing pull into something strange, something different. I cannot say that I welcomed these pulls. I can only say that I tried to withstand them and do what I could to discover and come to know both the stranger within and the person who evoked "him" in me. With each new love I became a more mature lover, a person more alert to the demands of love. Finally I have settled into an enduring partnership with my husband, my most thoroughly destined love, and amazingly I still fall in love with him from time to time and confront something new in both of us.

While I have been studying the complex mystery of heterosexual love and doing other things as well, I have followed my night dreams in order to see better how they might correct the blindness of my waking state. From my early childhood I remembered my dreams and wondered whether they had meanings different from waking thoughts. I believe now that night dreams are antidotes to the narrowness of our sense of self in waking life. They confront us with novel images that rework the emotional conflicts of life. Most of us do not remember these antidotes although we live roughly six years (of a seventy-year life) in their charged landscapes. Marvelously, dreams do their work without any help from us. Managing the complexity of the human personality requires more than a conscious self. Dreaming allows us to review ourselves without any harm to self or others. Dreaming gives us a different view, in which we *are* dreamed as well as *in* the dream. Dreams narrate the whole personality and tell the story from another viewpoint, different from that of the waking self. They allow us to see ourselves with the Others.

When I was twenty, I had a dream that fully expressed the nascent idea I had found in the Nemerov poem. The dream came at a time of great distress during the loss of this first love. When I lost the relationship, not having even finished the romance, I retreated into a morbid state of self-hatred and humiliation. I felt as though I had lost myself. About four bitter months after the relationship was over, I dreamed the following:

> I am standing in the doorway, looking through a glass into the backyard of the house where I live. My best girlfriend is standing in front of me. Outside everything is a mauve fog, very eerie. The fog is moving about and some of it coalesces into a giant ghostly form. It is huge, manly, and frightening. From the distance, the form moves toward us. Just before it closes in, a male voice says, "Destiny is a man." My friend drops dead. I wake before it gets to me because I know I will die also.

This dream was so powerful and moving that I kept it in the back of my mind for months. In my spare time, I would bring it into awareness and ponder its meaning. It strikes me now that its images are obviously quite similar to the Nemerov poem, although I had never consciously known this.

At the time of the dream, I thought I was being alerted to my morbid state and the necessity of separating from my beloved, on whom I feared I had become wholly dependent for my existence. My relationship with him was a life-and-death matter, the dream seemed to say. Now I realize that my recognition of my own dream lover, of the creative and edgy Other within, was a matter of life and death. The dream was alerting me to my own destiny in terms of the Man Within, the changing and evolving aspect of my female personality that would from time to time be wholly projected onto a man. My job, says the dream, is to take this seriously and die. The metaphorical death here is the cessation of the old self, in this case represented by my closest adolescent girlfriend. My own adolescent self was threatened by the force of the Man dream lover. He was powerful, exotic, gigantic in his meaning, and I was still a girl in my parents' home.

Dreams like this one convinced me privately in my early twenties that falling in love was the beginning of a process that meant more than eventually getting married. As with many other things in my experience at that time, I felt confused about my conviction because I could find little confirmation of it in things I read or people I talked with. Now when I look back, I realize I was reading (with very few exceptions) only works written by men and taking seriously, alas, only things said by men. Men were my authorities.

One of those authorities came to be the psychiatrist Carl Jung. My best girlfriend (the one who appeared in the dream) also seeking authorities, told me to read Jung in order to discover an attitude toward the unconscious that was different from Freud's, whose then-ubiquitous version of the Oedipus complex (a childhood romance with the opposite-sex parent) made absolutely no sense to me in terms of my relationship with my father. In Jung I discovered the term *anima*, which I had already found in the poem. Jung had discovered the Other, his own strange gender, in his dreams and fantasies. His theories initially appealed to me because he too believed that love was more than an attachment bond, something more like a projection of an aspect of the self.

Later in life, while I was training to be a Jungian analyst and had half forgotten about my early attraction to Jung's theories, I came across an essay he had written in 1925 called "Marriage as a Psychological Relationship." This essay lays out the premise that heterosexual relationships, especially committed relationships as in marriage, are avenues for our psychological development. Facing another of the opposite sex will eventually mean facing our own Otherness. First this happens through the disillusionment of the romance and taking back idealized projections of dream lovers. This taking back provides an opportunity for taking on parts of the self, for seeing and experiencing wishes, fears, and ideals that we had unknowingly placed in the other. After projections have been identified and understood, after we have increased ourselves with the shadowy meanings that we would like to deny, then we have the possibility of actually knowing another person who is different from us. This other person sees the world and knows the self through a different kind of body and a different gender lens.

Developing the skill of dialogue, as I described in the last chapter, means being able to understand empathically a partner's experience while simultaneously holding on to one's own truth. Dialogue, as a conversational exchange of views, allows a couple to learn from their differences, their conflicts. A major part of this learning will be the ongoing expansion of oneself. Expanding oneself to include what has been projected onto the partner but belongs to the self is a work of *integration* and *humility*. What I feared in you (believing, for instance, that you compete with me) is discovered to have come from me (actually I compete with you *or* I experience you as a rival like a sibling) due to one of my dream lovers that I tried to exclude from my awareness. Integrating this into myself brings a new humility.

Clarifying oneself to exclude what is an aspect of the partner is a work of *differentiation* and *boundary setting*. Becoming responsible for the range of one's own wishes, fears, and ideals is a terrific challenge, often overwhelming in its implications. In my view, the best definition of *autonomy* is taking responsibility for one's subjective states. Accepting the subjective states in another is a good definition of *compassion*. Accepting the ideals and failures of a partner can increase empathy for the entire opposite sex, for all of those others who are suffering and trapped (as we all are) in their limitations of body and gender.

psychological complexes

Why is it so hard to follow this path of claiming and disclaiming parts of the self in a relationship with the opposite sex? Have we learned so little since 1925 when Jung wrote the seminal essay that introduced the idea that marriage could be something like psychotherapy? In part, I think we have ignored the challenge. Until women could speak in their own voices, there was no possibility of dialogue. Until women could be respected as equal partners, there was no possibility of trust between the sexes.

Of course, many men have said much about romance and romantic love, about the inspirational and motivational "power" of a dream lover. In the history of Western civilization we find the muse, the *femme inspiratrice*, and the spiritual medium extolled for their power to motivate change. But when has one of these been associated with a *wife*? Expanding the self through a woman's influence has almost always excluded a wife. "She" had to be "the other woman."

On a broader cultural level, we have *all* been encased in silence because we thought that heterosexual love was "doing what's natural," and that if tough problems gripped us, then something in our relationship must be wrong or pathological. And finally, women and men are not equals. The problem of power—of envy, competition, idealization—often blocks our access to dialogue and understanding our differences.

All of these barriers have been in place for a long time. Although we have begun to knock them down by exposing them, the challenge of true dialogue continues to exist for every couple. (This is true even for dialogue between same-sex friends and partners, but for slightly different reasons than those I review here.) Dialogue is an especially heroic encounter for the cross-sex friendship because of the psychological complexes that are connected with our dream lovers.

A psychological complex is a collection of associations from past experiences held together by an emotional core. Remember that the emotional core contains image traces (sights, sounds, smells, feelings) that may go back to our earliest relationships when we were helpless and powerless. A complex can strongly influence our personal style, behavior, and beliefs and be out of our awareness. It can put us into a "mood" that we cannot seem to shake. Often people feel possessed by something almost trancelike and say, "I was beside myself when I did (or said) that." This signals being captured by an Other. When Joe raises his voice to Patty, this sound can trigger her Terrible Father complex. Patty experiences fear and dread, the core emotional state, and then she may yell at Joe, "Stay away from me! Don't you touch me!" as though Joe were making a full-scale attack on her. Even after Joe has apologized for raising his voice Patty may continue to feel apprehensive and irritated, not being able to trust Joe. She does not see that her overwhelming fear comes from her own subjective state and originates in her early dependence on a caregiver who was sadistic and attacking. Less dramatically, Pamela feels rejected by Charles every time Charles "gives her a look" that, in her view, scans her body. She believes that Charles is "disgusted" by her because she projects her Terrible Father—whose contemptuous inner voice critically reviews every detail of her appearance.

When a psychological complex is activated, we may act out the mood or message of an Other from our emotionally charged unconscious life *or* project an Other onto a partner, colleague, child, or friend. When we act out a complex, we dramatize the emotions or images held in the complex. I may *become* the Terrible Father and attack another person cruelly, for instance. When we project a complex, we "see" it in another person. Thus I would become afraid of the Terrible Father that I believe to be in my husband. We may do both, interweaving identification and projection in which we alternately feel like the Terrible Parent or the Victim Child, both poles of the same complex. The state of being in a psychological complex is *just like* being in a hypnotic trance. We snap into it and can snap out of it, but while we are in it we are "elsewhere." Better not to go in at all. Often we do not have enough awareness to step aside and simply take note of what Otherness is arising.

Remember when Patty discovered that Joe really did want to change and develop? Prior to her discovery, Patty would become infuriated with Joe when he tried to explain why he didn't want to join a self-help group or read a book she suggested. When Joe would say, "Look, Patty, I'm just not interested in that stuff," Patty would feel him pulling away from her influence and quickly she would fall into a dark vortex of fear. Often she described this as a "black hole feeling" in which she became overwhelmed with panic. She would envision Joe as "totally the opposite of me," as a fat, bald old man, demanding his dinner and turning on the TV defiantly in front of her. She would imagine him using improper grammar or obscenity, humiliating her in public, and finally limiting her freedom to follow her own dreams. When the Terrible Father was activated in Patty, it inevitably led to a conviction that she would have to divorce Joe because she would never be able to influence him and he would always hurt and humiliate her. This whole fantasy might take place if Joe even refused to read a brochure Patty had received in the mail!

Not all psychological complexes are dream lovers, but all dream lovers are psychological complexes. Recall that a complex is a whole collection of associations from many experiences bound together by a powerful core. The core of a psychological complex connects back through image traces to overpowering earlier experiences, either when we were powerless and very young, or when we were faced with a trauma (abuse or an accident) that overwhelmed us. The image traces—visual, aural, kinesthetic, or olfactory cues that can signal the complex—are not simple blips, but configurations that represent "self" and "other" in the original experience. When we reexperience the emotions and meanings that are stored in a complex, we can identify with either pole of the complex. One pole is some version of a powerless, helpless self; the other pole is an overwhelming, powerful other. *Both* of these poles are internal states of Otherness. An individual can swing back and forth between these two states when in the grip of a complex.

When Joe complained that Patty "demanded" he follow her every wish, Patty would silently concede that this seemed true. Patty thus colluded with Joe's projection of *his* Terrible Mother: He believed that Patty was trying "to control" him through her demands. At these times Joe would feel like a "little boy" who was being "criticized" by his fault-finding mother, *and* alternately like an "angry, critical, and dominating" parent who was "sick and tired" of listening to Patty. The Terrible Mother complex has an emotional core of fear. The image connected to the fear may be of one's own mother screaming and waving her arms while the "self" is small, silent, and helpless. The image could as easily be connected to an older sister who was punitive and cruel in taking care of her infant sibling. There are many associations (and usually many events) connected to the core emotion and image traces of a complex. Many core emotions of complexes are *primary emotions.*

Primary emotions are wired in before birth to arouse us and send out communication to our caregivers. From birth on we each express basic dislike, disgust, fear, aggression, sadness, joy, and curiosity. We do not learn them, but we learn to modify and fine-tune them. They organize us before we can speak and they have a validity that falls *outside language*. We cry in fear, or kick and push in aggression, long before we have words. When an image or emotion triggers a psychological complex, we feel the validity of the emotion. If someone raises a fist at me, even if I don't speak his language, I will feel afraid in response to what I perceive as aggression. I don't wonder if I am "right" because I "know," but I may be wrong. Maybe the other person is demonstrating a dance move. Obviously context is important, but we don't pay attention to current context if we are in a complex.

To complicate things further, primary emotions are expanded into hundreds of subtle meanings and joined by other emotions as infants and children develop. Language eventually takes over to modulate meaning, and sometimes emotions are *hard* to understand because the connotations of the words used to express them may differ by context—for instance, for one person an obscenity signals attack, but for another it may be a familiar buzzword.

A different kind of emotion shows up around eighteen months of age. It is *self-conscious emotion*. Self-conscious emotions are pride, envy, jealousy, shame, embarrassment, and guilt, which imply something about the self in regard to others. In order for me to feel ashamed, I have to recognize a self in me, and someone else in whose presence I want to hide or die or disappear. Human beings are so complex that they do not simply discharge their emotions. They store them in memory and abstract them into cues and scripts that will direct actions. Many of these scripts are psychological complexes based on childhood experiences.

Psychological complexes are necessary forms of organization in the human personality. They are ways of encoding memories and directing our behavior so that we adapt to our early circumstances. Often the term *complex* has a negative connotation in our culture and we may feel ashamed when we are "caught" in a complex. I want to stress that one is not to blame for one's complexes and that, without them, we would not have survived our early lives. Not all complexes are negative. Some have core arousal states of joy and curiosity. In the last chapter, for example, we were introduced to Jonathon's Great Mother complex. Image traces of satisfaction, admiration, and fulfillment are associated with the Great Mother. When Jonathon projects his Great Mother onto Karen, he wants to be her Golden Child. Whether positive or negative, complexes are adaptive to our early lives, but are generally unadaptive later. Even when they fit a partner's expectations and projections, psychological complexes get in the way of trust and intimacy. Most of us are especially troubled by the negative ones.

When I was a helpless little girl and my father screamed and waved his arms, I formed an overwhelmingly fearful image of a demon, giant Father. When my husband speaks in a forceful or stern manner, I may feel the old emotion (overwhelming fear) and experience an image (giant, frightening man) that will introduce a set of reactions in me that are irrelevant to the present situation. I may feel paralyzed with fear or feel a great need to calm my husband, for example. At those times, I cannot be convinced rationally that my experience is "not true" because rationality cannot explain the emotion and the image traces.

My only hope to recognize the complex comes from self-awareness of my own subjective state. I can "stop" believing my complex if I notice that it is coming from me, is owned by me, is my past. If my partner calmly refuses to play out the Other pole of my psychological complex, I may be able to resist believing it. If, for example, my husband says "Wait. Think about it now, I did not really yell at you. You're reacting to something other than me," I can usually alert myself. But if he tries to analyze or interpret me, by saying something like "You always react to me as though I'm your father," I will tend to believe that he really *is* a punitive parent and go on in my complex. The image traces that fuel our complexes usually fall outside of language, either because a complex formed preverbally or because we were so overwhelmed by emotion (as in the case of abuse) that only images can encode it.

Although complexes can be experienced and expressed (for example, in a temper tantrum) alone as well as in relationships, I believe that they cannot be recognized and overcome without a mirroring partner.

The partner may be a close friend, a spouse, or a psychotherapist. It must be someone who is deeply trusted and willing to challenge the complex.

Challenging a complex is especially difficult because of the emotional core. The core is made of emotional image traces that are linked to survival, adaptation, and universal patterns of relationship. Certain emotions (for example, aggression, joy, fear) are universally connected to certain relational themes (domination, attachment, submission) through images. The spontaneous expression of the same images, such as the Great Mother and Terrible Father, among different peoples was considered by Jung to be evidence of an innate organization of human expression. He called these image-themes *archetypes*, meaning primary imprints. Archetypes, in Jung's last theory, are not mysterious forms that lie outside experience. They are not Platonic ideals or aspects of a fuzzy collective unconscious. They are ordinary human experiences of emotionally powerful images that predispose us to action. Such an image is a cue, a stimulus, that re-presents a highly charged relational theme. My teenage son barks at me when I interrupt his television watching. The harshness in his voice (the image cue) *can* evoke the fear and powerlessness I felt in the presence of my father's harshness. In such a state, I am out of touch with my son. I may collapse into a trance of hurt rejection *or* I may identify with the aggressor and attack my son. At the core of every psychological complex is an archetype—an image connected to emotion and a relational theme. Archetypal images (Great Mothers, demons, devils, powerful seductresses) are represented in dreams, art, myth, and literature. In my view, they come from the universal organization of emotion in the human personality.

the unique meaning of dream lovers

A few pages ago, I slipped in a claim that I did not expand on: Not all psychological complexes are dream lovers but all dream lovers are psychological complexes. What does this mean? Our primitive emotional states and their image traces encompass more than cross-gender issues. We all have complexes of our own gender—such as my Terrible Mother complex, which criticizes me and my aspirations, or my Great Mother complex, on which I sometimes rely in nurturing my own children. Some people have complexes of thing images or animal images, but all complexes involve relational themes, mostly with other people, because we are so emotionally attached to each other.

Dream lovers are uniquely important complexes. They link our strange gender to the dramas of our early lives (which may be lost through repression and denial) and to our dreams and wishes for the future. For example, Louise would feel much better if she took responsibility for her Hero dream lover and developed further her own initiative-taking and planning capacities. Charles would be revitalized if he could claim the Maiden Lover as his creativity and find a way to express it at home or work. Taking responsibility for our dream lovers is a direct way to transcend stereotypes and expand the gender scripts that we have received from society. When the nineteenth-century French woman writer George Sand took a man's name and dressed in a man's clothes (so she could move about the cities freely), she was not trying to be a man. She was trying to be a *free woman*, and she incorporated her own dream lover into that vision. When I decided in my late twenties and early thirties that my Underground Genius deserved to be respected by me, I began to write and publish, developing an aspect of myself that I would never have believed could be *me*. I had always hoped I would marry a creative, artistic man, but now I saw that "he" was me, my energy and vision.

Gender is more flexible than sex and our gender identities *can* change over time to include more and more of the Others. Gender is not a matter of choice when we are youngsters, and sometimes not even later. In order to be accepted as "normal," we have to be "nice girls" and "tough boys." Some children go against this grain and suffer the social isolation of peers' excluding them. Even later as adults, we are all constrained by stereotypes that narrow our possibilities, stereotypes that are rooted in the psychological complexes of dream lovers. Breaking through these stereotypes is the work of women and men in friendship and intimate relationship as they develop the patience to see what is self and what is not.

psychological awareness and mythic traditions

In heterosexual relationships we have the possibility to encounter and claim our dream lovers after we are mature adults. Only then can we begin to free ourselves of stereotypes of *us* and *them*. A mature state of self-reflection, in which we can review our own thoughts and feelings and understand how they are related to our personality, is a requirement for integrating dream lovers. This kind of self-reflection needs a certain detachment, a kind of objective view of our own thoughts and feelings. I "step back" from the immediate sense of being in my thoughts and feelings, and get a bigger picture of what is going on. Contemporary Zen teacher Charlotte Joko Beck calls this step the ABC: getting A Bigger Context. In order for me to come to know my own Hero dream lover, I have to stop projecting my strange gender onto my partner or any other man. I have to step back and recognize that I am accusing or blaming him for something that is going on in me, either something I am doing or want to do, or something that was done to me before, when I was a helpless child. (When my partner *is* doing something to me, it is of course *not* projection. It is hard to "catch" oneself projecting because it requires knowing just what is happening between us.) *Then* I must claim this as myself. I may believe my partner could be a brilliant lawyer and keep "suggesting" that he apply to law school, but in fact it is I who has that ambition. When I claim it, then I will also have the responsibility for living it out or deciding against it.

Prior to the capacity to reflect on ourselves, and become responsible for our own subjective states, we are incapable of this kind of self-expansion. The capacity for reflective thought develops in adolescence. All parents notice that in early adolescence their children become "egocentric," believing they are the center of attention, as though they had a "public" that followed them around. This is a natural side effect of the onset of reflective thought: For the first time, a child is able to review thoughts and feelings and know they come from the self, rather than just come. Children become especially self-centered and self-conscious when this capacity is developing. Unless there is a mental disability, everyone acquires this form of thought by the end of adolescence. The ability to use it to understand *oneself* does not come automatically, however. All adults are capable of reflecting on their experiences, but not everyone uses this ability to examine the self and come to self-awareness.

Self-examination depends on many things, but especially on being able to use this *psychological awareness* of the self. Some people are uninterested in this kind of awareness and refuse to examine their subjective states, or cannot examine them. Others embrace psychological awareness when they encounter it. I do not know which is the "right" way. Psychological awareness complicates life and can result in even more stereotypes and defensiveness. For instance, it's a problem when self-awareness leads to armchair analyses of one's partner. A wife who says to her husband "You're mad at me about my cleaning because you were furious with your mother's sloppiness" is making an attack. Psychological awareness can be used in power struggles, to defend oneself and silence a partner. It also opens us to a range of subjective states, and becomes a major avenue of development. We become divided selves and we become aware of a wider range of possibilities in ourselves. Through self-reflection and psychological awareness, people grow by recognizing and taking back into themselves parts they have put into the world and others.

A lack of psychological awareness is the ground of another perspective, often called the "mythopoetic" way of life. This is a life based on externally given traditions and beliefs. Some contemporary people seem nostalgic for the mythopoetic life in their search for rituals and ceremonies that will transform them—through which they can pass to another stage of development. Ironically, though, when most of us actually encounter the mythopoetic way of life in our parents or other elders, we find it unpleasant, narrow, distasteful. When our elders insist that they "know" exactly the right way to do things, we protest. Often we argue, from our psychological awareness, that we have found a different way and then label them as prejudiced or narrow-minded. The way of myth *is* the way of conformity. People grow through methods, rituals, or states of being endowed with meaning by external authorities. An individual is commanded to behave according to the rules. When a person moves through a rite of passage, the person does not devise an individual method, but follows a tradition, one that has been devised over generations. By and large, mythopoetic traditions do not leave much room for gender flexibility except perhaps for the oldest elders. Most everything is set and carried out for the smooth functioning of the group or society. Gender roles are conveyed not only through peer socialization, but also through storytelling, inspiration, and guidance by elders whose words are to be respected.

Self-reflection and psychological awareness leave room for individual changes throughout the lifespan, beginning in adolescence. Stereotypes and gender socialization continue to limit us, but psychological awareness can remove some barriers (not all) by allowing us to become aware of assumptions, origins, and meanings connected with our gender identity and our dream lovers. Development through self-awareness is more arbitrary and chaotic than the orderly rites of passage of the mythic tradition. Psychological awareness means that we learn through our mistakes, failures, neuroses.

I use self-reflection and psychological awareness in all the work I do in psychotherapy. In both individual and couple psychotherapy my methods are designed to increase reflective self-awareness, although at times there are surprises of inspiration and awe. A change in a client's life circumstances, an illness or a new job, for instance, may suddenly produce the psychological change of insight or the action that we had been seeking through self-awareness. To make that a permanent shift, however, the client will still need the tools of self-awareness.

I grew up in a mythopoetic family environment and so I am familiar with that way of life. I did not specifically choose to leave it, but when I lost my first love, I was somehow "chosen" by my dream lover to feel the force of my own divided self. Once this force is felt one cannot turn back. One sees too many meanings, too many possibilities, too much complexity to accept conformity to tradition. The metaphors of "breakdown" (for personality), "breakup" (for a relationship), and "coming apart" (for both) depict the felt experience of division, multiples rather than unity.

The unity of the self does not usually break down within a well-regulated tradition. It is transformed in an orderly way through rites and ritual, but it does not fall apart. In our North American societies, we have a mix of different cultures and traditions. We are confronted by different truths and most of us cannot inhabit a wholly (holy) mythic space, unless we live in a highly restricted community, such as some traditional religious communities. Most of us have to confront the way of "not knowing"—the way of chaos and personal confusion. Most of us fall apart and feel lost at some point in the lifespan. Some people are fortunate enough to transform this experience into psychological awareness, others are lost in the chaos, and a few others return to communities in which they try to resurrect the mythopoetic way of life.

The reason I am talking here about self-awareness versus the mythic tradition is because in certain aspects of the women's movement, feminism, and the men's movement, I find the desire to resurrect the mythopoetic way. Goddess groups, goddess ceremonies, men's retreats, and ceremonies of sweat lodges and drumming are examples. Not everything that occurs under these banners is a search for the mythic (some are more like experiments in lifestyle), but many are activities that express a nostalgia for the traditional. That nostalgia, as I said above, is often not in keeping with value-laden negative reactions that may be felt in brushing up against the traditional views of parents and elders. Although I have an interest in understanding these recent mythic manifestations, I see my work as quite different. If anything, I am most interested in breaking down stereotypes, in opening up gender constraints, in finding the strange gender in oneself. I do not want to renew traditions of masculinity or femininity.

All of this said, I enjoy making use of traditional stories, folktales, mythologies, and religions. From these texts I have learned a great deal. The book I published in 1984, *Hags and Heroes: A Feminist Approach to Jungian Psychotherapy with Couples*, was framed around a medieval folktale, the story of Sir Gawain and Lady Ragnell. I was inspired by the old hag, Lady Ragnell, to understand better the resentment and bitterness I repeatedly encountered in certain kinds of women who were also wives and mothers. I found that the character of the hag who cannot be kissed on the lips (because she is capable of sucking out your soul) expanded my understanding of the fear of abandonment in these women. Also the young hero, Sir Gawain, is a fine illustration of the young man who bravely carries out the bidding of his elder (King Arthur) only to find himself developing integrity that goes beyond his elder's. The dilemma of moving beyond the old authorities is beautifully drawn in this tale when finally Gawain turns to his new wife (a transformed Ragnell) and consults her, rather than the king, for advice. The story of Gawain and Ragnell taught me how to see heterosexual intimacy as a struggle for both partners to maintain their own sovereignty (especially difficult for the woman), in an atmosphere of trust and closeness.

Then, when I wrote *Female Authority: Empowering Women Through Psychotherapy* with Florence Wiedemann, I found that traditional Greek myths, expressing as they do the dilemmas of gods and goddesses in a patriarchal (god-dominated) religion, were inspiring. We did not use these stories for instruction or advice (as I had done with the Ragnell story), but rather as analogies to current struggles between the sexes. For example, the enraged earth goddess Demeter trails after her lost daughter Persephone through the worlds above and below. Defying the great god Zeus in her search, she threatens to destroy all humanity and thus prevent him from receiving sacrifices ever again. Why is she in such a rage? Her daughter has been raped by her uncle Hades who is the brother of Zeus. Zeus, Father of Persephone, condoned the rape. Demeter would rather destroy the earth itself than let this injustice go unchecked.

Zeus and Hera figure in another scenario. Zeus possessed Hera as *his* property after she had earlier been a free earth goddess. Hera's revenge is to stick like glue to her husband and punish him for his endless affairs. This is an attempt to reclaim her power. Most of us hear only about the unattractiveness of Hera's jealousy, not about the meaning of her indignation. These Greek stories are maps for many of the problems that develop between the sexes in an environment of male dominance, when men try to make women into objects ("objectify" them), and when men and women are unable to communicate. Zeus is almost always on Olympus (when he is not out flirting with a young woman) and it is very difficult to see him there. Olympus is too remote.

Myths and folktales can be used to expand insight into our own emotions because they depict the playing out of psychological complexes in human life. They warn us about the dangers of our own natures. I like to use stories and images from folktales and myths to illustrate the relational themes and emotional meanings of dream lovers.

In presenting the dream lovers that follow, and suggesting which emotions might accompany them, I am not assuming that these are the only complexes we can have of the strange gender. Emphatically, I am not saying that everyone everywhere has these particular dream lovers. I am speaking mostly from my clinical work and my life experiences, and from psychological theory and research. I do not have the last word on dream lovers. In fact, I am sure that you have had fantasies or dream lovers that are different from the prototypes I describe here. The reason for singling out these images is that they are ubiquitous in our society and they depict many of the barriers and ideals that are commonly found in cross-gender relationships. They are so common, in fact, that many theories have been erected about them.

the strangers in men

The *Terrible Mother* complex is the most widely cited barrier to men's intimacy with women. There are several common variations of this complex. Joe's dream lover is the one I see most often in therapy: Critical, demanding, and dominating, she wants to control his life. (Recall that Joe is married to Patty and they are a "liberated couple" in early adulthood who have working-class backgrounds.) In stories and myths the Terrible Mother is depicted as the hag, nag, witch. She is especially feared by a man because she can suck out his soul, disempowering and devitalizing him. Her power derives from humiliation and contempt. She barks and bitches and "rides" men with her complaints. Men imagine she is taking her revenge for male dominance. She usually derives from the powerlessness felt by little boys in the face of dominant female authority—mothers, teachers, sisters, aunts.

Another version is Larry's depressed, empty, suffocating Terrible Mother. (Larry and Louise are a midlife couple struggling with the effects of changing sex roles and the promise of autonomy for women.) She is like a ghost from Hades who consumes her son's blood in order to live herself; sometimes she is the "Vampire Mother" who may be the historical prototype for Dracula. This empty, depressed Terrible Mother resembles death itself in the way she snuffs out vitality. She wields the power of guilt and shame. She has sacrificed herself in order to be Mother and now the Victim Child must be sacrificed to her. Woody Allen's portrayals of his guilt-inducing Terrible Mother complex are entertaining because of the widespread recognition of the crippling psychological residues of the self-sacrificing mother.

Finally, there is the seductive and raping Terrible Mother, the Jocasta who abandons her infant Oedipus and then uses him for her own sexual pleasure. She is the most malignant version of the Terrible Mother (artfully portrayed in the novel and film *The Grifters* as the seductive and abandoning mother of the protagonist). She uses her son for her own purposes, but always *promises* more. She implies that someday she will be transformed into something authentic, but she is not capable of that. In the meantime, she is full of manipulations and seductions, sadistic and sexualized power plays that seem intimate but are in fact self-aggrandizing. A man who suffers from this kind of Terrible Mother complex has usually experienced sexual abuse or stimulation by a mother figure, sometimes an older sister. He has a profound and debilitating confusion between intimacy and sexuality with a woman. Frequently he can imagine women only in regard to their desire for sex or his desire to dominate them.

The *Great Mother* has been depicted as the fullness of nurture, especially in the mother-and-son combination of fantasied "completeness" in which the two sexes become one unity. One form of the Great Mother is Aphrodite, the mother of Eros—seductive, gratifying, and extremely adoring. She infuses her son with confident expectation as long as he belongs to her. Jonathon suffers from this kind of dream lover. (Recall that Jonathon is married to Karen; they are an urban couple in their thirties who are upwardly mobile and see themselves as feminists.) No man alive can really *leave* her because she appears to be "all." She is the domain of limitless love. Everything comes from *her*—good fortune, fame, and beauty. If Jonathon were to part with this complex (his mother's fantasy of him), he believes he would die. French psychoanalyst Jacques Lacan talks about this kind of Great Mother complex as the imaginary "phallus of the mother," meaning that the son actually stands for the mother's phallic power and may be captured forever in a Great Mother complex. If the Mother permits the man to marry, she will choose his bride (although no woman is really his match), but internally he will belong to no one but *her,* his life sustenance. He will carry out the "mission" designed for him by his mother or mother figure. The bond woven in the darkness of nurturance mixed with sexual desire (or even sexualized love) threatens to bind Mother and Child forever. Jonathon has problems with sexual inhibition and premature ejaculation; unconsciously he imagines himself bound to the seductive Great Mother, destined to be her Eternal Son. He can thrive *only* in an atmosphere of her adoration because he is nothing without her.

Another form of the Great Mother is the traditional version of the happy selfless mother who is supposed to be content to serve others and nurture, nurture, nurture. She appears in the psyches of men as an ideal, a sort of Queen of Heaven who is desexualized (it was an immaculate conception). She is The Mother enshrined, whom the man sees as perfectly happy to have been his Source and support system. She has no being and no meaning other than having created and sustained him. She is the beatific nursing mother and he the full-fed son. Her power is giving life and sustenance. The psychological problem with her powerful presence is the difficulty in separating and the impossibility of a real woman's stepping into her position in the man's psyche.

The two poles of these Mother complexes are Mother and Child; they are *both* available to be played out whenever a man is captured. In the case of the Terrible Mother, the Child pole is a guilty, ashamed, humiliated, castrated, overwhelmed little boy. He is the Victim Child. In the case of the Great Mother, the Child pole is an arrogant, demanding, self-promoting, confident, admiration-hungry good boy. He is the Golden Child.

The *Mistress Lover* is perhaps the strangest of men's dream lovers because she is given birth in the male psyche and yet she is often assumed to have come from the female. She is the Whore, the overwhelmingly seductive female appearance in whose presence men are driven mad with desire. She is Aphrodite and Circe, the dangerous female power that can be defeated only through death (his or hers). She captures men through her looks and what is under the surface cannot be trusted. Pandora, in Greek mythology, is a wonderful version of the Mistress Lover. Pandora is the first female human being. Zeus issues an order that she be created in revenge for man's theft of fire from the gods. She is crafted by a lesser-known god, Hephaestus, to look like a goddess. The god Hermes places lies and deceit in her bosom (in place of a heart, it seems). Then she is adorned with gold and beautiful clothes and sent out to be the enemy of man. Her story is strikingly clear about the meaning of power in female appearance. The power of female appearance means trouble and was invented in the male hierarchy, in a power struggle. (In my clinical experience I find that women willing to play Pandora do so because they find no other way in which to enter the world. They do not seek this role or even want it; it is the only one available. Usually it is perceived by a woman as being the dubious "attraction to my appearance, not to me.")

Pandora's counterpart in the Judeo-Christian tradition is Eve, another seductive liar. The negative emotional power of the Mistress Lover is her sexual attractiveness, which confuses and deceives. Men like Larry are vulnerable to Mistress Lover complexes in midlife when they feel their own sexual powers waning. I believe this attraction to Mistress Lover fantasies and projections is less about the fear of death than it is about the fear of losing power among men.

What is the other pole of the Mistress Lover complex? The Bully or the Brute, the man who identifies his worth and esteem with being "macho" in an intimidating way. Some men are addicted to sex fused with aggression, and imagine the Mistress Lover everywhere, using impersonal sex as a way of handling anxiety, especially anxiety about self-esteem. The popular depiction (in movies, novels, TV) of this dream lover is an objectification of women, turning women into objects and devaluing them. As ancient as Pandora is, if she were not also thoroughly modern the pornography industry would not be thriving as it is.

The Bully companion of the Mistress Lover is felt by a man as freedom to "do as he pleases" because he is a man. In this state, a man may believe that "she wants to be fucked," that "she is begging for it" or "tricking me into it," even if she is a little girl. The girl or woman caught in the man's projection may *clearly* indicate that she is not interested in sex (or objects to being sexualized, for example, on the street), but the Bully voice will respond that "she doesn't mean it, she needs this, she's asking for it." Sexual crimes against women, from pimping and prostitution to child sexual abuse and rape, are connected with this psychological complex.

Although I do not entirely understand the origins of this complex, I believe it is built on envy, hatred, fear, and aggression. Underlying it seem to be both fear and envy/hatred of the female body and female sexuality, unconsciously expressed as a desire to dominate and possess it, to show "who's boss." French feminists like Luce Irigaray, and many contemporary feminist literary theorists, have written about this phenomenon. They tend to believe that the Mistress Lover and the fantasy of female as sex *object* are a male compensation or a revenge for the reproductive powers and complex sexuality of women. They may also be a revenge against a seductive mother or sister.

The *Maiden Lover* is the soul mate, daughter, or sisterly dream lover who is either the match or the potential match for the perfect relationship. Larry saw Louise as a Maiden Lover when he first met her: He would "bring her into herself" by guiding and helping her. Louise was supposed to emerge as a strong and successful woman who would be his perfect match. The long tradition of the soul mate, expressed by the Greeks in the brother-sister pair of Apollo and Artemis, seems to be a longing for oneself in the opposite sex. The self-conscious emotions of pride, envy, jealousy, and embarrassment fuel this complex with narcissistic motives to reproduce what is loved in oneself and to avoid what is detested and depreciated. When this complex discourages commitment to a current partner (in favor of finding the "perfect" one), it may live alongside a stirring Mother complex, either negative or positive. An overwhelming need or wish for a soul mate is often a refusal to commit to anyone (and by default, then, to remain the Mother's son).

When the Maiden Lover is projected onto an actual woman, usually the woman has evoked feelings of admiration, hope, and idealization in the man. She appears to him to have the virtues, qualities, talents, and intelligence that he respects. These are usually the ideal qualities in himself that he disavows. He may see her as more promising than himself, as Joe tended to see Patty. He wants to assist her in developing herself and becoming the "strong and independent" woman that she could be. Sometimes the man seems patronizing with such a woman, but more often he is laudatory and supportive. Like Joe, many men project the Maiden Lover onto women they consider to be strong, heroic, or equal counterparts to men. The "maiden" here is a metaphor for the independent, unattached, free spirit who does not live under male dominion. The Amazons and virgin goddesses, such as Athena, are examples from Greek stories. The range of feminine vulnerability in such a dream lover stretches from the ingenue-daughter image at one end of the spectrum to the free spirit–warrior woman at the other. What distinguishes the Maiden Lover is the potential to match or mirror a man.

The other pole of the Maiden Lover complex is Father, Brother, or Guide. In this state the man feels enabled to be special or unique in assisting, supporting, or encouraging the woman. He may feel that his worth or future depends on her agreement to his plan. The image of great teacher (guru, distinguished professor) in consort with promising student is one that captures many university professors and leaders of religious groups as they fall prey to the Maiden Lover complex.

As for the origins of the complex, I would guess that it is related especially to loving and admiring an older sister or successful mother, or identifying with the power of the Great Father complex, the provident patriarch.

All of these dream lovers may inhabit a man's psyche and his relationships with women, although usually one or two predominate. Many contemporary theories of gender and sex differences seem dictated by the Great and Terrible Mother scripts, in which the adult man is driven to emotional distance and anxious, angry conflict with women because of anxiety about his own masculinity—feeling like a boy with his mother. Although I think Mother complexes are indeed troubling, I find the Mistress and Maiden dream lovers to be equally disruptive to heterosexual intimacy.

The complexity and range of the strange gender in men has yet to be fully explored because the distinction between men's imaginations and women's lives has not been clarified. The powerful Terrible Mother is an aspect of a man's inner life and the seductive Mistress Lover is shaped by the male mind. If men were able to see that these dreadful images of women arise from their own imaginations, they might feel more inclined to be intimate and vulnerable with actual women. Once when I was giving a lecture on couples in dialogue, I began with a statement about women wanting to be closer to men and to speak in their own voices, but not wanting power *over* men. After only a few sentences, a man in the back raised his hand. "Yes?" I said with some irritation at the interruption. "What about the Amazons?" he asked, completely out of context. I felt embarrassed and momentarily blocked. Then a voice from within me (not what I was thinking at all) said, "Amazons are the invention of men. They have nothing to do with women." The man was shocked (and so was I), but I got thundering applause from the women in the audience, and I thanked my dream lover for speaking up.

Jonathon might feel the return of his own passionate sexuality if he could understand and objectify his inner state instead of seeing Karen as a whore. In Jonathon's case, the struggle will be especially difficult because he will have to recognize that being loved is not the same thing as being admired. His self-esteem may fall in the process of understanding this, but if he can claim his own Maiden Lover, he will take himself and his goals more seriously.

The projection of the Maiden Lover onto successful women is a problem in contemporary men who feel they have lost their ambition or independent-mindedness. A man feels deeply freed up when he realizes that the Maiden Lover is an image of his own inner life and resources that he must claim for himself.

the strangers in women

The *Terrible Father* is the most debilitating of women's dream lovers. It is impossible to chronicle here the cases of childhood sexual abuse, physical and emotional intimidation, and neglect or abandonment of girls by fathers, stepfathers, uncles, and other men who have been in supposedly protective roles. The national statistics on childhood sexual abuse show that one of every three or four adult women living in the United States now was sexually abused. This is a phenomenal tragedy. My own practice reflects these statistics. The legacy of abuse is the Terrible Father complex in the adult lives of women. If it were not enough to have suffered horrors as a child, the ongoing inner life of an abused daughter is fraught with terrors.

Many times these inner fears and terrors are a permanent barrier to trusting one's adult love partner, if a woman cannot or does not get therapeutic help. Even with the best help, some women never recover even a rudimentary trust of a man, especially as a sexual partner. This is why "survivors" of sexual abuse are said to be surviving and not recovered. At a Jungian conference on clinical issues several years ago, a woman from the audience stopped me in the women's room. She said that I had somehow implied in my talk or comments that I thought a woman could "recover" from childhood sexual abuse. She wanted to correct me. She said, "I have been a psychotherapist myself for fifteen years. I have been in psychotherapy for at least as long. Four years ago, I *remembered*. There is no way I can ever recover, because it was *my father* who hurt me. I am sexually dead." I was stunned. I was caught short because of her obvious pain and her definiteness. I thanked her deeply for sharing with me her own feelings of hopelessness. Although I cannot afford to feel hopeless about helping survivors, I was deeply touched by this momentary confrontation with the reality that many women feel. As we will see later in the chapter about sexuality, I believe that some survivors of sexual abuse can recover trust in sexual functioning, but it depends on many factors (some of which are completely out of the control of the survivor—such as her relationship to the abuser). In couple therapy, my husband and I have been successful in helping couples recover slowly when the nonabused partner is able to aid in the healing.

I have not been sexually abused, nor was my experience of the Terrible Father complex ever the product of my father's intention to hurt me. I do not have the most debilitating form of this complex, the one in which the child's felt (and imagined) experiences of fear are *mixed* with the reality of a malignant enactment on the part of the parent. Whether it is the boy with a seductive mother or the girl with an abusive father, when any parent actually carries out what the child most fears, there is no way to know *ever again* exactly what is the distinction between the imagined and the real. Consequently, even when things go very well in the relational life of the adult survivor, the childhood abuse stands in the way of knowing that "things are okay now" because the parent (who was *supposed* to be a protective, safe haven) turned into the monster (who was *supposed* to be imaginary).

Actual physical and sexual abuse of girls by protective male figures is so common that I, like most other couple therapists, find that heterosexual couples having intransigent sexual problems are much more likely than not to be dealing with sexual abuse—usually of the woman in childhood. I have worked in therapy with many women who have overwhelming, arresting Terrible Father complexes, whose dreams and fears of demonic men, of overpowering and sexually greedy monsters, must be seen and understood as the emotional residue from actual sexual or physical abuse in the past. It is extraordinarily difficult to take responsibility for this kind of emotional state while in a heterosexual couple relationship. (In a later chapter I will discuss how this process works.)

The most devastating version of the Terrible Father, then, is the devil, demon, monster, who mixes protective love with torture. He is the inner figure who promises to love or sustain and then turns on a woman and rapes her, empties her, or destroys her worth. The rape of Persephone by her uncle Hades, condoned by her father, Zeus, is an example from Greek mythology of the use of rape to strengthen bonds among gods. More relevant to contemporary women are Christian images of the devil as the god figure who "turns bad" and uses his power only to do evil.

Another version of the Terrible Father is a critical, attacking, belittling man who diminishes a woman's worth, especially her worth in the world. This Father complex attacks the mind, creativity, authority, body, sexuality, or nurturance of a woman and diminishes it according to some "standard" for truth or beauty. Women experience this Terrible Father as an overwhelming aggressor. When they project the complex onto men in authority, women feel intolerably afraid.

Louise, for example, turns on herself and enacts a sort of inner tyrant. She must "get things right," and when she doesn't, she will find a way to swamp herself with negative feedback. Frequently I find that women attach the Terrible Father to language and achievement. If they don't get the right words or get their words right, they attack themselves mercilessly.

Patty fears speaking out in her classes and often devalues what she has to say prior to saying it. Patty also fears Joe irrationally when Joe gets angry. If Joe makes even a small complaint about her housekeeping, Patty feels overwhelmed and defeated by her Terrible Father, whose attacking voice gets mixed with Joe's criticism.

Mythologically, Zeus is a good depiction of the Terrible Father of criticism, complaint, and female devaluation. He is remote and judgmental. His greatest interest is in keeping his own power. He is never interested in seeing something in a new way nor in hearing any opinions differing with his.

The emotions associated with the most malignant form of the Terrible Father are humiliation, shame, terror, disgust, aggression, rage, hate, and fear. The critical form of the Terrible Father is driven by humiliation, shame, guilt, embarrassment, aggression, fear, and hate. Both forms of the complex have another pole, the Victim Child. Usually a woman projects the Terrible Father onto a man or men and then identifies with the Victim Child. In the identification with the Child she feels totally diminished and helpless, sometimes wholly humiliated or even absent. She may go into a sort of dissociated state in which she feels "out of her body." Women who experience this are numb and nonreactive in situations where they should defend or protect themselves. This state is especially troublesome because the woman "has no words" and later feels enraged at herself. When a woman identifies with the Terrible Father she may attack herself or someone else. Attacks on herself are filled with hatred and abuse, sometimes resulting in self-mutilation, starvation, and other forms of torture. Attacks on other people can sound murderous, enraged, demonic. I have experienced a Terrible Father attack from a client who had been physically abused by her father as a young child. She would threaten to kill me and would malign everything about me, especially the therapeutic work we had done together. "He" wanted to destroy the bond between us and would stop at nothing.

It is difficult to talk about the Terrible Father complex without feeling hopeless and overwhelmed. Even in writing these pages I tend to recoil at the abuse directed against girls by fathers and father figures. This emotional response is what I find in women dealing with their own Terrible Father complexes. Often they are enraged or disgusted with men, themselves, and the world they inhabit. At those moments we have to objectify the complex and recognize that it grips us from within, and can be loosened by understanding and accepting ourselves and our pasts. This is not to say that it is "imaginary" to fear abusive men, but rather to say that a psychological state is different from a physical, actual state (when things are as they should be).

The *Great Father* complex is a common image in the psyches of women I see in therapy. He is the provident, protective, lovable, wise, authoritative, ideal, and powerful father-god-king. His image and the admiration he evokes are projected onto male leaders, heads of government, professors, writers, and philosophers. Although god images from many religions express this kind of power, an ordinary man can carry the same meanings. We witness the Great Father in Sophocles with his followers, in Franklin Roosevelt with the working class, or in Nelson Mandela with the African National Congress. He is the wise old man, the sage, and the protector. He does not engender direct feelings of sexuality, but rather more distant idealization.

Louise, early in her relationship with Larry, thought Larry was the protective Great Father and relied on him for guidance and inspiration. When Louise needed to make a decision about the children or to buy something new for herself, she always asked Larry's advice because she assumed that "Father knows best."

The film *Mr. and Mrs. Bridge*, like the novels on which it is based, presents a full portrait of the Great Father complex as it fuels the relationship of India Bridge with the man onto whom she has projected this aspect of herself. In the movie, Mrs. Bridge sees her husband as filled with meaning and goodness that others cannot see. In one amazing scene they are sitting in the dining room of their country club during a tornado because Mr. Bridge has refused to go to the basement. He does not believe that weather conditions are serious enough to disrupt his dinner. Although in fact he turns out to be right (the dining room is not blown away), the Bridges are set apart from all the other guests, who retire to the basement. The couple become the laughingstocks of the moment. India Bridge clearly does not want to remain upstairs, but she is too overwhelmed by the authority of her complex to make a conscious choice.

Intimidated by authority—this is the theme of many women's Great Father complexes. As a dream lover projected onto a partner, the Great Father may infuse the partner with power or may reduce him to dust when he fails the patriarchal test. Pamela had thought that Charles was a Great Father when they got married. (Recall that Pamela and Charles are a traditional, patriarchal couple in their sixties.) Over time, she saw his achievements as "trivial" compared to her own father's. Still, because Charles consistently received Great Father projections from his colleagues and their friends, Pamela had a hard time challenging his authority. Even to say she disagreed with him in private would precipitate a nervous attack, but to say it in the therapy office led to stuttering and squirming. She was afraid of his criticism if even she *thought* he was a failure.

The other pole of the Great Father is the Golden Child, the loving, worshipful, shining daughter—the Goldilocks or Alice in Wonderland who trips alongside her patron and feels herself to be the follower, student, promising young one. She will be cared for and sustained if she cares for him, if she obeys him—sometimes if she worships him. The emotions that feed the Great Father are joy, pride, love, guilt, fear, and anger. In the protection of the Great Father, the daughter can be happy and proud of herself. If she fails to admire him, she is afraid; if she becomes bored or finds him lacking, she is bereft.

The *Underground Genius* is the most common dream lover I see in women in their twenties and thirties. He is seductive, sensitive, passionate, full of dark exotic powers. He's also somewhat androgynous and the "artist type"—good with words, music, painting, film, something that reeks of *culture,* from the woman's point of view. You may remember how Karen felt about her lover, Jerry. She thought he was erotic, driven, and creative, and she felt his wanting her made her this way too. When a woman projects the Genius onto a man, she tends to believe that she must have him in order to possess herself.

The Underground Genius is depicted in the Greek god Hephaestus, who is very un-Olympian. He is dark, rather ugly, and very creative. Because of his beautiful work in metallurgy, he was worshiped as the god of craftsmen. Hephaestus is also the god of fire, especially of volcanic underground fire. Hera gave birth to him in a grand rage against Zeus. She produced Hephaestus without any male partner at all, impregnating herself with her rage. Her rage over her husband's constant affairs was fired further by her envy of Zeus's solo birthing of Athena (it turns out, though, that he had swallowed Athena's mother, Metis, and so it wasn't really solo). Hephaestus, fiery and dark, is an image of the first raw stirrings of a woman's creativity. This is not a creativity openly welcomed or fully valid, because the woman lives in a male-dominated world, just like Olympus. Both the woman and the people around her may feel apprehensive about these stirrings, as they may conflict with other roles such as mothering.

Another image of the Underground Genius is Dionysus. I find many Dionysian dream lovers not only palpably on the surface of women's imaginations but on magazine covers and in movie stars. This woman-man image, expressed in a Michael Jackson, a Grace Jones, or a David Bowie, is something that seems to have evolved from the effects of feminism on our culture. Dionysus is the god of ecstasy, and he was followed by crowds of women who participated in great spiritual mysteries through his and Demeter's cults. I tend to see contemporary Dionysian images as erotic expressions of the female psyche, just as I see the whore as an erotic expression of the male. Both combine sex and power; the Dionysian is not "power over" but rather "power of" the erotic-exotic. In the extreme, it too can become a harmful addiction.

A woman is vulnerable to projecting her Genius and then resenting the loss of her own talent, inspiration, or ambition. From feminist biographies we are now discovering how many women artists projected their Genius onto their male counterparts (for example, sculptor Camille Claudel with Auguste Rodin), and then gave up their own work. Similarly women psychoanalysts (such as Marie Bonaparte with Freud or Toni Wolfe with Jung) would endow the male authority figure with Genius and then fail to protect their own creativity. Perhaps the role that has replaced the traditional "wife" in contemporary younger couples is that of "midwife to the man's creativity." This is the projection of a woman's Genius onto her male partner, followed by her investment in his development. She financially supports his returning to school, his staying at home to paint, sculpt, or write, or his following some great spiritual teacher. Secretly the woman resents this arrangement from the moment it begins.

The other pole of the Underground Genius is the Empty Maiden, identification with female inferiority. How does this evolve? I believe the origins of the complex lie in the envy girls feel of the cultural privileges boys and men have simply because of their sex. As soon as gender is completely clarified (by six or seven years of age), boys and girls are aware that boys' games and ideas are more important than girls'. Envy, jealousy, desire, pride, curiosity, rage, and hatred are some of the emotions felt by a woman when she is captured by the Genius. When a woman projects the Genius onto a man she feels empty. If she wholly identifies with the Genius she may feel superior to her male partner, as though he is unworthy of her. Like any archetypal image, the Underground Genius refers to an emotional state, the deep arousal of creativity, that is beyond any real human being. No one is *really* filled with genius. Any creative ability or inspiration requires a lot of work and the help of many people to bring it to fruition.

The *Hero* dream lover is the man a woman would be: He is courageous, long suffering, virtuous, idealistic, and sensitive to feelings. He may be projected onto her partner, friend, brother (or brother figure), or son. His heroism comes from his optimistic willingness to take life as it comes and overcome the obstacles along the way. He is brave and responsible. There is no good representation of him among the Greek gods, but he is present in medieval heroes such as Sir Gawain and Sir Perceval who are idealistic, virtuous, sensitive, and brave. In the story of Gawain and the Green Knight, for example, Gawain's integrity is tested in terms of a seduction. It is arranged that the wife of his host seduces him, to test both his loyalty to his host (a nature god) and the strength of his integrity. Gawain shows only a little vulnerability by accepting a small gift from his seducer. This vulnerability can be forgiven, indeed makes him more lovable, like the bashfulness of Sir Perceval in the story of the Holy Grail.

In contemporary culture a woman's Hero complex is often projected onto the kind of man who is pejoratively called a "soft male." He is a man who cannot identify with the Great Father images around him. He is not a patriarchal man. He may see himself as a feminist and it is likely that he is idealistic, but his female partner will probably criticize him for falling short of the Hero she projects.

Women are perfectionistic about their Heroes. In the female imagination, the dream lover *always* chooses the noblest, most honest, most responsible course of action. *He* would know how to care for the children without making a mess in the kitchen, *or* he would at least apologize for his mess (not let it stand without comment). There are so many subtle ways that the Hero should act against wrongs or fight for what is right. Above all, whatever his values, the Hero would not watch television every evening!

The main emotions involved with the Hero dream lover are joy, expansiveness, love, excitement, courage, curiosity, disappointment, fear, and anger. The other pole of the Hero complex is the Lost Child. The woman may project the Hero and hope she will be rescued by him, like Cinderella by Prince Charming. Patty actually experienced Joe as rescuing her from her disastrous childhood and abusive father. Joe was a natural candidate for Patty's projection of the Hero complex—especially in her expectations that he would "always be ahead" of her. Because he was older and because he seemed adventurous, Patty thought that Joe would provide her with ideals, values, a future. When he was not interested in Patty's methods of self-improvement, she criticized him for falling short of her standard. In her imagination, he eventually became the Lost Child, a sort of failed adult. It seems to me that wives who feel they are "mothers to a son" see their husbands as unable to meet standards of their Heroes.

What happens then, as it did with Joe and Larry, is that the woman feels *she* is the Hero and judges rather harshly and idealistically the "failures" of her partner. Women in individual therapy with me have characterized their male partners (often of many years) as "little boys."

Sensing how humiliating this must be for the man—and how much it could play into his Terrible Mother complex—I look deeply with the woman into her inner state. Usually the man has failed her in some way she considers fundamental. He may have betrayed her sexually, failed in business, failed in self-improvement, been a bore over years, or the like. When she comes to believe he is the Lost Child, unable even to find his socks or make his dinner without her, she is implying her contempt or disdain for his failures. He may not even know there has been a test, much less that he has failed. When I note that he seems to do well enough at work, she usually draws the distinction between home ("He's a child") and work ("Somehow he manages to look competent").

The Hero complex seems to represent a desire in women to be mirrored for their courage and worth. They want to be seen as heroes. When a partner can appreciate this and a woman can acknowledge it, she often feels a soul-mate connection of the sort the man is seeking in the Maiden Lover. (Of course, this can reinforce the sense in the man that she *is* indeed his Maiden Lover.)

In adulthood, especially in heterosexual relationships, we have the opportunity to be set free. We can see the Others within ourselves and feel less afraid of the actual others in our lives. We can take up our own wishes and fears and stop criticizing the others. This requires an attitude of objectivity about our inner states. Not that we depersonalize them, but that we can be open-minded, curious, interested in examining our own thoughts and feelings. When we take this attitude we identify with neither pole of the dream lover, neither the powerful nor the oppressed. Instead, we begin to understand how this trance is evoked and what it means.

contemporary psychologies of gender

Many feminist psychologists offer theories of gender differences. Many Jungian analysts presume that healthy sex differences reflect universal principles of Masculine and Feminine according to which the two sexes should be operating. Since I am a feminist psychologist and a Jungian analyst, you might assume I hold these theories. I do not. I don't subscribe to a theory of distinct sex differences that characterize men and women everywhere—or even distinct gender differences that relate to the supposedly different effects on development that accrue from a *woman's* having been the primary caregiver—making men more separate and women more related. I also do not subscribe to universal principles that structure the two sexes into certain behaviors, strengths, or weaknesses. I see gender as a cultural division into two groups that serve different purposes and meanings *depending* on the society or family.

Two important issues stand out in my analysis of gender: Everyone belongs to only one gender group (and so must look at the others from the standpoint of an outsider) *and* men have significantly more power (in terms of decision making, resources, and status) than women under most conditions of everyday life. Although we can perform the tasks, roles, and styles of the opposite gender, we are still members of one group. Even if we take on the ways of the opposite gender, we do so as members of our own group. No matter how many tasks I perform that are traditionally masculine (such as being the family breadwinner), I perform them as a woman and so they take on meanings that are related to my gender. Those meanings typically include less power; for example, doctors in Russia, who are mostly female, have less status and make less money than doctors in our society, who are mostly male.

Many contemporary theorists (and many women themselves) believe that women are fundamentally better at intimate relating than men. They may also believe that men are more rational or emotionally distant than women. Jung's theory of sex differences was one of the first psychological theories to make this claim. In a 1948 lecture, Jung said:

> In men, Eros, the function of relationship, is usually less developed than Logos. In women, on the other hand, Eros is an expression of their true nature, while their Logos is often only a regrettable accident.

Very few current gender theorists cite Jung, probably because he was sexist. Jung assumed that women, by nature and biology, were inferior thinkers. In many current gender theories there is an analogous insult to men, implying they cannot relate adequately.

There are so many popular movements and theories about how men and women relate that you might be confused about what I am saying. Here are some of the main points. Beginning with Jung and Freud, most models assume a "dichotomy" of gender differences. Usually women are assumed to be more relational or emotional, and men more separate or autonomous.

In the 1970s, feminist theorists Jean Baker Miller, Nancy Chodorow, and Dorothy Dinnerstein published books on the differences between men and women, books that were widely influential. While these books criticized Freud's theory of female inferiority, and placed the psychological analysis of women in a broad sociopolitical framework, they also continued to affirm a strong dichotomy between the personality traits of male and female people. Male people were understood to develop *in opposition* to a female caregiver, while female people were understood to develop *in identity with* a female caregiver. In general, men were assumed to lack certain capacities for intimate relationship, especially with women, while women were assumed to relate more easily, but to "lose their boundaries" in accepting others' needs and demands too readily. Psychoanalyst Nancy Chodorow provided an especially rich analysis of the effects of female mothering in reproducing in every generation the autonomous, distant male personality, unable especially to show dependence and relate well to women and children. At the same time, female mothering reproduced a more empathic, emotionally secure female personality that was better suited to caring for others.

In the 1980s, similar ideas were extended by Lillian Rubin, Marion Woodman, and others—including myself. In *Hags and Heroes,* I fused feminist theories with Jung's psychology. (At the same time these theories were developing, other feminist theorists, usually from philosophy or sociology, made claims against this dichotomy.) Many of the most popular theories about gender differences came from one psychodynamic assumption: Because a woman is the primary caregiver in earliest life, the two sexes will develop differently. The following account of gender flows from that basic assumption. Mother and daughter are the same gender, and so a girl will never have to separate herself completely from her mother. She can have "flexible boundaries" in relationships. She can be comfortable relating intimately to another (man or woman) without anxiety about her identity. A boy, on the other hand, must completely and irrevocably separate himself from his female caregiver. He must become other, different, distinct. His individual identity is rooted in an anxious definition of himself based on an "opposition" to the mother. She is the most powerful influence in his infancy when a lot of psychological complexes first form, including his sense of self. In order to split himself off from his powerful Mother complex, the boy forms defenses that rigidly separate him. Throughout his life he will continue to be somewhat distant in relating, especially to women. As a young boy, he will anxiously identify with his penis because it is the "sign" of the difference between himself and Mother.

A girl's mother tells her she will grow up to "be like Mommy," but the boy's mother tells him that he is not like her, that he cannot have babies, that he will grow up like Daddy. This is the first betrayal of a boy's life. The boy is enraged at this betrayal spoken by a woman. The boy locks up that part of himself that trusted and depended on his mother. Later, the man will feel a split between words and feelings when it comes to close relationships. He will prefer to relate through *doing something* (without words) rather than through saying something. The girl, on the other hand, will struggle to feel herself as separate and distinct. She'll have problems with setting *boundaries* for herself. Although the woman will be confident of her gender *identity* (whereas the man will tend to be anxious), she will abhor disagreements and conflicts. She will do all that she can to stay close and connected in adult relationships.

Lillian Rubin, in a book about friendship, writes eloquently of these differences in adult relationships:

> The boy child, whose developing sense of himself is so separate from others, easily learns to become the competitor. If relationships cannot be trusted to provide safety and security, then strength is the answer and winning is the goal. If emotions are dangerous because they make him feel that old vulnerability again, then reason and logic offer protection.
>
> The girl child ... with her permeable boundaries and

> clearly felt need for connection . . . moves gracefully in the world of relationships, comes easily to the tasks of soothing and smoothing in order to make them work. For her, it's relationships that seem to offer safety, isolation poses a threat. Consequently, if competition means distance, she'll reach for cooperation.

These descriptions are moving and sound convincing. They seem to reflect our experiences. I embraced this way of thinking myself for about five years.

Initially I was attracted to this dichotomous model because it was helpful for couples like Patty and Joe, Larry and Louise, and Pamela and Charles (but not Karen and Jonathon), typical visitors to my consulting room. As I said in the first chapter, these women were furious with what they had found in the hearts of men. Why couldn't these men just learn how to relate? Was there something developmentally *wrong* with them? The theory answered that nothing was exactly *wrong,* but that men had been disadvantaged through the absence of fathers as caregivers, in a way that daughters had not because their same-sex caregivers were available.

Over time I became uncomfortable with the dichotomous model because it seemed to support stereotypes about men and women. I began to see that the model left out the importance of peers, the media, and adolescent socialization in developing gender identity. Recently this point was driven home for me when I was reading a psychoanalytic book on the influence of the mother, written by a French psychoanalyst, Christiane Olivier. She set out the usual premises: We all suffer from the early overinvolvement of the mother and the relative absence of the father. But then she claimed that girls suffer *more* from the father's absence than boys do! Girls forfeit the experience of being sexually desirable, which they can get only from the father. Okay, I thought, it's interesting to make this reversal, but what about the *advantages* girls have from staying close to the mother? Here's where her analysis shocked me. There are no advantages, only disadvantages, she claimed. This Frenchwoman uniformly saw women as competitive and unable to feel close to each other! For instance, she says:

> Women do not trust other women in anything that has to do with recognition: they are afraid, when in the company of women, of finding themselves once again facing the rivalry they knew with the first woman of all, their mother. The war with the mother . . . has ushered in the reign of mistrust. . . . And women find it very hard to get through their mistrust of one another.

Because the little girl's body is so different from her mother's (no breasts, no waist), she cannot identify with her mother, according to Olivier. All she can do is "make believe" and try to "act like" something, feeling all along that she is nothing. Because she cannot identify with her mother and because she is not seen as "desirable," as an adult later she

> is never satisfied with what she has or what she is. She is always yearning for a body other than her own: she would like a different face, different breasts, different legs. Every woman, by her own account, has something about her body which does not look right.

Olivier theorizes that the girl's closeness with her mother results not in a comfortable, connected gender identity, but in a hatred of herself and her body.

Her analysis of the male child's situation is not so different from the American one, but she emphasizes that the boy is the "love-object" of the mother and that motherhood for the man is "paradise lost, haunting him so much that he wants to be master of it, be the one who decides on it." Yet this paradise is also a prison because the mother's "tenderest of all loves" is one that refuses to let go. From it "the man emerges showing signs of distrust, silence, misogyny; in a word, all the things women reproach men with." Olivier interprets the absence of the father as a greater difficulty for the *mother* (in the sense that she has no partner) than for the son.

What is so eye-opening in this French analysis is that early closeness to Mother is understood so differently from the American psychodynamic model. Women in France probably are more competitive with and distant from each other than American women appear to be. Frenchmen apparently are more self-satisfied than American men. Olivier attributes emotional distance between the sexes to women's self-hatred, not to men's anxiety about the mother. American and French societies apparently spawn different versions of the genders. These different gender styles cannot *both* be unconditionally explained by closeness to the mother. Women are the primary caregivers of infants in both countries.

Gender differences in relational style need to be explained from some other angle. The feminist theorists I mentioned above (Chodorow, Dinnerstein, Rubin) have been extremely helpful in opening our eyes to differences in relational styles. These theorists have put on record a form of subjectivity—the relational self—that was largely new to psychology in the 1970s. Before that, only the autonomous self, the independent adult, was seen as "mature" in terms of developmental outcome. Feminist theorists of the female relational self have introduced a new story, one in which a mature outcome can still include dependence on relationship. I am grateful for this work, but feel that now we need to move beyond gender dichotomies and the emphasis on *female* relatedness.

In looking to the future, I can see that socialization, peer influence, and adolescence are important areas of research for understanding gender differences. A recent paper by psychologist Eleanor Maccoby reports on twenty-five years of studying sex differences. First and foremost, she says, the sexes are far more similar than they are different. Most aspects of intellectual performance show gender equality. Personality traits do not differ by sex in any predictable way. She says, "This no doubt reflects in part the fact that male and female persons really are much alike, and their lives are governed mainly by . . . a given culture." What about the relational differences between the genders we often observe in North America? According to Maccoby, both genders use different *interactive styles* depending on whether they are in the company of the same or the opposite sex. When females and males are among members of their own sex, their interactive styles depend on need and context. When they are with the opposite sex, they tend to play out the dichotomous model (females are more relational, and males are more autonomous/aggressive). Being with the opposite sex evokes the constraints of dichotomous gender styles. Dream lovers are active when the sexes face each other.

But why do the sexes repeat these patterns? If gender differences are not psychologically or biologically driven, why do we tend to play out certain scripts with the opposite sex? According to Maccoby, gender identity emerges most fully at the beginning of the school years when children interact with same-sex peers. They develop styles characteristic of their genders and *then* parents more strongly support these characteristics. Maccoby claims that *children socialize their parents* in wanting more gender-specific relating from five or six years on. Prior to this time, only fathers relate differently to the sexes and only in some subtle ways. *After* the beginning of the school years, mothers and daughters develop greater intimacy and reciprocity, and fathers and sons exhibit more friendly rivalry and joking, more interest in rough play. Same-sex peer groups in childhood and adolescence are the settings in which boys first discover the competitive requirements of the male hierarchy, and girls first discover the importance of maintaining friendship.

The research of linguist Deborah Tannen supports this view of gender differences. She explicitly rejects the idea that men are less feeling or less capable of intimacy than women. Instead she shows how male conversational style, emphasizing the "report talk" of giving facts and reasons, *is* supportive. While men emphasize *content* and women emphasize *process,* both speak with alert concern for the other person. Tannen calls female speech style "rapport talk," but she doesn't imply that women cannot deal with facts or description. Neither sex has a corner on facts or feelings.

and so . . .

A major implication of tracing out the bigger picture here is that changing the interactive field *between* the sexes would be a revolutionary step. Women and men have never before tried to relate as equals and intimates. If the patterns for sex role behavior get formed with same-sex peers, and reinforced when the sexes separate, then the only way to break up the patterns is to change them *between* the sexes. Learning to hear and "translate" the gender style or language of the other sex is one step. But the real test is to be able to handle conflicts and differences that arise from different embodiment and gender lenses, *without* projecting dream lovers, *without* stereotyping the others. It is precisely in encounters with the opposite sex that we are captured by dream lovers.

Often I sit face-to-face with Louise, or another woman in couple therapy, and describe the way her partner is experiencing her attacks: He feels humiliated and ashamed, and these emotions lead to his withdrawing. Louise can hear this from me and she will openly agree when I say that aggressive attacks are not part of intimate relating. But when she and Larry are back face-to-face, Louise will attack again. She may couch it in "I" statements, like "I feel you never pay attention to what's going on with our son." Under the guise of "I feel" she returns to her attack, because when she is faced with Larry, she automatically sees the Terrible Father. Her dream lover will continue to overtake her until she can develop the awareness to hear her own voice. Her only opportunity to understand the meaning of her attacks is *with* Larry. She can "get" it with me, but she can't change with me because she doesn't project her Terrible Father onto me. (In individual psychotherapy, of course, the complexes *are* projected onto the therapist.)

Sexual stereotypes form among same-sex peers. They are supported among our own kind. When our trust is reduced and we experience inequality, these stereotypes protect us from the others. They infuse and reinforce our dream lovers and we can imagine the others as more powerful, more exotic, more intimidating.

My goal is intimacy between the sexes and the place to practice it is face-to-face with the other sex. At work and at home, we break down our projections and stereotypes of the others only in dialogue with one of them. I am not suggesting that intimate friendship takes place *only* between sexes; that would be absurd. Our same-sex friends provide much-needed empathy, concern, support, and sometimes objectivity. Same-sex friends cannot, however, provide the basis for intimacy with the opposite sex. Only dialogue with the opposite sex can. If true dialogue can be accomplished, our century might be known as the period when men and women discovered they could understand each other.

chapter 3

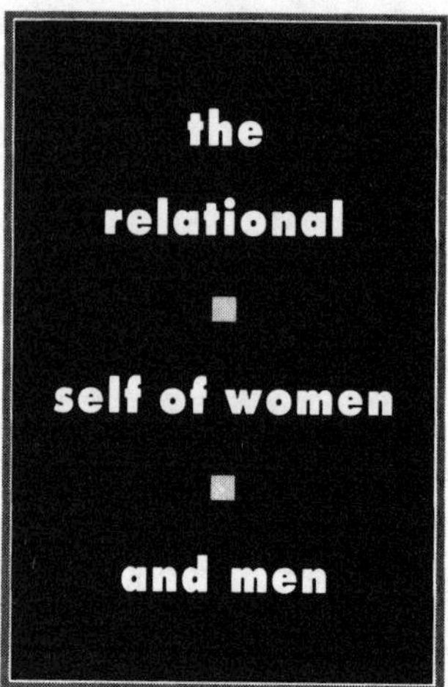

the relational self of women and men

I am an advocate of dependence on intimate relationship. When I speak about this publicly, my beliefs are challenged, probed, and questioned. Women tend to challenge me about the problems and "pathology" of codependence, a state they have learned to see as bad and symptomatic of their "addiction" to relationship. A woman like Louise might say, "I spent the better part of my adult life fused with my husband, serving his needs rather than my own. I see how I encouraged him to behave like a child. I'm out of that now and I never want to go back. I thought dependence was bad for adults." Men tend to point out the advantages of self-reliance and personal responsibility. A man like Jonathon might challenge me by saying, "I was tired of those clinging, dependent women. One reason I was attracted to Karen is that she seemed independent and self-sufficient. Are you saying that adults shouldn't be independent entities, surviving on their own?" Both women and men are anxious about dependence, especially dependence on a partner of the opposite sex.

It makes sense that people are anxious. Women are still stereotyped as childlike. The Maiden Lover is still idealized by women and men when that powerful mix of erotic seduction and learning blows through college classrooms and therapeutic cults. Men are still stereotyped as reliable and protective. The Great Father is imagined by some young women to be the safe haven for a secure, protected life as a spouse. Wives still depreciate their husbands by calling them "little boys," criticizing them for their passive behaviors at home. We haven't freed ourselves from the entrapments of parent-child dream lovers, either culturally or personally. How can I imagine then that dependence might be ideal for health in adulthood?

The answer is that dependence on intimate relationship, in marriage, friendship, and therapy, can lead to development. Defensive self-reliance, on the other hand, often leads to stagnation. From what I've said so far perhaps you can see that the first step of development is self-awareness. In the last chapter I described my first love and the recognition that "he" was an aspect of me, that I had the responsibility to develop myself in the direction that my Genius dream lover was headed if I wanted the satisfaction he promised. What about the relationship with the man who was the target for my dream lover? In this first encounter with love, I lost my partner. My lover and I separated, mired in a bitter entanglement of projection and counterprojection. In my later loves, however, I managed to do better with the relationship. Ideally the bond with a partner survives reclaiming dream lovers.

When an intimate bond survives the disillusionment after romance, it does so because the partners both acknowledge their dependence on each other. For that dependence, people are willing to face the strangers in themselves.

mature dependence

Vitality and health in adulthood are enhanced by *mature dependence,* a term borrowed from British psychoanalyst W. Ronald Fairbairn. Mature dependence, as I see it, is an appreciation of close relationships as the ground of the self. It is a willingness to give as well as take, and to value a friend as much as oneself. In my marriage now, I feel dependent on my husband in a way that is very different from the clinging, powerless dependence of a child. We survived the breakdown of our romance and the disillusionment of seeing each other as disappointments. Now we depend on our partnership as basic, enduring friendship. Most of the time, we can determine what is "my stuff" (dream lovers and complexes) and what is his. We have a "no-blame" attitude about the strange gender in both of us, as long as it is claimed by its owner. We depend on each other for understanding and support. I don't want to call this "interdependence" because there are times when each of us is simply dependent and not dependable. I want to emphasize the notion of dependence, pure and simple, in its mature form.

Because we are both competent adults, we depend on each other's *strengths*. Mature dependence derives from a recognition of strengths rather than weaknesses. If my husband is better at fixing our car and I am better at cleaning the kitchen (which is true in both cases), then we each depend on the other for those tasks. Rather than sort out cooperative tasks by weaknesses (I can't or won't do that), we ask ourselves who wants to do them (who is better at that?). Usually we find that one of us is able and willing to take on what needs to get done because that one feels competent to do it. Occasionally neither of us has a strength to cover a situation and then we have to negotiate how to handle it. In these cases, we might base our decision on weakness or vulnerability. For instance, if one of us has a physical weakness (such as an allergy) or an emotional vulnerability (such as a dream lover) that is likely to be worsened by doing a particular task, the other partner may agree to step in. This kind of agreement is a far cry from "rescuing," because both people have talked about their vulnerabilities and made the decision together that one of the two will handle the problem.

Some of my husband's and my strengths are gender-typed. I like tidying the house and he likes working on things outside. Other strengths are not gender-typed. I enjoy public lecturing (although I get nervous about it) and he prefers to be in a "supportive" role, showing and discussing our videocassettes of therapy demonstrations when we are presenting our work together. The capacity to determine strengths and weaknesses is increased through psychological awareness of the meanings of one's gender and dream lovers. Some of my strengths come from my dream lovers. (Some of my greatest fears and weaknesses also come from my dream lovers, as I've said already.) They have to do with my writing, creativity, scientific interests, and objectivity. Other strengths come from my own gender development and they have to do with empathic relating, personal and household decoration, and nurturing others' development. Weaknesses and fears (for example, low self-esteem) are also connected to my gender. It's the same for my husband.

Men and women have strengths that derive from both their own and their strange gender. My scientific interests and desire to be objective are not male or manly, although they may be related to a masculine dream lover in my personality. They are feminine, the product of a female psyche. My husband's nurturance is not womanly. It is masculine because it comes from him, a man, and yet he has access to it through his Great Mother. I am always ruffled when people use stereotypes such as "women's relatedness" and "men's objectivity," because I witness these same competences in both sexes and know how they develop through the integration of the Others into self-awareness and responsibility.

Developing my strengths does not necessarily lead to compensating for my weaknesses. No matter how much I have published or achieved, I continue to have problems with low self-esteem and fears of failure. I accept these aspects of myself, related to my dream lovers and my socialization as a female. I can overcome them temporarily by seeing how they arise from my own subjective states, but I will never be able to eradicate them wholly. When I talk with my husband about my weaknesses, he listens with an open heart and often just reminds me that I have a "habit" of putting myself down. He takes no responsibility for "curing" me or talking me out of my state. Only I can work with this material, but he can be supportive. At these moments he is relating to me empathically (seeing my struggle from my point of view) and yet he is differentiated from me (not advising me on how he would handle it).

Empathy and differentiation are the twin components of mature dependence. Empathy requires differentiation. If I understand you and feel your pain, I will not confuse you (or your pain) with me—that would be fusion. Sometimes sympathy, just feeling sorry for someone, is helpful, but fusing with another and taking on another's pain is not. If, for instance, I were to try to "solve" my husband's problems with disorganization (of his desk and closet) by giving him advice from my stock of "wisdom" about organization, I would not be empathic. I would be fusing him and me. I would be telling him how *I* would do it if I were in his shoes. But I am not in his shoes and he might find my advice belittling, intrusive—or helpful. Even if it seems helpful, he will usually not be able to carry it out. It wasn't his idea and probably doesn't fit his worldview. This doesn't mean that advice is never helpful, but most of the time intimate partners already *know* each other's strengths. My husband is familiar with how I organize my things, and if he wanted to incorporate my scheme he would have done so years ago.

Mature dependence feels good when it's working. It is an affectional bond that provides a secure base for the rest of life's happenings and struggles. This is not to say that we experience it as a happy or easy or comfortable state all of the time. It is more like a reliable common ground that can be recognized by both partners as the place where they seek comfort and help. Dialogue is the conversational style that leads to the possibility of mature dependence. Mature dependence is the result of many successful dialogues and experiences of receiving and giving help. It is also an open acceptance of the fragility of human life. From birth to death we are all dependent.

A philosopher of this century named John Macmurray was the first theorist whose work introduced me to the primacy of dependence in human life. When I read his major work in graduate school during the 1970s, I was awakened to a way of thinking about development that was otherwise unknown to me. This way of thinking is now part of some feminist psychological theories, but it was almost unknown in the 1970s. Seeing adults as primarily dependent is still somewhat revolutionary. Instead of taking independence or autonomy to be the goal of development, Macmurray claimed that a mature form of dependence is the ideal outcome of healthy development. Mature dependence is an intricate, delicate skill based on trust and love. Over the course of development, other forms of dependence precede it.

developing dependence

Life begins with the dependence of infancy (a form of dependence we tend to call infantile if it goes on too long). It is a powerless dependence on another's care. Of this, philosopher Macmurray says:

> The baby must be fitted by nature at birth to the conditions into which he is born.... He is made to be cared for. He is born into a love-relationship which is inherently personal. Not merely his personal development, but his very survival depends upon the maintaining of this relation.... He cannot do himself what is necessary to his own survival and development. It must be done for him by another who can, or he will die.

Each of us comes into life dependent on love.

The ways in which our caregivers are *incapable* of loving will become the basis of *defensive* self-reliance in our young years. Their adequate care and love will become a part of our desire to depend again in the future, and our willingness to explore new things. Where our parents fail we must become prematurely "independent," even in infancy sometimes. Where they succeed we can go on to develop more mature forms of love, trusting our feelings of dependence to lead us into greater satisfaction. I am using *dependence* here to mean a willingness to receive care and concern from another. Normal independence in children is grounded in a willingness to trust that they will be cared for. Children who are able to trust can engage their own curiosity. They are not passive or excessively fearful in new situations and so in this way they show an independence grounded in love.

As psychoanalyst D. W. Winnicott has made clear, we are *all* marked by limitations of love because all parents are limited. No parent (not even you or I) can provide a perfectly loving, perfectly suited environment for any developing child. Really good parents provide only a "good enough" environment in which the child feels both the trust and the anxiety of depending on powerful others. This means that everyone feels prematurely separate and independent in some ways that are unconsciously designed to overcome parents' limitations. But some parents are so unpredictable and needy themselves that their children cannot trust at all. These children cannot feel dependent. Instead they will feel anxious, afraid, timid, angry, or depressed, although they may seem to be self-sufficient. They will be faced with grave limitations in their ability to trust and sustain themselves through love. Instead of being able to trust, they will anticipate abandonment or rejection in their relationships with others, especially an adult partner.

When parents are only somewhat limited (as most of us are), then children develop a sense of being "individual" in a way that makes them self-reliant over against their parents' failures over time. Normal self-reliance develops when parents fail to be empathic with the impulsive aggression and demands of a developing child. The parent is justly punishing the child's behavior. This is an expected and right kind of failure of empathy. This normal parental failure occurs many times over childhood and adolescence when children are being self-centered or impulsive. Children then come to feel self-reliant gradually, based on experiences of not being understood, seen, or heard. In this way everyone (under the best conditions) develops a private and separate feeling of self. In this separateness, we feel ourselves as reliable or independent beings, taking care of our own needs. This ordinary kind of self-reliance is also rooted in anxiety about not getting needs met. It is fending for oneself. It is one aspect of an adult self, but it is not adequate to the full range of adult behaviors, especially those involved in an intimate relationship.

Patty fights for what is "right" because she cannot trust Joe to provide for her in moments of need. She developed premature self-reliance. Patty could not rely on her parents because they were unpredictable and often looked to her to meet their needs, feeling overwhelmed by the many competing needs of eight children and the limitations of poverty and their own personalities. As an adult now, Patty must learn about her lack of trust and her habitual aggressive tendencies when she feels in need.

Jonathon seeks admiration in place of love because his mother adored him when she should have loved him, indulged him when she should have frustrated him, and imagined him to be more powerful than he was. Jonathon could not depend on his mother to see his needs because he was flooded by her adulation of him. He was primed to respond almost exclusively to her wishes and fantasies of him. Nor could he feel his own self-reliance as Patty did. When he attempted to become independent of her, his mother intruded and tried to gratify him further. As an adult, Jonathon must learn about his desire for admiration and his tendency to seek it by pleasing a woman, wanting to be "just what she needs."

Because we begin life in utter dependence and develop through childhood by adapting to the needs of our parents (in order to be sustained ourselves), we are structured by our parents' limitations. As Jung says in his essay on marriage as a psychological relationship, "Children are driven unconsciously in a direction that is intended to compensate for everything that was left unfulfilled in the lives of their parents." For most of us this means that our dependence on our parents shapes us to search for a partner who will fulfill what the parent wanted (either in a love relationship or in achievement or status). Late adolescence and early adulthood are times of increased self-reliance and independence for young people in our society. During these times, a developing adult may oppose parental complexes and defend against the unlived life of a parent. Whether we choose a partner that is a parent's dream lover or seems to be the opposite of our parents' dreams, we will be faced with the difficulties of dependence as soon as the relationship becomes committed. Then our capacity for trust will be challenged full-force as we face the task of developing our dependence.

the relational self

What I call self is fundamentally and continuously dependent on relationship. Self is the story we tell about our sense of being a single person and existing continuously over time. In order to have this story and this existence, we depend on other selves. We were talked into being by our caregivers before we could talk, and we continue to be explained by others and to explain ourselves in terms of the meanings they lend us.

When people are engaged in a relationship that yields some support and intimacy, they tend to acknowledge this directly. As an exercise in couple therapy, I ask people to rate the value of their partnership on a scale from 0 to 10, where 0 is "I can take it or leave it; I'm indifferent" and 10 is "I couldn't live without it; it's as valuable as oxygen." Even when couples are just entering therapy, many people rate their relationships at this highest value. Rarely have I *ever* seen a rating below 5 unless the couple were about to separate. This exercise encourages reflection, getting a bigger context. Moments later when the couple engage in conversation, the person who rated the relationship as 10 may say things like "I *never* get anything from you that helps me at all, and I'm tired of trying to explain why." This is a strange contrast to rating the relationship as "valuable as oxygen," but now a dream lover is being projected onto the partner and the speaker is sounding defensively self-reliant.

When they are mired in childhood complexes and dream lovers, people feel the pull of defensive self-reliance, wanting to erase any need for the partner. An adult love relationship can be a path that leads from defensive self-reliance to mature dependence and a relational self. It can also be a path that leads to acting out of complexes, projecting dream lovers, and feeling defensively self-reliant. Love relationships in adulthood can easily repeat the trauma, rejection, and abandonment of the past.

Neither sex has the edge on developing mature dependence. Although women may have more empathic skills and expressive language (what Deborah Tannen calls rapport talk), they are as apprehensive as men about recognizing their dependence. Although men may have autonomous skills and greater privilege and/or power in the world, they are as apprehensive as women about surrendering defensive self-reliance and fantasies of independence. Experiencing directly the relational self is different from believing that your partner is there for you. It is more like *acknowledging* how much you need, depend on, and value your partner. This knowledge is difficult for both sexes.

My understanding of the relational self has evolved from theories of early psychoanalysts such as Carl Jung, Melanie Klein, Harry Stack Sullivan, Ronald Fairbairn, D. W. Winnicott, and later psychoanalysts such as John Bowlby, Heinz Kohut, and Daniel Stern. These psychoanalytic theorists have originated models in which the relational self is more or less central. Most of them acknowledge the critical importance of early attachment relationships for later development, but only Bowlby, Kohut, and Sullivan (and their followers) claim that the self is primarily and fundamentally relational over one's lifespan. Holding together the experience of a single self in a body (instead of falling apart), and remembering the connections to a continous past, depend on human relationships throughout life. If you think for a moment about your own experiences of "falling apart" (feeling beside yourself or disembodied), you will see that they occur when you feel afraid or anxious, either because of a past relationship (a complex, for instance) or a present one. Similarly, people forget parts or all of childhood because of relational traumas. Adult traumas can produce the same thing. These three theorists emphasize that we never outgrow our dependence on others for a self of our own.

Feminist psychologists Judith Jordan, Alexandra Kaplan, Jean Baker Miller, Irene Stiver, and Janet Surrey call their model the "self-in-relation," but they take the mother-daughter relationship to be the model case. In their view, it is primarily women who have relational selves:

> The basic elements of the core self in women can be summarized as: (1) an interest in and attention to the other person(s), which form the base for the emotional connection and the ability to empathize with the other(s); (2) the expectation of a mutual empathic process where the sharing of experience leads to a heightened development of self and other; and (3) the expectation of interaction and relationship as a process of mutual sensitivity and mutual responsibility that provides the stimulus for growth. . . .

Their definition is close to how I see mature dependence. However, I believe that a strong sense of being a separate person (*differentiation* is the term) is an ingredient in successful empathy. They deemphasize separateness of the self.

In my view, feelings of separateness come originally from defensive self-reliance against early caregivers' failures to be perfectly attuned and empathic. I believe that both women and men are defensively self-reliant at times when they feel overwhelmed. Both also have the need and capacity to develop mature dependence if early attachment bonds led to some pleasures and security. Under the best conditions, the recognition of the need for dependence tempers defensive self-reliance into the independence of responsibility for oneself, one's own subjective life. At the same time, strong feelings of connection and appreciation pervade intimate relationships and love.

Men and women have different interactive styles—especially with each other, as we saw in the last chapter—and they are stereotyped and socialized differently. These differences in North Americans may appear to lead to different selves for the sexes: a separate, bounded self in men and a communal, shared self in women. Taking this view may account for some gender differences, but not for the complexity of the strange gender as it affects the self.

Carol Gilligan, Mary Belenky, Blythe Clinchy, Nancy Goldberger, and Jill Tarule offer a model of development in which the story and meaning of the self are defined by relationships with others. These theorists do not exclude the possibility that boys and men can develop this kind of self, but they believe that girls and women have the advantage because of the interactive style of their gender. This is a matter for further research. Future study should include understanding the strange gender in both sexes, how it interacts with stereotypes, and how it can be integrated into development when it is consciously claimed.

Mature dependence and the relational self are not the exclusive property of either sex, in my view. The relational self is limited by defensive self-reliance. This limitation comes mostly from the effects of early caregiving, not from sex or gender. Adult love relationships with the opposite sex provide a mirror in which we can see our dream lovers and perhaps claim them as ourselves. In this process we become openly dependent on a good friend. We can come to feel enormous gratitude for a partner who is willing to sustain contact through difficulty. We can also feel compassion as we witness a partner struggling to become responsible for Otherness instead of projecting it onto us. A balance between taking responsibility for one's own states as separate (differentiation) and valuing dependence is present in mature dependence.

Reclaiming dream lovers opens the arena for all gendered (but not all biological) experiences to both sexes. If Pamela could have claimed the Great Father in herself and developed its potentials through her work, she would not be so bitter and resentful of Charles now. When Patty finally develops the Hero in herself she will have greater compassion for Joe because she will understand more fully how difficult it is to orient oneself into meaningful work in the world.

An intimate partnership can itself become what Jung calls a psychological relationship, saying, "In order to be conscious of myself, I must be able to distinguish myself from others. Relationship can only take place where this distinction exists." When partners are able to use their relationship to understand themselves, to soothe hurts and ills, and to lean on one another's strengths, they gradually awaken to the experience of a self embedded and completely dependent on an interactive matrix. I witness the relational self as the vital core of personality development in many couples in which mature dependence reigns.

Two contemporary philosophers, Charles Taylor and Rom Harré, seem to have witnessed the same thing. They insist that we shift our theorizing about persons into a forceful acknowledgment of the relational nature of the human self. They come to their conclusions through reviewing the history of the self in Western philosophy, not through clinical observations. Taylor and Harré claim that models of the wholly autonomous self are ultimately indefensible. Taylor, in a recent book on the history of the self, states simply, "One is a self only among other selves. A self can never be described without reference to those who surround it." Harré stresses the necessity of "psychological symbiosis" in the ongoing lives of adults. In a symbiotic interaction people attempt to complete or fill in for each other in order to assist each other. Although he sees this practice beginning in infancy, he does not believe it is "infantile." He claims that all adults engage in conversational practices in which they offer theories of self to each other as ways of sustaining experiences of unity and individuality as persons.

The movement from defensive self-reliance to mature dependence is a process that begins in infancy and flowers in middle adulthood or later, if it reaches its goal. Defensive self-reliance grows alongside dependence in our early years. In our society we grow up with caregivers on whom we depend and from whom we must separate. If their love is "good enough" we form a secure base for trusting later dependent relationships. We also have an ability to become self-reliant in a timely way, in sync with our peers. The private or unique way each of us feels early self-reliance depends on how our caregivers were limited in their ability to sustain us. Our self-reliance is first and perhaps always defensive.

If our early caregivers are unpredictable and unreliable, sometimes supportive and helpful, and then unavailable or aggressive without warning, a secure base of love is compromised. Prematurely we become self-reliant in too many situations. Patty repeatedly relied only on herself (even at two or three years old) for protection against her father's attacks and for soothing the wounds he inflicted. Her mother never intervened to protect Patty.

Still worse are caregivers who completely abandon a child to its own devices, setting few or no restrictions, providing meager and irregular sustenance. The effects of abusive caregivers are similarly disastrous. Without a modicum of sustained, predictable love, children cannot develop a basis for later trust. The most severe kind of trauma and abandonment, when children are beaten and left hungry and used for their parents' ends, leaves a person unable to trust adult bonds. Few of these people will ever develop close ties that could lead to mature dependence. Although they may succeed at work (if the work does not primarily depend on relationship), they are unlikely to succeed at love. As parents themselves, they are vulnerable to repeating the abuse and rejection they experienced.

Defensive self-reliance in a child or adult can give the appearance of independence. It has been called a "false self" by psychoanalytic theorists. Charles developed a false self because of his mother's narcissistic demands on him to be bold and intelligent and save her from boredom. Like Jonathon's mother, Charles's mother flooded him with her wishes and ideals rather than allow him to develop his own. Consequently Charles enclosed his needs within a shielded privacy. From the time Charles was four or five years old he appeared to be self-contained and self-sufficient, although he often longed for reassurance. Till this day Charles has a defensively self-reliant attitude in place of a relational self. To others he appears to be charming, able, and entirely independent, but in himself he is insecure and afraid that he is unlovable. Although he seeks admiration from others, still unable to see how it differs from love, he cannot express his actual needs and desires and often he feels ignored and unappreciated. A false self is difficult to change because it is unknown to its carrier and it protects against feelings of rage and impotence that can be overwhelming if they are felt directly.

When romance breaks down in a committed relationship, most people resurrect their defensive self-reliance from late adolescence. When this is not a false self, it is the first step in a process of coming to know oneself and one's partner in the development of mature dependence. Karen is a good example of what often happens. When she became disillusioned with Jonathon, she went out to find another man, not that she intended to do this. In adolescence, Karen could not depend on her parents to understand her wishes and ideals. Although her parents, who are Jewish survivors of the Holocaust, were nurturant and supportive through her childhood, they were sometimes overwhelmed by memories and consequences of their own enormous suffering. What pain or difficulty or desire could Karen have that could compare with their suffering? Karen cooperated with them in every way so as not to distress them. In adolescence, as Karen wanted to move into the world, her parents were apprehensive and even paranoid at times. Karen then became defensively self-reliant by having lots of dates and eventually by becoming sexually involved with several young men. Her Genius dream lover was activated through her wishes for a freer, more exciting life. She projected her dream lover onto several men and tried to use the relationships to escape from her parents. When Jonathon seemed unable to respond to

Karen's sexual desires and she felt helpless to influence him, she tried to escape from Jonathon, through projecting the same dream lover onto another man.

Defensive self-reliance is often the signal that disillusionment has set in. It is not a reason to leave a relationship, however. In order to move forward, one has to recognize how one's strange gender is influencing thoughts and feelings. When I became disillusioned with my husband I felt like packing up and leaving. (My defensive self-reliance of adolescence involved moving *far* away from my family home as soon as I could.) Instead I noticed how afraid I was of my husband's depression and fears. When he expressed very negative feelings, I felt overwhelmed by dark intimations. I felt responsible for his feelings and then disabled when I couldn't "cure" them. Mostly I was afraid, but I came to see that my fear was not engendered by my husband's depression, but by my own feelings of helplessness against my Terrible Father. The internalized aggression led to fear and helplessness. There was much to understand and claim for us both in the process of developing mature dependence, but the transformation from self-reliance to greater trust meant increasing trust of each other at every new step of the way.

As we watch our four couples move through this process in the following chapters, some of the subtleties of development will be clarified. When partners of the opposite sex come to know their own dream lovers it is usually through suffering. They are almost always disappointed in each other and the relationship. The courage that allows them to move closer and trust again, when they want to feel more independent, is rooted especially in the love they have received in their early lives.

working models for dependence

Three different styles of early attachment to caregivers have emerged from studies done by psychiatrist and psychoanalyst John Bowlby and his followers. In particular, psychologists Mary Ainsworth and Mary Main have studied young children and their mothers in situations that allow an observer to rate the level of trust or security in the relationship.

I offer these three interactive styles as "working models" of the relational self. They describe the developing child's sense of trust or mistrust in parental care as well as a general personality style that has been shown to carry over at least into adolescence. Our four couples have interactive styles that repeat the patterns they learned in childhood.

The first style is called *secure attachment*, in which the child experiences the parent as stable and reliable. A secure attachment is apparent to an observer in a child's readiness to share in play and feelings, to explore, to meet someone new, and to be comforted in distress. Children and caregivers who relate in this way show the desire to be in contact after even brief separations, are happy to see each other, and take strong initiative to relate to each other. This is the basis for a strong, secure relational self. Certainly Karen shows indications that she has the capacity for a secure relational self in her desire to be close to Jonathon and in her willingness to repair their relationship. Although she is troubled by dream lover projections and a defensive habit of looking to a "new man" to solve her problems, it is likely that she will trust herself and Jonathon enough to begin a process of repair. It seems also that Joe had a secure attachment to his parents and can believe that relating to Patty will eventually be fulfilling, even though Patty appears to be hypercritical of him. Joe shows a kind of determination to remain differentiated (to do things in his way and according to his timing) that is not defensive because he also stays in contact. Neither Karen's nor Joe's parents had many material resources at their disposal, but they were able to be reliable and effective in providing care for their children. Their signals were predictable and consistent. In general, they loved their children not only as extensions of themselves, but also for the children they were.

The second relational style is a *resistant attachment*, in which the child experiences the parent as unpredictable in providing care, sometimes attuned and available but at other times not. Here we see distress when the child separates from the caregiver because little trust exists that care will be forthcoming when the child returns. Sometimes the caregiver is able to attend to the child's needs, but other times the caregiver is preoccupied, angry, tired, or depressed—unavailable. The child has become anxious about trusting. The child may seem passive in the presence of the caregiver and usually will not express joy on reunion. Instead, there will be continuing distress or even an attack on the caregiver. Patty certainly shows signs of an anxious, resistant relational self. She fears that Joe will "turn into someone else" without her influence and she repeatedly relives the fears she felt when her father showed unpredictable rage at her and her mother was unable to protect her. Sometimes, though, Patty's mother could be adequate, comforting, and available. Sometimes Patty felt reassured by her mother's singing at night and her hugs and kisses to the younger children. Other times, her mother was unable to meet Patty's needs, especially her need to be protected from her father. Patty's attachment to her mother was resistant, but her attachment to her father was avoidant (see below).

Jonathon also has an anxious, resistant relational self. He fears his own sexual feelings because he assumes he will be inadequate to Karen's needs. His mother flooded him with her wishes, ideals, and desires, and praised him when he carried these out. She could not attune herself to what Jonathon needed or wanted because she was so consumed by her own needs.

Louise also shows the effects of a resistant attachment in childhood. Her mother often ignored her and her father predicated his love on her performance and intelligence. Consequently she was not secure in feeling loved, nor was she able to explore the world based on her own curiosity. Larry was trapped in infancy and childhood with a mother who was sometimes available and loving, and other times extremely depressed and self-centered. He shows the kind of passivity in the presence of Louise that resistant children show in the presence of the caregiver.

Pamela and Charles both came from early attachments that were of the resistant type. Their marriage is an example of a bond that hasn't worked because they have difficulty trusting and difficulty being separate. They are punitive to each other when they reunite and they are always afraid to let down their guard.

The final relational style is *avoidant,* and it is the most problematic for adult attachment bonds. In this kind of attachment, due either to the unavailability of the caregiver (for example, a parent who is ill or has died suddenly) or the special needs of the child (for example, autism), the child withholds contact from any caregiver. The greater the need of the child (the greater the stress of the circumstances), the more the child withholds, until the child may aggressively attack a caregiver in the presence of need. This type of child shows a lot of premature self-reliance, readily separating from the caregiver in new environments. But there is little affectionate sharing and a lot of avoidance of the caregiver. Often such a child seems to prefer the help of a stranger to that of a familiar caregiver. The child shows no trust of having needs met in the primary relationship. This avoidant relational self extends into later attachments. People like this usually do not seek intimate relationships in adulthood. If they do, they prefer to remain defensively self-reliant under conditions of need and may even be aggressive if help is offered.

The first two relational styles promise greater opportunity for developing mature dependence. With a secure relational self from childhood, a person will tend not to develop a false self unless there is some later trauma that interferes with trust (rape, combat, or sexual abuse, for example). Such a person is open to feeling dependent and able to be dependable.

A resistant relational self can be transformed, if a consistent and responsive caregiver becomes available at some point while the child is still young. In adulthood, people like Jonathon and Patty can transform a resistant self into a secure one. A false self is harder to crack. People like Charles are perceived by others as being capable and independent. They have a hard time believing they are in need because of the stories told by others (as Taylor and Harré point out). The chances for Charles to develop mature dependence are very slim at this stage in his life, but if he is confronted by loss (through the death of someone close, for example), he might be awakened to his dependence on those he loves. Larry and Louise can come to trust and develop mature dependence through psychological self-awareness. Knowing the fears and fantasies associated with one's dream lovers allows a person to become alert to subjective states that interfere with being close to a trusted partner. With this knowledge comes a responsibility for one's inner life. Expanded self-awareness means stopping to reflect on one's own internal states (instead of blaming or cajoling a partner). Taking responsibility means stating one's own wishes, fears, hurts—knowing that they arise in oneself and are not "caused" by another. For Jonathon, of course, this will be especially difficult because Karen has betrayed him. When betrayal enters into adult attachment, both partners tend to become resistant and afraid to trust again.

Transforming defensive self-reliance into a secure relational self is the work of dialogue. When partners can be empathic and differentiated, they can look together at their difficulties and find a way to share the strengths they have. The ability to carry out this rather complex task belongs only to adults. Prior to full maturity we do not have the psychological complexity or the range of knowledge to develop our dependence fully. As we follow our couples over the next chapters we will see how they take responsibility for dream lovers by claiming their own needs and feelings—and how this knowledge expands their strengths.

speaking of differences and connections

When Mary Belenky and her group studied the ways in which women come to know themselves and the world, they discovered two styles of learning and conversation. The first one they called *separate knowing* and they linked it to the traditional forms of education and the ways in which men tend to debate issues. The second one they called *connected knowing* and they linked it to the relational ways in which women learn by finding similarities between themselves and others. I believe that these two ways of speaking and knowing are both necessary for dialogue between the sexes. The degree to which any person can speak in both styles depends on that person's motivations and experiences, but most people can learn to understand both.

Separate knowing is the work of differentiation, distinguishing between things and taking an objective attitude. Formally this procedure is an impersonal method for establishing truth through logic or evidence. It has been honed through the development of mathematics and the Western sciences. It is a form of doubting or standing apart from intuition and immediate belief.

Less formally, separate knowing is energetic and engaged debate. I work with a seminar of mostly male colleagues, along with one other female, and the loving atmosphere of our meetings is charged with debate. "How do you know that your premise is accurate?" and "Where did you get *that* information?" are the kinds of questions my colleagues ask. They search for errors, contradictions, and gaps in one another's viewpoints and they examine problems through this search. In this way of knowing, authority is assumed to be impersonal and nonarbitrary, resting on some objective truth. My friends are not interested in the personal contexts of theorists—their personal histories, class backgrounds, effects of gender, and the like. These are irrelevant from the point of view of separate knowing.

When I first met with this group of colleagues, I was frightened most of the time. I thought they were in combat! I have now come to see that the adversarial style of debate is (in this case) an expression of interest, even love, and dedication to our joint relationship. Although I still sometimes freeze in my boots in the face of their challenges, I recognize that they are not attacking me. They are engaging me. Many men and some women engage me this way in all kinds of contexts from parties and family gatherings to therapy sessions and lectures. I am less likely to be afraid that I am being attacked now that I know this is simply a form of conversational exchange, one that carries a sense of affective sharing for many people. Men especially express their concern and care through finding ways to disagree rather than agree. Although this has never been my style, I now know more about using it when it comes up and see it as a legitimate way to carry on conversation.

Connected knowing is the way of similarity and sharing. It builds directly on personal knowledge and experience. The methods of connected knowing have not been formalized. Although they are used in the humanities and in creative writing, they are not encoded in rules. For most of us connected knowing is familiar through intimate conversation and gossip. The underlying assumption of connected knowing is that truth comes from experience. The major way to elucidate truth is to discover the experience that led to an idea or viewpoint. The procedures for connected knowing relate to grounding oneself in one's *own* experience and believing in one's own terms. People then share by comparing and finding similarities in their experiences. When I am with my women friends we tend to talk almost entirely by supporting each other and saying "Wow, I had exactly the same experience. I can't believe how close your perception was to mine!" When we have differences, we ignore them and instead find something that is similar to mention. Using this method exclusively precludes bringing up challenges and doubts. Paying attention to self and others, and supporting everyone's right to make claims to personal truths is the way of connected discovery.

Expanding horizons through belief and similarity leads to "analogous" thinking, finding ways in which our thoughts or ideas can be extended by analogy. Expanding horizons through doubt and difference leads to "logical" thinking, eliminating contradictions and errors in reasoning. Both of these ways are necessary for empathic dialogue between men and women. Together they allow us to see our similarities and differences, to examine our states of being, and to see where they overlap and where they are distinct. Patty wants Joe to speak the language of connection—to share his experiences without giving advice and without challenging her thinking. Joe wants Patty to "be more logical" and see that he is not against her, but merely needs to go his own way in making certain choices for his own growth. In a dialogue, neither Patty nor Joe can claim to know the "right" way of speaking about truth and experience. Both must accept whatever the other presents and try to understand the other's words and meanings. This is extremely difficult because of the emotional states evoked by dream lovers and envy between the sexes.

steps to mature dependence

To cross the difficult terrain between disillusionment and mature dependence, heterosexual couples must develop the skill of dialogue. Same-sex couples can sometimes rely on simple exchanges to move them smoothly into dialogue. They may speak the same language and have similar ways of knowing. Heterosexual couples have to accept differences in speaking and knowing in order to achieve dialogue, and this acceptance of difference seems "unnatural" to both parties. Every day I see women and men fighting over these differences.

It goes something like this:

He: You complain so much about your work, I think you should quit.

She: I complain because I want *sympathy* and that's what you never seem to give me. When you come home after a long day you're not exactly a comedian yourself. I hear a lot about what bothers you. I always listen and say comforting things. Isn't that true?

He: Yes, you're very good at that.

She: Anytime I open my mouth about something that's bothering me, you just tell me how to change it.

He: But I see how badly you're treated by your boss and I want to help. You know how much I believe in you, and I see you suffering through so much stuff that's not your fault. I just think you should quit and find something that's better for *you*. We don't really need the little bit of money you make.

She: The little bit of money! I hate when you say that! I *reject* that. Of course we need the money and I can't help it that women are paid less than men. This is why I hate talking to you about my feelings.

If these two people could value how they are trying to *help* each other, they might enjoy their time together. The man is not empathic, but he is sympathetic. The woman is unable to be empathic during this exchange because she has projected a dream lover, a critical Terrible Father. She may be capable of empathy, but once she gets into a power struggle, she loses it. The power struggle she is enacting here is "You should love me just like I love you, and if you don't, I won't cooperate." This is a common problem. Many people believe in the unwritten contract "What I give should be given back to me." I don't know why so many of us have come to believe this, but we do. Both men and women look to get a return on their investments, usually in exactly the form they give.

The fundamental principle of dialogue—to be able to understand another's viewpoint, while retaining your own—is violated when you legislate your own way as law. If you eradicate another's language or method by claiming it is wrong or invalid, you cannot be interested in it. Ideal dialogue involves an exchange of different views on the basis of trust that permits difference. Each partner must be able to formulate a point of view and sustain it while trusting that the other is doing the same. Each partner must be open to accepting the other's language and style of knowing.

When Pamela and Charles try to talk, they eradicate each other. Pamela says that Charles is "never interested in sharing anything with me" and Charles says that Pamela is "illogical and irritating in her demands, a problem I cannot cure." If Pamela asks Charles "How do you feel about that?" and Charles responds "Okay," or "It's all right," Pamela is incensed. "See, that's what I mean! You *never* say anything! You hide everything from me." Charles may then resume his attack on Pamela's "irrationality" based on her statement that he is hiding something. This kind of repetitive exchange is influenced by the projection of dream lovers: Pamela projects the Terrible Father and Charles projects the Terrible Mother. At that point they lock into projective identification (which I described in Chapter 1) and confirm their fantasies again and again. Neither one is listening to or interested in what the other is saying because they both supposedly *know* in advance what will be said.

Dialogues between women and men can be limited by rights and privileges (because of their social status, many white men feel free to interrupt women and to talk more than women, as has been shown in many studies). They can be limited by the interactive styles of the genders: men attempting to maintain "independent thinking" and women wanting to "share." They can also be limited by the differences between separate and connected knowing. All of these differences *can* enhance dialogue when it is working because they provide for surprise elements and keep interest high in both parties.

Something that I recommend as a simple way to prevent eradicating another person is paraphrasing. In a dialogue between the sexes it is often necessary to repeat and check out what you thought you understood, because there are so many possibilities for misperception. Paraphrasing is especially important during emotional conflicts, and especially difficult then too.

Here is how Louise and Larry sound, first when they fail to understand each other and then when they are paraphrasing.

Louise: A lot of times I don't think you know how much effort I put into raising our sons. It's not just that I cook and clean, but I think all the time about them. I'm always hoping and praying for the best for them. All I hear from you is how I get in their way.

Larry: Don't blame me for the lip they give you. I try to stay out of it.

Louise: I know. That's what I mean, you don't ever support me.

Larry: What am I supposed to do, make them talk nice to you?

And now let's paraphrase.

Louise: What a minute, I have the impression that you think I want you to talk to *them* for me. Is that what you mean?

Larry: Yeah. I think you want me to tell them to be nice to you.

Louise: That's not what I mean. I just want you to show your appreciation *to me* for the effort I put into raising our sons.

Larry: You want me to tell you about what a great job you do?

Louise: Yeah, that would help a lot.

Larry: That's no problem at all. I think you do a great job and I don't mind saying that anytime.

Larry was projecting a controlling Terrible Mother onto Louise before he understood what she was saying. Louise said a few things about needing his support and he felt blamed. He responded only to the presumed blame, snagging Louise into saying something different from her first request. Louise finally stopped to paraphrase and allowed them both to check out the meanings that were being tossed around.

With couples in therapy, and in my own life, I have seen the development from defensive self-reliance to mature dependence taking a certain shape. The shape follows five steps or stages. These are probably not the only ways to traverse the difficult terrain of disillusionment, but in general I find them to be characteristic of couples who succeed in transforming disillusionment into trust.

Stated simply, the five steps are:

1. Recognizing the vulnerability of the self and accepting an attachment relationship as the ground of self
2. Reclaiming one's own dream lovers

3. Learning how to relate and function through dialogue, especially in areas of conflict or difference
4. Claiming (not shirking) one's ability to engage in dialogue about all sorts of things so that partners feel the common ground that provides basic trust
5. Expanding the uses of dialogue into daily activities with others that encourage greater empathy, concern, and interest

This last step is a movement beyond the couple relationship into a new way of being in the world. Not every couple takes this step. If it is taken, the partners feel even more secure in their development together. The use of dialogue to understand differences outside the couple relationship is an enhancement of the couple.

When mature dependence is born and supported within an adult love bond there is a significant transformation in how a person sees the world. Respect for dialogue comes to be respect for difference. The possibilities for knowing oneself through relating to another open up. Dependence on others becomes the rich soil of knowing oneself, and this in turn reinforces the desire to sustain others. This is true for one's attachment relationships, but it may also be true for less personal contacts. Learning to value friends and colleagues for themselves, rather than as extensions of oneself, makes silencing another almost unthinkable.

Maturely dependent people do not eliminate all dominance-submission in their relationships, however. They simply keep it out of intimate relating. Many people continue to use power dynamics in the workplace and to represent their authority as primary in certain settings (with their children, for instance). But in these arenas, power is used more consciously and recognized as a limitation to intimacy.

The core step in the process of developing mature dependence is reclaiming dream lovers. The rest of this book provides examples of how this works under different circumstances of conflict between the sexes. I've already said quite a bit about how it works, but I want to lay out the components here so that you can refer back to this section if you need to. We will see how each of the four couples comes to deal with its differences, but here is the skeleton of what they must learn in regard to their own dream lovers:

- Seeing how early attachment patterns carry over to current relating: Am I secure, resistant, or avoidant when it comes to this or that relationship?
- Discovering one's major dream lovers by examining the fears, ideals, and wishes one feels for one's partner
- Knowing how one's dream lovers fit with parents' lived and unlived lives, hopes, and dreams
- Taking responsibility for one's subjective states: dream lovers and other complexes
- Claiming one's desires, ideals, wishes, fears, aggression, jealousy, and envy by actively changing to make them one's own
- Acknowledging the hurts one has caused in the past by projecting all of the above onto one's partner or others
- Putting into action one's strange gender in some way that keeps it a conscious part of oneself

If you don't understand some parts of the list, don't worry. We'll be witnessing how all of this works repeatedly as our couples move through their disillusionment and on to mature dependence.

As an illustration of how this works, let me describe how I use the last four parts of it to reclaim my Terrible Father complex when I project it onto my teenage son. When I am afraid that my son doesn't love or respect me, or I feel overwhelmed with a kind of hateful rage about a simple comment from him (like "Don't bother me now"), I look to myself. Rather than address him with blame, I notice, what was I just doing or how am I feeling? Usually I have some belief that he is rattled or anxious and I am approaching him for evidence that things are "okay." How much anxiety I have about any negative emotion coming from a male person! In my fantasy, this is a signal that I should *change* that person's mood or mind because I read his unhappiness as a threat to me. As a child I repeatedly experienced my father's unhappiness as an attack on me and so I was very anxious when he was in a bad mood. I would try to change him, either by getting out of his way or by telling him how he should be different. Knowing that I have often done the same thing to my son—that is, tried to change him by telling him how he should be different—I try to be sensitive about how I advise him. I've also told him on a number of occasions that it is *my* anxiety or fear that gets in the way of our relating, not a problem of his. Most of the time I can stop myself from acting out my impulse with my son, but when I can't, I apologize.

I put all of this into action on another level when I work with others in therapy on the same issue. Being a therapist gives me an exceptional opportunity to work in a lively way with my own foibles through helping others. Though I rarely mention to my clients how I am struggling with similar complexes or dream lovers, many times I am engaging a client in an area of my own difficulty. My depressed and aggressive Terrible Father complex produces impulses in me to remedy negative feelings in the male people I love. Most people (maybe even all people) as children felt responsible for their parents' moods. A chronically unhappy parent often has the effect of producing a sort of moral obligation in the child to convert that parent to happiness. When we know how this tendency derives from childhood, we can examine whether it is a strategy for the present. As I work with people in therapy to discern their dream lovers and vulnerabilities, I feel an enormous gratitude. Their suffering teaches me about my own. In this way I feel a mature dependence on them.

In my view, the central goal of heterosexual intimacy is freeing the relational self and developing mature dependence. To me, this is what Jung meant in suggesting that marriage could be a "psychological relationship" in which one could discover a "true self." My version of the true self, different from Jung's, is the knowledge of oneself embedded in a matrix of relationships, in the past and present, out of which personal experience emerges. In realizing this, a person knows directly what Charles Taylor observed in his review of Western philosophy: There is no such thing as a self that is separate or private. There are only selves in relation who sometimes believe they are self-reliant for purposes of the moment. Through this recognition, I have the deepest appreciation for the common ground of trust in which even the two sexes can share.

chapter 4

fighting—to stay together

Imagine this. You are paddling a little rowboat against the current in a small lake. Your friend, seated across from you, is busily conversing, and you are using all the energy you can muster to keep the boat moving. The two of you are heading across the lake for lunch. It's a bit late and you are very hungry. Out of nowhere, crunch! Another boat has collided with yours, apparently moving into your path. You are furious and spin around to attack the boat's pilot. But no one is in the boat, which is drifting by itself across the lake. What happens to your attack? Unless you are a very tense person, your attack will dissipate. You realize that no one is at fault, so there is no one to blame. While you may still be a bit frustrated, it is likely that your blood pressure will normalize quickly and you will continue across the lake. No explosion will disrupt your continuing action.

This little story comes from a Buddhist tradition and it is often repeated. It reminds us how easily we attack a person (oneself or another) whom we hold responsible for our difficulties, *and* how easily we can calm our distress if we don't hold anyone to blame. Finding a "no-blame" attitude toward those we love allows us to differ without fighting, to be angry without being aggressive. When I named this chapter "Fighting—to Stay Together" I was alluding to this condition of anger without aggression.

Psychologist Carol Tavris, in her book about cultural and emotional aspects of anger, offers her view of the culture from which this story is taken. She draws a strong contrast between Occidental and Asian styles of expressing anger and aggression:

> In this country [the United States], the philosophy of emotional expression regards self-restraint as hypocrisy. The cultures of the Far East do not have this conflict; a person is expected to control and subdue the emotions because it is the relationship, not the individual, that comes first.

In developing mature dependence with a partner of the opposite sex, this Far Eastern philosophy comes in very handy. Controlling and subduing negative or explosive emotions does not mean hiding them, but putting them into words. One's words must be chosen with care to avoid cruelly attacking a trusted partner. No direct attack should ever be allowed if you want to maintain trust and minimize projection. You will see how some words and not others give the speaker a way to express difficulties without destroying trust. Our four couples, now in the second session of dialogue therapy, will illustrate the problems and some of the solutions in trying to resolve conflicts without aggression.

Let's begin with the worst of it. In the second session of therapy, couples do not yet understand how to use dialogue. They are in disillusionment and full of blame. They attack each other through hateful parental projections or they blame each other for the pain of lost romance. Most of us are unpracticed in seeing the empty rowboat. Following are some examples of the fights I have heard between heterosexual partners in therapy.

At the beginning of each therapy session, my husband or I give the cue "We would like to hear the two of you talk about what you hope to achieve from today's meeting. You can talk about it in any way you want, and you may have already discussed this matter between yourselves, but we would like to hear you talk together now. Don't worry about informing us of the details of your situation. We'll get those later. Just talk with each other as you normally would." In only the second session, many couples begin with "pure meanness."

the malignancy of pure meanness

Pamela: I know that your skin *crawls* every time you look at me, Charles. I see the way you wince and roll your eyes, and I know *exactly* what you are thinking. You hate the way I look! The wrinkles and the bags under my eyes, and all of the sagging flesh. I know you hate them and so I don't expose you to my body anymore. Don't bother denying it because you have already proved my point.

Charles: I suppose I could say "Yes, I find you utterly disgusting," and you would feel better then? I *am* disgusted by all this self-pity. Pull yourself together, woman; you *are* old and you should have wrinkles! I might enjoy your company if you ever had a kind word to say to me. I can't help it if you hate yourself. I happen to *like* myself quite a lot and I wouldn't want to end up like you.

Pamela's strange gender has the voice of a critical, attacking Terrible Father from whom Pamela expects derision. Of course, "his" voice has become her own in this exchange, and she is "thought-reading" her husband and blaming him for her own negative self-appraisal. This is a projection of her Terrible Father dream lover. Projection is the psychological defense of oneself through externalizing an internal state. It puts one's own subjective states under another's control, or so it seems. Because Pamela has the fantasy that Charles hates the way she looks, she feels under his control. She wants Charles to change her feelings, so she keeps hounding him with negative comments about her appearance, hoping he will counter them.

In their early years together, Charles frequently did. No matter how much he said she was "lovely" and "beautiful," though, she always had a way to forget or diminish it. Pamela's self-hatred and feelings of insufficiency transcended any attempt to change them. Eventually Charles got bored and discouraged. His projection onto Pamela shifted as he "gave up trying to convince her that she's attractive." Pamela was obviously not his dreamed-about Maiden Lover who would shine with his warm praises. Nor was she going to be a Great Mother who would admire him and take his advice. Charles began way back then, when he and Pamela were in their thirties, to vibrate on the wavelength of Pamela's projection. He began to attack Pamela back. Then they entered into a delusional arrangement of projective identification in which Pamela is convinced that Charles *is* the Terrible Father and Charles is convinced that she *is* the Terrible Mother. Charles is contemptuous, haughty, and belittling in response to Pamela's attack. This seals a fated malignancy (harmful evil wishes against each other) into their attempts to talk about difficulties. Whenever they enter into an important conflict, for example about their sex life, they lock into a mean repetitive exchange. Because neither Pamela nor Charles has been "bred" to "fight it out," they withdraw after a few nasty rounds. Over the years, the cold rage of withdrawal has seeped into every aspect of their relationship. Mostly, they have stopped trying to talk about anything of significance. The rowboat is never empty.

Karen has always been openly and combatively aggressive with Jonathon. Their second session of dialogue therapy was a shocking demonstration of this. Jonathon's response to her was equally shocking.

Karen: I don't know why I have no sexual interest in you, Jonathon, but I think it's because you *never* seem to want to do what I want. No matter how small a request I make—like when I asked you to weed the garden with me last Sunday—you find a way to turn it down. You were watching TV, for—

Jonathon: Baseball, my favorite team, and it was a good game.

Karen: What*ever*. It's always something, but the point is that you never just initiate doing anything with me that you know I like.

Jonathon: (*Silence.*)

Karen: Well?
Jonathon: Well what?
Karen: Where the hell are *you* anyway? I mean, are *you there*? I am so *fucking* tired of all this passivity. You *never* say what you want out of this relationship! I'm sick and tired of doing all the work.

Of course Jonathon remains quiet in return until Karen jumps out of her seat and threatens to leave the therapy session. My husband and I suggest that Karen switch seats with my husband so that he can sit face-to-face with Jonathon and talk with him about what's going on. Karen sits down with a huge sigh. Jonathon immediately opens up to my husband and says he is still furious about Karen's affair. He doesn't want to do anything with her until he can trust her again.

Karen and Jonathon are an excellent example of active and passive aggression. All human beings and many complex animals have aggressive impulses. Aggression is the innate desire to attack another either out of fear or need. Eating is aggressive: We consume another life for our own sustenance. Ordinary self-protectiveness (like the self-reliance I discussed in the last chapter) is aggressive. We are willing to sacrifice another's welfare for our own. Aggressive attacks give signals that the attacker is going to "get" the attacked in some way. Ordinarily in an aggressive attack between people, the targeted person will fight, take flight, or freeze (try to disappear). This is called a fight-or-flight reaction. Usually we call people like Karen aggressive because her attack is open and active. We often think of the Jonathon-type person as "doing nothing" or just "trying to withstand the attack." But in fact Jonathon is making his own aggressive attack through his passivity. Jonathon stonewalls Karen. He doesn't answer and he doesn't engage. He "forgets" what she has asked him to do or he "ignores" her signals. Passive aggression can be just as infuriating and frightening to the target as naked hostility. When a conversational partner walks out of the room because she or he is "just tired of talking about this," you feel the impact of passive aggression quite directly—rage. Karen expresses her aggression through sound and fury. Jonathon expresses his aggression through self-pity, iciness, and barriers. *Neither* of these kinds of aggression belongs in an intimate relationship based on trust.

Aggression is an attack on another. If it occurs frequently, it will silence the other, eliminate the other's presence. When only one person is actively or passively aggressive in a relationship, that one person will become dominant. The dominant person will use aggression to get the other person to submit to her or his wishes. Often heterosexual couples fall into a pattern in which the person who makes the most money (especially if it is the man) becomes dominant. When a pattern of dominance-submission takes over in decision making or initiative taking, then relating is narrowed into the confines of the strange gender, especially the parent-child configurations (for example, experiencing the man as Terrible Father and the woman as Victim Child, or the woman as Terrible Mother and the man as Victim Child).

Things are different for Jonathon and Karen, however. Jonathon has stopped imagining Karen as the Great Mother. Recall that the Great Mother is the supreme nurturer and sustainer of another's growth; as an archetype, she is imagined to sacrifice willingly and to be boundless in her resources. Jonathon has changed his projection onto Karen; now he imagines her as the Mistress Lover. The Mistress Lover (or the Whore) is the sex-crazed, seductive dream lover—the product of male fantasies of sex and longing. Jonathon now perceives Karen as the Mistress Lover who withholds her sexual favors from him, and provides them to other men. Unbeknownst to Jonathon, his strange gender has shifted. When he was being a "nice guy," he was struggling to be Karen's Golden Child, the opposite pole of the Great Mother complex. Unconsciously, now he has been overtaken by the Bully side of the Maiden Lover complex, because he perceives Karen as the Whore. His refusal to communicate implies that he wants to bring "her" under his control. He doesn't want to "deal with her" until "things have changed around here." Jonathon's response to Karen's betrayal is to be expected. His projection of the Great Mother would not have changed had she not broken the trust between them and mightily roused his separation anxiety. Jonathon is now beside himself with envy, hatred, fear, and aggression in response to Karen's betrayal. No wonder his image of Karen has changed. A different psychological complex, the Mistress Lover, has been triggered by separation anxiety. As we will see, separation anxiety creates awful barriers between partners as each imagines the other in ways that threaten the attachment bond.

Karen, of course, has seen Jonathon as the Child for quite a while. She implies "Stand up and be a man" almost every time she talks to him. Her attack comes, at least in part, from the shadow of her mother. Her mother enacted the Great Mother to the Lost Child (Failed Hero) with Karen's father. Karen's mother was "devoted" to her father's needs and obviously filled with bitterness and martyred resentment about it. Karen vowed to herself, "I will *never* do what my mother has done. I will never sacrifice my life for a man!" As I said earlier, Karen wanted a man who would "inspire and excite" her. She thought Jonathon could do it, but when he failed, she reverted to her mother's pattern (bitterness about the Lost Child). Many daughters live out their mothers' scripts with men, even when the daughters have consciously committed themselves, as Karen did, to a different script.

Why are these patterns so hard to escape? As children we were repeatedly exposed to the situational patterns of our parents' relationship. In those moments of conflict, joy, love, or attack, we were swept into the emotional power of image and sound. As Jung says, these affective moments give way to universal images—archetypal images of the Terrible Parent, the Mistress Lover, the Hero, and so on. We cannot easily change the scripts that we learned in the first drama of our lives because these images are almost immune to rationality and later learning. They express universal emotional states and the power of the human dilemma. Archetypal images do not "tell the truth" about what people are really like. In fact, human beings are never as powerful as the images. The images point to the essence of emotions and situations that overwhelm us, that are much bigger than we are (for example, the creation myths about the Great Mother). They connect us to the emotional image traces that depict the history of our earliest relationships, wishes, and fears. Similarly, the working model for the relational self is difficult to change.

Dream lovers and our early attachment patterns *can* be made conscious, although perhaps never really altered in their ability to capture us at a particular moment. What I mean is that our dream lovers and early attachment patterns have a hold on us that is never entirely broken, even with increased consciousness. Increased consciousness and self-awareness render these internal states much less powerful, though. This happens as we learn about them, their origins, and their meanings. We become alert to how certain environmental stimuli are the signals that activate a dream lover. We can step back from the dream lover and see what has just happened. No longer do we have a knee-jerk reaction of projecting or identifying with that state. Instead we acknowledge it as an "old habit" or an "old way of seeing things" and let it go. When we take responsibility for our own internal states, we can get A Bigger Context (ABC), recognizing that no one in the present is to blame for our powerful inner states. (Note that I am talking about subjective states and not about the reality of another person's actions in our lives, such as Karen's betrayal of Jonathon. His reaction to Karen was due to Karen's actions and not to his early life patterns.) Then we can move ahead with our own actions, consciously. Look for the empty rowboat.

Although Karen had a secure self with her mother, her relationship with her father was more distant (although not unpredictable). Her father was passive-aggressive in a way similar to Jonathon. Her mother adapted by trying to "read his mind." Karen fears a similar outcome for her and Jonathon when she screams at Jonathon, "Where *are you*?" Attacking Jonathon only brings about the dreaded Lost Child suspicions in Karen now that Jonathon has withdrawn from her.

Charles and Pamela, and Karen and Jonathon, hear from my husband and me the rule we tell every couple: NO AGGRESSION IN AN INTIMATE RELATIONSHIP. By this rule we mean that you must always look for the empty rowboat. (You may not always find the empty boat, but if you make an attack you can learn to ask quickly and sincerely to be forgiven.) Aggression is an attack. Attacks do not belong in intimate relationships with partners, friends, or children. These relationships are sustained through trust, and protecting the common ground of trust comes over and above the individual impulse.

Conflicts between intimate partners become habituated and mean (as in repetitive exchanges and monologues) or are completely avoided (as in passive aggression and withdrawal) when aggression is regularly expressed through either open attacks or stonewalling. To develop mature dependence, to come to understand oneself and one's partner, anger must replace aggression. Anger, the subject of a later section of this chapter, is a "moral emotion" and requires an assessment that an injustice or an unfairness has been done.

Charles Darwin equated anger with aggression (seeing them both as rooted in needs and fears), but I strongly distinguish between them on many of the same grounds that psychologist Tavris argues. Aggression is expressed by animals and humans alike. Anger is expressed only by humans. Human beings can feel angry and express it in hundreds of ways (in language, works of art, organizing a political protest, or cleaning the closet). Conversely, aggression requires no preference or conscious judgment at all, and is expressed impulsively to hurt, destroy, or diminish.

The distinction between aggression and anger is the most important emotional distinction that can be learned by a heterosexual couple in search of intimacy, in my view. In order to protect the development of mature dependence, in order to ensure the right of each partner to bring difficulties openly to the other, in order to provide the ground for discovering one's own dream lovers (by examining fears, ideals, wishes one feels for one's partner), and in order to make dialogue possible, aggression must be avoided.

Similar to aggression and also different from anger is rage. Rage, whether cold or hot, is fury and violence that is purely and simply destructive. Tearing down or tearing up is not part of an intimate relationship. (Aggression and rage *are* useful in separating from an intimate relationship. They are feelings that break the bonds of attachment and need to be put into words during the period of grief that follows breaking an attachment bond.) Rage and aggression are functional in power struggles within a dominance hierarchy (as in work settings in which competition and dog-eat-dog patterns are the mode) and when there is a serious threat to one's safety or resources. If a couple relationship has been transformed into a dominance hierarchy in which one or both partners are threatened, then there is little chance for mature dependence and intimacy without a deep commitment to change. The relationship between Pamela and Charles appears to be such a case. None of the other couples has reached the kind of crisis experienced by these two, as they both feel threatened (although Charles can only imply it) by the specter that they will be badly cared for in their ailing years, that their resources may be hoarded or dissipated by the other. In order for Pamela and Charles to heal the ground of trust and forgive each other for the battering, they must feel the threat of losing their relationship.

separation anxiety

In the last chapter I talked about the work of psychoanalyst John Bowlby and his followers in discovering the character and meaning of human attachment bonds. The human experience of a self depends on sustaining relationships. As I described earlier, different attachment patterns carry over into adult relational selves, described simply as secure, resistant, and avoidant. Stories about self (as shared or individual, as open or private) are sustained in communities of people who have certain beliefs about selves, especially same-sex peer groups in childhood, adolescence, and adulthood.

A bonded couple relationship of adulthood is a critically important matrix of the self. In case you are confused about what I mean by *bonded couple* (not a couple in bondage, I assure you), I am referring to a couple relationship in which the two people have come to identify themselves as a couple. Earlier I explained that when this happens (and it occurs at different moments for different couples) for either partner, the experience of disillusionment begins to emerge. No longer is one able simply to project an ideal dream lover and believe the partner (or relationship) is ideal. The very act of commitment brings terror to the soul. Why? Because somehow we know "instinctively" (whatever that might be) that this person is now a part of the self and yet is not under control of the self.

Of course we have each spent a very long period under similar circumstances when we were absolutely powerless in infancy and early childhood. Whatever frightened us then will frighten us now, whether or not we remember it explicitly (for example, childhood trauma and abuse). For absolutely all of us, though, separation anxiety will also be a threat.

What is separation anxiety? John Bowlby's early research on orphaned children showed that children who have been permanently separated from their earliest caregivers fail to protest after a while and become apathetic and unreactive. Walking through a refuge for war orphans, including infants in their cribs, Bowlby did not see rooms of screaming, aggressive, or demanding children. He saw frighteningly blank children. Some even died because they showed no interest in food. Apathy, lack of interest in life, is the final product of being separated from a bonded caregiver. As we saw in the last chapter, when the caregiver is sometimes available but is cruel and unpredictable, we find a premature self-reliance developing in the child. Some of the war orphans showed this quality also, but they were not the very youngest.

Studying this phenomenon in greater detail, especially as it was explored by psychologists Mary Ainsworth and Mary Main, brought out a fuller picture of separation anxiety. After an attachment bond has been formed and a lengthy separation occurs (lengthy by subjective standards; this might be a matter of hours for a young child), the attached person—especially a dependent child—experiences a range of predictable emotions: protest or rage, despair or sadness, and apathy. The final stage of apathy is a protective withdrawal from the world as though one no longer needs anyone else. In normal grief, apathy is followed by recovery to a normal equilibrium, if the grief is completed. In grief over a lost loved one (through death or divorce), the grieving person *knows* the relationship has ended, so completion is possible. If, however, a child is too young to know (like some of the war orphans) or if the relationship has not clearly ended, the grieving process may not be completed, and the result may be lingering apathy and disengagement in the form of depression.

In adult love relationships in which loss is threatened (as, for example, when Karen betrayed Jonathon with her affair), one or both partners may experience a cycle of separation anxiety—rage, depression, and apathy—on an ongoing basis. Because the bond has not been clearly broken, the full grieving process cannot be completed. Because the bond is not secure, the partners feel threatened. This is why "trial separations" are usually unbearable and unproductive; they are neither secure bonds nor clear separations. This extends the cycle of separation anxiety over time and generally leads to apathy and depression. Healing the trust and securing the bond again will usually relieve separation anxiety (unless projections from childhood relationships are too troubling). Breaking the bond and grieving over the loss will also relieve separation anxiety as rage and despair bring an end to the bond.

Separation anxiety can be a troubling ongoing state for couples like Karen and Jonathon, and Charles and Pamela. In the first couple, the relationship is threatened. In the second couple, the fragility of the bond is always under pressure. Charles and Pamela do little to encourage their bond (other than sleep in the same bed), and do much to destroy trust and intimacy (such as cold withdrawals and periodic attacks).

The cycle of separation anxiety is also troubling in situations in which a couple's ongoing commitment is under question. Their security in the relationship is always under pressure and the instinctive response is to feel a round of protest, despair, and apathy about it. Many young couples, like Patty and Joe, suffer this kind of anxiety when they live together without a promise or commitment to a future. The "let's wait and see" attitude can kill a relationship after the romance has ended. The phase of disillusionment sets in and no commitment has been made. Both partners become vulnerable to making attacks on each other, and in the presence of these attacks, one or both of them feel a threat to the relationship. This threat produces separation anxiety (often experienced as rage followed by depression), which tends to produce more accusations and questions about the relationship—like "How come I felt much better before I got involved with you?" When people choose to get married under these waves of disillusionment and separation anxiety, they frequently doubt their bond for many years. And yet marriage (or a similar commitment) is the only solution that leads to further development—other than the loss of the relationship and a grief process that may free up the individuals for further relationships.

Another important thing to remember about adult attachment

bonds is that they are closely related to sexual intimacy and can be confused with sexual intimacy. It seems that we are "programmed" to feel intimately bonded with people with whom we have continuing sexual contact—unless we suffer from defensive self-reliance or an avoidant relational self. A sexually intimate relationship, or even sexually approximated situations (like sleeping in the same bed), can fuel an attachment bond with someone, whether or not we love that person. An attachment bond is the experience of being identified with, somehow personally bound up with, another being. It is different from love, which is based on affection, on more or less conscious respect for and approval of the other. It is quite possible to feel attached to someone we hate—as many abused children feel about their abusive parents—because of the strong relational needs of the human self. Many people in our society confuse attachment and love, especially when attachment is based on sexual intimacy.

Once when I was speaking publicly on this topic of adult attachment and separation anxiety, a young woman raised her hand and asked me if it was possible to feel attached to someone after having sex only five or six times. I said "Yes," with the proviso that the number of sexual encounters varies by person (remembering that people with avoidant relational selves may never feel bonded because of excessive and defensive self-reliance from early attachments). She sighed with great relief and said that several male psychiatrists had told her it was impossible, but she felt that she "could become bonded to Mussolini" if she "slept with him more than five times." I advise everyone, young and old, to take very seriously any sexual encounters, because even after sleeping with a partner relatively few times, that partner takes on new meaning. In order to promote the promise of an enduring relationship, it makes sense to have feelings of love (affection, respect, approval) in place *before* becoming deeply involved sexually. After the attachment bond is formed—and I believe that sex is the act that was "designed" to foster it—it is more difficult to separate from a partner (even when we want desperately to do so) because we must encounter separation anxiety and grief. The full course of grief includes both the rage and the despair—as well as a temporary sense of emptiness in one's life.

Bowlby and his followers have hypothesized that attachment relationships are biologically designed to keep human beings (fragile creatures that we are) in close proximity to each other, in little clusters we call families. Separation anxiety prevents the young from wandering far away from caregivers. In adults, this form of anxiety produces a sort of anxious watchfulness over our loved ones.

The modern world tends to increase this anxiety because of the inherent dangers to children and the typically long daily separations from our attached others, especially our adult partners. Karen and Jonathon were considering a "commuter marriage" before Karen's affair. She would take the train to work in a nearby city and remain there four days a week. They imagined that the three-day weekend would be a lot of fun and Karen hoped it might increase her sexual interest in Jonathon. Although Jonathon now refuses even to consider it (because of the threat he is already feeling to the relationship), I believe that this kind of commuting would have weakened the affectional bond between them because of their current disillusionment and the fallout from separation anxiety.

The specific fallout I am referring to is the "feedback loop" of separation anxiety. Researchers on attachment have found that even brief separations of bonded partners (parents and children or spousal partners) can bring about a kind of "punishment" reaction at the time of reunion. This is especially true for people who have a resistant relational self, and many of us do, I believe. After a separation, a child may attack or punish a parent even if the child initiated the separation. When disillusioned adults frequently separate for a few days and get back together, they find the first hours of reunion difficult. Instead of blissful reunion, what they experience is anger, touchiness, and testiness. Then they begin to question the relationship (again the old "If I am so unhappy when I am with you, are you really the right person for me?") and the threat of separation is increased. There is even a risk for securely bonded, intimate couples that the stress of periodic long separations (more than a day or two) will produce separation anxiety. Separation anxiety is a breeding ground for projection and identification with dream lovers, as partners experience a round of negative feelings in the presence of each other. Obviously partners separate and reunite frequently in our culture now. Knowing about separation anxiety, and the testy feelings that result from it, usually makes reunion easier. When my husband and I are apart for the weekend, we anticipate a "reentry adjustment" of a few hours. Preparing for reentry by planning some comfortable time for dialogue is usually enough for us to get past the desire to "punish" the person who went away.

more dangerous conversational styles

Before I can move into what is "good fighting" or the kind of conflict that keeps a relationship together, I have to illustrate a few other problems. Let's listen to Larry and Louise in their second session of couple therapy.

Larry: (*To Louise*) Do you want me to start?

Louise: (*Silence.*)

Larry: I mean, last time you said that you really wanted to hear from me about my feelings, honestly, and that you wanted me to take initiative. So I'm saying to you now, do you want me to start?

Louise: Your question ruins it.

Larry: What do you mean?

Louise: I mean if you really took the initiative you wouldn't sit there waiting for me to tell you what to say. This is always the problem. It's always me who has to identify all the feelings. I'm not helping you with this one.

Larry: Okay. Here's the way I see it. You are always so tired and played out by the end of the work day, and I know your boss is unfair. So the most supportive thing I can say to you is get out of that job. I think the boys and I would be much better off with you feeling happier and you could—

Louise: Shut up! Just shut up!

Larry: Wha?

Louise: Leave *my* problems out of this. I am so sick and tired of being the focus of what's wrong. Why don't you fix yourself instead of trying to fix me!

Here we have a classic projective identification of Louise playing the Hag (Terrible Mother) to Larry's Hero. Louise is acting out the role of aggressor in what is often described as "identification with the aggressor." Because her father was so critical of her and because her mother was often bitter and depressed, Louise has access to a very bitter, critical voice that can annihilate Larry's every attempt to be "helpful."

Of course Larry is not being helpful. He is neither empathic nor sympathetic to Louise in the above exchange. He is identified with the Victim Child who must fix the depressed Mother. In his view the only problem in their relationship is Louise. This plays directly to Louise's assessment of him as a "little boy" because he has failed to meet the standards of her Hero. As we saw in the first chapter this has produced a kind of monologue that keeps going between them. She also identifies with being the hated, imperfect, but "fixable" Victim Child of an overwhelmingly perfectionistic father. If only she could somehow find out how to *fix* herself then she might be able to do other things (like be Larry's partner). Larry constantly reinforces Louise's fears by implying or stating that she is "the problem." Larry's images of Louise as the Terrible Mother (nag, hag, bitch) often tilt the delicate balance within Louise by which she maintains her thin thread of self-esteem—the sense that she can be "fixed" somehow. If she slides into believing that she is "unfixable" and deeply, horribly bad and destructive, she loses hope. Then she attacks Larry in a bitter and demanding way, renewing his belief that she is indeed the Terrible Mother.

Within each of us is a very aggressive voice, based on those moments in childhood when our needs were not met, and more significantly based on encounters when caregivers disciplined us fairly or unfairly. We all have the potential to "identify with the aggressor," as psychoanalyst Anna Freud called this defense, when we are in conflict with a partner. Because of this, we need to be especially conscious that we do not wound in the ways we were wounded. Although Louise is accurate in calling on Larry to speak for himself, she has no right to be so judgmental and demanding.

How about Patty and Joe? How do they sound at the beginning of their second session? If you remember from the first chapter, Joe wanted Patty "to be happy" but Joe was unwilling to do the things that Patty wanted—like going to individual therapy, following self-help programs, attending church more often, and so on. In the second session, Joe decided to "take a stand" about his limits.

Joe: One thing I learned by being here last time is that you sure don't know everything. You've been putting all this pressure on me and now I'm going to put some pressure on you. We don't have any sex life at all anymore. You ration sex in exchange for me doing the things you want. This is the thing I want to deal with here. As far as I'm concerned this is the *real* problem between us and it always has been. The last time we were here I learned that I don't have to follow your orders and that I have a right to find the things that develop me, so now I want to know, are we never going to have sex again? I mean, I refuse to follow your rules—

Patty: I have never wanted you to follow my rules. That's just the problem. You don't try to think of things you can do to improve our relationship. I've tried to tell you again and again that I *can't just have sex*. I can't even tolerate being close to you because you *never* can understand anything that I'm going through—and then you're such a bully with the kids, trying to be the Big Daddy when you haven't even spent time with them all week!

Joe: Me! What about you! You've been out every evening with your *groups* and your classes and all. I've been making dinner and you can only complain. I'm so tired of hearing you complain about everything I do.

Of course, this is also an example of projective identification in the form of conversation that I call repetitive exchange, in which both partners argue the same points again and again. Neither is influenced by the other and both are projecting very negative images. Patty is projecting the Lost Child side of her Hero complex, seeing Joe as the disabled partner who cannot meet her standards for responsibility taking. Joe started out as a kind of Bully, which is unusual for Joe, but he became the Victim Child with the Terrible Mother by the end of the round.

What can account for the change in Joe? Is it that the therapists actually precipitated his attack on Patty? I think not. Joe is suffering from envy of Patty. In the first chapter I talked about the problem of envy between the sexes and I want to use Joe's conversation here to illustrate something that is common. From the theories of psychoanalyst Melanie Klein, I have come to use the term *envy* to mean a form of aggression or hate that expresses the desire to *destroy* what another possesses because one cannot possess it for oneself. Envy is an emotional attack that diminishes, empties, or belittles another in an effort to deal with the feelings of emptiness aroused by the other's resources. In the next chapter I will treat the topic in more detail, looking especially at envy of biological and gender resources. Here I want to look at Joe's envy of Patty's intelligence, as he sees it.

Joe imagines that Patty is "smarter" than he is and has more "initiative." In this way Joe sees Patty as his Maiden Lover who is full of potential to become someone great in life. Joe often finds himself "devoted" to her development, especially in regard to "helping her" with the children and the housework. In this view of Patty, Joe imagines that Patty has resources and abilities that he does not have, and so his best bet for developing these is to promote Patty. The emptiness that arises in Joe when Patty is out and he is cooking and putting the kids to bed is a problem. Sometimes he feels depressed and unable to relate to the children or enjoy anything about these times alone with them. Sometimes he's just seething with a hatred of Patty because "she thinks she's better than me and even my family." Sometimes he longs to do what Patty is doing, but feels it is impossible for him to try. His view of Patty as the Maiden Lover full of promise is "balanced" by belittling and diminishing her in terms like "She doesn't know what she's talking about."

The problem of envy exists as a barrier to further development in both sexes. Envy disempowers the self through identifying with the image of being empty of one's own resources. Envy of biological or gender resources often leads to belittling one's partner. Envy can fuel false comparisons of one's own and others' potentials, rights, or privileges. The first step in coming to terms with envy is recognizing the resources that belong to oneself. This is the only way to resolve envy. A sense of one's resources replaces the feeling of emptiness—and this in itself may transform envy into jealousy, a more related negative emotion. Envy is the desire to destroy another's resources, but jealousy is the desire to compete for them or to possess them for oneself. Jealousy is a functional negative emotion in couple relationships, but envy is not. When Joe recognizes his envy of Patty (as he will later in this chapter), he will have to claim his own intelligence and initiative. He may find they are different from Patty's or similar. If they are similar, he may compete with Patty for achievement in school, but if they are different he may be satisfied that he and Patty are in the world in different but equally valuable ways. This will be a process of developing a sense of himself as a resourceful person and an understanding of who Patty really is. In the meantime, Joe owes Patty an apology for belittling her. Patty has a right to be angry with him.

anger: the moral emotion

I hold a strong distinction between anger and aggression. Aggression is an attack, but anger is the feeling connected to a perceived unfairness or injustice. Anger requires reflection. It is not a knee-jerk impulse. Anger is expressed in words that suggest a *boundary:* Stop! Don't do that! I don't like that! I won't tolerate that! Anger is not—never, never, never—an attack on someone else. I define anger in this way from years of experience in psychotherapy and life, and from contemplating the issues of human conflict. Anger is a way to deal directly with conflict without escalation (when it works).

When I first read Carol Tavris's book on anger, some years ago, I was looking for a conceptual model that could fill out my intuitions about anger. I found it. In this fat volume on anger and aggression, she reviews libraries of other studies, beginning with Darwin's. Based on these studies and her own experiences, she comes to conclusions that are almost identical to mine. She says:

> Human anger is far more intricate and serves many more purposes than the rage reflex of lower animals. We do not

> need to deny our mammalian, primate heritage, but we do not need to reduce ourselves to it, either. Judgment and choice are the hallmarks of human anger.

Judgment and choice, exactly. This is why anger was called "the moral emotion" by the ancients. Anger is based on the judgment that we or our values have been wronged, treated unfairly or unjustly. Choice here means the assessment of what to do. Since anger involves reflection, we have a choice about whether or not to express it. What is most important? Expressing the anger with hopes of righting the wrong or at least being heard? Recognizing the anger in oneself and making a decision to wait some more and evaluate? Turning the anger into a piece of creative work or a protest in a larger context? Anger is rooted in reason; it is equally of the heart and the head.

In a couple relationship, some kind of evaluation must take place in order for a partner to decide if expressing anger on a particular issue is worth it. Often it *is* worth it, provided the anger is expressed in an effective way, as I'll describe later. Individual patterns of expressing anger match dream lover projections or parents' patterns. For example, if you have projected the Great Father onto your partner, you will probably say something like "Uh, excuse me, dear, I'd like to talk with you" before raising an issue of perceived unfairness.

If your parents never expressed anger directly, then you are likely not to feel able to do so, although you can learn. What often happens then is that difficulties get handled through passive aggression: stonewalling, put-down humor, procrastination, and forgetting. Anger is the best way to handle difficulties with a partner, much preferable to passive aggression.

Most people do not distinguish clearly between aggression and anger. If they describe their parents as "angry all the time," usually they mean "aggressive all the time." If your parents attacked each other constantly (euphemistically referred to as "bickering"), you are more likely to believe that aggressive attacks are okay. You are likely to confuse aggression and anger. You are likely to be aggressive.

There is *no* evidence that discharging anger or aggression is, in itself, beneficial. In other words, there is no basis for the idea that "getting your anger out is good," including expressing it through dialogue. Anger in, or anger out, is a choice that should be based on A Bigger Context. Getting aggression out *always* destroys closeness and intimacy. It is useful to let out aggression in some situations of danger or risk, as long as you are in a position to protect yourself. Tavris reports extensively on research on "ventilationist" theories of discharge—that getting out negative feelings somehow helps (physically or psychologically). After reviewing both physiological and psychological studies she says:

> Most of the time . . . expressing anger makes people angrier, solidifies an angry attitude, and establishes a hostile habit. If you keep quiet about momentary irritations and distract yourself with pleasant activity until your fury simmers down, chances are you will feel better, and feel better faster, than if you let yourself go in a shouting match.

Of course this passage blurs the distinction between anger and aggression. Her point is that expressing anger or aggression does not somehow magically "free up" new energy or good feelings so that people act in some better way. On the contrary, expressing these negative emotions typically involves us in further expressions of them. When anger is directed in words to an intimate partner, it will arouse at least frustration in response. Usually anger leads to an involved conversation for which we should be prepared if we bring it forth.

Differing with Tavris's overall belief that "civility" should win the day, I am in favor of anger. Mind you, my definition of anger excludes all attacks on and blame of another person. Anger expresses feelings of unfairness, offense, and boundary setting. It allows us to keep track of our individual preferences and principles. Without it, a couple is likely to fall into patterns of active or passive aggression. I think it is an important "policing" emotion in a couple, but it should always include the element of choice (to express it or not) based on context. When it is well practiced and well expressed, anger provides a way to handle grievances and conflicts in important areas of decision making—such as parenting, sex, money, and affection.

Anger should be expressed in "I" statements. If these are not easily accessible and the moment is tense, then the next best thing is a command to the other person: Don't, stop, wait, get away. When anger is put into a self-statement it is often easiest to begin, "I am angry because . . ." This framework leads to the *reason* or *judgment* that goes with the feeling. Another, equally good format is to describe what the other person has done—"When you criticized my cooking in front of the guests"—and then give your reaction—"I was angry and hurt." Sometimes I say something like "Don't insult me" when I am angry. Usually I hear back, "That wasn't insulting." I have to be prepared to say something more than "Yes it was," because I want to convey my specific judgment about the meaning. So I might say, "When you use a harsh tone of voice to tell me where to put your things, I feel upset and angry. If you used a quieter tone, I'd feel okay about it." Anger gives feedback about what is acceptable and unacceptable to a person. Other people may or may not want to hear or follow the feedback. Giving the feedback does not improve the situation in itself, but it opens the possibility that things could be improved. Then, usually, much more has to be done.

what to say and what to keep

In the last chapter, I said that the core step in developing mature dependence was reclaiming our dream lovers. In confronting a partner's or our own anger—and in recognizing our fears, aggressions, envy, hatred—we begin this process. In the rest of the chapter, we will witness our couples changing their malignancies of pure meanness into statements of anger and hurt that reveal their own subjective states. Sometimes this leads to seeing the empty boat and ceasing to blame a partner for one's inner states.

After speaking with Pamela for a few moments, I said these words as her alter ego or "double" (turn back to Pamela and Charles on page 137 for their dialogue and to page 29 for a description of doubling):

Pamela (Double): Often I hate my body and I worry that you hate it too. Do you?
Charles: Not at all. I find you very attractive.
Charles (Double): What I dislike about you is your criticism of *me*. I really want you to stop. Do you know what I'm talking about?

As alter egos or doubles, my husband and I often name the negative feelings—fear, hate, hurt, anger—that are being implied about oneself or the other, but we never allow an aggressive attack to be made on the partner. Instead we reformulate in terms of the speaker's subjective states or dream lovers. I knew that Pamela reflected on *herself* from the critical, self-hating perspective of the Terrible Father. She had attacked Charles for hating her, but I put her statement in terms of her own experience and asked a question of Charles about his. Pamela, or anyone else, is free to disagree with her double, to change what was said or ask a question about it. Since Pamela accepted my formulation, it was treated as though it had been spoken by her.

A basic rule of dialogue is to remain interested and curious about your partner's experience instead of trying to read your partner's mind (silencing or trivializing). Some hypotheses about the partner need to be kept silent while a question is asked instead. As the double, I asked Charles if he agreed with "my" (Pamela's) self-hatred of her body. He said that he did not. Then my husband (as Charles's double) changed Charles's earlier attack ("I might enjoy your company if you ever had a kind word to say to me") into a statement of anger. His question allowed Pamela the freedom to confront Charles's projection of her as a "bitch, witch, hag." Pamela had become teary over what I had said about her self-hatred.

Now she responded to Charles's question with vulnerability.

Pamela: Yes, I am aware that I criticize you. I don't like that tendency in myself. Sometimes I just don't know how to get your attention because you are always so busy—
Pamela (Double): I don't know how to get your attention and then I

imagine that you are too busy to care about me. How could I get your attention when I need you?

Pamela has claimed her critical voice and admitted that she doesn't like that aspect of herself. I stopped her when she began to attack Charles by telling him what his experience is ("you are always so busy").

Charles: You could come over and give me a little kiss or hug. I'd like that very much.

Charles (Double): I have a hard time recognizing your needs. I have so many needs of my own, like to be touched or kissed by you. What do you want from me?

My husband reformulated Charles's statement because he did not really address Pamela's request of him. Instead, he indirectly aggressed against her by returning to his needs. My husband put this into words that mirrored Charles's unconscious desire to be the Golden Child with the attentive Great Mother, or the Great Father with the Maiden Lover. At moments like this, when a partner's dream lover has been revealed in a negative light, sometimes it is tempting to the other partner to attack based on the "evidence" the therapists have turned up. For example, Pamela might blurt out, "That's exactly right! You are so self-centered that I never can get your attention!" If she were to say this I might ask her to paraphrase what Charles has just said (through his double) and check to see if she's right. This allows Pamela to get A Bigger Context and to stop blaming Charles (and begin listening to him). If her paraphrase was accurate in Charles's view, we would look into her experience of the moment and ask why she had made such an aggressive attack. We might find that she can barely control the self-hatred connected to her Terrible Father. She would need to recognize this as belonging to her, not being generated by Charles. As her double I might say, "I often feel so overwhelmed with self-hatred that I hardly know how to speak about it. Could you help with these feelings, Charles?" This could lead into a dialogue about Pamela's feelings and how Charles might treat them—and how Pamela should take responsibility for them too.

Eventually in the second session, Pamela and Charles came to a point of confrontation.

Pamela: Charles, I cannot go on living as we do. Either we have to become more intimate or we have to separate. I am a constant wreck.

Charles: Intimate? I thought *you* had given up on sex, I—

Charles (Double): I have a hard time talking about intimacy and get very afraid when you say we should separate.

Pamela: Do you really feel that way?

Charles: Yes. I don't want to lose what we have together.

Pamela: Why can't you say it's *me* you don't—

Pamela (Double): I want more of a commitment to me personally, not in terms of our children or things.

Charles: How can I commit myself to you when you refuse to be my sexual partner ever again?

As you can see, Pamela and Charles are learning to have a dialogue of give-and-take about the issues that trouble them most.

By the end of the session, Pamela had promised Charles that she would work toward having an active sex life again, but Charles was not able to say he "wanted" Pamela. He did say that he desired a "new Pamela." Charles has a resistant relational self with a "false self" defense, as I said in the last chapter. He does not *feel* his dependence on Pamela. Instead he looks to be admired by Pamela and is confused and frustrated because this almost never happens. He feels defensively self-reliant. When confronted by the potential loss of the relationship (when Pamela said she would rather separate than continue as is), Charles was shaken. Feeling a threat to the relationship aroused enough separation anxiety in Charles that he could begin to respond to his wife. If Pamela can voice her anger directly—saying what she will and will not tolerate in terms of Charles's responses to her—it is likely that Charles can remain responsive. If Pamela backs down at all and seems to be the Maiden Lover (needing Charles in order to *have* a future), Charles will easily revert to his identification with being her protector.

Doubling Karen in the second session was more difficult than it had been with Pamela. Although Karen had initially agreed to make her best effort in saving this relationship, after the first session she had met with a group of women friends. Several of her friends agreed that she shouldn't "settle for less" than an active, intimate sex life. Jonathon didn't appear to offer this. Karen's fantasies of an exotic Genius dream lover were fired up again. Instead of trying to improve her understanding of Jonathon, she had been "looking around" at other men at work and other social situations. She was finding herself less and less convinced that she could remain with someone as "dull" as Jonathon. Because Karen makes considerably more money than Jonathon and has career possibilities that are somewhat better (although not as stable as his), Karen could form a defensive self-reliance in response to the fears she felt about needing Jonathon. In the second session, her initial attack on Jonathon was so massively aggressive that I was speechless at first. Eventually I doubled her:

Karen (Double): I am really afraid of the possibility of losing this relationship and I feel myself moving farther and farther away from you.

Jonathon: *You* had the affair. How do you think I might feel here?

Karen: I *assume* you don't feel at—

Karen (Double): I want you to pay attention to how I feel. I am afraid because I cannot see how we could solve the sexual problems we have.

Jonathon: I'm afraid too. I can't imagine how I will ever trust you again, with my feelings or my body.

Jonathon (Double): I hold back everything from you. I would like to forgive you for what you've done to me, but I don't know how to bring that about. Right now I can't forgive you.

Betrayals of trust cause a break in the foundation for intimacy. Intimacy includes the feeling of being open, vulnerable, close. It is impossible for human beings to feel this way unless they can trust in a secure base for the relationship. Karen has threatened this base. Jonathon is feeling a cycle of rage, despair, and apathy. Separation anxiety and stereotypes about women have brought Jonathon to see Karen as a Whore, a Mistress Lover. Unconsciously he would like to "control" her and be a Bully. Consciously Jonathon is immobilized and hopeless (except that he showed up for the therapy session). Because Jonathon has generally perceived Karen as the Great Mother (and himself as the devoted Golden Child), he is not in a good position psychologically to do what must be done. He must be confrontationally angry with Karen, but this cannot blur into the aggression of a Bully. My husband tries the following:

Jonathon (Double): Karen, if you want this relationship at all, this is your last chance. I am very insulted by the way you treated me here—and during the time since the first session. I want to know what you intend to do.

Karen: I really don't want to lose our relationship, but I can't see a way to handle our problems.

Jonathon: The problems begin with what you've done to me.

Jonathon (Double): I want to know why you weren't faithful to me, why you didn't come to me to talk about your disappointments in our sex life.

Karen: I really didn't think you could take what I had to say. I worried about your self-consciousness and your feelings of disappointment in yourself.

Jonathon: Tell me now.

Karen: I think there's a lot wrong with you—

Karen (Double): I am uncomfortable with taking the lead sexually. I wish you'd take the initiative because—

Karen: Because I wanted to be *desired* by you. I have a lot of insecurity about my body and appearance, and I've always wondered whether you really found me *attractive*.

Jonathon: My God, yes! I think you're beautiful and strong and intelligent.

Karen (Double): I'm uncomfortable when you put all those together, as though I need to be superhuman for you or something.

Karen and Jonathon began to open up the fears and fantasies buried in their projections onto each other. By the end of the second session, they were able to take some beginning steps to rebuilding trust. Karen asked Jonathon to forgive her. She backed that up by clarifying how she understood his feelings about the affair. (She was pretty accurate.) This took most of the session. Unfortunately, Jonathon sometimes felt guilty (Great Mother/Golden Child), as though he had caused the affair. My husband sensed this and helped him reveal the hidden anger—his anger that Karen was always unwilling to reveal any problems at all.

Unconsciously Jonathon was furious that Karen had not taken any responsibility for her problems in the relationship, but had always focused on his. This was another way that Karen kept "one foot out the door" in terms of looking for her ideal dream lover elsewhere. Karen had never been vulnerable with Jonathon. She played into the projection that she was the "strong one" (Great Mother or Whore). This left both partners disappointed. There are no "strong" people. Everyone needs support and reassurance, although some people defend against it. When Karen accepted the strong-independent-woman hype, she fit Jonathon's ideal dream lover. When this happens, distance appears between partners as one (the supposedly weaker, childlike one) lets the other one take initiative on all major issues (like sex and money). The supposedly stronger one may move into this more dominant position enthusiastically or apprehensively. In the end, however, the idealized partner will feel cheated, burned, alone. It's always lonely at the top. The parent-child relational configuration of dream lovers (for example, Great Mother and Golden Child) is a deadening influence on intimacy. Parents and children don't have sex together. They are not partners (if they're a healthy team) and they don't lean on *each other*.

Anger with one's partner is difficult to address. In the above examples, I hope you can see how necessary it is. And yet, this is no license to "say what you feel" without reflection. In the interchanges between Pamela and Charles, and Jonathon and Karen, you observed how the therapists cut off attacks, mind reading, implied hostilities, and statements about the other person's experience. The point of expressing anger in an intimate relationship is either to address a problem (which may or may not get resolved) or make a boundary. Anger helps a couple differentiate and claim dream lovers. When Pamela refuses to be the Maiden Lover with Charles, Charles has to confront something in himself. When Jonathon draws a line against Karen's projections of him as the Lost Child, she has to face herself. Intimate relationships are full of problems and projections. Anger is a functional emotion when it is handled through words and without attack. It helps us reclaim dream lovers.

passive-aggressive men?

Jungian analyst David Hart has presented some insightful papers on the phenomenon of passive-aggressive men. His thesis is that some men are afraid to claim their own aggression and insist on appearing as "nice guys" around the clock. Their aggression seeps out, but they claim they are "doing nothing"—just making a joke, showing up late without an explanation, forgetting to do the promised favor, and the like. Because men in our culture are socialized to be aggressive, to be "at the top" and "walk over the little guy," perhaps the passive-aggressive man is aberrant in both a negative and a positive way. Negatively, he takes no responsibility for his own aggression. Positively, he doesn't accept male dominance as a virtue. Hart believes that male passive aggression is a topic that needs further study.

In three of our couples, we find men who tend to be more passively than actively aggressive. Jonathon, Larry, and Joe prefer to believe that their wives are the aggressive ones in the relationship. How common is this? Psychologist Tavris reports on many studies that have surveyed the kinds and causes of expressed anger in men and women. Very few have uncovered any sex difference. Neither sex seems to have a corner on the difficulty of expressing anger or discontent. (Since these studies did not use my definitions of anger and aggression, I cannot say how they might fall along the lines I have drawn.) Tavris summarizes the situation between the sexes by reminding us that both girls and boys are forbidden to express anger openly to their parents. Girls are told it's "unladylike" and boys are told it's "unmanly." Both men and women have trouble expressing anger directly to the boss. People who believe they show anger too readily want to control it. People who believe they back off from anger too quickly wish that they could more readily express it. There are representatives of both types of people distributed fairly equally between the two sexes. The sexes differ notably only in expressing fear and sadness, probably because women do not have masculine standards of stoicism to live up to. One study reported that more women than men said they were likely to cry when they got angry. Women also said they were more likely to deny the targeted person some "customary benefit." Although this wasn't specified, what comes to mind is sex or some personal favor. (That is certainly a passive-aggressive stance.)

Probably, then, neither men nor women are more likely to be actively or passively aggressive. Either way, the translation of aggression into anger is the work that needs to be done to protect the ground of intimacy in a couple.

Passive aggression is harder to identify than active aggression for people who use it. It seeps through conversation in myriad ways. The target of the aggression, however, feels the attack. Passive aggression is so widely unrecognized that its expression may be missed by everyone except the target. When Larry began the second session by asking Louise if she wanted him to start, he put Louise in a double bind. If she said "Yes," then she would seem to be giving orders, and if she said "No," then she would still be giving orders. Double-binding is aggressive. Her silence was the only viable answer. Larry likes to give advice and his advice is usually designed to control Louise's actions without making him look bossy. Here is how his advice giving can be transformed into straightforward anger.

Larry: You really need to quit that job, Louise, because it's so hard—

Larry (Double): I can't tolerate you coming home in such bad moods.

Louise: Why does it affect you so much? It's my job.

Larry: I'm affected by your moods. The moment you come through the door, I get nervous that you're going to yell at me or the boys.

Louise: I don't think that's any of your business. My therapist told me that I should let people know exactly what is bothering me, and I don't intend to cover it up.

Louise is taking a position that I often hear in couple therapy. It is the "expressing your feelings is good" position.

In a committed couple relationship, expressing your feelings cannot follow any specific rule. The only rule about feelings that I recommend is "*Knowing* your feelings is good." It is important to recognize what is taking place within your own being; that is the territory of your personal responsibility. What you do about the recognition of your feelings—whether you express them or make a silent note—depends on all sorts of things: context, desire, level of trust, and many more. To reiterate, the impulsive expression of aggressive, hateful feelings is never good for increasing intimacy in a couple relationship. Many people have learned in therapy (whether this was intended or not) to say aggressive things if they feel like it. This freedom comes with an unwritten law that we should all be "honest" about our subjective states. Honesty *is* an important component of trust, but if your partner has not *asked* you to express your feelings (especially your negative ones), there is no dishonesty in keeping them to yourself. Louise frequently causes quite an upset at home when she grouses about her boss and the unfairness at work.

Larry: I want you to quit—

Larry (Double): I want you to take responsibility for what you're feeling. In general, I don't like to hear a lot of complaining, but if you want to get some support or advice, ask me directly.

I ask Louise to paraphrase what Larry's double has just said.

Louise: You don't want me to complain without having some goal in mind, like getting your advice, right? (*Larry nods in agreement.*) I don't know if I can do that. I get so afraid when I walk through the door. I'm afraid of seeing you and the boys. So instead of dealing directly with you, I usually complain about work.

Larry is asked to paraphrase.

Larry: You mean you're actually *afraid* of coming home? Why?
Louise: Because it seems like I'm the problem around the house. I never get any good—
Louise (Double): My impression is that no one cares about me, appreciates me. I don't feel at all appreciated for what I contribute to the family.
Larry: That's funny, because I feel the same—
Larry (Double): I am sorry that you feel so unappreciated because I know how hard you work. Sometimes I feel exactly the same way.

Larry's passive aggression has to be transformed into active statements about his desires without blaming Louise. Louise's more actively aggressive statements need to be transformed into statements about her experience, her perceptions.

Passive-aggressive men want to appear as nice guys, either because they project the Maiden Lover (and identify with the Great Father) or because they project the Great Mother (and identify with the Golden Child). Sometimes they want to fix the Terrible Mother, as in this case. Larry feels he has to rid Louise of depression in order to feel good himself. His complex drives him to fix Louise, with the presumption that *he* will then be happy. Louise is well aware that she comes off as the "identified patient" and she doesn't want that label. Her attacks on Larry only strengthen the projective identification, though. They imply that he should change in order for her to feel better. In the above exchange, Louise is able to speak directly about her fear. She fears being hated by her husband and children. These are fears based on a very punitive Father-God complex in her childhood. Louise needs to work on recognizing the meaning of her own dream lovers. This should be done in her individual psychotherapy, where she can gradually become familiar with a range of idealized and terrifying inner states. In couple therapy, Louise can ask Larry for reassurance, understanding, or patience with her struggle.

Larry eventually will have to do the same. Larry still has a lot of defensive self-reliance. He often describes himself as "very independent, a real problem-solver." When he finally accepts that his wife and children have problems that he cannot solve, he may be more able to take responsibility for his own subjective life.

In the earlier exchange between Joe and Patty, we saw Joe's passive-aggressive style transformed into an actively bullying attack. The slide from passive aggression to active attack is one I see frequently when one partner envies the other. Joe has yet to recognize that he envies Patty. Envy is a feeling that should be kept silent, however. There is no good way to put into words "I would like to destroy the resources you have because I can't have them for myself." Instead, envy must be transformed into jealousy. Jealousy can be spoken of and accepted: "I would like to have what you have." As I said earlier, envy changes when the envying person can claim the resources of the self. In the meantime, what does the envying person say?

Envy can be translated into underlying fears. Here is how my husband worked with Joe.

Joe (Double): Sometimes I am afraid that you will leave me, Patty, if you continue in school and change a lot.

Joe: No, I am afraid that I will leave *you* because I won't have anything in common with you anymore.

Patty: There's nothing I can do about that.

Patty (Double): Tell me more about what frightens you.

Joe: I guess I get afraid that you will get very sophisticated or something and not want to do stuff like bowling with our friends or going to football games.

Patty: I don't know why you think that. I like our friends and I want to continue socializing. I just want you to develop *yourself*—

Patty (Double): I guess I get afraid that you won't like me if I change and you won't want to hear about my interests. What I want from you is involvement in my life, not distance.

Joe: I don't know how to do that when you criticize me so much.

By speaking in terms of fears rather than put-downs (envy), Joe invited Patty to empathize with him. Patty was able to do that at least in part because she wanted Joe to tell her his feelings.

Patty has not yet claimed her own aggression and her desire to attack Joe when he doesn't measure up to her Hero. Patty has a lot of defensive self-reliance—a feeling that she can "make it on her own" and fantasies of being without Joe. Also, Patty's Father complex is so contemptuous, aggressive, and belittling, it will be difficult for her to claim it as her own. Patty is unaware of how aggressively she attacks Joe, and when this is brought to her attention she often feels indignant and justifies her attack. "He *never* listens to my feelings!" is usually the response she makes to my drawing attention to her attacks on Joe. In order for Patty to understand fully how aggressive she is, she will have to experience it in both couple and individual therapy. For Patty now, an attitude of "no blame" is impossible. There simply isn't an empty rowboat on the lake.

claiming emotional power

In the first chapter I talked about the disclaimed emotional power of men, the ways in which men imagine that women are "in control" of all feelings. Under these circumstances men experience themselves as powerless in the face of women's emotions. Women can experience something similar when they are in Patty's situation. Patty has a severe, aggressive, and debilitating Terrible Father complex, which contrasts entirely with the way she sees herself. Patty sees herself as a kind, generous, emotionally open person; indeed, she is this way most of the time. But occasionally, she is captured by her deadly strange gender. In those moments she may identify with the aggressor. Then *she* can make an emotional attack that is as powerful as her father's were, although she is typically attacking Joe, who is a grown man. Patty inhibits attacks on her children because she can identify them with the Victim Child in herself. From her therapy, Patty knows the "child within." As yet, however, she has no knowledge of how she can also be the Terrible Father within.

Most people tend to identify themselves with the "victim" or "ideal" side of a complex. As the victim (for example, the Victim Child or Lost Child), we feel helpless and powerless. As the ideal (for example, the Great Mother or Hero), we feel impeccable, beyond fault. Most of us fail to see how we could be an emotionally powerful aggressor. Like the women I see in therapy, I have difficulty identifying and claiming my Terrible Father in my actions or words. Contempt, aggression, envy, hatred are difficult emotions to claim in oneself. And if they remain unclaimed, then they can be used unconsciously in projections or actions against loved ones.

I find that men are somewhat more able to acknowledge their aggression (although not necessarily other negative emotions, such as sadness or fear) than women are, but usually men disclaim the force or power of their aggressive responses. They tend to discount the physical differences between themselves and women or children. Physically, men are much bigger (on the average) than the women and children around them. When a man who outweighs me by a hundred pounds demands a certain outcome (for instance, that I "better fix" his sexual relationship with his wife), I don't take it lightly. Many times he believes I would. The physical disparity between men and women, men and children, gives greater force to men's aggression, hatred, envy and rage. Men need to recognize this force as their own and take full responsibility for it.

Dream lovers are emotionally powerful complexes. When we project them, we feel overwhelmed by the "power" we assume others hold over us. When we identify with them we can enact very powerful scenes. If we enact them against relatively helpless or powerless others (such as children or the elderly), we become the "monsters" of their experience. If we enact them against our equals, we can be swept up into *their* projections of Terrible Parents, or even abandoned if our partners find us intolerable. Practically speaking, the only way to come to terms with dream lovers is to know them in ourselves. Then we can explore their meanings and eventually live out the ideals or values represented by the positive ones, while taking responsibility for the inner states engendered by the negative. Of course, this is not a simple matter of the will. Because the strange gender is always active in our unconscious life, we can be captured at any moment. We can fall in love or make an attack without any forethought. But if we recognize "whose voice" that is, or (roughly speaking) which self we are falling into, then we will emerge enriched by the knowledge that we are "multiple personalities" with multiple responsibilities. Most important, in times of conflict and frustration we can see how we may be creating the problems we face. We need feel no blame for having unconscious complexes; they are fate. Understanding that, we may see an empty rowboat.

chapter 5

sex as desire

Think with me about desire. Desire is longing for something that is not present. Desire is yearning for what is missing. In order to yearn we must *already* have known or experienced what we desire. I cannot desire a pleasure that I have never known. I can imagine a pleasure that someone else describes, but I cannot long for it. Suppose someone tells me that a raw Colombian yam is irresistibly delicious, a delicacy of pungent sweetness. I know nothing of this yam, but I am told it is the perfect dessert, light but sweet. When I am next longing for a sweet dessert, will I desire a raw Colombian yam? Probably not. The description, no matter how powerful, cannot supply the experience. Only those pleasures that have been known directly can become the focus of real desire.

On the surface this seems peculiar. Many people insist, at the beginning of psychotherapy, that they desire to be loved or approved or admired in some way that they have *never* known. "All I want from my wife is to be acknowledged as a person, something I never got in childhood, but she can't give me this" is the kind of claim I mean. A man like Joe or a woman like Louise might say something like this, insisting that the desire arises from nothing, out of the void of never-having. I may counter by saying, "If you have never experienced this, how could you know that you want it?" and the other person is alerted to the possibility that the desire *reveals* a previous experience, something that has been known but forgotten or disclaimed.

Heterosexual sex is often portrayed, in everyday conversation and in the professional literature, as a conflict of desire. He wants sex in order to feel intimate. She wants intimacy in order to feel sexy. Although this is an intriguing formulation, I believe the problem of desire in heterosexual sex is more like this: He desires sex (and sometimes intimacy) and she desires intimacy, but not heterosexual sex. She will "tolerate" sex if it is part of intimacy. Assuming that both she and he have experienced intimacy in this or another relationship, they can both desire intimacy in its absence. He has experienced direct pleasure in heterosexual sex, and he can desire it again. She has not and so she cannot desire it.

You may be saying, "Now wait a minute, you've already acknowledged how much Karen desires sex, so how can you say that women lack sexual desire?" You're right, Karen *has* experienced a lot of pleasure in heterosexual sex. (Karen also has difficulties with her sexual pleasure. She makes dream lover projections onto men like Jerry, her former lover, that she needs to integrate into herself. All the same, she has known sexual pleasure with a man.) Karen has discovered her own pleasure and knows how she can reexperience it. She is among what I consider to be the lucky minority of heterosexual women who have experienced direct pleasure in heterosexual sex, enough to have *desire*.

If desire is based on missing something that has already been pleasurable, then a majority of heterosexual women feel little or no sexual desire because they have not discovered or developed pleasure in sex. Often women feel ashamed of their lack of desire. They hide it or defend against it with "excuses" (like the old "I have a headache" or "I have to wash my hair tonight"). To discover that lack of desire usually means lack of pleasure (with the important exception of those women who have been abused or raped and fail to desire because of such trauma) is to feel less ashamed of lack of desire. If you haven't had the experience, *how* could you miss it? By the way, I am *not* claiming that lack of pleasure is a result of a flaw "in the woman." In my view, only trauma (such as physical or sexual abuse or pain) will inhibit a person's desire to have pleasure. When pleasure is possible, generally people will seek it, unless they have some higher goal that supersedes it. My point is that heterosexual women too often lack access to pleasure in sex, and so they don't miss it. What's there to miss?

Shere Hite's 1976 survey of sexual pleasure in women showed that only 30 percent of women have orgasms regularly from intercourse; others can achieve orgasm through masturbation; and 11.6 percent don't have orgasms at all, ever. Helen Kaplan's 1974 research showed that 8 to 10 percent of women never have orgasms and up to 45 percent can have orgasms during intercourse when they are clitorally stimulated. Although these studies may seem dated, they are probably the best and broadest data we have available.

More current and smaller studies tend to show similar results. In a 1983 survey of 1,453 married women (conducted by the Institute for Advanced Study of Human Sexuality in San Francisco), for example, 52 percent of those surveyed said they were "somewhat" or "not very" satisfied with their sex lives; 48 percent said they were satisfied. This survey is described as representative of middle-class married women in the United States. In a more recent survey by *Redbook Magazine,* published in 1992, a rather shockingly high 56 percent of more than 1,000 women respondents confessed to faking orgasm with a "current partner." Full-time homemakers were less likely to fake orgasms than working women. Perhaps the working women were too exhausted to enjoy sex and wanted to get it over with through faking. Age was also a factor. Women between 18 and 24 were much less likely to fake orgasm than those 35 and older.

In *The Kinsey Institute New Report on Sex,* published in 1990, less than half (44 percent) of women surveyed said they initiated sex about as frequently as their male partners. Another 42 percent said they initiated sex "sometimes" and 4 percent said "not at all." What is going on here? Why are so few women taking pleasure in heterosexual sex?

One kind of answer is given by Naomi Wolf, a writer and journalist who has explored the effects of our cultural standards for female beauty on women's sexual desire:

> Heterosexual love, before the women's movement, was undermined by women's economic dependence on men. Love freely given between equals is the child of the women's movement, and a very recent historical possibility, and as such very fragile.

She believes, as I do, that love given freely is the only recipe for heterosexual intimacy in sex and this means equality between partners. For heterosexual sex to be pleasurable for both partners, it must be given freely by both—desired by both.

Along with Wolf, I believe that heterosexual intimacy is revolutionary in its implications. If tenderness and mutual respect were a practiced component of heterosexuality, then both men and women might well become dedicated to the transformation of a male-dominated society into one of shared power. Both partners might find equality as desirable as sexiness because they would recognize the link between equality and desire. Sexual intimacy could be a central means by which women and men would feel their mature dependence on each other. As things are now, though, there is a barrier to women's desire for heterosexual sex. The cultural maintenance of male dominance keeps most women "in the dark" about the sexual pleasures of their bodies, especially in regard to what they might want from men. This darkness or silence about female sexuality is quite damaging to heterosexual intimacy as things now stand.

As *The Kinsey Institute New Report on Sex* shows, orgasm rates for women appear to be related more to psychological than biological factors. Women generally experience their highest rates of orgasm from their mid-twenties to mid-forties. Men report their highest rates of orgasm in their adolescence or early twenties. The idea that orgasm is governed by hormonal levels cannot explain the age difference between the sexes in orgasm. At puberty, hormonal levels are high in both sexes, but only males exhibit higher rates at this time. If women learn about orgasm, they learn when they are older, at least in their twenties. Then it depends on how quickly an individual woman can feel secure enough about sexual pleasure to practice having orgasm. As women grow older, they usually learn more about their sexual capacity and engage in longer periods of stimulation. If women were exposed to adequate learning about their own sexual pleasure in adolescence, as men are, then it is more likely they would feel competent in seeking pleasure at a younger age and probably over a lifetime. From the Kinsey data we can conclude that being "in the dark" about female sexual pleasure is a major problem of female sexual desire.

Darkness or silence here means the absence of *female* portrayals of female sexuality in art, media, books, and paintings. As I said in the second chapter, we have vast archives of men's depictions of their dream lovers, and male views of women's lives are often the only resource some people have for portraits of *women's desire*. Circe, Pandora, Aphrodite, and Eve are illustrations of "classical" dream-lover depictions of female desire, and *sex, lies, and videotape* and *Presumed Innocent* are contemporary examples from movies. These and countless others depict female sexuality from a male perspective, giving nuance and meaning through the lenses of men's fantasies about female desire. Men's dream lovers depict female sexuality in terms of its appeal or its terrors for men. From pornography to classical art, we are steeped in images and stories that portray the female and her desire as "objects" (of male desire) and not as "subjects" or active participants. As objects of male desire, women's bodies can be imagined as seductive and exotic, as power withheld or freely given. As we'll see, many men imagine women as bestowing or withholding these powerful sexual resources *from them,* rather than as wanting or freely giving something.

Only recently have the voices, writing, and portrayals by female artists and experts broadened our cultural arena to include images that affirm active female pleasure in sex from a female viewpoint. These images and accounts show women enjoying and wanting their own sexual experiences, being active or passive based on their pleasure, and freely giving and receiving. Women portray the comforting, relaxed positions of the female body poised for orgasm and the easy passion for multiple orgasms in a woman who knows her own sexual pleasure. The rich and colorful exploration of female genitalia in literary and artistic expressions has more often been the product of lesbian than heterosexual women artists. I believe this gap primarily results from the absence of heterosexual women's pleasure and understanding. Mostly, though, both young and older heterosexual women are exposed to depictions of men's dream lovers as examples of female desire. Wolf describes this problem in terms of girls' learning to be objects of desire:

> What little girls learn is not the desire for the other, but the desire to be desired. Girls learn to watch their sex along with the boys; that takes up the space that should be devoted to finding out about what they are wanting. . . .

Wolf stresses the pressure that develops in girls and women to be the perfect image of a man's desire. Slenderness, sleekness, prettiness, and being well presented are qualities that most women come to associate with being sexy. Instead of developing their own *experiences* of sexual pleasure, women project their dream lovers onto men and try to imagine how *a man feels* in response to the female body. Women strive to meet the standards for female appearance and often feel sexy in relation to how well they believe they meet these standards.

Pamela despairs of ever feeling sexual again because of her wrinkled body, which she believes is unattractive to Charles. Pamela is wrong, but until she discovers that her standards originate within her own Terrible Father, she is likely to continue to believe she cannot ever feel sexy again. Patty feels sexy about her body because she holds herself to a tight schedule of exercise and diet. Yet Patty does not feel much sexual desire for Joe. She has never had an orgasm in making love with Joe. Although Patty masturbates easily to orgasm, she has not said much to Joe about how she would like to be touched and stimulated by him because she feels "embarrassed, as though there is something wrong with me because I can't have an orgasm through intercourse."

Many, if not most, women cannot have an orgasm simply through intercourse. This fact is often taken to be a sign of women's inadequacy, a falling short of a "natural" goal or objective. The most recent source of support for the vaginal (presumably intercourse) orgasm was the "discovery" of the G spot, a sensitive spot at the back of the vagina that, when stimulated, was supposed to produce an orgasm and an ejaculation comparable to a man's. Psychologist Carol Tavris, in her recent book about misinformation in "expert accounts" of women, takes up the long tale of how the G spot evolved and was named. Although the media reported on this supposed discovery as though it were a fact that any woman *could* have a vaginal orgasm if she found her "spot," Tavris shows the contrary.

> To date, research finds that: The G Spot is not characteristic of all women. Of those who do have a "sensitive area," most do not "ejaculate"—i.e., produce a fluid at orgasm. And for most of the women who do produce fluid upon stimulation of the sensitive area, this response does not always occur with orgasm.

Although no consistent research findings have supported the uniform existence of the G spot, women have been subjected to "expert" accounts that challenge them to develop this orgasmic skill. Naturally, this is confusing for women who either don't find a G spot in themselves or find themselves uninterested in looking.

Once again, many (if not most) women cannot have an orgasm simply through intercourse. Sensitive stimulation of the clitoris is the surest way to orgasm. Whether the clitoris is stimulated by a penis (before or during intercourse), a hand, or some other object, it offers a relatively certain path to pleasure. A lot of women I've seen in therapy are similar to Patty in that they can have orgasms through masturbation, but they feel ashamed or embarrassed that they have not met what they perceive to be *the* standard of orgasm through intercourse. Often women do not disclose to their partners the fact that clitoral manipulation is a fairly sure route to orgasm, because they feel ashamed or inadequate about this. Some men do indeed hold the orgasm-through-intercourse standard. Many do not.

If the multiorgasmic nature of female sensuality and sexuality was made well known through the popular media, I think both women and men would benefit immensely. Preparatory relaxation and easy clitoral orgasm are simple behaviors to practice as components of heterosexual lovemaking. Holding women to a single (male) fantasy of sexual pleasure confines both sexes to a stultifying routine that is often boring or unpleasurable for women. The fact that much of female heterosexual pleasure has been left unspoken and unexpressed, or even undiscovered, also means that female heterosexual desire is often filtered through fatherly or heroic dream lovers rather than boldly erotic ones. Only in the last two decades has the Underground Genius been a major fantasy expressing female desire in more active and erotic ways. Influenced by female expressions of pleasure in sex and the link between sexual and creative expression, women dreamed up the Genius from their own desire. Still, I find that the Genius is often more hotly desired because of his creativity than because of his sexuality. Perhaps as we heterosexual women explore our own sexuality more openly and with a fuller range of expression, we will develop images of our strange gender that include a more explicitly sexual nature.

The standard for female orgasm is harmful to male desire too. Men are socialized into believing that "beautiful women are sexy" (like a formula, "beautiful = sexual") and that girls and women desire pleasure from the penis as much as or more than men desire it. In adolescence especially, boys are initiated into fantasies of dream lovers through pornography, stories, and masturbation. This initiation usually takes place within male peer groups and carries with it a range of stereotypes about female sexuality—for example, that when girls say no they really don't mean it. In this awakening of sexual desire in heterosexual boys, pleasure becomes associated with pictures and fantasies of the female body, especially as it could be "used" by males. A central psychological complex is formed around the core state of male sexual arousal: the "power" of female appearance must be brought under a man's control. A man's desire becomes bound up with *his* potential control of his lover, either because, as he imagines her, his lover is initiated by him into the pleasures of his penis (the Maiden Lover) or because she is driven by desire for his penis (the Mistress Lover). He has the penis that will bring this powerful female beauty under control. Nothing in these fantasies involves making a relationship with the person who is in the female body. Rather, the beautiful woman is understood to be "sexy" and her imagined power is to be added to a man's own when he can possess her.

In a committed couple relationship, after the romance has ended and power struggles of disillusionment are activated, a man can feel deeply ashamed when his partner does not crave his penis or have orgasms through intercourse. Men like Joe or Jonathon who have other difficulties with self-esteem may feel crushed by their partners' lack of sexual responsiveness. They take it to mean there is some inadequacy of their own sexual performance or endowment, such as penis size or sexual endurance. Feelings of shame can then inhibit a man's sexual desire because sex is no longer associated with pleasure, but with humiliation. Men like Larry and Charles may also feel ashamed, but they will tend to blame the partner and feel indignant themselves. Under the surface, though, Charles (because of defensive self-reliance and a false self) feels humiliated by Pamela's sexual rejection of him. Most of the time he handles this feeling by assuming the fault is Pamela's (she's "frigid").

Both men and women are motivated to be the object of desire for the other, but women are more often exclusively motivated in this way. Men seem to be aroused directly by their desire for sexual pleasure as well as by their desire to be desired. When Patty is wearing a pair of tight jeans at home in the evening, it doesn't matter to Joe if she is scrubbing the floor or conversing with him when he feels sexual arousal. He "goes for it," but he is often shocked and hurt when Patty flatly turns him down because she "doesn't feel connected." When his female partner is unresponsive, a man tends to conclude that something is wrong with him (his sexual performance, for instance) or with her (she's frigid). Rather than talk with her about her preferences, most men retreat into silent shame in which they blame themselves or their partners. If they blame the partner, usually she is seen as "withholding," either because she is in a power struggle (punishing him for shortcomings he despairs of correcting) or because she is unable to surrender herself. Either way, he is ashamed that sex is not under his control as he imagines it should be.

Mostly, women are not withholding. They honestly don't feel desire because they have never felt pleasure in an extended, satisfying, and reliable way. Without a direct experience of pleasure in heterosexual sex, without the background of portraits and fantasies of female desire, and without words and images as information about female sexuality, women are at a loss for desire.

Women like Karen, who have found words and images that appealed to them, and who then have sought pleasures directly, are the exception to the rule in my world. To be clear about it, though, some Karen-type women have identified with their male partners' dream lovers. That is, they have become a version of male sexuality as their partners have imposed its meaning on them. In Karen's affair with Jerry, for example, she was willing to conform to Jerry's rules about not disclosing much personal information to each other and making sexual contact the sole purpose of their meetings. Although Karen wasn't comfortable with this, she pretended she was because she wanted Jerry to know that she valued "pure sex" as much as he did. I don't mean to imply that something is wrong with Karen's sexual excitement, but rather that Karen still has some developing to do in order to discover why she would simply "follow" Jerry's dictates. On the other hand, I recognize that Karen's open and felt desire *is* an advantage. She has some knowledge of her pleasure and how to seek it. For most women I see in therapy, this is not true.

The lack of female sexual desire is probably the number one complaint I hear from heterosexual couples in dialogue therapy. Until the woman has some regular, direct sexual pleasure in her own experience, she cannot be expected to have desire. Neither can her partner be expected to take responsibility for her lack of desire. Together both partners must look into what the woman finds pleasurable and build these activities into lovemaking. The woman has responsibility for discovering and shaping her own pleasures. The man also has to develop an interest in discovering his partner's sexual pleasure—not assuming that he already knows from his dream lovers. Both women and men have to claim the meanings and images of their dream lovers as their own, and free their partners to express themselves. This is where the issue of sexual desire becomes complicated and requires greater depth of knowledge of oneself.

the problem of desire

This chapter confronts me with discomfort because I wish I could write something lighter, more hopeful, or even juicier about sex in heterosexual couples. Most of all, I wish I could write about the "synchrony" of heterosexual lovemaking in the way that researchers describe the synchrony of infants and mothers, the delicate dance of desire and meeting of desire that the "infant couple" learns. It would give me joy if I could feel confident in the "dance of intimacy" of heterosexual sex. But I do not feel confident. For more than fifteen years I have been seeing individuals and couples in psychotherapy, teaching in graduate schools, and carrying out my responsibilities as a mother and wife. In all walks of my life I encounter a lack of sexual desire in heterosexual women. This pains me greatly. Female sexual pleasure is a relatively easy achievement, whether a woman is straight or lesbian. The myriad problems that disrupt women's trust in their own pleasure, their bodies, and their male partners I detail below. None of them is the fault of women. Some of them are the products of a male-dominated culture in which women have been trivialized and silenced. Neither men nor women are individually responsible for this situation and only men and women together can change it. Some problems for women *are* the responsibility of men: Incest, violence against women, and rape can be stopped only by men. I hope that my account here alerts heterosexual men to what they lose if they promote or ignore these atrocious actions against the vulnerability of female sexuality. In an environment in which women cannot trust known or unknown men, women will never feel their own sexual pleasure. Until a woman has enough regular pleasure in sex to feel her own desire, a couple will have no synchrony of sexual desire, no rhythm of give-and-take that sustains the pleasures of both people. When they both feel their desire, sex is an easy and intimate way to relax together.

When this is not the case, sex can take on negative emotional meanings: violence, pain, rage, and humiliation are a few. For men too, heterosexual sex can become a burden, accompanied by shame and indignation. I say a lot here about the pain and troubles imposed by some men on heterosexual sex. Some men ruin the experience for the rest of us by failing to control the impulses connected with their dream lovers. The majority of heterosexual men are not like this. They want intimacy and trust with their female partners. Unfortunately, the cultural context and a minority of men have robbed many couples of the trust that permits intimacy. I want to reach the majority of heterosexual men who desire intimacy with women and say to them, *try to understand* what is going on with women and their trust. Look and listen to the scenes around you. Pay attention to the fears and inhibitions of your female partner. Many of these can be soothed or eased *if you really understand* the dangerous situation that surrounds women's sexuality. When you understand this, and when your partner trusts that you do, then the two of you together can form your own trusting exchange of pleasures. In a section called "Trust" below, I give details about how this can take place. Much of it has to be negotiated on an individual couple basis. There is no reliable model for heterosexual intimacy in any society that allows and even promotes sexual violence against either sex, and our society promotes sexual violence against women.

You will probably get the impression from what I say here that I think all projections of dream lovers are "bad" for heterosexual intimacy. In a sense that is true. Projections get in the way of knowing each other. Projections can be sexy, though. They are necessary for falling in love. But projections of dream lovers cannot sustain an intimate relationship with the same partner. Only knowing the partner through dialogue can do that. Sometimes I see my husband as my Hero—and sometimes as a Great Father (I confess). Both of these projections inspire me with respect and admiration that can be translated into sexual desire if the situation is right. But I also recognize that my Hero and Great Father are, in fact, parts of me, not really of my husband. I am much more likely to be passionately moved by recognizing my husband's actual strengths and attractiveness, not my projections. Sometimes he and I share our night dreams in the morning; occasionally we recognize the sexualized dream lovers that we projected onto each other when we were falling in love. Versions of his Maiden Lover and my Underground Genius still seduce us in our dreams—sometimes embodied as other people (known and unknown) and sometimes as ourselves, eroticized by the dreamer's mind. These dreams and other momentary flashes of dream lovers in daily lives *can* turn us on sexually. That energy can be used to develop intimacy. That turn-on cannot, however, replace intimacy in a sustained relationship.

In my view the most erotic dream lovers are the Maiden Lover in men and the Underground Genius in women. The Maiden Lover is a soul mate, the image of a developing female who needs to be "initiated" into sexuality. "She" is imagined as sensitive, delicate, tender, and freshly erotic. "She" allows the actual female partner to speak and emerge gradually.

The Underground Genius in women expresses a creative, erotic, pleasure-seeking, and quiveringly sensitive image of a male. When it is projected it encourages the actual male partner to reveal his creativity and sexuality. It is not a demand on a man, but an invitation to "show" his most expressive, creative sexuality. Women's other positive dream lovers, the Hero and Great Father, do not generally connect directly with sexuality, although many women project these in falling in love. Women feel romantic about the Hero and the Great Father. The Hero is an image of the sensitive male who would be a woman if he could be. He is so careful, correct, and sensitive (in a woman's imagination) that he would not put any sexual pressure on a woman. He would only wait for her. When a woman tries to hold an actual man in this projection she may feel romantic about him, but not at all sexually motivated—a perplexing state for both partners. The Great Father, of course, is the god-king protector who is supposed to know everything. When a woman projects him she suspects that the actual man "knows all about sex," but she waits for him to introduce it to her and she takes it as a lesson in duty. It seems clear to me that the Genius is the dream lover that expresses a woman's emergent sexual desire. Any dream lover can help us fall in love and any dream lover can later interfere with trust and intimacy. The three I discuss at length here are, however, the most troubling ones.

the terrible father

Let's begin with the most troubling disruption to heterosexual intimacy. There are several ways in which women's Terrible Fathers disrupt the possibility of sexual desire, but the most wounding image of the Terrible Father is that of incest and sexual abuse. Our couples are now in the third session of dialogue therapy and are beginning to confront directly the problems of sexual intimacy. In her individual psychotherapy, Louise has begun to remember scenes of sexual abuse, incest with her uncle, one of her father's brothers. This uncle was a trusted figure in Louise's childhood family and he frequently took her and her two brothers for summer outings to his cabin on the lake. Louise always wondered why she had negative feelings about these trips, but she had assumed that her feelings were connected to the bickering among her brothers and the discomfort of being the only female in the group. Now she has begun to uncover another reason for her discomfort.

From the time Louise was six years old until she was ten, her uncle would come at night into her room at the cabin and stimulate Louise's genitals through touching, and eventually oral stimulation. Although he never had intercourse with her, Louise felt "terribly dirty" about her childhood desires for this pleasurable touching combined, as it was, with terror and disgust. Apparently her uncle threatened that if she ever told her parents or brothers, he would drown one of her brothers in the lake.

As I mentioned earlier, the malignant legacy of childhood sexual abuse is the way in which fantasy and reality remain forever mixed. Because Louise learned not to trust the protective role of the fatherly uncle, she has never been able to fully trust Larry when he tried to have sex with her, especially oral sex. Even when they were first married and still in the early romance of ideal dream lovers, if Larry offered to give Louise oral sex she would jump out of bed and say, "Please don't!" Larry would feel hurt and rejected because he had always imagined that oral sex was especially enjoyable for women.

Through most of their marriage Louise's fears and apprehensions about sex were assumed by her and Larry to be part of "her problem." Larry believed that Louise's upbringing in a minister's home was the root of her sexual inhibition. He would say she was "sexually repressed." He wanted to tease and cajole Louise out of her fears, but she tended to attack him when he tried this. "Stop talking to me about this stuff and just leave me alone!" would be her usual retort. Eventually Louise and Larry pretty much gave up sex. They would attempt it once every few months, but mostly they "tried to forget it."

Now in this third couple session, Louise began to tell Larry what she had discovered about her past. (Notice that Louise and Larry are beginning to have a dialogue, but they still need some help from their doubles.)

Louise: There is something that I want to tell you, but it is very difficult to say it. I want you to listen to all of it before you say anything, okay?

Larry: I don't want to agree to that unless it's not about me, like your disappointments in me.

Louise: No, it's not about you. It's about me but it's very difficult to talk about. Over the years I know I've blamed myself for not being able to get comfortable with sex. You've blamed me too, haven't you?

Larry: You want me to answer? (*Louise nods.*) No, not exactly. I've sort of assumed that a strict religious upbringing and your father's repressive attitude about sex have made it difficult for you to enjoy it.

Louise: Well, it's much more than that. (*Starting to weep*) I've been hiding something awful from myself over all these years because I guess I couldn't allow myself to think it. You know Uncle Rob, my father's younger brother? The uncle that I always thought I liked so much? He sexually molested me (*sobbing*). It wasn't just once either. It (*sobbing*) happened every time we were at the summer cabin from when I was about six until I was ten. I feel so disgusted about it and so afraid about what it might mean for me now.

Larry: Oh my God, Louise! I am so shocked! We've visited Rob so many times at his farm and I would never have imagined that he could . . . Do you want me to confront him?

Louise: No! Absolutely not! *I* don't know who I will tell or how I'm even going to understand this. Don't give me advice or try to solve this.

Louise (Double): I want your help in coping with my feelings and the fallout from so many years of feeling so numb sexually.

Larry: What can I do for you?

Louise: You can listen to my feelings about what happened and you can help me try to restore my sexuality, although I don't know how that will happen. My therapist believes I can feel safe again, but probably not for a long time. I guess I want you to stop pressuring me in any way to have sex and—

Larry: I *never* pressure you to have sex!

Larry (Double): How do I pressure you to have sex?

Louise: You talk about it a lot, like on vacation and at our summer cabin—my God, I never thought of that connection! I have never felt safe having sex with you at our summer place and now I know why. Sometimes I just feel like you're mad at me—

Louise (Double): At times when you mention sex I get very uncomfortable and I imagine then that you're mad at me or something.

Larry: I've never felt mad at you about this. I just wanted to get things fixed. I really want to have a good sex life with you.

In the remainder of the session my husband and I talked about rules that Louise and Larry must follow in order to prepare gradually a new basis for mutual sexual desire. We lent them copies of psychotherapist Laura Davis's books on surviving childhood sexual abuse and on being a partner of a survivor.

Specifically, we asked Louise to remind Larry that she loves him whenever she makes a rejecting remark or gesture when she cannot endure being touched or held close by him. We asked Larry to spend some time studying the whole picture of what abuse is and what it does to survivors. Larry will need to become more empathic with Louise, and also to retain a sense of himself and his sexual desires. How can he do this?

First, by sharing with Louise his own observations and understanding of what she has endured from this trauma, Larry will open a door to her trust. Then Larry needs to speak about what he wants from Louise, both in the present in terms of gestures of support and love, and in the future in terms of their sexual life together. Larry and Louise need to have many good dialogues, being empathic and differentiated, about what has happened to Louise—and to Larry—as a result of an uncle who abused her.

Almost one in three adult women and one in ten adult men in the United States have been sexually abused as children. About one in three heterosexual couples is affected by the tragedy of childhood sexual abuse, usually incest in some form. When I contemplate the vastness of this problem for heterosexual intimacy, sometimes I am overwhelmed. This linking up of aggression and sex in the psychological complexes of so many people staggers my imagination. Some of this violence against children takes place so early in life that the emotional image traces can barely be captured in words. Even when the abuse happens after the development of language, the overwhelming and shocking nature of the events makes it very difficult to translate the feelings into language and to associate the memory traces with actual people and circumstances. Because so many women are survivors of sexual abuse, I alert myself to this possibility when I hear about a woman having no sexual interest or about a young girl who has a repetitive, "driven," overly seductive manner. Sexual deadness in older women and sexual drivenness in younger ones are often signs of childhood sexual trauma.

Is it possible for a couple like Larry and Louise to survive this trauma and build a vital, trusting sexual partnership? It depends. If Louise can forgive her uncle and remember much of what happened to her, she probably has a fairly good chance of restoring some trust in Larry's touch, as long as Larry maintains dialogue with her throughout this process. She will guide Larry in doing what gives her pleasure and in refraining from what does not. Larry will have to accept the finality of his wife's trauma: She cannot erase it and it will mark them as a couple forever. He will also need to understand how this trauma disturbs and disrupts his sexual needs and desires. Both people will have to cope with limitations in their sex life—calls for "time out" and flashbacks of fresh memory traces. If they can do all of this with support and empathy for each other, then they have the possibility of making a mutually desirable sex life, one that is shaped by both people's needs in the context of limitation.

Limitation is a general theme at the intersection of the Terrible Father and sexual desire. Sex and violence or sex and oppression mix together in this dream lover, because male dominance means aggression turned against female people. Earlier we encountered Patty's Terrible Father, who is connected to her memory traces of childhood beatings and attacks. This is another form of the complex that interferes with sexual desire for heterosexual women. When a father, a stepfather, a brother, or another fatherly figure has physically attacked a young girl, especially when there has been no resolution or even explanation of the attack, the adult woman carries not only the dark vortex of fear about a man's touch and closeness, but also memory traces of having been physically hurt by a man she thought she was supposed to love or respect. (By the way, I do not count ordinary spankings that seemed "fair enough" to the child to be traumatic physical attacks.)

Far worse for female sexual desire is the violence of male partners against their lovers. This kind of violence makes heterosexual intimacy impossible, unless the male partner is willing to go through a change process, and take full responsibility for the pain he has caused.

Lenore Walker, a pioneer psychologist in investigating violence in heterosexual relationships and marriage, has uncovered a cycle of violence between men and women. The cycle begins with an attack, sometimes on the environment (the door, table, dishes, and so on), from an irate male partner who wants his way or is furious with his lover. The attack causes damage to the environment or pain to the woman. The attacker becomes apologetic and penitent after the attack because he withdraws his Terrible Mother or Mistress Lover (Whore) projection at the moment he recognizes the destruction he has caused. At this moment, the man's projection transforms into the Maiden Lover or Great Mother: He promises he will never attack again as long as his partner is willing to forgive him. If the woman is willing to do this, often he begins to feel amorous or sexual. He wants to make love. She may find this attractive because he appears to want intimate contact now. Although she may feel little of her own desire and even continue to fear her partner, a battered woman often accedes to sex with this "penitent aggressor" because now she sees him as the Lost Child. If she engages in sex, things return to normal. When power struggles recur, he is likely to resort to violence again, usually in a more intimidating form.

This cycle of violence—attack, repent, sexual encounter, attack again—is an all too common drama among heterosexual couples of all classes, races, and backgrounds. In this cycle, men are entrapped by their projections. When they see the Terrible Mother or the Whore in their mind's eye, they feel compelled to bring this female "power" under control. Frequently their partners are realistically afraid of the consequences of trying to prevent or escape the situation. A woman is at greater risk for serious injury, even murder, if she resists or tries to escape from an abusive male partner in the heat of an aggressive attack. Frozen in fear, the woman may seem to be identifying with the projection. Much more likely, the recipient of the projection does not *know* how to transform the moment without increasing the risk of harm to herself. In a couple in which a cycle of violence is being enacted, the woman's best strategy, whether she ultimately wants to leave the relationship or to change it, is to contact a shelter or domestic abuse project in her geographical area. If the man has any possibility of recognizing the power of his own projection (and how and why it arises in him) in order to stop acting out, it will come through a third party who is trained and organized to assist the couple.

From national surveys of American people, it is a conservative estimate to say that one in four or five couples has experienced violence. One third of that violence is likely to be serious assault—punching, kicking, hitting with an object, assault with a knife or gun. In an assault it is the female partner who gets hurt in 94 or 95 percent of the cases. According to several major surveys, violence against women is the most common crime worldwide. Women's violence against men is often in retaliation for an attack. (Note here that I am talking about physical violence and not emotional aggression. In the last chapter, I talked about how both women and men are aggressive against each other in an emotional way.) Some men refuse to inhibit their impulse to use violence against people they love, and this creates difficulties of trust with their victims and observers (their children, for instance).

None of our couples has endured a battering relationship, although Joe and Larry both hit their partners once in their early years together. When Patty and Joe were talking about Patty's lack of sexual desire in the third session, Patty remembered what had happened.

Patty: I want to trust you, Joe, and I'd like to enjoy having sex, but I often feel completely disconnected with you when you just want sex. I think it's because of the way my father attacked me when he wanted something from me. I wish you could spend some time talking with me first.

Patty (Double): I want you to talk with me about your desires and to ask me about mine.

Joe: I know you do, but I am afraid you will criticize or reject me or something. I can't seem to get through to you with just wanting sex. Like you seem to think I don't *love* you because I want to have sex, but it's just the opposite. I wouldn't want to have sex if I didn't love you. I can't understand why you confuse me with your father.

Joe (Double): I would like you to stop confusing me with your father. I've never attacked you like he did.

Patty: That's not true. You hit me once the first year we were living together. I don't know what we were fighting about, but I know that you got mad because I was shouting in your face. Then you punched me in the chest. I was really shocked and I have never forgotten it.

Joe: Yeah, I remember it too. Even though I was really mad about the way you shouted at me, I know that I shouldn't have hit you. I felt real bad about it then, and I still do. I don't consider myself to be that kind of a man.

Joe (Double): Help me understand more about what bothers you still. I would like you to forgive me for it.

Patty: I guess it's just the image of you slugging me and the feelings like a dark hole that go with it. Sometimes I'm afraid that you still want to slug me and that you don't know how vulnerable I feel when you and I are fighting. I never feel strong. I'm always afraid.

Joe (Double): I'd like you to remember that you're not afraid of me in the same way you feared your father. I did hit you once, but I vowed I'd never do it again and I haven't. I want your trust.

Joe: That's true. I really want your trust because I love you and I want to be close, which includes sex, for me. I understand now how afraid you get when I'm mad. I really try to keep my temper down because I want you to trust me. I have never hit you again or even threatened. Do you think you could forgive me?

Patty: So you do understand about how I get afraid? That's the most important thing to me. If you know about that I can believe in your words. I really need to be *protected* from your rage because I already got too much rage from a man in my life.

Joe: Yeah, I see that.

Patty: I forgive you.

It is possible for couples to repair trust after one or two incidents of violence if the responsible partner is willing to claim the action *and* empathize with the other's hurt. More than two incidents, in my experience, are the beginning of a cycle of violence.

Couples in a cycle of violence are not suitable for dialogue therapy because they cannot establish a basis for trust. Special programs are set up nationally for partners caught up in violence and I recommend such a program to couples snared in the cycle. When violence has become a cycle, it can easily become an addiction. Physical aggression overtakes conversation when there is conflict, and destroys the possibility of intimacy.

The Terrible Father complex robs legions of women of the possibility of sexual desire for men. The legacy of childhood sexual abuse (especially by fathers and father figures) is often sexual deadness with a male partner in adulthood, even with a trusted partner. Physical and emotional violence against women and children (including children's witnessing an attack on their mother) is a form of male oppression that continues to be widespread. The fear of rape and other crimes against women at home or on the streets is another dimension of the Terrible Father complex where fantasies of male violence mix with the reality of male dominance. When will daughters be able fundamentally to trust their fathers? When will women be free to open themselves to sexual pleasures with male partners because they feel certain that female equality will be unquestionably protected?

Authors Robert Bly and Sam Keen plead for fathers' involvement in their sons' development and suggest that this is more essential than a father's involvement in a daughter's life. I want to cry out, Wait! Look what is happening to our daughters' sexual desire! How can our daughters come to trust and enjoy male partners if their fathers not only remain distant or critical, "merely" trivializing a girl's importance in the world, but also give rein to violence and sexual impulses with their daughters or stepdaughters? In this contemporary world where the media, pornography, and men's dream lovers portray the female body as a sexual resource for men, loving fathers must form personal, caring relationships with their daughters in order to help them resist the pull of male dominance. Loving fathers are essential for their daughters' later ability to love a male partner freely (as an equal) and to experience sexual desire for him. This is not a simple rehashing of the "romance with Father"—although for some daughters, Father romance is an aspect of later sexual development—but it is a plea that fathers become conscious of the circumstances in which their daughters are sexualized. Pornography, rape, violence against women, incest, and portrayals of the female body as a sexual resource are conditions that severely constrain the sexual development of women. If fathers could become fully alert to the enormous loss of female desire in this mix of violence and sex, perhaps they could become more protective of trust. Perhaps they would work openly to transform heterosexuality into a relationship of mutuality and reciprocity. More than in any other historical era, ours is a time in which young people are persuaded (at some level of the imagination, conscious or unconscious) that sex is violent and violence is sexual *as long as the violence is against women*. The connection between violence and sex is inescapable in everyday life, from the nightly news to MTV and contemporary art and literature.

The Terrible Father complex—women's images of critical, dominant, oppressive, and demonic men—haunts many women in their attempts to trust a male partner and develop sexual pleasure. Like Patty, some women can forgive the mistakes of their partners and come to recognize that their deepest fears connect to the powerlessness of childhood. These women can move beyond oppression by the Terrible Father and enjoy their partners as equals. Like Louise, some other women cannot easily free themselves from the emotional image traces of abusive and incestuous relationships with fathers or father figures. They must learn to live with the frightening residues of impulses that were not contained by their male caregivers. In order to feel any heterosexual desire, they have to find activities and conversations that give pleasure in the presence of their partners. About one in three women is faced with a dilemma like this. It is a dilemma whose origins can be traced back to our fathers.

the terrible mother

The greatest barrier to male sexual desire is shame, humiliation. Criticism, degradation, and failure to meet standards are the experiences that men report as interfering with pleasure in sex. One major aspect of male sexuality is profoundly different from female sexuality: the early discovery of, enjoyment of, and identification with the penis. Boys and men often find pride, comfort, and satisfaction in their mastery of sexual feelings. Finding pleasure in masturbation and fantasy is a sexual outlet for many adolescent boys and mature men, one they have under their own control.

Some men come to believe, though, that having a heterosexual partner "should mean" that masturbation is unnecessary, and so they begin to associate masturbation with shame (lack of control of one's sex life).

When a female partner withholds sexual contact but continues to be present physically (sleeps in the same bed or room, for example), her partner is likely to feel humiliated, even degraded. He is aroused by the closeness of her body and ashamed that he cannot bring his sexual needs under control. Masturbation no longer seems like an option because sexual pleasure has become associated with the female body. Only bringing *that* body under control would bring the desired results. The condition of needing the female body, but not having it under control, tends to evoke emotional image traces of the Terrible Mother. The Terrible Mother complex—controlling, dominating, attacking, critical, and withholding—is the dream lover that is likely to replace the Maiden or the Mistress under these circumstances.

A man like Jonathon, who has had a Great Mother projection onto his own mother (who was sexually stimulating in her constant admiration and gratification), is especially confused when his partner rejects him sexually. From his early attachment relationship with his mother, Jonathon concluded that his mere physical presence was "exciting." And he wanted to please Karen, to create the environment that *she* wanted. Jonathon sees himself as "doing everything" for Karen that she wants (and eager to do more if she asks), and so he is doubly humiliated when she complains about him. Her criticisms and corrections of his sexual performance and personal style are intolerable to Jonathon because they link him to his earliest experiences of discontent, rage, and pain (the ways in which his parents failed to meet his needs when he was powerless). Jonathon turns this pain and hatred onto himself at present. Rather than see Karen as the Terrible Mother (spiteful, hateful, withholding), he tends to see himself as the Victim Child whose body and appearance are not "masculine enough." Without help, over time this would tend to turn into blaming Karen as the "bitch"—the manipulative power broker who withholds her affections.

In the discussion of the Terrible Father, we saw how "control" enters into male sexual desire in a big way. Men want to feel control over sexual pleasure. Most men have already felt this through masturbating and fantasizing or using pornography. The expectation of control was transferred to the female body. Many cultural traditions openly promote sexual dominance by the male over the female body. Young men and women may assume this as a "norm," even including images of sexual violence against women. When a man is faced with a female partner he loves, who inhabits a body he would like to control, he can easily become confused and ashamed. Ashamed of his desire to dominate her body, and of his inability to dominate her and meet his sexual needs directly, he is mostly ashamed that he cannot keep all of this under control.

In this atmosphere, critical comments and actual rejections from his female partner seem acutely wounding. He will tend to withdraw, doubt his sexual desire (because now sexual pleasure has been clouded with humiliation), and blame himself or his partner. Inevitably his partner will seem more and more like a Terrible Mother (critical, withholding, demanding) because he has attached such power to her body and finds himself unable to control that body and his access to it.

When Karen and Jonathon try to talk about Jonathon's sexual performance they come up against his humiliation. Karen, however, is learning now to paraphrase and empathize with Jonathon, instead of insisting on her own needs only.

Jonathon: I just want to know that you like my body and that you enjoy touching me.

Karen: You want me to tell you that I enjoy touching you? (*Jonathon nods.*) It's hard for me to say something like that unless I know *you* are paying attention to my needs too. I don't like it when you sort of jiggle my breast, pat me on the rear, hump me, and it's over. I do like your touches, but I want more.

Jonathon: I hate your criticisms and can't stand to hear—

Jonathon (Double): I want to please you, but my own feelings of shame get in the way when I think you are mostly unhappy with our lovemaking.

Karen: You mean you really feel *ashamed*? I didn't know that. What do you feel ashamed about?

Jonathon: It's hard for me to say. It seems like I'm ashamed of my body and size, like I'm not masculine enough or something. I hate to talk about this stuff because I think that talking makes it worse.

Karen: I really appreciate your talking with me about it. I can tell you that I *love* your body. I don't see anything wrong with it. All along I thought that you really didn't enjoy sex and that was why you came so soon.

Jonathon: Just the opposite. I get so excited when we make love, sometimes because it's so infrequent . . . and then I can't seem to control my own ejaculation. I enjoy your body enormously. I think that I could control ejaculating better if we made love more often.

Karen: Why haven't you wanted to make love more often? I've been complaining about that since we've been together.

Jonathon: Your complaining actually stops me. I don't know how to explain that.

Jonathon (Double): When you complain, even when it's complaining about wanting to make love more, I feel ashamed of myself, like I'm not good enough for you. I guess I need more reassurance.

A lot of men need reassurance from their female partners in regard to their capacity for lovemaking. Because we all seem to be operating under the unfortunate assumption that the man should be in charge (even of the female body), men are confused about their role in actual lovemaking. Perhaps even more perplexing, neither partner often knows *what* to do with the woman's body in order to stimulate it. It's clear to the man what he likes (generally speaking, unless he has had a very repressive development), but it's unclear to him how to bring pleasure to his female partner except to do what the stereotypes say: dominate, control, overwhelm her with his penis and intercourse. These stereotyped images, drawing on the Maiden and Mistress dream lovers, encourage the man to move toward his partner's fantasy of the Terrible Father. When the woman then withholds her desire (and trust), she begins to look like the Terrible Mother to the man. She seems dominating and controlling although she may actually feel vulnerable and afraid. The woman imagines her partner as a judgmental or abusive Terrible Father and he imagines her as the denying, rejecting Terrible Mother. These negative archetypal dream lover states encourage both partners to identify with being children or victims. Neither partner then feels able to initiate an adult love relationship. Both feel "dominated" by the other, when in actuality it is the Other within—not the partner—who is dominating.

When couples speak about sexual inhibition and lack of desire, generally both partners are caught up in believing the other is the negative parent. It is the *power* of the negative parental image that invites a childish identification in an adult. Most of us feel disgust at the fantasy of having sex with a dominating, intrusive parent, and so when we are making projections of the Terrible Mother and Terrible Father onto a partner, we feel a kind of disgust (or shame) in place of sexual desire for each other. Although we may have had sexual fantasies about our parents in childhood, these were erotic specifically *because* they were under our own control. If sexual stimulation or contact is forced upon a child, it is perceived with disgust and shame (even if it is also erotically stimulating). The parent has *power over* the child. It is this state of *power over* that is recreated in a negative parental projection with an adult partner.

Many men complain of feeling powerless and ashamed about the lack of sex in their lives. They complain of feeling held hostage to their wives' lack of sexual desire. Above I named what I consider to be the root cause of the lack of female sexual desire for men: the lack of pleasure in sex with men. In order to increase female pleasure in heterosexual sex, both partners need to awaken to the fact that they may not know what is pleasing for the female. Rather than the woman waiting for her partner to take the initiative and show her what is pleasurable, or the man assuming that he *knows* what a woman wants and then trying to *give it to her*, both partners need to study, investigate, and discover what is actually pleasurable for the woman. In the meantime, the female partner must remain empathic with her male partner—reassuring him, supporting him, and appreciating him for his willingness to go through the darkness with her. The darkness of female sexual pleasure is not a condition that either partner likes. Neither partner brought this on the relationship. It is a cultural condition—one that mediates directly against heterosexual intimacy. In order to overcome this darkness and allow both partners to feel their sexual desire directly, pleasure must be guaranteed for both.

If a male partner has not discovered pleasure in heterosexual sex, he too will walk a dark path with the help of his partner—gradually finding what is pleasant and increasing that. As psychologist Carol Tavris points out in her book about contemporary misjudgments of sex differences, men also have a variety of sexual styles and preferences, based on learning and development. Some are slower and some are quicker. Some prefer the use of the entire body in sex and others prefer focusing on the genitals. On the topic of how we learn to be sexual, Tavris says:

> An appreciation of male diversity in sexual response would help to dispel the prevalent myth that male sexuality is natural, unlearned, and entirely beyond a man's control. This myth harms both sexes. It is cruel to women, for it justifies sexual coercion and rape, and it requires women to learn to "manage" and control male sexuality instead of putting the responsibility for men's behavior squarely on men. The myth is also cruel to men, many of whom are desperately afraid of hearing that something psychological might be affecting their sexual performance.

Men like Jonathon would benefit enormously from a recognition of the range of differences in male sexual behavior and preferences. If men were readily aware that their sexuality is learned and not *found,* they would feel better about asking questions and needing help from partners. When men perceive themselves as having sexual problems, they blame themselves (their body parts or "performance"), their mothers (usually for being "dominating" or "intrusive and overinvolved"), or their partners (for being "frigid" or too critical). Men often feel better about their sexuality when they remember that it is learned behavior, not a simple drive like hunger.

But, how much of a role do actual mothers play in initiating their sons into a Terrible Mother complex? Naturally mothers have major influence on children since mothers are the primary caregivers. How much mothers are themselves *responsible* for the negative mother complex is not a simple calculation because of the *conditions* under which problematic mothering often takes place. Being a single mother, carrying most of the household chores while mothering and wage earning, and being blamed by society for one's children's flaws are just a few of the vulnerabilities that may produce overly anxious or intrusive mothering. Many women are functioning under conditions that make fatigue and anxiety ordinary components of mothering. Empathic mothering is difficult if not impossible if the mother is exhausted, overburdened, and impoverished.

In some cases, though, the personality of a mother (especially perhaps her conscious or unconscious desire for vicarious fame, pleasure, intelligence) may interfere with a child's development in a way that predisposes a child to a resistant attachment with an adult partner. Sons especially are vulnerable to being the target of a mother's dreams for success. When the son becomes *identified* with the mother's fantasies about him, he has come under the sway of what I call "narcissistic mothering." This style of mothering has had repercussions on many men I have seen in therapy. When mothers try to meet their own dreams through their children, by molding *them* into dream lovers or using them to substitute for creative development, their sons may become especially compliant or oppositional with the mother's wish. This childhood adaptation leaves a man later unable to agree and support his female partner without becoming anxious about her "power." He imagines that any dependence on his female partner will result in her having power to "manipulate" him into doing and thinking things from her point of view, instead of his own. (Obviously this is a fantasy based on childhood powerlessness, because adults do not control each other's thoughts or feelings.)

Abusive mothering continues to plague children all over the world. Physical battering, aggressive attacks, and neglect or desertion are the traumas that often go hand in hand with poverty and oppression. Cases of abusive mothering in my experience have many times been associated with the mother's limited resources, lack of support from her family or anyone else, or mental illness. When these circumstances are not present and a woman has become openly critical of her children, blaming and attacking them, then surely we should hold such a woman personally responsible for the abuse. Some of us were mothered by women who were critical and demanding and we may tend to repeat that pattern ourselves if we do not become self-aware enough to stop it. Sometimes becoming conscious of such a tendency in oneself also helps develop empathy for one's mother, understanding her in context.

The critical demanding mother is the bane of any son, no matter if he conforms or rebels. Until he becomes conscious of his Terrible Mother complex, the emotional image traces of her manner and voice will arouse rage, shame, and hatred when his female partner sounds, smells, moves, or demands in a way reminiscent of his own dream lover. In this way his mother complex has interfered with his ability to love his wife or partner, and to see her as vulnerable (not powerful).

the mistress lover

The Mistress Lover is the expression of a particular kind of male sexual desire—demanding, exotic, captivating, cruel, and even brutal. This is a desire for power, not love. Men imagine that "she" has power over them and so they want power over her. My reading of this dream lover is that she is probably connected to the envy men feel of women's reproductive powers and complex sensual bodies. The Mistress Lover or Whore is disruptive to heterosexual intimacy as she intrudes "power" between vulnerable men and women. In its worst form this projected male power becomes a motive for rape.

Rape, defined as sexual intercourse forced upon a woman without her consent (including situations in which she is unable to give consent, as when she is unconscious), is a shockingly common event. Somewhere between 25 percent and 45 percent of American women have survived a situation in which they were raped or rape was attempted. These statistics may seem impossibly high, but they are consistent across many studies. Rape can occur anywhere—on a date, on a dark street, on a college campus, in a woman's living room (by her lawfully wedded spouse). The legacy of such a trauma is a deadening Terrible Father complex that will haunt victims and survivors, as self-hatred of their (female) bodies and an inability to trust men and male love for many years, perhaps the rest of their lives. My focus at the moment, though, is the Mistress Lover and her effects on *men* everywhere in terms of the rape mentality that can enter into heterosexual relationships. The rape mentality prevents intimacy and encourages a deadly mix of sex and violence.

Rape mentality is common among men in Western societies, according to writer Tim Beneke, who investigated men's attitudes about rape after working to rehabilitate male rapists. What he conveys preeminently is that male-dominated cultures are full of "rape signs" indicating that rape is to be expected, natural, even attractive. Rape signs, which show up in our society in jokes, cartoons, MTV, pornography, advertising, art, and literature, are indicators that it is right and natural for a man to force sex on a woman. For example, television ads and videos on MTV often portray women as willingly surrendering to violent or aggressive moves from men. On a motorcycle, a man dressed in black leather speeds by a blond teenage girl dressed in a lacy open blouse and a short leather skirt. He skids to a stop a block later, turns his motorcycle around, and speeds back to scoop her up onto the back of his bike. She looks perturbed but intrigued, and off they ride. On another level, we all hear jokes in which the woman "deserves what she gets" because she is "coming on" to the man in a way she denies, but must *obviously* intend.

These communications may be direct or subtle but the message is clear: Rape cannot be prevented and is sometimes necessary. The implication is that men cannot control their sexual feelings when under the influence of the Mistress dream lover. Women should "just know" this and bring about the necessary controls through their behavior—by wearing modest clothing, walking only in neighborhoods that are "safe," refraining from getting drunk at a party—or else. Or else it is inevitable that the "uncontrollable male urge" will take over. Rape signs invite men to have fantasies of rape that make it acceptable. As Beneke says:

> In all of the sexual fantasies of rape that I have heard men recount, the experience as described by women, with its terror and fear of death, is denied. Just as rape signs make it difficult to think clearly about rape, men's fantasies of rape may make it difficult for men to think about the reality of rape.

Beneke's findings are supported in surveys that show upward of 50 percent of male college students believe they would force a woman to have sex if they could get away with it.

Many men and women believe that rape is somehow "natural" because men, especially young men, are "driven" by sexual desire and women's appearances. As it turns out, though, anthropologist Peggy Sanday in a study of ninety-five tribal societies discovered that 47 percent were virtually rape-free, with others being rape-prone or somewhere between. Sanday believes that respect for nature distinguishes rape-free societies. She says, "Men who are conditioned to respect the female virtues of growth and the sacredness of life do not violate women. It is significant that in societies where nature is held sacred, rape occurs only rarely." This kind of respect for growth and the sacredness of life does not enter into the Mistress Lover image that our society boldly promotes.

The Mistress Lover—especially the young, slender, nubile woman—is broadly portrayed as a sexual resource that should be available to a man, especially if she displays her beauty publicly. When I introduced the Mistress Lover in Chapter 2, I briefly told the story of Pandora, the first woman on earth in Greek mythology. She is made by the gods to be beautiful but evil, to be merely an appearance that distracts men. In the place of a heart are lies and deceit. She is not human like men. Her power is sexual, a force she holds over men. This force is used as a weapon against men, who become distracted and confused in her presence. I stress the Mistress dream lover in my account of rape because she is an image of male strange gender. She is not a product of women's lives or psyches. The Pandora story is an apt one for the accounts given to Tim Beneke by contemporary men of how they imagine rape. From Beneke's extensive research and clinical work with rapists, he concludes that "rape is a *man's* problem. It is men who rape and men who collectively have the power to end rape."

Beneke talked with rapists, lawyers, judges, and ordinary men about how they view rape. Before he began his study, he was troubled by the fact that rapists sounded much like himself and his friends when the rapists discussed their motives for raping women. Beneke began to see that he shared beliefs about women with rapists, and he was determined to understand how this could be so, because he considered himself to be a sensitive, ethical man. He discovered that everyday life in a male-dominated society is filled with rape signs that indicate rape is natural and sometimes inevitable. He also discovered a hidden metaphor of female beauty. It is the metaphor that female beauty = force. Here is an example of how this metaphor is used. The following is excerpted from an interview with a twenty-three-year-old man, called Jay, who works as a file clerk in Pittsburgh. Jay is an "ordinary guy" who would never rape a woman (because it's wrong and unlawful, not because he doesn't want to). When asked how he feels when he sees sexy women, Jay says:

> Let's say I see a woman and she looks really pretty and really clean and sexy, and she's giving off very feminine, sexy vibes, I think "Wow, I would love to make love to her," but I know she's not really interested. It's a tease. A lot of times a woman knows that she's looking really good and she'll use that and flaunt it, and it makes me feel like she's laughing at me and I feel *degraded*.
>
> I also feel dehumanized, because when I'm being teased I just turn off, I cease to be human. Because if I go with my human emotions I'm going to want to put my arms around her and kiss her, and to do that would be unacceptable. I don't like the feeling that I'm supposed to stand there and take it,

> and not be able to hug her and kiss her, so I just turn off my emotions. It's a feeling of humiliation, because the woman has forced me to turn off my feelings and react in a way that I really don't want to.

When the Mistress Lover is projected onto a woman, a man feels humiliated, even degraded, by the power the woman supposedly holds over him. Most men will say this woman is "flaunting" her power and knows about the force she holds over men.

According to Beneke's findings this force is the "power" of female beauty, not under the control of the male viewer. This imagined power is said to "drive" men to violate and attack women in "retaliation" for the force that is out of a man's control. Beneke details how many male metaphors of sexual desire for the Mistress Lover are commonly used in a way that implies the mix of sex and violence in men's fantasies. Here are just a few:

> I tried to get her into bed but *got shot down*. If I can *wear down her resistance,* I'll score.
> He's always *hitting on* women.
> I really *put it to her, stuck it to her*!
> I'd like to *bang her box*.
> He *knocked her up*.

In almost of all of Beneke's interviews there is an implication that if a woman is raped, the act must have *something* to do with *her* behavior. Some men claim that the responsibility for the action, the force or power that drives the action, is within the *victim's* behavior alone. These men seem to be saying that rape would stop if *women* changed their behavior. Apart from the absurdity of this position, it is important to remember that the Mistress Lover can be projected onto any female person—not only those who are attractive, scantily dressed, or young. Children, eighty-year-old women, and disabled women are among rape victims. Even in these cases, though, my guess is that the rapist would tend to explain his behavior in terms of "her" power. Somehow he would tell the story that she "asked for it" or "wanted it."

This peculiar form of reasoning arises in all forms of sexual harassment. The idea that a woman must be doing *something* to provoke a man's assault or harassment of her is explained by the metaphor that female beauty = force and by the projection of a Mistress Lover who "says no when she means yes." This projection colors the female with force and power, at that moment of a man's projection. "She" (the dream lover) controls the man's feelings and "she" must be subdued or he feels degraded, ashamed, humiliated. To avoid the humiliation, the male viewer can walk away in an attempt to escape with as much of his pride as he can muster. Or he can attack verbally, physically, or financially to try to bring this force under his control. This dream lover, this image of male sexual desire, creates a narrow and dangerous structure for heterosexuality. Tragically, the Mistress Lover—the sex-starved bitch who must be possessed and dominated—is one of the major images through which young people come to understand sexual arousal. Sexual behavior is learned or acquired by humans (not built in), and our children are learning a dangerous version of it.

The metaphor of female beauty = force and its attendant Mistress Lover appear in so many arenas of everyday life, dominating our images, fantasies, and depictions of heterosexual desire, that all of us are steeped in their meanings. It is hard for a couple to escape the Mistress Lover when he says he's "just admiring" her body. She responds, "I want you to *love* me and not my body." When Joe grabs Patty because she "looks so hot in her jeans," Patty has a difficult time trusting Joe's sincere and personal expression of love, because Patty has been tolerating hoots and suggestive remarks on the streets (for wearing the same jeans). Women know that force may be used against them by known or unknown men, but often women *don't know why*. They may realize that a metaphor exists that female beauty = force, but it makes no sense to them because they know how limited their actual powers and privileges are. Sometimes women translate this metaphor into one of their own: female trust = danger.

This translation may be the result of trauma, such as rape or harassment. It may just be a matter of surviving on the street, following the "rules" set down about where women should walk and how they should dress, intuitively recognizing rape signs around them. One way or the other, female trust = danger is hard to overcome when a woman finally faces a trusted male partner. It's hard for her to believe that he *knows* how apprehensive she is, how confused she might be about her own desire and the meaning of her appearance. Most women are unable to free themselves from concerns about their appearance; some women have wholly confused their appearance with sexiness. They, in fact, have no clue that sexiness would mean actually knowing and seeking out their *own* sexual pleasures, eventually living out their desires. They only want to be *seen* as the object of male desire because this is what they have learned about their sexuality. But they cannot feel powerful about their beauty (even if they can be beautiful) because they know that beauty is transitory, that they will inevitably lose it as they age, or even if they gain a little weight. The cultural standards for beauty are not under women's control.

Pamela and Charles are a poignant example of a couple trapped by cultural metaphors.

Pamela: If you want to touch me in bed, I'd like you to do it at night with the lights out.

Charles: You want the lights out because you are ashamed of your body? (*See how Charles is improving.*)

Pamela: It's just that I'm afraid if you see my body and all of its wrinkles and other imperfections, you will compare it to the bodies of younger women. I worry that you've been sleeping with younger women. And even if you haven't, you see them on TV, in movies, at the beach.

Pamela (Double): Are you attracted to younger women?

Charles: I'd be a fool to say I'm not, but that doesn't prevent me from being attracted to you. I always enjoy the way you look, your clothes, your figure—

Pamela: (*Weeping*) I don't. I hate myself for being old and there's *nothing* to do about it! I feel like I have lost everything that brought me confidence—my face, my skin tone, even my graceful movement.

Charles: I *am* sorry that you feel that way. I'm just at a loss about how I—

Charles (Double): How can I help? What could I say to you that would be reassuring?

Pamela: I guess if you complimented me more or showed your interest in doing things with me. Taking me out occasionally—not for business or family purposes—for a "date."

Men need to be alert that the Mistress Lover can be a very hurtful projection for women, expecially when older women see their male partners projecting it onto younger women. This dream lover is the epitome of male dominance. The metaphor that female beauty = force is, after all, a metaphor invented by *men* and their desire to control the female body (and the associated feelings of shame when they can't). The Mistress Lover is harmful to men on the level of their belief in their extraordinary "domination" by female beauty, and it is harmful to women through the equation of women and sexual resources. Dehumanizing on so many levels, the prevalence of the Mistress Lover in all male-dominated cultures obscures the sexual feelings of women and confuses all of us about our vulnerabilities in attempts at heterosexual intimacy.

trust

Almost everything I have said so far about sex in heterosexual couples sounds pretty dreary. The lack of sexual desire in women and the mix of violence and sex in men are barriers to intimacy. Yet, I count on sexual intimacy in my relationship with my husband and I assist many other people in finding it for themselves. What is the secret that these couples have? First, they *developed it together*. Heterosexual intimacy, the experience of freely giving sexual pleasure to each other, has to be learned and developed within a relationship. It cannot be learned through books (not even this one), with other partners, or through "nature" or "sexual chemistry." Because sex is a most private and fragile communication (allowing another into your body space), it requires dialogue for its development. Lovers need to be able to talk empathically and for themselves.

This of course is especially true for heterosexual lovers. The main reason why heterosexuality is so "unnatural" is not because we have different body structures or speak different languages, in my view. It is projection. Projection of dream lovers takes over in sex more than it does in any other arena, except perhaps parenting (where partners tend to project parental Others). I think this is because of the vulnerability we feel (if we are not defensively self-reliant) in allowing someone to bond with us, to become part of us, through sex. It is very difficult to be conscious of the risk involved in allowing another person deeply into one's being. So the strange gender takes over and we often use projection to find our way rather than ask questions. Apparently simple matters such as lighting, temperature, posture, position, manner and place of touching, verbal commands or expressions, extent of clothing, and many other mundane details are frequently handled by each partner through projection. Instead of *asking* what the other would like and then working out differences through dialogue, most partners feel they "know" in advance. This knowledge is based on one's own sexual fantasies and dream lovers. It may not match the partner's preferences at all.

Often I have witnessed conversations like the following between women and men in dialogue therapy:

Karen: There's something I want to tell you, Jonathon, and I don't want to hurt you with it. I guess I am learning how important it is to be careful and supportive.

Karen (Double): I have something to say that will probably hurt you, Jonathon, but I would like to understand your reaction.

Karen: I really don't like the way you touch me when you want to make love. You come up behind me and grab me and start patting me all over like I'm a teddy bear or something. Do you know what I mean?

Jonathon: I guess I thought you liked to be surprised and hugged like that. I always liked that when someone did it to me, but you don't, I guess.

Karen: No, I don't. And I *really* don't like it when you lean your head on my breast and talk to me like you're a baby or something when we're making love. It's totally unsexy to me.

Jonathon: It hurts a lot to hear you say that, because I thought you wanted me to be vulnerable and open, and that's what I was trying to be. It wasn't *serious* either. I was trying to be playful and light. Sometimes I think you want a macho type or something.

Jonathon (Double): I am afraid that I'm not the kind of man you could love, that I'm too "childish" for you.

Karen: I *do* love you, but I can't feel sexy when you are acting like a baby. If you want me to stroke you or if you want to get reassurance, tell me and I'll try.

Jonathon: Okay, right now I would like to know what you *like* about our lovemaking. What really appeals to you about it?

Karen answered him in detail, saying how much she enjoyed being held and caressed and how much she liked looking at his muscular body (even certain specific parts of it). Jonathon was surprised and visibly pleased because Karen had never before detailed for him what she *enjoyed*. She had told him only what she did not like.

Taking back projections means asking questions of your partner. Finding out what the other person likes or dislikes is the basis of developing a lovemaking *routine* that guarantees pleasure for both partners. I stress "routine" because many people believe that spontaneity should always be a part of sexual pleasure. For most couples, spontaneity fades with the romance. After a couple have committed themselves to shared responsibilities and demands, they have little spontaneity. The routine of knowing when and what will happen is reassuring to both partners, as long as (1) the routine can be renegotiated through dialogue, and (2) it includes tried and true pleasures for each.

There is nothing like pleasure in sex to promote desire. And when you don't enjoy what is taking place with your sexual partner, then you are not going to want to return to it. Sex is learned behavior and it follows the "reinforcement schedule" of most simple learned behavior: Success reinforces; lack of success and failure diminish interest and desire. Many people feel a mere "lack of success" rather than out-and-out failure in lovemaking. Partly this is due to the orgasm-through-intercourse standard that couples impose, partly to the problem of female sexual desire, and partly to the cultural climate in which the Mistress Lover is the major symbol of sexual desire for heterosexuals, men and women alike.

Trust is the basis of sexual desire between the sexes: trust on the part of the woman that she can have sovereignty over her own pleasure, and trust on the part of the man that he can have access to sexual pleasure with his partner. I have tried to show why these two forms of trust are difficult to establish, and how the sexes differ in terms of the barriers they are confronting in the search for pleasure. Let me add one more fact: Women need to feel relaxed in order to have an orgasm, and men do not necessarily need to be relaxed (otherwise they wouldn't be able to rape). Trust for the woman includes a basic feeling of security that she will relax when she and her partner engage. To have sovereignty over sexual pleasure, relaxing is a given, a base. This means different things for different women, but often the surroundings and environment are the issue. No children, no pets, no TV, locked doors, or whatever is necessary so that she can feel "relaxed" and unhooked from the responsibilities that she normally feels.

Because trust for the man does not usually include the relaxation key, he sometimes argues against the "requirements" his female partner imposes.

Joe: I don't know why we have to wait until Sunday night when the kids are in bed to make love. It's like we have this one night a week when you are willing even to consider it.

Patty: It's true. I like the feeling that the kids are worn out from the weekend and have to get to bed early for school on Monday. I feel free for the first time all week.

Joe: I understand. It makes sense that it's the time you don't feel responsible for their needs. (*Joe is improving in his paraphrasing* *and empathy*.) I would just like to get maybe a different plan so that you could feel that way on another night too.

Patty: I'm glad you didn't argue with me like you used to. That really feels different to me. Yeah, I'd be willing to talk about another evening as long as you're willing to ask your mom to take the kids.

Joe: I'm willing to find someone to take the kids. I don't see why it has to be my mom.

Patty: Because I want someone who can keep them *overnight*, like maybe on Friday night. I know you want to make love more often and I do too, but I know that I need certain things in order to be comfortable and enjoy myself.

Patty and Joe had a very good dialogue here. It was empathic and differentiated, responding to their own and each other's needs. Instead of trying to talk Patty out of her need to have the kids asleep and elsewhere, Joe accepted it as important to *her*. Then he could suggest that together they might find a way to meet his need for more lovemaking.

Through this kind of dialogue, partners expand and change their routines. To have a basic routine is the first step, though. Many couples spend a few months in dialogue therapy trying to find a routine that brings them both sexual pleasure, while taking back the projections of how it "should" be with the other person. Larry and Louise struggled mightily to find some situation in which they could both meet their (very different) needs and retain a sense of closeness. Because Louise was slowly integrating her memories of incest, she asked that Larry touch her only in the ways she could openly assent to. Sometimes this did not go beyond hugging her. Larry asked that Louise reassure him that she loved him whenever she asked him to stop touching her. He also wanted Louise to know that he had a lot of sexual desire that he was managing through masturbation, but that he did not enjoy masturbating (beyond the mere relief of tension). He asked that she progress as quickly as possible in her individual therapy so that she could return as his lover. Louise, who still was not confident about her body and appearance, haltingly agreed to this (and I alerted her to confront her self-hatred in individual therapy so that she would not expect Larry to solve it for her). Together Larry and Louise set aside two hours a week for "private time" in which they would take a walk holding hands or spend time lying in each other's arms. They decided the exact days on which these hours would occur and promised each other that eventually these would be hours of lovemaking.

These routines of trust in finding pleasure combat the despair of women and the shame of men. Pleasure has to be the goal for each person. Although I see each partner as directly responsible for her or his pleasure (that is, how to reach it and what is pleasurable), I also hold the *couple* responsible for integrating the activities of each partner into a routine. In other words, you need to know what you find pleasurable and be able to describe and direct your partner. If your partner objects that what you want would not be comfortable, then you have a dialogue about this. For example, you may want to be stimulated in a way that your partner finds difficult (because it is boring or humiliating). Together you find a way that it could be pleasurable for both of you with enough of what you want.

The integration of two people's pleasures, a woman's and a man's, is complicated and requires a lot of good talking. The dialogue should take place, by and large, outside of the love bed. Negotiations about sex need to be carried out in some situation that is intimate and safe; the occasion of lovemaking is usually too vulnerable.

Sometimes couples like Pamela and Charles say, "Why do we have to be sexual?" They seem to be saying that life together is good enough without sex, but when I listen to their complaints about their relationship, I always hear them implying otherwise. She talks about her desire to appear beautiful and he talks about his "not caring" that his wife "has given up sex." Unconsciously, unintentionally, they are saying, "Why can't we be sexual like we used to be, like we'd want to be?" but they feel too ashamed to say this openly. I believe this is true of most heterosexual couples that do not have sex.

Living together intimately in a context in which sex is expected means "being sexual." Increasing trust in finding heterosexual pleasure means taking responsibility for the fact of being a sexual couple. Couples married for decades will appeal to me, "Couldn't we just pretend we're dating and go out but not have sex?" No. To me this is tantamount to saying, "Couldn't I just pretend to be a teenager at the age of forty, get a punk haircut, and watch MTV?" One cannot go back in time. One cannot pretend not to have a sexual bond. Pretending not to have responsibility for a sexual relationship is a problem that many couples bring to therapy. They seem to be waiting for a "parent" to "solve" the problem, and of course in the interim each partner sees the other one as a Terrible Parent and feels completely turned off sexually. Claiming responsibility for having a sexual bond is the first step to increasing trust and increasing pleasure. At this point the partners can say, "Hey, we have a sexual relationship, and so how do we make it work to our advantage?" (The question should never be "How do we get a sexual relationship?" for a couple that has already committed itself through sexual attachment.)

Working out a sexual relationship with one's partner is rarely what one imagined it would be. One's ideal dream lover would be different. The ideal dream lover is one's own fantasy, is one's own Otherness. Only through the recognition and integration of this Otherness can a person develop what has been projected or left out of the conscious self (but is nonetheless a part of the self). A partner helps in this development by refusing to take on one's projections, by resisting being stereotyped, and by supporting changes and development.

A partner should be more complicated, ornery, and difficult than an ideal dream lover. When fantasy and reality seem to match, then it is impossible to maintain the tension necessary for development. This is a tension between what is imagined, feared, or expected and what is actual. In the gap between the imagined and the actual, people grow. This is a central way that human beings change and develop—by coming up against resistance and learning how to deal with it. Considering this, we recognize that dream lovers are neither "good" nor "bad" for us; they are necessary aspects of Otherness. They promote relationships between the sexes through projection, but they can be the basis of development when they are reclaimed as the self. Once they are reclaimed, we have the possibility of knowing ourselves (and our dreams) more completely—and of taking responsibility for our own ideals and fears.

envy and betrayal

In order to establish an environment in which both partners can trust each other with the vulnerability of sexual pleasure, couples have to become conscious of envy and avoid betrayal. These two—envy and betrayal—are the emotional killers of trust when they are enacted against a partner. As we have seen, shame and humiliation interfere especially with men's sexual pleasure, and fear and confusion with women's. When envy is used against a partner, through making attacks or belittling the partner's resources, these threatening emotions emerge strongly. When betrayal is enacted in a committed relationship, as when Karen betrayed Jonathon, it destroys trust until the betraying partner can be forgiven. This can happen only when that person thoroughly understands and takes responsibility for the pain that was inflicted on the partner.

Envy, in the way I use the term, means an attack on what is good or resourceful in the other, but cannot be brought under control of the self. As I said in earlier chapters, envy is a destructive, hateful way of trying to "equalize" unequal resources by diminishing the worth of those resources. Envy is at the root of a lot of violent and aggressive attacks between the sexes. Men rape and attack women because men envy the "force" that women supposedly have under their control in having female bodies and the options of makeup and dress that men don't have. Women belittle and depreciate men's careers and wage earning because they envy the "power" men supposedly have under their control through their freedom to develop their skills and talents in a culture that "welcomes" them. Projections of dream lovers (without understanding that they are projections) can fill a partner with envy and stimulate aggressive attacks.

When a couple want to develop the basis for sexual pleasure (exploring what is pleasurable for both partners), they have to recognize how hurtful and destructive envy has been. Let's listen to Charles and Pamela talking about her envy of him.

Charles: Over all of these years we've been together, you have never appreciated what I have given you in terms of wealth, property, or privileges to travel and be a broad consumer of culture.

Pamela: You're saying that you feel hurt or angry that I've belittled you in terms of what you've contributed to our relationship? (*Pamela is improving too.*)

Charles: It's a relief to hear you say that! Exactly! I've felt belittled by you, almost *hated* for the way I have consistently taken responsibility for making the needed money for you and our children. Why have you treated me this way, do you know?

Charles (Double): I would like you to stop treating me like this. I wonder if you understand why you do it well enough to stop it.

Pamela: I think I understand. I've always envied your freedom in the world. You've developed your knowledge and abilities in ways that I can hardly imagine. (*Weeping*) It's been difficult for me to see what I have given you that is as interesting or developed or—

Pamela (Double): I have knowledge and abilities that I regret not developing. Sometimes my regret and sadness are so overwhelming that I can hardly see anything else. That's why I belittle your achievements.

Charles: I *am* aware of all this. You may not know how much I admire your decorating skills, your musical talents, and the closeness you have with our children. These are things I have missed.

Charles (Double): I would like you to stop belittling my contributions and I will also show greater appreciation for yours.

Pamela: I really am sorry for showing so little appreciation and admiration for you. In fact, I admire you and your work greatly. I always feel proud to be your wife. You are revered by so many people and I *know* how much you have done in the world. Not just the world, but in our family also. I wonder if you can forgive me for so many years of bad behavior and put-downs.

Charles forgave Pamela because he could see that she empathized with his dilemma in having been taken for granted so long. It was Pamela's ability to paraphrase and expand on what Charles said that allowed him to trust her goodwill.

Charles also came to terms with his projections of the Maiden Lover and Great Mother onto Pamela, assuming that she had "fewer responsibilities" and was "endowed with biological mechanisms that make her better with children." These envying fantasies had been used against Pamela for years, when Charles would trivialize her complaints and tease her about her work. Charles and Pamela had attacked each other on so many fronts that there was scarcely anything they enjoyed about each other. Instead of appreciating their strengths or celebrating their good fortune in the world, they attacked each other's resources. These attacks resulted in enormous hurt, resentment, and even rage.

Pamela was beginning to understand how she had first projected the Great Father and then the Terrible Father onto Charles, always assuming that "he" had so many more privileges and resources than she had. In this way, Pamela had divested herself of responsibility for her own development. She began to see that there were still possibilities for her to develop her own talents. In this therapy session, she openly entertained the possibility of taking some classes in graduate school—in an area of arts education that had always interested her. If Pamela does this, it will increase the possibility that she can find sexual pleasure with Charles. She will appreciate Charles more and feel better about herself.

Charles, for his part, always imagined "how easy" Pamela's life must be, identifying himself with the Great Father who "provided everything" for her. When she began to turn against him and withdraw sexually, he saw her through his Terrible Mother fantasy as being manipulative and controlling, just wanting "everything her way." As Charles began to see that these were aspects of himself—both the dependence and the desire to control—some of his false self began to crack. Charles began to feel depressed. I recommended that he enter individual psychotherapy. Charles was not eager to make this leap, but when Pamela said she was willing to work on making a sexual relationship with him if he would go into therapy (because she felt "safer" if he did this), Charles said he would seriously consider it. He was beginning to feel his dependence on Pamela and to desire her once again.

Envy of biological resources, psychological differences, and cultural differences occurs regularly between the sexes through projections of dream lovers. When the others are imagined to be our Others, we feel this distinct oppositeness to them: What "they" have we could never have, and we cannot spare them our hatred for this. As I said in an earlier chapter, envy is cured by claiming one's own resources—and is forgiven by one's partner when one can empathize with the pain it has caused. Some envy cannot be discussed at all because it would be too debilitating (for example, envying someone else's physical illnesses or traumas because of the "attention" they bring). What can always be discussed is the *lack of appreciation* for the other's skills, talents, hard work, or whatever. Lack of appreciation—belittling, trivializing, withholding praise—is a symptom of envy. We can ask forgiveness for not having appreciated what the partner brings to the relationship after we understand the pain we have caused. Almost all heterosexual couples in therapy have a lot of forgiveness to seek in regard to envy. This is a common path to greater sexual pleasure because of the enhancement of trust.

Betrayal is a complete break of trust. By *betrayal* here, I mean specifically a sexual betrayal of one's partner—sexual intimacies and/or a full sexual relationship outside of the attachment bond. Whether or not betrayal is "agreed upon" (for example in an "open marriage"), it is deadly to trust. This is so because of the arousal of separation anxiety—a cycle of rage, despair, and apathy—that affects the attachment bond when a relationship is under the siege of betrayal. Betrayal constitutes a separation threat to the bond. Whether or not it is disclosed, at least one of the partners *feels* this separation threat and the accompanying separation anxiety (unless the partner has a false self or an avoidant relational self). Separation anxiety transforms an intimate relationship into a minefield of bad feelings. Rage, despair, and apathy are disruptive and unpleasant, even to the partner who has broken the bond. Consequently the original bond always "feels worse" than the affair.

In order to heal the trust broken through betrayal, a couple must go through a very difficult and demanding transformation. If they want to keep their relationship, as Karen and Jonathon do, it is possible to make this transformation. It is never guaranteed that it will work, however. Both partners will have to engage in knowing and understanding why the bond was broken and *what happened*. The second part of this is extremely difficult because it involves asking and answering questions about the outside lover.

Jonathon: Why didn't you come to me and tell me how disappointed you were instead of going off with Jerry?

Karen: I was afraid that I would humiliate you. I wanted to say the things I've just now said about our lovemaking, things that I knew had to be changed for me, but I was afraid you'd just clam up.

Jonathon: God, I'm so angry that you didn't give me a try at least. When did you first get sexually involved with Jerry?

Karen: It's really hard for me to talk about this because I promised Jerry that I'd never tell you the details.

Karen (Double): I will tell you all about this if you promise you will hang in there with me.

Karen: Okay, I got involved with Jerry when you were away on that trip to Colorado for a week. I was so hurt that we hadn't made love in a month and then you just went away.

Jonathon: I just wish you had talked to me. I thought you were so pissed at me that you didn't want to make love and I didn't want to force you. What was it like being with Jerry (*sobbing*), I mean, did you like him better than me?

Karen: (*Weeping*) Not at all. I always missed you, but I felt somehow more confident that he *wanted* me sexually. I was so confused about what was going on with you. I thought you didn't like sex with me because you kept avoiding it.

This is the kind of interchange that is difficult to negotiate in repairing trust. Both partners will have to reveal their dream lovers and their hurts and resentments—to themselves and each other. Sometimes this increases shame, indignation, fear, and confusion for a period of time. Only when the truth has been adequately told and reasonably forgiven can the partners work to build a new sexual relationship. Otherwise, love cannot be freely given with the goal of sexual pleasure for both. By the way, some couples have an infusion of erotic feelings when one of them confesses or discovers an outside affair. These feelings are not based on trust or intimacy. They are connected with dream lovers projected onto each other. The projections don't last long before separation anxiety sets in.

Repairing trust after a betrayal may take years. Only when both partners are free of separation anxiety (the feeling of threat to the relationship) is the trust actually repaired. Some couples can begin a sexual relationship again before all the trust has been repaired. Others cannot.

Envy and betrayal are barriers to sexual pleasure. They occur largely through the projection of dream lovers on all sides. Taking back the projections and asking for forgiveness can be a transformative turning point for the individual development of partners in a committed relationship. Partners who complete the process of forgiveness discover they are different people at the other end than they were at the beginning, but not all partners complete it.

love and dominance

It should be obvious now that I believe that love, an affectional bond, supports sexual pleasure in a committed relationship between the sexes. Dominance erodes it. Many people seem surprised at this observation. Because power and sex are mixed in the erotic fantasies of men and women in our culture, some people believe that dominance can go hand in hand with sexual pleasure. By dominance, I mean *power over* the decision making, personal autonomy, body, or manners of another person. I have tried to show here that dominance has no place in heterosexual intimacy—in sex freely given, based on love freely given. Sexual pleasure comes with sovereignty over one's own body and activities. Knowing and describing what is pleasurable, negotiating for the pleasures of both partners, and freely giving these are the components of an ongoing sexual relationship based on equality. Such a relationship breeds desire in both partners.

Most couples suffering from sexual difficulties, couples I have seen in therapy, are captured within a realm of projective identification. Usually the projection of negative dream lovers onto the partner is the issue. As we have seen, this takes the form of imagining the partner to be more powerful than oneself. Dominance enters here through the psychological realm rather than through any actual offense by the partner. Dominance or the desire to dominate is connected with one's own strange gender—the way the partner is imagined to be. Sometimes fantasies of being victimized lead to actually taking control of another's sovereignty. One begins to order the partner's life, manners, or appearance in some way. To change this, one must give up control of the other and take responsibility for oneself. This means one must *stop* imagining a beloved partner as a terrifying parent, a sex-starved whore, an ingenue, or an impulsive child. Then one claims responsibility for these images, fears, fantasies, or ideals. In regard to sexual pleasure, reclaiming dream lovers often leads to feeling quite vulnerable. Never before has one so exposed the hidden parts of the self and taken responsibility for them.

This kind of vulnerability between partners is an avenue of increased intimacy, provided both partners protect its ground of equal influence and trust. Under these circumstances, both sexes can open up and have an "honorable human relationship," as in the words of poet Adrienne Rich:

> An honorable human relationship—that is, one in which two people have the right to use the word *love*—is a process, delicate, violent, often terrifying to both persons involved, a process of refining the truths they can tell each other.

chapter 6: partners in money and parenting

Is money really important to feelings of personal worth? Is it possible to have good, strong, worthwhile feelings about yourself as an adult and be financially dependent (although healthy and able-bodied)? I've rolled these questions around in my mind so many times that they've formed well-worn ruts in my thoughtways. The reason they bother me so is that I have seen smart, endearing, and creative women in psychotherapy over the years who "believed" that their worth "shouldn't be tied to making an income." Some of these women have been talented writers or artists who decided consciously to become financially dependent to pursue their art. Others have surrendered high-powered professional roles to have and raise their children. Still others, like Pamela, accepted financial dependence as part of being "wife and mother" in the 1950s script for the successful woman. I have tried to keep an open mind to the possibility that financial dependence does not preclude mature dependence, because I have wanted to be empathic with these women.

The evidence, in my experience and from large studies, is otherwise. Financial dependence in adulthood appears to be hazardous to feelings of self-worth and a barrier to mature dependence. Mature dependence means respecting each other as equals. In our society, feeling like an equal includes earning money for oneself, to meet one's needs.

Children, the disabled, and the elderly are "legitimate" financial dependents in our families. Even for them, this form of dependence is often accompanied by shame and anger. My teenage children sometimes express "hostile dependence" (biting the hand that feeds them) when they rudely demand money from us, their parents ("*Yes,* I need money *again*! How do you expect me to *get* money while I'm going to school full-time?"). Clearly, they hate being in the role of "begging" just as they are beginning to feel like free agents in a free-market economy. Our culture promotes the ideal that freedom = money, and though I may dislike this formula, I cannot wish it away.

When I was in my late twenties I spent a year fully out of the labor force, the only such year in my entire adult life. I was pregnant with my second child and writing a master's thesis (with my other child, under two years old, at home with me). We had just moved to a new state so that my husband could take a better teaching job. He and I reasoned that I couldn't easily get hired while I was visibly pregnant. I thought I'd be busy enough (and I was). I also wanted to experience the "full-time mommy" role. Suddenly, after a few weeks, I felt cut off from the world, from feedback, from paychecks, and even from the right to spend money. It wasn't just that we had moved away from our old community. We had a lot of new and old friends in the city we'd moved to, but I felt too ungrounded to be in touch with most of them.

I learned about depression that year. By the end of my year of unemployment, I was so depressed that I could barely sign my name—and sometimes I even *forgot* it! I saw a social worker for a consultation. She suggested that I "get out more" with my husband and hire an occasional sitter for my babies.

Some days later, my husband and I were on our "therapeutic outing," watching a movie that was supposed to be captivating, and I was feeling even more depressed. Being at the movie reminded me that I had been teaching film criticism only a year before, and now I was feeling hopelessly unrelated to this new movie. A light bulb went off in my head. I saw that my problem was being unemployed, not being underentertained. I began applying for jobs the next day, and after a few interviews, life returned to my being. Just as I had earlier decided that falling in love involved more than meeting the "right" person, I had now stumbled onto another piece of wisdom: Paid work keeps confidence and self-esteem afloat—at least for me, I added. Although I knew that Freud stressed the importance of both love and work for psychological health in adulthood, I didn't know then how to translate "work" for women. Clearly women worked at home. Was earning money the real "magic" that supported good feelings about myself? I had to conclude that it was, although I assumed that this was probably due to a psychological lack in me.

I assumed that if I were a "really healthy woman," I would be happy to serve the needs of my loved ones at home and feel the satisfaction of their successes. But being at home for a year with healthy babies and a successful husband hadn't been enough. In fact, I could see that my family suffered from my lack of enthusiasm about life. So I made the switch, went back to work, got additional care for my children, and jokingly (with some embarrassment) told my friends that I was the "type of woman" who needed to have *both*—children and paid work.

Seven years later when I was teaching in graduate school myself, I came across a landmark study by psychologists Grace Baruch and Rosalind Barnett empirically verifying that my "type" of woman was more likely to feel satisfied, happy, and competent in midlife than other types of women. In a survey of more than 350 women, these psychologists discovered that the most content and confident midlife women were those who had families *and* paid work, those who were juggling a complex interplay of needs and duties. Women who stayed at home (with no outside employment) to tend to their children often felt pleasure in their relationships but lacked a feeling of competence. Women who worked but did not have intimate or family relationships often the felt the opposite: competent but without much pleasure. Only those women who did *both* felt both competent and satisfied. Other studies have supported the findings from this one to show that paid work enhances health, in both women and men, even when it is combined with housekeeping chores and child rearing.

In this chapter, I elected to combine relational issues of money and parenting because they are connected to many of the same dream lovers. They both activate parental dream lovers—either as saviors (the Great Father or Mother who will finance or nurture me) or demons (the Terrible Father or Mother who fails to support me or overwhelms me). I will make the case that financial dependence is a form of "infantile" or "immature" dependence for adults—incompatible with mature dependence as an ideal for a healthy couple. In regard to parenting children as it affects a couple relationship, I will claim that if a parent forms a couple relationship with a child (for example, spending most recreational time with the child and actively wanting to leave the spouse behind), that parent is meeting infantile dependence needs through the child. Many childish fantasies are tied to dream lovers through whom we imagine fulfillment of wishes and needs. Women often imagine financial support and protection from a Great Father. Men imagine domestic support and protection from a Great Mother. With children, parents may attempt to fulfill all kinds of needs and fantasies—from ordinary dreams and wishes for their success (which is to be ours by extension) to forbidden sexual and power needs. The process of development in adult life challenges us to take back these wishes and fantasies and integrate our dream lovers into ourselves, and into the give-and-take of mature dependence with an adult partner. When partners behave like children with each other (demanding to be financially or domestically sustained and protected) or make idealized couple relationships with one or more of their children, the partners are enacting infantile dependence—and preventing the development of mature dependence. Mature dependence relies on strengths, both in oneself and a partner. It is a relationship based on recognized strengths, negotiated in an atmosphere of trust. It requires a feeling of confidence and competence that is almost antithetical to financial dependence in adulthood.

parental complexes and financial dependence

In the conclusion of her book of interviews on and analysis of the meanings of money in the family, sociologist Marcia Millman reports:

> Being financially dependent is a set-up for becoming a child. In these times, anyone who would choose this position for an extended period is probably looking for a parent-substitute. Those who keep forcing others to pay for their expenses are symbolically extracting revenge from a parent who, they believe, neglected them.

There are many adults among us, especially women, who are unaware of the shadowy implications of financial dependence.

I am pained by the felt powerlessness of many midlife and older women who try to cope with their situation of financial dependence. Many feel hopeless about ever feeling like an equal partner. They should realize that lessening financial dependence does not necessarily mean becoming self-supporting. Making or inheriting money of one's own, even if it does not supply all one's needs, can serve as a foundation for increased self-esteem and claims to equality. Some women have the courage to take on something new, even late in life, and look forward to a time when they can earn money. I applaud any step toward feeling financially equal and able to make claims for one's own needs and desires. Taking steps to prepare for earning money and having a place in the world is something that can be accomplished by people of any age as long as they have their health.

In her fourth session of dialogue therapy, Pamela was stymied in talking with Charles about her new commitment to graduate school. She had recently enrolled in a graduate program in arts education that would allow her to teach or direct community arts programs. Pamela had claimed her desire to go further with her education as a result of reclaiming her Great Father dream lover, but now she was having a difficult time telling Charles just why she wanted this degree.

Pamela: In all of our years together I've always taken *your* work so seriously, even when I haven't said as much. You've been the "important one" in all of our social circles and . . . or, at least, it has seemed that way to me.

Charles: Yes, thank you for saying that latter bit, because I've always thought *you* were the mainstay socially.

Pamela: I guess you mean because I usually plan social events? (*Charles nods.*) Well, that wasn't what I meant. I mean that people respect you for your contributions to the world. I want that kind of respect for myself. I'm just afraid that it might be too late—for me to succeed and for people to notice me.

Charles: You're afraid because you don't know if you'll succeed in your studies? Or after you graduate? (*Pamela nods.*) It's difficult for me to see how this studying will benefit you *or* me.

Pamela: (*Weeping*) I know what you mean. I guess I'm doomed to never being more than *Charles's wife,* but I'm angry about that most of the time. I'm so tired of following you around and doing your bidding.

Pamela (Double): Because I feel so little self-worth, I often believe that I've followed you around. I can't see my own worth and meaning, except in regard to the children, and that's over anyway.

Charles: Yes. Of course, I agree with the double that your problem is self-worth because, in fact, we own both houses that *you* wanted and I feel *bound* to your needs and demands.

Charles (Double): I am angry about a lot of your demands over the years—for certain material things. I guess I see this graduate school business as the same kind of demand.

Pamela: It's not. Finally I want to direct *myself,* but I can't seem to find the conviction for doing it.

I turned to Pamela at this point and expressed my concern and sympathy. She seemed to feel that she didn't have enough self-esteem to get more.

In other words, it was very difficult for her to claim her desire to become "somebody" this late in life—in her mid-sixties. And yet this was the necessary claim. I mentioned to her the lines from a poem by Adrienne Rich called "Transcendental Etude":

> *But there come times—perhaps this is one of them—*
> *when we have to take ourselves more seriously or die*

I sat across from her and talked about the projections of Great and Terrible Father she had placed on Charles for all of these years. In order to withdraw these and stop feeling like a Victim Child, she had to claim her own competence. Pamela acknowledged the importance of this claim, and yet she wondered if "going back to school at my age" could be worth the enormous trouble that she imagined it would be. What is the alternative? was my response. She couldn't come up with one, because she knew that volunteer work and organizing social occasions were alternatives she had already tried and they had not worked. Taking seriously her desire to make a contribution to the world was the only alternative. We both acknowledged the struggle ahead—being a student who is much older than the others, establishing herself in a paid job afterward, and hoping to have some years to work while she still was healthy enough.

In a free-market economy, freedom = money. Women are still encouraged to ignore this central message, and when they do, they regret it. Even though Pamela is a few years away from being prepared to earn money, her return to graduate school is a signal to herself, her friends, and Charles that she is going to take herself seriously in a new way. Some of her friends will support this and some will challenge it, but everyone will feel the aura of new meaning associated with Pamela's making a claim for herself in the world. Obviously, Pamela and Charles do not "need" the money Pamela could earn as a community arts teacher or director. Although her income has nothing to do with survival, it will carry two significant meanings: It will be her own earned money that she can choose to spend or give away without consulting Charles, and it will be feedback from the world that her work is worthwhile.

When men are forced to retreat from a place in the world, because they lose their jobs or (less often) they have to care for children or other family members, they too become caught in Child identifications. Although there is some evidence that women are less likely than men to expect special favors from a partner who earns less, men also suffer when they are financially dependent. Marcia Millman describes a case in which the wife was the solitary wage earner for twenty years. The husband stayed home, did the cooking and cleaning, and cared for the couple's three daughters. After twenty years, the wife took a lover with whom she openly spent each night after her daughters went to bed, leaving her husband behind to clean up the dinner he had cooked. Here is her husband's reaction:

> Far from complaining about this arrangement or making ultimatums, her husband meekly accedes to the new routine without a word. In fact, since she's started the affair, he's so worried she'll divorce him that he's making a real effort, for the first time, to hold a conversation during dinner.

His financial dependence promotes a childish accommodation that is tragically depressing. He is afraid of having to support himself financially after all these years out of the job market.

In the fourth session of couple therapy we learned that Larry might be laid off. His company was trimming back middle management and Larry was slated to be either let go or moved to a less desirable situation. The prospect of financial dependence opened a new vulnerability in Larry.

Larry: I worry about how we'll cope with my unemployment, how it'll affect all of us, but especially the boys. I can't imagine them seeing their father without work.

Larry (Double): I'm ashamed of being at risk for a job loss and afraid that you and I won't be able to handle the feelings aroused in our family.

Louise: I know that you're afraid. Although I'm afraid too, I feel confident that we can get through this thing together. We're both healthy and I have a job that's reliable. I'm sure we can get through this.

Larry: I worry about depending on your income, like you won't respect me. I know how many times I've encouraged you to quit your job, thinking that you would feel better just being a housewife, but now I'm glad you didn't.

We encouraged Louise to accept Larry's feelings of fear and shame and to see them as part of his reality. In doing that she would be better able to understand why he wanted to hide the news from their friends, and was willing to "take whatever I can get" at work. We also encouraged Louise to express her affection for Larry, especially because she was still recovering from the memories of incest that she had discovered in her individual therapy.

In this very difficult fourth session we witnessed two surprising outcomes: Larry and Louise were affectionate and vulnerable for the first time, *and* Louise began to take on her own Heroic qualities.

Louise: I really love you very much (*weeping*). I would never want anything to break up our relationship, because you really *are* my best friend. (*Larry crosses over to embrace Louise and they weep a little together. They sit back down.*)

Louise: Please don't worry so much about losing your job. You have been the most responsible father I can imagine. You've never let us down at all and now it's time that you can rely on us to help *you*. I can make some job contacts through the college for you, if you want, and I am sure that I can work extra hours to bolster our income while you're on unemployment.

Larry: Thanks, thank you so much, Louise. It's hard for me to accept help, but I've never felt like this before. Losing my job would be like losing my mind.

We alerted Larry to the possibility that he would attack Louise as a Terrible Mother (not supportive enough, not giving enough) if he were to slip into feeling like a Victim without any options. In order to feel like an equal partner, Larry would have to struggle uphill if he lost his job. We suggested that he join a local self-help group of unemployed people who meet regularly to assist each other in looking for work. They wear business clothes to their meetings and help each other in networking and résumé writing.

When a person is laid off it's vitally important that he or she still have a place in the world. As Baruch and Barnett discovered, the role of stay-at-home child rearing may be today's "high-risk" occupation. It's full of powerless responsibility. Married women who are unemployed at home with children report higher levels of dissatisfaction and distress than any other group of midlife women, except unemployed women at home with no children. Back in the 1970s, sociologist Jessie Bernard discovered through her studies of marriage that (1) marriage benefits men more than women, and (2) single women report greater happiness and pleasure than married women. My guess is that these results are related mostly to conditions of financial dependence and confinement to the home that many women suffered in the 1960s and 1970s. I see Bernard's study now not so much as a condemnation of heterosexual partnership as a statement about the impossibility of partnership when one partner is financially dependent. In other words, I would guess that financially dependent husbands who are confined to the home (with or without child-rearing responsibilities) would report the same kinds of distress that Bernard found in the wives—depression and low self-worth.

Mature dependence means relying on each other's strengths. When it comes to earning money, the only way that partnership can work is to recognize the inferior earning and decision-making power of women. Although women constitute 52.4 percent of the world's population, they own only about 1 percent of the world's property. Even after the effects of the recent wave of feminism, women in the United States make only about sixty-six cents for every dollar men make. Although 72 percent of women with school-age children work outside the home—putting the working couple in the majority—women lack the earning power, status, and decision-making capacity that men have. In the unusual and infrequent situations in which men (such as Larry) are vulnerable to financial dependence, men are faced with some of the contradictions that women regularly experience: for example, seeing one's worth and value measured in financial terms that diminish one's competence, skills, or labor.

Sociologist Arlie Hochschild suggests that some women trade their "work" on love for financial support in an attempt to legitimize their contribution to intimate relationships. Women often speak in terms of "working on our relationship" or "doing the work of relating." When women lack money, power, or status, they may trade on emotions with their partners. Hochschild is not implying that women are manipulative in doing this, but rather that they view their relational contributions as "worth something," and they assume the something should be money. In North American societies, women are expected to feel and express emotion more than men. Women often try to keep "good feelings going" to enhance the well-being of their loved ones. As we saw in Chapter 3, some women then believe that they are better at relating or more relational than men. From Hochschild's work, we can see that claiming greater emotional skill than men may feel like a source of power for some women. Being experts on feelings carries status and is socially acceptable for women. The only other socially condoned power that women are openly afforded is the power of appearance. This "power," however, is bound up with the Mistress Lover in men—with all of the risks and stereotypes of the Whore. Many women recognize the dangers of identifying with Mistress Lover projections, especially for making financial claims in exchange for sexual favors. Trading on good feelings and making the most of relational "superiority" is a safer means to feel their strengths and to demand compensation.

Ironically, this work of love often is financially unrewarded until divorce. Claims of "emotional superiority" can provoke projections of the Great or Terrible Mother in male partners. Many women are not openly supported or rewarded for their emotional skills. Instead, they feel angry that they "have to do all of the emotional work" and many men are indignant that their spouses make such statements. As Millman points out, the financial underpinnings of emotional work are often clarified in divorce. She says:

> One woman, divorcing a clinically depressed husband, claims she earned a share of his inheritance because she kept him sane and functioning over many years. Another woman, dumped by her husband, argues in court that she deserves half of the marital property, though she didn't work for wages, because her husband was a "full-time job."

What was perceived as "love" going into marriage is translated as "money" coming out. I have often thought how unfortunate it is that a woman's financial security and worth cannot be clarified outside of divorce court if she is financially dependent. She literally does not know what "she is worth" unless she divorces to find out.

Acknowledging the inequality between women and men in terms of compensation for work done, and recognizing problems of dream lover projections under conditions of financial dependence, is a first step toward partnership in money. By recognizing the limitations or constraints between the sexes, both partners are able to see more clearly how difficult their "partnership" is likely to be. Without some sense of equality in money, intimacy between the sexes is not likely to come about. By "equality" here, I do not mean equal income, but rather a sense of oneself as "equal" in a financial partnership with a spouse or lover. In order to feel like an equal partner, one has to have some financial resources of one's own and to embrace the power to negotiate in conflict.

money as a trust fund

Back in 1984 when I read the massive study of American couples published by sociologists Philip Blumstein and Pepper Schwartz, I was struck especially by the finding that couples who pooled their financial resources were more likely to stay together. I was also interested to discover that lesbian couples, of all the different kinds of couples interviewed, were most able to be equal partners in finances and to feel like equals.

These findings have guided me in working with heterosexual partners on money matters over the years.

First, pooling resources, even the impulse to do so, can be taken as a sign of trust or incipient trust that may lead to mature dependence. The absence of pooling (or even the impulse) is often a symptom of underlying anxiety and insecurity about finances and dream lover projections.

Second, lesbian couples teach us about equality in the ways they negotiate financial issues. Both partners are sensitive to the inferior financial status of women and accept the limitations of each other's earning power: For example, one partner may be of a higher social class, better educated, or simply luckier in finding well-compensated work than the other. They teach us that mature dependence means pooling all resources, financial and otherwise, and learning to appreciate and cherish whatever strengths a partner brings.

Patty and Joe had had a difficult time with their finances over the years. When Patty moved in with Joe, she was loath to pool her resources because it was the first time in her life that she'd had any financial independence and she wanted to enjoy it. During the years before they got married, Patty and Joe kept separate checking accounts and compulsive chit lists of each person's expenditures. Although this solution brought Patty peace of mind, Joe was always anxious about it because he saw the arrangement as a symptom of Patty's having "one foot out the door." He didn't like the fact that Patty regularly reminded him that she made enough money to "support herself." When they got married, Patty and Joe pooled their resources.

Joe makes considerably more money than Patty (almost ten thousand dollars a year more) although they both work the same number of hours. Until last year Patty did much more of the housework and cooking than Joe. Now Joe cooks dinner for himself and the kids three nights a week while Patty attends night school studying for a college degree. Joe has wanted appreciation for his "contribution" to Patty's education since he took over cooking and caring for the kids like this, six months ago. Patty has been unwilling to give him any sign of appreciation. In this fourth therapy session, Joe insists on being seen as an equal partner rather than as a version of Patty's Terrible Father.

Joe: You know, Patty, you really couldn't go to school without me keeping the kids and making dinner three nights a week. I'm pissed off that you never mention this—

Joe (Double): I'm hurt that you don't show any appreciation for my extra effort.

Patty: How many times did you thank *me* for carrying our kids around in my body for nine months, or spending all those months nursing them, and then the years—

Patty (Double): I'm angry because of the unfairness in our situation, that I stayed at home for years just because you *expected* I would as the mother.

Patty: Yeah, that's it and more, also because you never really thanked me for all the time I spent doing housework and stuff *after* I went back to work. I feel it would *demean* me to thank you now.

Joe: Okay, I'm sorry that I never really noticed all the work you put into the kids over the years. You're right. And the housework. I took it for granted, because my mom raised us kids *and* worked in a factory. I never thought it would be different for you. I was kind of blind to how much work you did until I started staying at home with the kids. I really *do* appreciate you, how good a mother you are, and how smart you are in school.

Patty: Thanks. Thanks for saying that. I know how much your mom did for you guys and I don't want to get stuck with being as bitter as she is now. She really feels like she got stuck with the work *and* the complaints of you guys. Anyway, thanks. I wish I could feel grateful to you too. I guess I'm jealous that you earn so much more money than I do and that I work so much harder than you—

Patty (Double): Sometimes I believe that I've worked harder than you, when I think back over the years when I did all of the housework and child care *and* earned money. I'm still mad about those years.

Joe: I can see that, but there's nothing I can do but ask you to forgive me for my blindness. I think I just took you for granted once we had kids. I thought you were the Big Mother or something. I didn't know that you were so upset about what you were doing. I thought you just didn't like *me* and how I did things, because you complained and criticized me so much of the time. You have really stopped that. I feel good about coming home for the first time since we had kids. But I still would like you to thank me for the extra work I do. I only do it because I love you.

Joe is able to recognize his Terrible Mother projection onto Patty and to claim its effects on her. Patty is still unable to deal with her Hero standards for Joe as she feels keenly that he "should know" how hard it is for women with young children to work outside the home.

In fact, she is right about the conditions under which many working mothers labor at home. As sociologist Barrie Thorne has discovered, the home is no refuge for women in general. Almost all women identify "home" with "work," and time studies reveal a pattern of women doing much more housework than men. Wives with full-time employment put in an additional twenty-six to thirty-five hours a week doing housework. All husbands, whether or not their wives are working outside the home, average between ten and fourteen hours of housework a week. Other studies have shown that, in some households, when a woman returns to the work force her husband actually rebels by doing even less housework than he had previously done!

It's no wonder that many married women do not come home to relax, and are reluctant to spend a vacation (or even an extended weekend) at home rather than in some other setting. Being at home often means working harder than anyplace else for married women, even when they are employed elsewhere.

The challenge for Patty, though, is to recognize her wishes for a perfectly sensitive and responsive partner, someone who could understand her needs and conflicts from her point of view. This is her Hero dream lover and she is reluctant to recognize how only she can bring "him" into her life. Part of the reason why Patty is reluctant to appreciate what Joe brings to her—both the money he earns and the child care and housework he has taken on—is that she is envious of the money he can make. Envy results in putting him down, thinking, "Why should I *thank* him for the little bit he contributes to our children's lives when *he* gets all of the privileges around here anyway? He makes more money and he's always had more freedom than I do." The combination of her refusal to claim her Hero and her envy of Joe's status may stultify Patty's further development. She will continue to focus her "correctives" on Joe even though she is not openly criticizing him.

Feminist theorist and journalist Gloria Steinem, in her recent book about increasing self-esteem, talks about reclaiming a dream lover after she ended a wrong relationship with a man who was very unlike her. She realized that she was seeking refuge in him rather than having a relationship. Although Steinem doesn't articulate the concept of the dream lover exactly, she certainly understands it when she describes reclaiming her Great Father projection:

> Slowly, I began to realize there might have been a reason why I was attracted to someone so obviously wrong for me. If I had been drawn to a man totally focused on his own agenda, *maybe I needed to have an agenda of my own*. Finally, I began to make time to write. If I had felt comforted by the elaborate organization of his life, *maybe I needed some comfort and organization in my own*. Therefore, I enlisted the help of friends to take the stacks of cardboard boxes out of my apartment and started the long process of making it into a pleasant place to live. I even began to save money for the first time in my life.

What Steinem recognized was that the comfort and protection she felt in the presence of this man's affluence and influence were aspects of a new way of life for which she needed to take responsibility. Similarly, Patty needs to recognize more directly her own fears, inner conflicts, and wishes for success and a place in the world. By opening herself to her own inner life, becoming *sensitive* to her struggles, and *comforting* herself about the difficulties, she will provide the kind of Heroic stance she wants from Joe. In identifying herself as a *woman* who wants both children and a career, Patty will also be able to identify with other women who are doing both. Seeing and hearing their stories will help Patty accept the struggles of making a contribution to the world, especially for a woman in a male-dominated world. If Patty is committed to becoming a lawyer, she has before her years of education and conflict in which she must find courage to face difficulties and jump hurdles in a patriarchal hierarchy of which Joe knows nothing. Nor does Joe know anything about how a woman might do this.

By the end of their fourth therapy session, Patty said the following to Joe in an effort to reclaim some of her projections:

> **Patty:** It's been very hard for me to appreciate what you have given me over our years together. Although I know in my head that you've done so much for me, I get mixed up in my heart because I'm jealous of you and angry about how men take advantage of women in our whole society. I know it's not your fault, but I get afraid that I'll never be able to reach my goals of being a lawyer because I'm a woman and a mother. Then I kind of take out my feelings on you. I'm sorry. I see things more clearly now and I'm going to pay attention to my own fears and fantasies and say a few more "thank yous" to you.

Joe was grateful for this change in Patty's attitude, but he was unable to empathize with her anger about earning less money than he does. His position was that "someone has to make a pretty good income here and it may as well be me." It was hard for him to see that this inequality took away from Patty's belief and trust that Joe could understand her predicament.

The dilemma about unequal earning capacities has been disruptive of trust in many couples I've seen over the years. Generally speaking, though, if the male partner earns more money the female partner may resent the situation, but she usually finds some way to accept her lot and believe they are equals *as long as they pool their resources*. If a husband, while earning more money, makes special accounts for himself (for example, investments of his own), then his wife is more likely not to trust his love—fearing that he is preparing for her demise. If the situation is reversed and the female partner earns more money, as with Karen and Jonathon, then the issue of trust is even more complicated.

In the cases I have seen in therapy in which the female partner is the greater wage earner (from small divergences of a couple of thousand dollars annually to large ones in which the female partner earns two or three times the male's income) a certain mystery lingers. How much money exactly does the woman earn and/or bring in (through her inheritance, for example) to the couple? Because she feels embarrassed, even a little ashamed of their earning difference, she has implicitly or explicitly put him in charge of the cash flow. He does not like to make it very clear just who earns how much. He likes to explain things in terms of their joint funds. Often the man does not openly acknowledge that he earns less unless the woman brings up the topic. She does so either sheepishly or aggressively. Then the man acknowledges that he earns less, seems downright ashamed of the difference, and tries to change the subject. Let's listen to Karen and Jonathon in their fourth session:

Karen: I would like to plan a winter vacation with you to go somewhere like the Caribbean, but I don't know if we have the money available for an extra like that. I *never* know exactly how much money we have available and I have asked you many times for an account. Why don't you show me a month's review of what each of us earns and what we spend?

Jonathon: I don't know. I never seem to get around to getting the computer printout. I've got the records, but I keep forgetting—

Jonathon (Double): I am afraid to show you what we earn because I earn so much less money than you.

Karen: Is that true? (*Jonathon nods.*) That scares me too. That's what I've been thinking all along. I really would like to talk to you about my feelings and yours on this topic, but I'm afraid you'll end up being hurt or feeling unmasculine or something.

Jonathon: I find it really hard to deal with the shame or embarrassment I feel. My dad always made the entire income for our family and now I don't even make half. I even wonder what the therapists here think of me—

Jonathon (Double): I am very disappointed in myself.

Karen: I'm sad that you feel that way. I don't feel that way at all. I figure that I just happen to be in a more lucrative line of work right now, but your job is more secure.

Jonathon: Thanks for thinking that way, but I still have to cope with my own doubts. I will show you the printout though. I would like to talk with you about a vacation.

Karen: I am angry that you never acknowledge how much money I bring in. You know that we couldn't have bought our house without my contribution. I guess I would just like to hear that you recognize that I'm a good earner.

Jonathon: You're right. I've got to understand better what keeps me from saying that. Anyway, I do notice it and you are great at bringing in an income.

What interferes with Jonathon's ability to appreciate Karen's earning capacity is a little different from what prevents Patty from recognizing Joe's contributions. Although they both envy their partners, Jonathon's seeing Karen as the Great Father is more devastating to sexual feelings than is Patty's seeing Joe as the Great Father.

It's my hunch that men fear a female partner's greater earning capacity because it seems to put the female in the position of being Father—not just Mother, which is bad enough. If your wife feels like Father when you're going over financial accounts together, it's unlikely that you're going to cuddle up in the next sexual encounter. Many men feel ashamed to fall short of being the main breadwinner in the family.

I read recently that the *most* common definition of masculinity given by American men is "earning an income for my family." If masculinity is *defined* as being the family breadwinner, then women who earn more than their male partners are going to feel the pinch of competing. This is a very touchy subject in heterosexual couples because of the stigma for the man. I don't believe in "role reversal" between the sexes (since I believe that gender exclusion preempts any valid reversal), and I don't imagine that women are trying to "be men" or take over men's roles in earning more money. Nor do I believe that men who are outearned by their female partners suffer in the same way as women who are outearned by their male partners. The situation for men is more ambiguous, shame-producing, and confusing than the culturally condoned situation of women's earning less than men. For both sexes, however, different earning capacities are somewhat lighter emotional burdens than financial dependence—which can promote unconscious identification with the Child. Differing earning capacities encourage projection—often of the Hero or Great Father onto the male (by the female partner) and the Great or Terrible Father onto the female (by the male partner). Sibling rivalry and power struggles about who is "more important" are another kind of dynamic between the sexes in regard to different earning capacities. These projections are (generally speaking) easier to reclaim and digest when both partners are earning money than when one partner is entirely financially dependent on the other.

On the way to mature dependence, heterosexual couples seem to benefit from pooling their resources under conditions of honesty. This means that both partners need to know who makes how much money and where the money goes. Although this sounds like an easy task, it is not. Envy, inequality between the sexes, negotiations about unpaid work (housework and child care), power struggles, class differences, and different earning capacities all interfere with trust and honesty. The metaphor of a "trust fund" is a good one in dealing with issues of money. With the goal of intimacy, a couple is served by a focus on trust in open and honest communications. Let's listen again to how Karen and Jonathon worked out their negotiations about honesty.

Jonathon: Right now I'm in charge of all the bookkeeping. I don't particularly like that responsibility. I'd like to share some of it with you.

Karen: I really wouldn't like doing it *and* I guess I consider it "fair" that you do more of the work because I earn more of the money.

Jonathon: That doesn't seem fair to me. I would like to work out an arrangement in which you could take on the checkbook and bills for some period, alternating with me. That way you would get familiar with the bigger picture of income and expenditures.

Jonathon (Double): I want you to take some responsibility for how our money is handled.

Karen: Okay, I see your point. I guess we could rotate the checkbook and bills every six months or so?

Although Jonathon is emphasizing the task of shared responsibility here, his approach is very useful in helping Karen come to terms with her apparent wish to be buoyed up by a Great Father, even though she earns a good income. She is reluctant to take responsibility for her earnings.

When it comes to trust and money, partners seeking intimacy need to focus on the theme of equality in terms of responsibility taking and honesty. Otherwise pooling resources can become a cover-up, as sociologist Millman says:

> Pooling can ... be a way of covering up unacknowledged conflicts and power imbalances and other problems, but it doesn't make them go away. I think of the woman who put her entire inheritance in joint names with her husband, and allowed him to spend it all on himself, because she didn't want to face the fact that he was using her.

Dialogue and negotiation of conflict, honesty, and responsibility are the bases for trust in regard to money. A family inheritance, however, tends to complicate the picture, increasing power imbalances and distrust.

inherited money in couple relationships

Parental projections, more than any other type of dream lover, are stirred by financial dependence and inequality of money and support. Although the Hero is sometimes projected onto a male breadwinner, couples struggle mostly with Parent and Child dynamics in regard to money. Inherited money from one's family of origin complicates the picture because it introduces directly the monetary links of the past between parent and child. Inheritance is a problem for both partners, the one who inherits and the one who doesn't. For the first, the problems have to do with the residues of meaning connected to the inheritance, decisions about how to spend it, and implications for changes in one's life. For the second, problems have to do with envy, jealousy, resentment, and feelings of neglect or rejection if the money is not shared or no personal inheritance is forthcoming from one's own family.

In most middle-class American families, inheritance is ambiguous and unpredictable. Consequently, it can come as a surprise. In most upper-class and upper-middle-class American families, inheritance is expected and its absence is taken as an affront. As Millman says:

> It's often joked that upper-class grandparents get revenge on their children by skipping a generation in their wills and leaving their money in trust to the grandchildren, to be distributed when their children die. Although tax considerations are probably the major motive for arranging trusts this way, the unintended consequences illustrate a general feature of money: whatever people may intend, money has a life of its own.

In working-class white and African-American families, pooling monetary resources in the extended family is more the norm because present survival (not the future) is the issue.

When partners from different class backgrounds marry, that difference is highlighted by inheritance. Jonathon expects to inherit money from his upper-middle-class parents, but Karen will not inherit money from her lower-middle-class parents. When they talked about this difference in therapy, they decided that Jonathon should keep a separate account and make decisions of his own about his "family money." When Larry inherits a small sum of money from his father, as he knows he will, it is likely he will use it directly to fund his sons' college education or some other family necessity. Louise is very supportive of this. If Louise inherits money, though, I imagine she will want to set up a separate fund for herself (if Larry is back at work) because she has dreamed about taking graduate courses in painting after her children leave home.

Many women have proprietary feelings about their inheritance, especially if it has come down through generations of mothers who have wanted their daughters to have "money of their own." Writer Virginia Woolf made famous the idea that inheritance can set a woman free. I have worked with many women in psychotherapy whose lives finally broadened into their own creativity and strengths when they received some amount of money through inheritance—which freed them from the condition of financial dependence. I have encouraged these women *not* to pool these resources, because they needed the feeling of "legitimate spending" within their immediate reach. Feeling worthy of spending money on one's own needs and desires is a prerequisite to mature dependence. Without this experience, an adult is unable to feel like an adult. For some women—women "of a certain age," as sociologist Lillian Rubin calls midlife and older women—inheritance may be the only means of feeling financially independent.

Apart from these cases, how do couples negotiate inheritance? Usually with jealousy, rivalry, and greed, I'm sad to say. I have rarely if ever noticed that inheritance readily and easily helped a couple, except in cases when a woman inherits enough money to help her feel like an equal partner (or when a partner freely gives the money to the common needs of the couple, like the college education of their children). More often, inheritance introduces more inequality.

Because of the peculiar conditions of inheritance—as an "unearned privilege"—I suggest that the person receiving the money have the final say on how it is to be used. I have come to understand inheritance as an aspect of fate. Each of us is born into a particular family, with certain patterns of relating and certain privileges. As far as we know, we have not "requested" the special fate we have. Inheritance, like accidents and illness, is part of fate. We all have to decipher the meaning of our own fate. In terms of a couple, this means that a partner with an inheritance needs to look at the bigger picture: What does this money mean to me? in terms of my parents? in terms of my relationships now? in terms of my children? Partners decide differently, but explaining through dialogue makes the decisive difference in terms of intimacy.

If a partner can speak openly and the other partner can paraphrase and respond openly, usually the meanings of fated money can be clarified. When this does not happen, bad feelings can go on for years because of the inherent unfairness of inheritance. In dialogue therapy, couples like Louise and Larry have come to decisions (with the individual receiving the inheritance taking the lead) that reflect both the fated meaning of inherited money and the needs of the contemporary couple. If inheritances are relatively small and manageable, often they do not create too much acrimony. If they are large and carry major implications for changes in lifestyle (as with one couple that moved from a suburban middle-class neighborhood into a mansion because of the husband's inheritance), inheritances can be a disaster to equality, intimacy, and trust. Sometimes I have the fantasy that inheritance laws should include requirements for couple psychotherapy when one member of a couple receives an inheritance over such-and-such an amount of money. I think this would make inheritance a more benign gift.

negotiations and special claims

You have probably noticed that I tread gingerly over this area of money and heterosexual intimacy. Social and political inequalities between the sexes are rampant in this part of couple life. In my own relationship and when I work with couples in therapy, my goal is to help both partners *feel* like they are equal. This feeling comes when each partner is able to have an effect on the other: It is a situation of equal influence. This doesn't mean having a fifty-fifty split of income or unpaid labor. In sharing housework and child care, for example, partners have to negotiate based on their strengths.

As I said earlier, and as many researchers have shown, men are not prepared (or ready to learn) to share household tasks equally with women. Although I might find it more ideal if my husband had been socialized to keep the kitchen counters clean and pick up all the ballpoint pens and loose change he casually drops, he was not. I have different standards for household cleanliness than he has, and I have to take responsibility for meeting my own standards.

I don't recommend keeping lists and accounts of who does what. Nor do I recommend trying to equalize or balance the columns of tasks versus income versus whatever. An intimate relationship is not an arena of sociopolitical justice. Generally speaking, women are going to do more work (paid and unpaid) and make less money; men are going to make more money and be less inclined to do household chores. This is an unfair and angering arrangement. It may help a little to recognize that cultural expectations and stereotypes are gradually changing, and that women are certainly more actively engaged in the world than they were two generations ago. Men are being challenged to become more actively involved in family and home; younger men seem to be moving in that direction. If couples continue to struggle for intimacy based on equality, daily life patterns will have to shift more in the direction of sharing labor at home, and sharing power in the world.

In any particular couple, though, some old patterns will coexist with desires for change. Accepting certain parameters of gender preference and personal style allows individuals to see their needs and contributions within a realistic framework. I don't like pumping my own gas, for instance, and I don't want to change my attitude (no matter how many gas stations I exit quickly after seeing that they're self-service). When I was a teenager learning to drive, I always enjoyed getting "waited on" at the gas station, and I still do. My two sons and my husband always pump their own gas and think it wasteful to do otherwise. Accepting aspects of one's own and one's partner's socialization in no way excludes working for social or political change on another level. In my public presentations and my work with organizations, I couldn't be clearer about the necessity of equalizing rights and opportunities for the two sexes, and for other groups as well. My relationship with my husband is not the ground on which I can work large-scale public changes. Sometimes even my relationship with myself requires my accepting my socialization and peculiarities about sex roles.

On the other hand, a lot of defensive maneuvering can take place in terms of negotiations around money and unpaid labor. Reclaiming dream lovers is not an easy task and often we prefer to have a partner carry the responsibility for our dreams of financial success or inability to claim our own needs. When Louise decided to stop being the "servant" at home, she angrily said, "I'm not making any more family dinners!" Somehow she hoped that another family member would jump in and say, "I will." No one did. Louise and Larry had a long and difficult dialogue about how to handle this new void in their lives. They finally decided that each of them and each of their two teenage sons would be responsible for getting one dinner per week—which could involve cooking or bringing in food. That covered four dinners. On the other three days, everyone was on his or her own. Individuals could make dinner or go out, depending on finances. This has worked well. Louise had to give up the projection that she "should" take care of "her men." She sustained this projection when she saw them as Heroes or Fathers. She also had to recognize that they weren't going to take care of her. If a partner is giving money or performing tasks resentfully, bitterly, then that person needs to take the responsibility to speak up and stop providing what is not given freely. Negotiated between adults, this kind of conflict can be solved by dialogue. Often the solution falls outside of what either partner would have imagined at the beginning. The solutions arrived at by dialogue are often free of stereotypes and "shoulds."

Special claims of either partner due to illnesses or protected money (such as inheritance) require dialogue. Although I have read a great deal about prenuptial financial agreements, I find myself somewhat reluctant to promote them as a general rule. (Perhaps this is because I live in a traditional city on the East Coast and not many of my friends have them. I understand it is different in California.) In couples I have seen in therapy, prenuptials have raised the same specter as separate accounts—separation anxiety about "What does this mean?" I tend to support increasing trust, over and above all other objectives, like protecting one's financial advantages. On the other hand, there are cases in which one partner comes into a relationship with considerably more financial advantages and wants to protect them. Careful dialogue about the partner's desire to protect these advantages can resolve the issues of trust for some couples.

In regard to a wholly different topic, the illness of one partner can put a lot of financial and other burdens on the other. Illnesses that require a week or more of absence from work and/or household chores require dialogue between partners. Sometimes people believe that illness is such a clear message that a partner "should just know" what has to be done. But in fact, the breakdown of the usual structure of activities of the couple for a period as long as a week creates a new kind of chaos that cannot be intuited. There is no way to "know" what to do without dialogue. Longer illnesses require a number of levels and layers of negotiations. The objective is to sustain the trust that allows for intimacy. Both partners have to feel equal in this process—being able to speak about needs and knowing specifically what is wanted. When I have had extended illnesses, I have felt ashamed of my complete and utter dependence. This is a different experience from mature dependence. Sometimes I have hesitated to map out particulars with my husband because I wanted to hide how completely dependent I was feeling. It is very important that partners speak up and claim their needs and listen to each other during times of illness that put unusual financial and household stresses on a couple.

Money and labor in a couple relationship are problematic especially because they elicit parental projections and tend to invite identifications with being children. Girls and women are still encouraged to be financially dependent and earning capacities are unfairly unequal between the sexes. These conditions and envy predispose all of us to fail to trust each other in negotiating equal and honest solutions to our conflicts. Our four couples have learned how to confront the difficult, enraging, and often shameful images that money and labor involve. Empathic dialogue about conflicts in this area are reassuring to the ground of trust. Parenting together is another challenge to trust between heterosexual partners, one that maps out in ways similar to conflicts about money and labor.

great and terrible parent scripts

I was very much influenced in my experience as a mother by two accounts of motherhood: *Of Woman Born* by poet Adrienne Rich and *Inventing Motherhood* by British psychiatrist Ann Dally. Both of these books emphasize, from different angles, the effects of the cultural institution of motherhood on women's experience of mothering. Rich gives her own and others' accounts of the wide range of ambivalent emotions associated with becoming a mother—terror and joy, hatred and love, insecurity and confidence. She contrasts these with "expert accounts" of how mothers should be: calm, pleasant, supportive, and caring. In describing her struggle to mother three sons after the death of her husband, she reveals the inner pressures that we mothers feel to be perfectly adequate in a role that is filled with responsibility and lacks any real power. As our children move into the culture of their peers in childhood and adolescence, we have less and less control over their values and ideals, and yet are usually held accountable by professionals and the public (and, alas, ourselves) for our children's actions.

Ann Dally shows how the institution of motherhood has developed historically in the image of Mother and Child. From the Middle Ages through about the middle of the eighteenth century, very little attention was paid to children as a category. Judging from journal accounts and doctors' records, mothers themselves often remained distant and somewhat emotionally aloof in caring for infants and young children, because it was not at all clear that the young ones would survive. Mothers also had lots of help in the form of extended family (among the working class) or house servants (among the middle and upper classes). Rarely were mothers at home alone with young children, even more rarely in an exclusive one-on-one relationship with an infant. Typically several caregivers were involved with each child and other children were in the household. Often mothers felt no particularly strong bond with individual children until the children had survived into adolescence, and then sometimes not unless a child continued to be close and sustaining of the parents in adulthood. It was adaptive not to become too attached to a young one who might die. Until the last 100 to 150 years, most women were pregnant or nursing throughout most of their adulthood. Typically a woman gave birth to fifteen or more infants, of whom about five would survive to adolescence. Our contemporary investment in individual infants and toddlers was completely unheard of, even among the wealthiest class. It wasn't that children were ignored or necessarily mistreated, but rather that they weren't doted upon as individuals—special and unique. A mother was not automatically seen as connected with her biological child, either in terms of explaining the child's behavior or in terms of assuming that the mother was devoted to the child.

The recognition of childhood as its own "period" of development, lower rates of infant mortality, and our recent cultural emphasis on the "important role" of mothering have resulted in our current belief in women's primary "maternal instinct." This belief has been used as an explanation for everything from confining women to the home, away from the workplace, to assuming that women are less rational and more emotional than men. The idealization of motherhood—and its underside, the Terrible Mother complex—is a constant presence in the feelings of individual women about their mothering. Additionally, many mothers feel absolutely responsible for producing healthy and happy children at a time when our society is full of violence, danger—and resistance to supporting child care and the educational needs of children. Rather than seeing that many of their children's problems have a larger social context, mothers tend to blame themselves when things go wrong. Our society also holds mothers (not fathers) to be accountable for children's behavior and outcomes. As Dally says:

> Mothers bear the burden not only as child-rearers but also as scape-goats. Their role [has] become increasingly at variance with the organization and way of life of our society, and this gap is filled partly by idealizing the mother and partly by denigrating and humiliating her. The situation is frozen by making it extremely difficult for her to see the situation realistically so she is unable to do anything about it.

What can result from all of these cultural and social conditions is the "coupling" of a mother with her child. Instead of remaining a partner with her husband, a woman can be captured by the belief (and then the experience) that her most powerful and important role is to provide for the needs of her children. With a first child, especially, a mother can be swept into a "love affair" that lasts well beyond the first two or three months of an infant's life—when a mother's preoccupation *is* necessary and natural.

Women like the mothers of Jonathon and Charles romance their sons (or daughters) while entertaining fantasies of future fame or fortune for the child. As Dally points out, our current preoccupation with making "the perfect child" has too often resulted in producing narcissistic adults who feel entitled to privileges or status simply because they *exist*. Jonathon's inability to distinguish between admiration and love, like Charles's "false self," is linked to the idealization of motherhood and the projection of the Great Mother onto women.

Recall that these archetypal images of the Great or Terrible Mother are not representations of real people. They are images aroused by particular emotional states—contentment and nurturance in an infant-parent bond in the case of the Great Mother; rage, unmet need, and aggression in the Terrible Mother. The images are depictions of universal emotional states of human life. These states are especially powerful in infancy prior to language use. When they are projected onto actual women—either our partners or our mothers—the images color the women with powers that are superhuman. No one *is* the Great Mother or the Terrible Mother.

When women identify with these projections, we have seen how disastrous the outcome is. Louise is attempting to "step aside" from the images of the Terrible Mother that Larry and her sons have projected—and with which she has often identified.

Louise: I just want to be clear that, number one, I am not responsible for how well our sons do in school. When Jack (*their younger son*) failed his math course last year, you reprimanded *me* more than him. I won't tolerate that anymore.

Larry: I'm sorry if it seemed that way to you. I was so upset about him failing that I expressed my feelings mostly to you—maybe in a way that sounded blaming. I don't blame you. I just don't know how to *reach* him on some of these things and I keep hoping that you do.

Louise: I don't either, but I'm tired of being the heavy with him. He's having some problems again in math. I just got a notice that he's missing a third of his math homework. I'd like you to deal with him.

Larry: Okay, as long as you and I together talk about it first, about the message we want to give him.

In this fourth therapy session, Larry and Louise were able to talk about Louise's being seen as the Terrible Mother without a lot of difficulty. Earlier, they would have fought about whether Louise *was* at fault and Larry might have said he wanted out of any conflict between Jack and his mother. In this dialogue, Larry and Louise were able to reinforce their partnership and come up with a plan for handling Jack.

Working with couples on their parenting, I often find that fathers want to be seen as the Great Father and are reluctant to play the heavy in dealing with discipline. Often this position is presented in terms of "not wanting to interfere" with the mother's disciplining the children. This is certainly a contrast to the role of father described by Freud in Victorian families, in which the authority and discipline of the reigning patriarch were the mark of a functional family. I'm not saying that contemporary fathers are only "nice" to their children. Indeed, too many fathers express rage and aggression, discharging destructive impulses that are irrelevant to limit setting or discipline. Taking the role of the responsible and rational disciplinarian is what I mean by playing the heavy. Setting limits, using parental authority wisely, and saying no to indulgences and excessive demands of children are examples of the kind of discipline that fathers have abdicated. I find men too often wanting the easy part of parenting—fun, play, and nurture—until they reach some personal limit where they blow up. This limitation may be due to emotionally distant fathering in recent generations—leaving contemporary fathers unsuited for dealing with the frustration of their children. This may also be due to the idealization of motherhood with its supposed virtue of supportive, empathic care. My experience in therapy is that midlife and younger men want to be seen as "good guys" as fathers, especially in providing positive, nurturant care for young children. This too often leaves such fathers open to coupling with a child as well.

One man in his mid-forties comes to mind. Emotionally and sexually distant from his wife of twenty years, he completely invests himself in his ten-year-old daughter. He spends his free time in the evenings studying with or reading to her. On the weekends, they go horseback riding or skiing. He can't imagine life without her. His wife is loath to criticize him because she also loves her daughter very much and feels this is "good for her." At the same time, the wife is jealous and resentful of the attention her daughter gets. The daughter does very well in school and has lots of outside achievements, but she shows little interest in her peers and wants mostly adult company.

There is such a large-scale problem with Terrible Father enactments in our society and so much concern on the part of sons (in the mythopoetic men's movement, for example) to rectify a connection with the father that idealization of fathering is wide open. The temptation for men to fill most of their needs for admiration and recognition through fathering may be almost as great as women's temptation to do so through mothering. From my husband I know how hard it was for him to surrender the glow of youngsters' smiling trust in exchange for teenagers' criticisms and complaints. He felt that parenting was one aspect of being a man in which he did not have to compete with other men (only with a woman). When he was a young father of small children, people openly complimented him on his fathering (sometimes even with oo's and ah's). He felt reassured that he was making an important contribution to society. Now he sees how transitory this public admiration was. Outsiders don't oo and ah over teenagers, and older children are themselves frequent critics of their parents. Deep feelings of satisfaction about the outcome of a father's efforts are delayed until the children's young adulthood, and then only if things go well.

You probably see what I am implying here: The primacy of the couple relationship should sustain parents—instead of their trying to get admiration and closeness too exclusively through their children. Parents have a range of good and bad feelings about their offspring, but can be easily taken by the narcissistic belief that their own children are "special" and "unique". Parenting is a tremendously important life event (also an ongoing "life emergency" for many years) for both parents. From time to time, it is a very rewarding experience. Often it is just plain hard work. More than anything, it requires courage, endurance, and enough foresight to control one's own destructive impulses (including impulses to live through one's children). If partners can work together to continue their dialogue and intimacy during their years of active parenting, they will discover countless occasions on which they are faced with powerful feelings and memories from their own childhood. Reclaiming aspects of oneself, lost from immediate memory but evoked through moments with one's child, is an opportunity for tremendous growth and development, especially when it can be discussed with a spouse. A healthy partnership in parenting gives parents greater possibilities for reworking what was troubling from their own childhoods rather than acting it out on the next generation. Without that partnership, parents are at risk for repeating the past and for coupling with their children—depriving the children of a secure bond in which they are free to be themselves.

sustaining trust in parenting

This book is about the search for heterosexual intimacy, not parenting. Rather than speaking about parenting per se, I want to show how parenting (like money) can interfere with trust as the basis of intimacy, and suggest how this interference can be avoided or at least minimized through dialogue.

When partners make idealized couple relationships with one or more of their children, trust in the couple relationship is wounded. Let me say clearly that I distinguish between a *child's* fantasy of an idealized parent—the Great Father or Great Mother—which may be filled with erotic and other desires of all kinds, and a *parent's* actual attempt to seduce a child. It's the parent's behavior that I am talking about, not the child's fantasy. Parents are vulnerable to becoming narcissistically, erotically, and/or aggressively paired up with a child. A parent wanting to fulfill an ideal, a sexual desire, or a power motive can use a child as a partner. When a parent turns to a child for a need that should be fulfilled by a partner, or should never be acted out with anyone (for example, beating up a child), then that parent has broken the trust of the couple relationship. Trust can be repaired when the partners are willing to face each other and make their relationship primary again, so that together they can repair the damage done to the child.

When either parent acts with a child in a way disapproved of by the other parent, trust may be disrupted and the partners need to confer. If one parent is abusive, neglectful, or otherwise inhumane to a child, there should be a break in trust in the couple. If no such break appears, then one or both partners are pathologically unconscious or consciously malicious. Parents should be responsible, predictable, and concerned caregivers for their children. I will not be speaking here of situations in which one or both parents act malevolently toward a child. That is a condition that may well lead to a breakup of the couple, and perhaps *should* lead to a breakup unless everyone (child, abuser, and other family members) gets help.

I am speaking here of legitimate disagreements in style, manner, and goals of parenting seen from the point of view of either partner. Often a mother says she cannot "trust" her partner to care for the children because he doesn't carry out a particular program in the way she would. Let's listen to Patty and Joe talking about Joe's behavior at bedtime with their daughter, Rita, five, and their son, Anthony, seven.

Patty: When I came in at nine-thirty the other night and you and Rita were running around downstairs, I was so pissed off I could hardly speak. It was an hour and a half past her bedtime, and Anthony was still watching television! I can't understand why you can't just follow the rules and get the kids into bed.

Patty (Double): I don't like it when you have the children up past their bedtimes.

Joe: I don't agree with the rules. Rita wasn't going anywhere the next morning and she and I were having a lot of fun. I was planning on settling down and reading her a book if you had stayed out of it. You come in with a whole agenda like you are the Big Parent or something. I don't see why I have to follow *your* rules—

Joe (Double): I would like to negotiate the bedtime rules so that we could both make the decision about how to handle them.

Patty: You know what I think: Rita goes to bed at eight o'clock every night except holidays or special occasions. Anthony goes to bed at nine. It's simple. The kids need a lot of rest, and when they don't get it they're crabby, and I'm the one who has to deal with them in the morning.

Joe: You're saying that every night has to be the same, no matter what's happening the next morning? (*Patty nods.*) I don't agree. I want to be able to spend extra time with them on Thursday night because Rita doesn't go out on Friday and Anthony likes to stay up extra just that one night. It's really important for me to have one evening when it's not all work to stay with them. I really look forward to the fun—

Patty: I didn't realize that the time meant so much to you, but I'm still worried about having them stay up so late. I think it's exhausting for them. Is there any other way to get extra time with them?

Joe: No. I've thought about everything—unless you want to miss church on Sunday. I really don't think a little bit of missed sleep is that important. I think having fun together is really more important.

Patty: I guess I understand, although I'd like to keep on thinking about it to see if we can find some other way.

Patty had based her assessment of Joe's parenting on her view of Joe as the Lost Child. She was assuming that he wasn't being responsible and that he didn't have the kids' interests in mind. Actually she was wrong and she found out that he had given his actions a lot of rational consideration. Many times partners base their assessment of each other's parenting on a dream lover projection rather than on actual knowledge or information.

Partners may also base their assessments of themselves on projections from each other. For example, Karen could fall into a Great Mother projection from Jonathon after they have children. He would see her as "the one in charge" of nurturance and development of the children. She would see herself as "doing the work of relating," as I talked about in the first part of the chapter. Her power would be based on his projection of the Great Mother, and she would feel guilty and afraid were she to make a mistake or have her own desires that fall outside of "selfless love." Women appear to gain status in society through seeming to meet the idealizations of motherhood. In fact, however, they gain very little status, power, or control from identifying with the Great Mother. As Ann Dally points out, the idealization of motherhood carries with it little real power, and much responsibility for children's development—responsibility that should belong also to fathers, the community, and the society at large. By contrast, there is a lot of emotional power (that is, powerful feelings) in parental projections because they are grounded in archetypes. Archetypal images are larger than life, carrying with them the emotional image traces of everyone's years of infantile dependence and powerlessness. On the other side of the parental coin, there's also archetypal power in projections onto children.

When children are very young, from infancy through about three years old, it is natural for parents to imagine the child as fulfilling all that the parent had hoped for, but failed to do or be. Little girls may be imagined to be sexy, beautiful, exceptionally verbal and intelligent, and so on. Little boys may be imagined to be strong, athletic, handsome, exceptionally talented and intelligent, and such. Carl Jung called this the archetype of the "Divine Child." When children are very young, they evoke fantasies of having every and any possibility of succeeding, of being special and unique. As they grow older and become individuals, their limitations become clearer, and they are less easy to idealize (until adolescence, when it's usually hard to idealize them at all). Especially during the early years, the parent-child relationship can be used as a substitute for feelings of intimacy with a partner. It's easy to project the Hero, the Genius, the Maiden, or the Mistress onto a young child. All of us do this and it's quite normal. When this happens (even with a same-sex child who may seem to be the ideal that the parent never has been), the parent feels a surge of erotic or narcissistic fantasy that is linked to this particular child. If the parent is alert and fully engaged in a couple relationship with a partner, it's likely that the parent will feel these feelings in only a passing way. When the partner relationship is in disillusionment, a parent may have a harder time parting with the fantasy and turning to a partner to meet intimacy needs.

With all of these various projections of dream lovers and possibilities for identification, partners need dialogue to help them understand each others' parenting actions, especially when they disagree. For the welfare of children and the intimacy of a couple, it is critically important that partners *ask questions* of each other when they have differences in parenting. What did you do? Why did you do it? What are your goals? What are your reasons? Without this kind of knowledge of each other's parenting, partners are likely to base their assessments on their own strange gender more than on reality. Many women imagine their partners are "just children themselves," irresponsible and unaware of the needs of their children. Some women believe their partners are unfeeling, too rational, too distant, and too uninvolved with the children. Asking questions and trying to understand a partner's reasons often opens a way to see things from another parent's eyes. For the welfare of children and intimacy with a partner, it is vitally important that partners respect the reasonable choices and approaches made by each other. When suggestions are made for change, they should be brought up in a framework of mutual respect. Shared parenting may not boil down to an equal split in the amount of time a child spends with each parent, but it should reflect a couple's ability to deal with conflicts about their differences. Many men admire their partners' parenting, but feel unable to reproduce it. To some extent this is a result of socialization. All people have limits and constraints on their personalities. But the "hands-off" admiration of mothering is harmful to everyone. It often leads to distance between partners (as parents and otherwise) and an alienation of the mother. She feels separated from her partner, even from her children at times, because no one asks her about her reasons or goals in parenting.

My husband and I spend hours talking about our parenting and our children. We find it an exciting topic in which we are both vitally interested. Often I ask him for detailed explanations of why he sees things as he does, and he does the same with me. In this way we can "try on" each other's parenting. Even when we don't see eye-to-eye and have to come up with a negotiated solution that we can both accept, we have a lot of understanding and empathy for each other. I don't think my husband is at all intimidated by my mothering—or that he particularly sees it as gender-bound. He provides some parenting (for example, an interest in watching sporting events) that *is* gender-based, but I have come to appreciate it, and to see his reasons for doing what he does. I enjoy sharing parenting with him in a way that opens up gender boundaries and clarifies our differences where they exist.

divorce and blended families

The two paragraphs above are especially important for divorced parents. This book is not about divorce and separation, but the simple rule of *asking questions* and not making assumptions is a good one for divorced parents to follow. Divorced parents, more than married parents, too often function entirely through projection of dream lovers onto each other. After divorce, trust is broken and the possibility of dialogue is gone. Yet parents must go on cooperating and relating for the sake of their children. Ideally this is carried out through conversations that resemble dialogue in that they include asking questions, paraphrasing, and attempting to understand the other parent's experience—as well as expressing one's own. We know now from studies of the effects of divorce on children that open aggressive conflict between parents is *the* greatest wound to children. Obviously this is true for children of married parents as well. After divorce, though, parents have only one shared responsibility: the welfare of their children. Asking questions and listening are the best tools available to assist divorced parents in responding to their children's needs without aggressive conflict.

Although none of our couples has a "blended" or stepfamily, I want to add this special case of more complicated shared parenting. My husband and I have a blended family. Our oldest son is his from his first marriage, and our younger two children are mine originally. Also I have a fully grown stepson from my first marriage, who was three years old when I came into his life. He is on his own now, but is still an involved member of our family. In our blended family we have good relationships with our former spouses and their new partners and the children produced by those partnerships.

Early in our relationship as a couple, my husband and I parted with the possibility of having a biological child of our own. Although we wanted one badly, we already had a lot of responsibility and parenting ahead, with three young children (my first stepson lived with his mother and stepfather). We decided to forgo having our own biological child in favor of becoming deeply committed to parenting together the children we had. Because I had been a stepparent in my earlier marriage, I knew the struggle that lay before us. My husband did not.

Stepparenting requires a deep, abiding commitment to dialogue about every question, decision, and instance of "mixed loyalty." Mixed loyalty is the conflict felt by all stepparents and stepchildren between the primary attachment bond to a given, usually biological, parent or child and a new attachment to a stranger. Mixed loyalty feels like a pull back into the comfort or protection of the original relationship, away from new developments. Children and parents feel this mixed loyalty as they attempt to relate across the gulf of strangeness, new rules, and revised family structures. Becoming conscious of these feelings and seeing that they emerge from the *condition* of blending families—not the fault of anyone—is a first step to forming new bonds. If this step isn't taken, the partners in the couple relationship will literally *feel* pulled apart by mixed loyalty. It feels like pressure against the couple's bond. When divorced parents remarry, they usually feel "coupled" to their original children in a way that competes with the partners' relationship. As I said earlier, this kind of problem threatens the development of partners and children alike.

It is possible (but not easy) to become comfortable and secure in a blended family, feeling as much like "family" as a biological unit does. My husband and I are very proud of our "extended blended family"—with our former spouses and all of the children. We are especially grateful for the opportunities to develop consciousness that a blended family brings. Although a blended family may find it difficult to feel close and comfortable at first, its members have the opportunity to build closeness through dialogue. A biological family generally feels close, but is often unable to deal easily with differences of individual members. In a biological family, the developmental task of its members is often differentiation, because a feeling of togetherness is usually present at the start. It's just about the opposite for blended families. A blended family begins more often as a "disunity" of competing and conflicting patterns and structures. The developmental task of its members is to develop trust and closeness that can accept existing differences. The blended family builds trust consciously, through dialogue.

Parenting in a blended family requires ongoing conversation and dialogue on all levels of decision making, in terms of all kinds of projections. Negative parental projections—the Terrible Mother and Father—are to be expected in stepparenting, especially from the children. Folk and fairytales about the terrible stepmother (not as often about the terrible stepfather) tell us how cruel and difficult stepparenting can be when self-awareness is limited or absent. Now that many people have greater possibilities for self-awareness, the enactments of Terrible Parents by stepparents can be reduced and even eliminated. (This is not to say that stepparents have necessarily become self-aware and responsible. Many stepparents continue to abuse their stepchildren.)

In the midst of conflict and mixed loyalty, partners may identify with their darkest dream lovers. Because stepchildren respond to us initially with so much fear, distrust, and jealousy, and even hatred, we stepparents may victimize our stepchildren because they awaken primitive feelings from our pasts. Men can be swept away by the Terrible Father and Bully experiences enacted from repressed brutalities endured in their own childhoods. Women can be caught up in Terrible Mother attacks, criticisms, and demands from the past that emerge now directed at a stepchild. Consciousness developed through self-awareness and dialogue is the only cure. Through consciousness of our psychological complexes, the impulse to enact our darkest dream lovers with our stepchildren can be avoided. If some impulses are enacted, we can recognize the hurts we have caused and ask for forgiveness.

Through reflection and dialogue, partners in a blended family can learn to examine the negative parent projections and enactments. Partners need to ask questions and remain interested in each others' parenting in just the way I described above. When we hear from a biological child that the stepparent is "mean" or "unfair," we ask questions about this as *partners* (not of the child, but of each other). Sometimes the accusation is true and the stepparent's behavior needs to change. Sometimes the accusation is false and the stepparent needs to be supported by the partner. Good resources for understanding the complexity of stepfamilies are the books by psychologists Emily and John Visher, who have a blended family and specialize in therapy with blended families.

When partners commit themselves to having and rearing children, almost everyone takes seriously the belief that the family will stay together. The biological family preserves the continuity and personal history of its members intact, over time. For its children this is an invaluable benefit. The break that occurs through divorce is not simple and is never entirely repaired, as we have seen from studies of adult children of divorce. For these reasons, no one would ask for a blended family rather than a biological one. However, when divorce has occurred or a partner has died in a couple with children, the only options available are the blended family (for partners who remarry) and the single-parent family (not to be discussed here because it doesn't involve couples).

When a couple has a blended family, pride in that form of family is as essential as it is for any other kind of family. Our society has prejudices against blended families (what we used to call broken homes) and couples have to resist stereotypes in order to feel proud. From my own experience, I can say that the fight is worth it. My own blended family is endlessly interesting (because of its high degree of diversity) and broadly supportive. Whenever possible, a couple with a blended family should develop cooperative relationships with ex-spouses and their partners and children. This extended blended family makes available many options of different parental models for children, but perhaps more important, it provides continuity in the personal history of its members. In our yearly family gathering, the members of our extended blended family meet to share meals and to reunite with each other. The children seem especially to appreciate this opportunity to have all of their parents and siblings together. The adults enjoy the richness of sharing stories from the past and feeling once again united with a history that spans decades. Naturally, the key to all of this is dialogue, and mature dependence that allows us to appreciate our attachment relationships even after they have been broken.

equality without equity

Throughout this chapter, I have been confronting issues of money and parenting that present heterosexual couples with dilemmas of equality. My premise all along has been that heterosexual intimacy is based on a relationship of equality and trust that fosters mature dependence and development of a relational self. How can we be equal partners in a relationship that includes vast inequities of income, paid and unpaid labor, and parenting roles? What could the concept of "equality" possibly mean between the sexes, when we are acutely aware of the unfairness of sex roles in this and other male-dominated societies?

I have two answers. They have been implied in all I've said already. First, equality in an intimate relationship means the give-and-take of honest and open dialogue: the willingness to listen and understand your partner's point of view *because* it is as important as your own. This equality of influence cannot translate into "equal pay" or "equal parenting" when these equalities are not under the control of a couple. Although some couples can work gradually into shared parenting, the strengths of individual partners usually preclude exact equality in parenting.

Wider societal and personal possibilities of equal pay and equal parenting can be opened up through the equality of influence, however. Appreciation of mature dependence with a person of the opposite sex often leads to greater respect for people of the opposite sex—and the hope and belief in gender equity. For men, greater respect may mean advocating women's rights, equal pay, and protection against violence and abuse. It may mean hesitating to interrupt, trivialize, or silence women's complaints about the unfairness of their situation in a culture that marginalizes them and fails to recognize their competence. It may also mean sharing more equally in parenting. For women, greater respect may mean ceasing to blame individual men for inequity between the sexes and coming to understand more fully how the process of development of self-awareness works, through the reclaiming of unconscious dream lovers. It may mean a willingness to remain open to diverse meanings and possibilities in parenting with someone who has a different view of bedtimes, cleanliness, and discipline. It may mean appreciating the contribution of breadwinning, especially the responsibility of carrying more of the burden. When equality of influence works, it opens up gender limitations and allows both partners to experience life from each other's perspectives.

That is my second answer. Through dialogue and taking back dream lovers, women and men open up their gender identities. Hearing and understanding what it's like to earn a living for a family, I can "try on" being the primary breadwinner for my family. Hearing and understanding what it's like to be primary caregiver for infants and toddlers, a man can try on being "home base." Without the questions, curiosity, and interest in knowing each other, we are stuck with the Others within.

Inequities between the sexes are rooted in our strange gender—in how we imagine, fear, and idealize the other sex. When men see that heterosexual intimacy and sexual desire depend on respecting women, men also realize that equality between the sexes is a goal for everyone. When women see that equality between the sexes depends on their speaking up and representing their own desires (as well as listening to others), women realize that equality depends on treating men as equals, not superiors. As women and men come to know what life is like for each other and to understand each other's strengths, they gradually reclaim their own strangeness. This is a process that frees each of us of idealization and fear.

Idealization and fear are the roots of sexism and all other power hierarchies. Injustice is freely enacted only upon those whom we consider our inferiors—those who fear us and whom we ultimately fear. When we empty the others of worth and meaning, we fill them with motives to retaliate and possess what is worthwhile. Even in the current atmosphere of inequity, the two sexes can operate according to principles of equality if they cease idealizing and fearing each other. Equal influence between partners in heterosexual couples on issues of money and parenting has revolutionary implications for a future of greater justice between the sexes.

chapter 7

TV or not TV? ■ that is ■ the leisure ■ question

In a recent popular movie, we (the audience) watch the middle-aged housewife heroine who is enraged at her husband use a hatchet to rip out an interior wall of their suburban home. Although we don't immediately understand why she is tearing out the wall, we are sympathetic with her because her overweight, stupid, and passive husband obviously watches too much TV. Everyone recognizes him as a familiar American character, even though he is a caricature. He arrives home after a day at work, looks at the lovely meal prepared for him by his wife, grabs a beer and his plate, and moves to the front of the television. She is infuriated, but disempowered. She cajoles or demands that they eat together. He mumbles and remains glued to the TV. She has taken countless classes on improving their relationship, tried all kinds of tricks from exotic foods to seductive dress to distract him from TV, but nothing has worked. She must resort to violence.

Although the movie is an exaggeration, even a farcical one, of a common problem in midlife couples, I was impressed with how much I felt this woman's attack was justified. I could easily identify with her utter exasperation. When I'm listening to couples in psychotherapy debate the TV question, fortunately I feel more neutral. I often find myself musing about the tone of seriousness in these discussions. Could television watching (to watch or not to watch) possibly be a moral issue? Couples engage in passionate debate as though it were. Usually the woman opposes it for herself, her children, and her partner. Often the man defends it. Both are vehement, claiming infringements of their "basic rights." Of course, not all women oppose television watching. Not all men defend it. In my experience, though, the argument for and against TV falls along fairly strong gender lines. I've wondered why this is so. Could it be an overflow from the way women associate being home with *work* (as either the "second shift" after an outside job or the scene of their primary responsibilities) and men associate it with *relaxing*? Or could it be that the TV means something different to men and women?

While planning this book, I decided to design a survey to ask questions of heterosexual couples about their use of leisure time—in large part because of my curiosity about television watching. Later in the chapter I'll report the results of the survey, administered to sixty-two married couples from mostly middle-class backgrounds. Many interesting patterns of difference emerged. One of them was that men like to watch television at the end of a busy day as much as they like to converse with their spouses, but women much prefer conversation to TV. On the way to understanding gender differences in television watching, I learned a great deal about the crucial importance of leisure time in the life of a couple.

Besides television watching, in this chapter we'll encounter the core difficulties that couples face in using leisure time. Much has yet to be understood about the ways in which women and men negotiate their differences in spending leisure time together, but one thing is clear and certain: Leisure is the heartland of contemporary couple relationships. In the past, for most of the history of civilization, couples and families spent their days working together. Now that people spend much of their working time apart from their families, leisure has taken on new and more crucial meaning. From research on leisure time, I learned that people evaluate the worth of their relationships with spouses more in terms of the pleasure that is shared in leisure (usually referred to as "companionship" and "enjoyment") than in terms of any other concerns (such as sex, children, or money).

In our society, increasingly partners and spouses spend longer times apart because of the extended workday, as economist and professor Juliet Schor shows in her recent book on the "overworked American." Separation anxiety (fears and insecurities that are experienced as anger, depression, and apathy) is aroused by long hours of separation from those to whom we are attached. When reunited with our partners and children, we cannot easily shift into enjoyment. We tend unconsciously to want to punish the person from whom we've been separated. Separation anxiety may interfere with a couple's ability to enjoy leisure time when partners have been separated for days and weeks, and then are reunited for a weekend or a few days of expected relaxation.

Long working hours tend to increase the expectations and significance of leisure. The longer I have to delay pleasure in favor of work (waiting for the weekend), the more significance I will assign to the "success" of that pleasure. When partners spend long hours apart and then have agitated, disagreeable, and conflict-ridden leisure time together, they will tend to depreciate what might work well between them (for example, parenting) because of the disappointment that conflicted leisure brings. If I waited all week to enjoy myself with you, and now we are bickering about how to spend our time, *or* I am angry about having gone along with your choice, I may evaluate the whole relationship in terms of my disappointment. I may say to myself, "What good is a relationship in which the few hours we spend together each week are spent either being bored or arguing?"

Even coming home at the end of the workday or work week can be a disappointment. As we saw in the last chapter, coming home after work has quite different meanings for women and men. For women (especially women who have children at home), home is associated with the "second shift" of work and generally is not viewed as a haven of relaxation. For men, home is the specific location in which they expect, indeed often believe that they "deserve," to relax. According to a number of surveys, most Americans spend much of their leisure time at home, and television watching is one of the primary types of leisure activity at home.

I have listened to countless heterosexual couples from a range of educational and economic backgrounds passionately debate the television issue. He watches *and* appreciates TV "for what it is, a form of entertainment and relaxation." She doesn't *and* depreciates it as a "silly waste of time that we could spend together." The contrast is often so strong that I have fantasized someday discovering a magazine article on the "biological basis" of sex differences in television watching—a single fiber of the corpus callosum of the female brain that blocks satisfaction from TV! Surely there is a sociobiologist out there who will want to see this gender difference as a biological sex difference. Sometimes couples themselves see it that way.

Let's listen to Patty and Joe talk about it in their fifth session of dialogue therapy.

Joe: I have a right to come home and switch on the news or whatever *because* I have worked hard all day. I want you to stop criticizing me on this. All the guys watch the news after work. I'm tired of feeling guilty.

Joe (Double): I tend to feel guilty when you criticize me and I don't want that feeling when I'm trying to relax.

Patty: I can't control *your* feelings.

Joe: I know that. I just want you to stop criticizing me for watching TV.

Patty: In my head I can say okay, but somehow my gut just believes that watching TV is bad for all of us. Mostly it's junk, even on the news. I would prefer your company when I walk through the door in the evenings—especially at dinner. I really hate it when you watch the news over dinner.

Joe: Okay, I'll cut out TV at dinnertime if you agree to stop criticizing me for watching when I come home from work. And Monday night football—I have to watch it and I don't want your comments.

Patty and Joe were able to negotiate this into an agreement that he would limit his evening TV watching and she would limit her criticism.

Each of them has worked to take back projections of negative parental dream lovers. They are less afraid of their differences now. They can negotiate conflicts much better. Watching weekend sports on television was a particularly difficult issue that they resolved in this way. Joe wanted Sunday afternoons to be free for television, but Patty wanted this time to be free for family outings or time together with Joe. Patty used Sunday afternoon to prepare herself for sex in the evening, to feel more involved and intimate with Joe, which was difficult if he was glued to the set. (Sunday night sex had become very gratifying for both of them.) She tended to depreciate him when he watched television all day. Through dialogue and negotiation, Joe agreed to spend dinner and the rest of Sunday evening doing something with Patty or the family. Patty had to acknowledge that Joe was not the Hero she imagined, and that watching television was not a moral or social failure.

This chapter is about becoming unafraid to confront differences. The differences that I explore here have to do with the use of leisure time. Choices for spending leisure time may seem to be a trivial matter in contrast with fighting, sex, children, and money (topics we've already covered), but as it turns out leisure may be the glue that keeps a couple (and a family) together—or the wedge that drives them apart. Shaping activities for leisure time covers a range of questions as diverse as whether one wants to engage in religious worship or whether one would rather take an evening stroll or watch the news on TV.

Conflicts about leisure may be the central access that couples have to an arena of equal influence between the sexes. Because most leisure activities are not determined as gender-specific in advance, and because leisure has few parameters (other than individual ones), leisure is a "wide-open" aspect of a couple's life. It's not like child rearing or breadwinning, in which socialization and role expectations have tended to sort men and women into specialties. Although some gender expectations may influence couples—for instance, expectations that women fill in the social calendar or that men do sports with their sons—much of leisure is left open for decision making by individuals.

playing together is staying together?

Leisure experiences provide bonding for contemporary couples and families in a new way, compared with other periods of history. In earlier centuries, families and couples defined themselves by their work, often spending most of their time engaged in the work that sustained them. Couple and family identity came through shared work, as described by family names such as Smith, Carpenter, Wheelwright, and so on. Families interacted mostly through their shared responsibilities and roles in the community. Performing a service or a craft, harvesting and storing food, and caring for others in and out of the family were the activities that brought members into sustained intimate interaction.

In this century, and especially now at the end of it, families and couples are not bonded through work. Work separates family members and leisure joins them. Many families with teenage children no longer even have daily family meals together. Coordinating schedules is too difficult, and the microwave provides the possibility for each person to choose when and what to eat. Family roles are no longer clearly structured, especially when it comes to choice and enactment of leisure.

Modern families are dependent for their satisfaction, in large measure, on their ability to negotiate differences and preferences for leisure activities. But if leisure holds out the promise of bonding and relaxing together for a couple or family, it can also be a threat. Because leisure is not well structured and connected to assumed roles, it is an arena of conflict. Different leisure preferences can have a negative impact on marital satisfaction and family relationships. Anticipating that leisure time should be pleasant and satisfying, adults and children are often distressed when conflicts arise and cannot be resolved. Unresolved conflicts about leisure time can threaten the intimacy established through other areas of a couple's life. If a couple can't play together, often they can't stay together.

Although patterns vary somewhat with each couple, the trends I have noticed as the strongest are women's desires for *interaction* in joint activities (talking together and finding similarities in experiences) and men's desires for *relaxation* or *entertainment* in "shoulder-to-shoulder" parallel activities with little direct exchange. Another trend is women's search for self-improvement (through church, education, or therapy), seen by them as an exciting development of the self through leisure time. Mostly I hear men rejecting self-improvement as "more work," not an ideal way to spend leisure time.

In studies of marital satisfaction, "companionship" appears to be the major benefit named by both men and women. Both sexes seem to believe that the success of marriage lies in the realm of leisure activities, in being able to share meaningfully. A 1982 national study of adults found that "spending time with your family" and "companionship" were the two most common determinants of marital satisfaction, more important than having children or financial security. This focal value of shared experiences is supported by many findings about the importance of leisure to marital satisfaction. A 1987 national survey of American families found that the most common leisure activities among American adults were home-based—activities like visiting with kin and watching television.

Most of the research that has looked at the leisure behavior of couples and families has examined its consequences for marital satisfaction. Most important is a consistent finding that husbands and wives who share leisure time together tend to be much more satisfied with their marriages than those who don't. This finding is pervasive in American and cross-cultural studies. A related finding is the negative impact on marital satisfaction of time spent in independent, individual leisure activities. High concentrations of separate leisure activities are consistently associated with lower levels of marital satisfaction, especially for wives. Individual activities are not by themselves a problem for marital satisfaction, but when time spent separately is greater than the norm or an individual's expectation, then marital satisfaction declines.

Here are Larry and Louise, in their fifth session, talking about Larry's extended commitments to sports activities in which he has both active and passive involvement with his teenage sons. Larry did not end up getting laid off at work, but he was transferred to another location. He now puts in more time driving to and from work, *and* he has committed additional travel time to fulfill his job responsibilities. One weekend a month he is away from home on business. Other weekends, he likes to play tennis with one or both of his sons or watch their sports activities. He would like Louise to "just accept" this. She feels rejected by Larry's preference to spend *most* of his leisure time away from her.

Larry: You know how much I love watching the kids playing soccer and baseball. My dad wasn't able to attend any of my high school sports because he was away so much. I don't want our sons to feel the kind of loss and humiliation I felt when all of the other fathers were there, but mine wasn't.

Louise: You're saying that you're afraid that our kids will feel rejected if you're absent from their games? (*Larry nods.*) I guess I'm saddened by that statement. I go to the boys' games when you're away and I'm their parent too. It's not just *dads* that count. My issue here is how little time you and I spend together. I'm angry because you only speak to me directly to give me your laundry or ask me how the boys—

Louise (Double): I feel rejected because you rarely seem to want to be with me personally, just for myself. I want more personal contact.

Larry: What would you like? I'd like more time together too, but I guess I'd like you to come with me to the boys' games and sometimes watch us play tennis.

Louise: I'd never get the Saturday chores and shopping done if I went along on all your trips. What I'd like is one Saturday afternoon or evening a month with you. Just with you and me.

Larry: Okay, I could do that. What would you want to do?

Louise: I'd like to take a walk together, maybe go to a movie sometimes. In fact, what I'd like best is for *you* to arrange a "date" with me. You set up dinner and a movie or something.

Larry: I'd be willing to do that if you would play golf with me every once in a while.

Without a lot of blame and accusation (having improved in their ability to hold a true dialogue), Larry and Louise were able to navigate through hurt and rejected feelings to reach a negotiation about leisure time. Differences in leisure preferences sometimes signal "rejection" to one or both partners. An absence of shared activities or a major commitment to separate, individual ones is a symptom of marital dissatisfaction—and can lead to more dissatisfaction, even instability.

Three types of leisure activity affect couple relationships in somewhat different ways. The first type is called *joint* activity, and it involves direct sharing and interaction. Generally speaking, joint activity enhances satisfaction. The second type is called *parallel* activity, and it involves doing something together without much interaction, like watching television. Parallel activities can have a positive, modest, or negative impact on couple relationships. A 1988 study, designed specifically to understand the effects of parallel leisure on couples, found that activities involving little or no communication provide little benefit for the relationship. They may even hurt the relationship because they suggest togetherness when people are feeling separate—and so may lower the experience of satisfaction. The third type is *separate* leisure activity, which has a negative effect on couple satisfaction if the amount of separate time exceeds a partner's sense of the "norm."

When I first read about these studies, I wondered about the fact that moviegoing is a very satisfying activity for my husband and me—and for our whole family. Although moviegoing, like television watching, is generally assumed to be a parallel activity, I realized that for us it is a joint activity. In our family, we spend a lot of time talking about movies after we see them. A really good movie can be the basis for breakfast and dinner conversations for several days. Even when we have disagreements about a movie, we find the communications satisfying.

For most families, television watching tends to be more parallel than joint. One researcher has suggested that television watching "anesthetizes" people by reducing tensions between them, minimizing their efforts to deal with conflict. A study in 1976 of American families found that higher levels of television watching were associated with higher levels of tension. Parallel activity may reduce surface tensions, but leave real differences untouched.

Because leisure time is so important to satisfaction in couple relationships, I have been especially interested in those factors that might inhibit or constrain possibilities for joint leisure. A most important factor for heterosexual couples is gender difference—a factor that I'll be discussing in the remainder of the chapter. Other factors include stress, depression, religious differences, ethnic differences, competence, and personal evaluations. Among the factors that are most disruptive is stress associated with the presence of preschool children. Preschool children in the family significantly reduce the amount of time husbands and wives spend together—leading to feelings of lowered satisfaction with the marital relationship and sometimes contributing to marital instability. Other stresses also create barriers to shared leisure. Older people, poor people, and single parents are those most likely to experience serious barriers to enjoying leisure activities. Overall, the greatest barriers to shared enjoyment in leisure among married couples are incompatible leisure interests and the inability to enjoy each other's company. Some incompatibility of interests is related to gender differences in socialization and interactional styles.

gender differences in leisure: a study of married couples

With the help of my friend and colleague, sociologist and educator Valeria Freysinger, I designed a study for the purpose of investigating certain trends in gender differences in leisure activities that I had observed in heterosexual couples in dialogue therapy. Because the study was designed specifically to provide data for this chapter, and because I was interested only in couples that had been committed to each other for at least a year (and I needed to tap both members of the couple at once), I wanted a simple format. The questionnaire—which appears in the Appendix and can be used by readers to measure their areas of difference and similarity with a partner—presents the beginnings of six statements about leisure preferences. Each statement has up to six different completions. Respondents were asked to circle a number on a scale from 1 to 10 in response to each completion. On the the low end of the scale, 1 meant "not at all," and on the high end, 10 meant "most of the time."

In summarizing the results of this survey below, I'll present the findings according to certain themes in the use of leisure time. These themes emerge often among couples I see in dialogue therapy. As I review each theme from the study, we'll hear from our four couples in terms of their differences. Before I do this, however, here is a brief description of the sample of couples that were surveyed.

Sixty-two couples, 124 men and women, responded to this four-page survey, completed quickly by circling numbers and giving us a few personal statistics about themselves. The respondents came from a midwestern state and covered a range of ages and years together. Fifty-seven couples were Caucasian and four were African-American (one couple didn't give their race). Although a few respondents did not list their age, approximately 100 of them were between 21 and 50 years of age, and 24 people were between the ages of 50 and 71. Their years together ranged from 1 to 50, with the majority together for 30 years or less. Only 13 people had been previously married, and so most of these couples were unaffected by divorce.

Educationally and economically, this was a solidly middle-class sample. Sixty-six percent of the men held college degrees ranging from the baccalaureate to an advanced graduate degree (Ph.D., M.D., and so on). Fifty-seven percent of the women also held college degrees in the same range. Sixty-four percent of the couples reported annual family incomes upward of $45,000. Fifty-five percent of the men reported working more than full time (41-plus hours per week). Twenty-nine percent of the women reported the same commitment to work (41-plus hours per week), with another 26 percent reporting 40 hours per week.

The respondents were not paid to answer the questionnaire; their responses were requested by college students in Dr. Freysinger's classes, who took home the survey forms to their parents and neighbors. I am very grateful to the students and the respondents. What did they tell us about gender differences in leisure?

conversational styles

Earlier, I reported on linguist Deborah Tannen's findings that men and women tend to relate in different conversational styles. Our study found support for this claim. We asked respondents to tell us about themselves when they are in conversations that are not work related. Four of the six completions for the statement on this topic drew significantly *different* responses from women and men. The topic of conversational style elicited the biggest gender differences we saw.

In response to the item "When I am talking in ordinary conversations with friends or family (not work related) . . . ," *women,* more often than men, said the following:

- I want to express my personal feelings.
- I am eager to understand the other person's feelings.
- I am eager to understand the other person's viewpoint.
- I see ways that I am similar to the other person.

In Tannen's terms, these women prefer "rapport talk" when they are in personal conversations. They prefer to express feelings, to understand the other person, and to see how they are similar to the other. They are relating through "connecting" to the other person.

The contrast to rapport talk is what Tannen calls "report talk"—the type that men may prefer. Report talk has to do with reporting on facts and descriptions, and with solving problems. Two of the completions for "When I am talking in ordinary conversations . . ." involved report talk. A slightly higher percentage of men than women chose these:

- I am trying to solve the problem at hand.
- I am mostly trying to make a point.

We did not find statistically significant differences (differences lying well outside of what might be random or chance) in the choice of these two.

As it turned out, though, educated women tended to choose "I am mostly trying to make a point" almost as often as men did. The better a woman's education, the more hours of paid employment she worked, and the higher her family income, the more likely she was to be trying to make a point in ordinary conversations. One final trend was also interesting. Those men who worked the most hours per week reported themselves as less eager to understand another's viewpoint.

In reviewing these findings, I am reminded of something I witnessed early in therapy with Pamela and Charles. Pamela had originally been less tenacious in holding on to her viewpoint than she became later in our fifth session of dialogue therapy. Because Pamela had returned to graduate school and was beginning to feel that she "had something to say," she was now able to tell Charles more directly what she wanted to do in their leisure time.

Pamela: On Saturday afternoons, I want to spend some time just touching and talking, just the two of us. When we do this, I always feel better about making love. I wonder how you feel about this.

Charles: Anything that in fact increases your desire to make love is very interesting to me. However, I do enjoy our visits and outings with the grandchildren on Saturdays and I wonder if you're hinting that we should give those up, in favor of ourselves.

Pamela: I agree with you about enjoying the grandchildren, but I think that Sundays are enough time to spend together as a group. Now that I'm away more during the week, and you're always busy too, I would like to reserve Saturday afternoons for ourselves—and then count on Sunday mornings for lovemaking.

Charles: Unbelievable! You'd miss church to make love! I'm shocked, dear Pamela!

Charles (Double): I'm pleased and really surprised how much you want to make love, but I guess I'm a little afraid that I might not be able to perform if we make love so regularly.

Pamela: Is that true?

Charles: Perhaps, I guess, maybe. I'm not accustomed to regular *intercourse*, and I wonder how you would feel if I didn't or couldn't get very amorous.

Charles (Double): How would you feel if I couldn't get or maintain an erection?

Pamela: That doesn't bother me, really. I just enjoy the closeness between us, especially when we can carry it over from one day to the next.

Pamela went on to explain that she didn't want to miss church. She only wanted to make love on Sunday morning and attend a later service. She talked about how much she enjoyed the physical closeness with Charles, now that they had established some emotional closeness again. She found that she no longer distrusted him with other women, or imagined that he was "chasing after" younger women. You probably noticed that Pamela spoke up for herself and sustained her own sense of worth, knowing what she wanted and trying to get it, throughout the dialogue. Although Charles did not respond in rapport talk, Pamela accepted his participation and responded to it feelingly. She was able to "feel past" his defensiveness. Charles, for his part, was happy to hear that Pamela wanted to make love more—even though he sometimes lacked confidence in his ability to perform.

Although women may strongly prefer rapport talk, both for themselves and their partners, they can learn to understand and respond feelingly to report talk and separate knowing, as I discussed in Chapter 3. In order to negotiate leisure time and to share that time effectively, both partners have to accept each other's conversational styles. In observing couples in therapy, I find that women—more often than men—reject their partners' conversational styles in favor of their own. Perhaps this is a power move or perhaps this is misunderstanding the desire for joint or shared leisure. Women may erroneously believe that in order to "share" in conversation during leisure, both people need to express and be interested in understanding personal feelings. My sense is that a couple can enjoy leisure time if both partners attempt to speak in their own languages and to understand enough of the other in order to see that person's viewpoint.

Of course, the men in our sample were less likely than the women to regard "understanding the other person's viewpoint" as important. Here is where men may interfere with sharing leisure through conversation. They may not put a high enough premium on understanding what a partner is expressing—not only the other's feelings, but even the other's viewpoint. Sometimes this shows up as a kind of "passivity" in men in heterosexual conversation. They seem to be waiting (or interrupting) until a woman finishes speaking in order to make a point themselves, rather than actively listening and trying to understand. Understanding another's viewpoint is obviously a necessity for any kind of shared or joint leisure activity.

television or idle chatter

In our survey we asked for responses to two situations that involved television watching and/or conversation. The first one was "At the end of a busy day . . ." and the second was "Over the weekend with my spouse, I am annoyed by . . ." On the first, we found no statistically significant differences in the preference ratings given by men and women. Both sexes seem to prefer the same things after a busy day. There was only one preference that came close to revealing a significant difference: Men, more than women, preferred to watch television to relax at the end of a busy day. Otherwise, men and women chose quite similar ratings for the following:

- I like to engage in good conversation with my spouse.
- I want to sit quietly (with snack or drink) and not be disturbed.
- I am annoyed when my spouse wants to talk.
- I am annoyed when my spouse wants to watch TV.

These couples were heavily engaged in paid employment, with 77 percent of the men and about 55 percent of the women working forty hours per week or more. Perhaps for this reason, the genders appeared to be more similar than different in how they want to spend the final hours of the day. The average (or mean) rating for "I like to engage in good conversation with my spouse" was exactly the same for both genders: up near the top of the scale. Both men and women like to talk to each other at the end of the day. On the other hand, men's average rating for watching television "to relax" was the same as their preference for conversation, although women rated television watching as a much lower preference.

Regarding the weekends, our respondents saw things differently. Men indicated being significantly more annoyed by "idle chatter" than women were, and women indicated being significantly more annoyed by television watching. When thinking about leisure time *on the weekends,* our respondents expressed what I have so often heard in couple therapy: He is annoyed by her chatter. She is annoyed by his television watching. Neither gender was annoyed by serious conversation. Nor was either gender especially annoyed by "criticisms of my activities."

Two interesting trends regarding the weekend were expressed. Women were more annoyed than men by unnecessary expenditures of money—and this difference was almost statistically significant. Because we know little about our respondents, it's impossible to say why this might have been so. In the studies about gender and leisure that I have reviewed, I have not seen anything that suggests women are more concerned about leisure expenses than men are, but this result raises some intriguing questions.

This sample included many educated and employed women; what is the relationship between earning money and concerns about unneccessary expenditures in women? In dialogue therapy with me, financially dependent women frequently complain about the "stinginess" of a spouse who does not "allow" large enough expenditures for leisure. Increased earning capacity in women might make them more alert to expenditures, especially unnecessary ones.

The other result was similar. The more hours per week women worked, the more likely they were to be annoyed by "unnecessary interruptions" of their chosen weekend activities. There were no significant gender differences on this issue.

Our results seem to indicate that weekends are the kind of unstructured leisure time that might invite conflict over gender differences, especially regarding television and conversation. Weekends are times set aside specifically (in our society) for the "rewards" that come from hard work. Protecting one's preferences over the weekend may be a more serious matter than relaxing at the end of the day. Weekends are microcosms of vacations. Vacations are notoriously difficult when family or couple needs are in conflict and everyone feels pressure to "have a good time." Our study looked at only one aspect of vacations—travel in the car.

in the car for pleasure

When the car is part of leisure activity, its handling can become a point of contention. The following dialogue took place between Jonathon and Karen, in their fifth session, when they were trying to determine what had gone wrong on a recent trip to a nearby city to visit Jonathon's relatives.

Karen: It's still hard for me to respect your way of driving, even though I feel better about most of our relationship. I mean, you get in the car and you don't want to stop for *anything,* not to ask directions or even to go to the bathroom. On Sunday, on our way home, I was really angry with you when you just refused to look for an alternate route home.

Jonathon: You mean when we were sitting in the traffic jam for about an hour? (*Karen nods.*) I can see now that you were angry, but then all I could think about was finding the traffic news on the radio. I just didn't want to hear your ideas about taking other routes home. The last time we went to Baltimore, you had us coming home through upstate New York or something.

Jonathon (Double): I don't trust your directions. I want to keep everything under my control when I'm driving.

Jonathon: Yeah, that's right, I guess. Driving *is* important to me and I don't like to feel that you are taking over when I'm feeling kind of vulnerable or confused, like when we're in a traffic jam.

Karen: It's interesting that you were feeling vulnerable and confused, because I thought you were just angry at me for making a suggestion. I would like to know that we have *some means* to communicate when we get into a delay or we're lost on the highway. Do you have a suggestion for what we could do?

Jonathon suggested that Karen ask for a "time-out" when they're stuck on some difference in driving. She would make a signal and they would each listen for a couple of minutes to what the other wanted to say. Karen agreed to this, although she believes she is more flexible about driving and willing to take Jonathon's suggestions directly without a special signal. Jonathon was clear that he needed a special sign indicating that Karen wasn't trying to "take over" but just wanted to confer with him about a dilemma. Still, Jonathon asked that he retain the right to make a final decision if he was the driver. Karen agreed.

Although this interaction might seem trivial on the surface, I have seen many couples almost come to blows about differences in the use of the car for leisure time. Car disputes are especially difficult on vacation when everyone (couple and children) is already a little tense about getting needs met. Traffic jams, getting lost, taking alternative routes, and the question of who's in control are all potential crises.

In our survey we asked people to respond to the situation "When my spouse and I travel by car on a pleasure trip . . ." One preference turned out to be statistically significant as a gender difference: "I prefer to listen more than talk." Which way do you think this one went? Men, more than women, preferred to listen more than talk when they were on a pleasure trip. This may seem to be a surprise, but when I thought about the men's responses, I pictured them *driving* and making the assumption they would not be having any serious talks. Another preference was no surprise at all: Women preferred the scenic route, even if it was less direct. Men preferred the highway. Working with couples in dialogue therapy and taking pleasure trips with friends, I have often witnessed preferences falling along just these lines, with men preferring the faster or more direct route while women want to see the best scenery.

Studies of vacations show that they can be both a source of satisfaction and a source of stress. In a 1989 study, researchers found that people returning from vacations reported greater overall feelings of life satisfaction, although they might not be feeling more comfortable with or closer to family members. People who reported postvacation blues were more likely to have had those feelings *before* the vacation. Their normal day-to-day feelings seemed to carry over to the vacation. It was the same for those people who had negative feelings about spouses and other family members. The negative feelings carried over and did not change with the vacation.

active or passive leisure

Women like Patty and Pamela often find themselves coercing their spouses into more active or self-improving leisure pastimes. Here is an example of Patty and Joe struggling to accept each other without his projection of the Maiden Lover (his ideal companion) or hers of the Hero (her ideal companion).

Patty: I would just love it if you would agree to go to Marriage Encounter at our church, just once more. When you went last time, you said that you really enjoyed it, didn't you?

Joe: That was before therapy. I was just telling you that because I didn't want to disappoint you. Actually I was uncomfortable being so personal with people I hardly knew, and I hated losing an entire weekend—not being with the kids *and* watching football. You know, I'd love it too if you stayed home with us more often. You're always out doing school or church or therapy.

Joe (Double): I miss being with you. You're my best friend now and I want more time with you.

Joe: I don't know if I would go so far as saying you're my *best* friend, but you're a good friend and I do miss you a lot. And, I wonder if you're going to change so much that you'll be bored with me.

Patty: You're afraid of losing me because I would change so much? (*Joe nods.*) That was a risk at one time, but it's not anymore. I realize how important our relationship is to my whole life, everything that I depend on. My problem is that I don't want to make these changes *alone*. I keep thinking how *wonderful* it would be for you to discover how much talent and potential you really have to develop yourself.

Joe: Thanks for the compliment, if it's a compliment. I just don't have the self-improvement bug. Maybe it's not right, but I like things just as they are. I want to enjoy myself on weekends, not improve myself.

Patty: Yeah, it's kind of paradoxical, I guess, because you just like "to be" and I keep searching for that feeling in all these experiences of self-improvement.

Patty and Joe were able to accept each other's differences in using leisure time as long as they had committed enough time to being together—on Sunday evenings and for Saturday night dates. So that they wouldn't feel rejected by each other's differences, they promised to spend some time each day getting a "review" of each other's activities and ideas from the day. In that way, they would keep up with each other. Additionally, they promised to show affection and appreciation for each other at every reasonable opportunity, especially at those times when their leisure activities separated them—knowing how hard separate leisure time can be for couples.

In order to investigate gender differences between active and passive leisure, we asked our survey respondents to react to the item "When I look forward to leisure time I imagine . . ." We found only one statistically significant difference: Women, more than men, gave high ratings to "learning or reading." This wasn't a surprise because I had made informal surveys of men's and women's leisure preferences at workshops conducted by my husband and myself. Usually I'd found that women preferred reading and talking to almost all other activities. Men's choices varied from passive entertainment (watching sports in person or on TV) to active participation in games and sports. In our study there were two interesting preferences that showed up much more frequently for men (although the difference between the sexes wasn't statistically significant). Men rated both of these higher than women did:

- Active play or exercise as leisure
- Imagining that their *spouses* would direct leisure activities

These two seem to contrast. One involves a physically active engagement in leisure, while the other implies a passive dependence on the spouse. The second item was worded "When I look forward to leisure time I imagine . . . My spouse will direct our activities." Men gave this preference a much higher rating than women did. This response seems to fit the traditional role expectation that the wife would arrange the social calendar for a married couple (as in "I don't know if we can come over this weekend for dinner or not; I have to ask my wife"). These educated and professionally active men still tended to anticipate being directed by a spouse in leisure activities. Some men answered a little differently. Men who were better educated were less likely to want to be directed by a spouse. Similarly, the higher his educational level, the more likely a man was to want active leisure—and the less likely to see himself "napping or passively enjoying life." Both men and women were less likely to see themselves in active play as they grew older.

Large differences in age or physical abilities can interfere with a couple's companionship because of the ways in which these factors are linked to different leisure activities. Couples I've seen in therapy whose partners have differed by more than fifteen years of age have often had difficulty finding leisure activities that they both enjoy—other than dining out and going to movies (and even movie selection can be difficult). Feelings of abandonment and rejection accompany partners, especially women, who are spending a lot of free time in separate activities. It's not so much a problem when *some* leisure activities are done separately, but when a majority, or more than the cultural norm, are. When separate activities slip over into the "too many" category (which is different for different people), then one or both partners will feel rejected and begin to assess the relationship as less satisfying. Large age differences mean different generational styles in North America—and different physical possibilities everywhere. When ages differ substantially, the typical combination is an older man with a younger woman, although recently the situation has sometimes been reversed for couples I've seen in therapy. Couples with large age differences can be quite effective as parents, as sexual and financial partners, but sometimes not as companions. Issues as seemingly trivial as one's taste in music on the radio (he likes the Beatles and she likes rap) can set people apart. Issues as important as who will be her tennis partner (because he's had a hip replacement) are often overwhelming. The theme of active or passive leisure comes up frequently with generationally different partners and it's a hard problem to solve.

how "should" couples be?

The final area that I wanted to know about in our survey was whether or not we would find gender differences in the way partners expected conflicts about leisure to be handled. Because difference is such an important aspect of negotiating leisure time, I wondered how partners thought about differences in general. Here is how the item was stated: "Ideally I think that couples should . . ." and these were the preferences to be rated from 1 to 10:

- Learn to talk out their differences
- Accept differences without talking them out
- Find a way to change their differences to be more similar
- Learn about each other's points of view

There were no significant differences in the ways men and women responded to these issues.

One preference showed the kind of difference that I anticipated we might see. Men gave higher overall ratings to the idea that couples should learn to accept differences without talking them out. Years ago in a couple therapy session, a newly married man was describing to his wife how much he admired the relationship between his parents. He said, "Most of the time they didn't have to talk things out. He just looked her in the eye and she knew." This is the Ozzie and Harriet fantasy from the days of wild projections. The belief that "she knew" rests on a dream lover. Because "she knows me" she will automatically know how to meet my needs. She will be the perfect Mother, Maiden, Mistress. In our survey, though, the more educated men saw things differently. The higher a man's level of education, the less likely he was to say that couples should accept differences without talking them out. Perhaps with greater education men have a more developed understanding of the complexity and worth of human difference, especially in an intimate relationship.

How about women's reactions to the idea that couples should learn to accept differences without talking them out? Women rated this preference lower than men did, but not significantly so. The longer a woman had been involved in her relationship, however, the less likely she was to believe that couples *should* talk out their differences and that partners should learn about each other's points of view. Possibly women become cynical about their ideals of talking things out and trying to understand each other's viewpoints. Certainly that was how Pamela and Louise seemed at the beginning of dialogue therapy. They appeared to have given up hope of even having an influence on their partners.

Throughout these chapters, I have stressed the importance of acknowledging and respecting differences—something I have often dubbed "differentiation." At the same time, I have insisted on the importance of empathy in responding to difference: the ability to see something from another's point of view. In regard to leisure activities especially, partners need to be alert to how they respond to differences. In a 1980 national survey of American families, it was found that one third of American families experience distress from leisure conflicts. Only household roles and sex were more likely to be a source of family conflict.

Similar findings came from a worldwide study of military families in 1980. Conflicts over the use of leisure time and opportunities for companionship were described as more stressful than problems of child rearing or finances.

In a 1985 paper summarizing research on leisure conflicts, researcher Dennis Orthner identified five factors that lead to stress over leisure in marriage. *Inadequate leisure time* is certainly one about which I hear many complaints from couples in therapy. As work and child-rearing responsibilities increase, companionship is likely to drop off. Because the American workweek has now expanded beyond the traditional forty hours (recall that 55 percent of the men in our survey work forty-one hours per week or more), the time for leisure contact is often severely limited. Larry will be away from home for a weekend each month, in addition to leaving at six in the morning and arriving at home after seven o'clock in the evening on workdays. Louise will tend to feel neglected because of his absence, and will complain about the lack of time for family and couple activities. Now that she has a more effective voice, Louise will have to negotiate for her side. Karen works over sixty hours a week, and she and Jonathon often disagree about whether she should attend a professional conference or go on a holiday with him. Feeling better about himself, Jonathon is more likely to be angry with Karen for "overworking" than to feel rejected by her. Larry and Louise and Karen and Jonathon will have to engage repeatedly in conflicts about the lack of leisure time in order to establish equality of influence, and a sense of trust in their companionship needs.

Inappropriate leisure choices are made when people choose activities that meet obligations or conform to social pressures ("things we should do") rather than pursue what the partners actually enjoy. Charles is often more motivated to meet social and family obligations than to enjoy himself with Pamela. Even though Charles knows that he and Pamela need a certain base of companionship to "repair old wounds," he still tends to prefer to ease his guilt and anxiety about obligations. Pamela and Charles will differ a lot in regard to the use of holidays, weekends, and vacations. Fulfilling obligations through traditional gender roles can interfere with appropriate leisure choices, leaving one or both partners feeling resentful—and perhaps "unentitled" (as women feel more often than men) to make leisure choices.

Differential leisure preferences are the sources of conflict I've discussed most in this chapter, especially in regard to gender differences. Feelings of neglect are the distressing outcome of different leisure preferences if these take partners away from joint activities. Early in marriage, both husbands and wives report greater preferences for joint leisure, but this trend tends to decline over time with greater work and child care responsibilities. Later in marriage, men report a greater gap between their preferences and actual activities, apparently indicating greater inner conflict about their activities. As we saw, men are more inclined to "go along" with a spouse's directive and then to resent it. Certainly Joe would attend workshops and conferences with Patty—before working through these differences—and resent it. Now he negotiates with Patty so that they spend some time together and some separately in leisure activities.

Interruptions in leisure patterns are the fourth area of conflict identified by Orthner. When patterns are interrupted suddenly, as with the birth of a child or an illness in the family, partners become especially irritable and apt to complain. The change in Larry's work schedule has brought on this kind of reaction in Louise. Here's an effective dialogue between them:

Louise: I'm sad and distressed about spending so much time separate from you, especially since we've been feeling much closer emotionally. I don't know how to change this. Can you help in any way?

Larry: I'm sorry that you feel so bad. I'm unhappy about the additional hours away, but on the other hand I'm very grateful that I have this job. Only last month we thought I'd be on welfare by now. I mean, really, I was lucky to get this position at a time when many of my associates were laid off. I guess the only way I can imagine *helping* is by trying to change my hours after some time has passed.

Louise: It actually *helps* when I hear that you are sorry to be gone so much. It also helps to know that you might be able to comfort me, just hold me and let me talk about how much I miss you.

The ability to express one's own experience directly, to listen and paraphrase the other's, and then to return again to one's own is critical to working on leisure conflicts. Because leisure is both so undefined and so central to satisfaction in a couple relationship, it demands good communication skills to bring good effects.

Conflicting circadian rhythms are the final area of leisure-related stress named by Orthner. Circadian rhythm is the rhythm of daily life—waking, tiredness, sleep cycles—that makes us "morning people" or "night people." When partners have vastly different circadian rhythms, they have difficulty planning leisure activities, especially those that occur in the morning and at night. Again, the only solution to such a conflict is dialogue about differences, and negotiations to a resolution.

How should couples be, in regard to leisure conflicts? Willing to talk about differences—that's the view I take. Although it may not be possible to resolve leisure differences when they touch as deeply as circadian rhythms or time obligations to one's profession, partners must be willing to talk and to listen (and paraphrase). Leisure time is the means of greatest companionship for most couples. Negotiating differences about it is as critical to a couple's life as is decision making about having children and sustaining an active sex life. Because leisure has not been tagged by experts as being critical to a couple's intimacy, many people feel embarrassed about the distress they feel over unresolved issues about television watching or disagreements about sports. I hope that this chapter will disabuse all of us of the belief that leisure is "trivial" or "icing on the cake" in a couple's life. It's right at the heart of a stable, satisfying relationship.

religion and spirituality

Although religious beliefs and spirituality are rarely considered under the topic of "leisure time," I have chosen to put them here. Contemporary couples are often faced with dilemmas about free time that include questions about church attendance and the development of spirituality.

Religious beliefs cover a wide range of possibilities in North America—everything from the traditional Judeo-Christian and Islamic religions to traditional forms of Buddhism and yoga to "new age" adaptations of all of these. Often I separate religion and spirituality because people present them as different issues.

Religion encompasses a specific system of beliefs about a deity and usually a form of worship. When speaking of such things as church affiliation, people often mention "organized religion," referring to the social and political structures that go along with most major forms of religious worship.

In a famous lecture on the topic of psychology and religion, Carl Jung characterizes religion more in terms of an attitude of mind.

> Religion appears to me to be a peculiar attitude of the human mind, which could be formulated in accordance with the original use of the term "religio," that is, a careful consideration and observation of certain dynamic factors, understood to be "powers," spirits, demons, gods, laws, ideas, ideals or whatever name man [*sic*] has given to such factors as he has found in his world powerful . . . and meaningful enough to be devoutly adored and loved.

In this passage, Jung broadens our understanding of religion to go beyond organized religion, and to include those values or ideals to which one may be "religiously devoted" or those matters that one "studies religiously." Jung emphasizes that whatever truth one takes to be most powerful and meaningful *is* religion. In this period of time, Jung's definition of religion would include science.

Contemporary understanding of spirituality often broadens religious beliefs to include greater idiosyncrasy, but most contemporary spirituality leaves out the note of seriousness that Jung sounds. Spirituality is usually considered more personal and wide ranging (maybe more arbitrary) than religion, including beliefs about *whatever* an individual holds to be sacred. Contemporary spiritual movements cover such diverse topics as spiritual practices, healing, ecological concerns, myth and ritual renewals, human rights, and rights of the unborn. This is hardly an exhaustive list. There is a spiritual movement to fit almost any ethnicity, cause, or practice that is a concern in the contemporary world.

It would seem that with this daunting array of possibilities for religious and spiritual activities, I would have encountered a lot of conflict among couples in psychotherapy on these issues, but in general I have not. Many couples—like Karen and Jonathon, Pamela and Charles, and Larry and Louise—have similar religious or ethnic backgrounds and rather a high degree of consensus about "religion." Patty and Joe, although they have both agreed to raise their children as Catholic, are a little different from the others because Joe grew up in a traditional Eastern Orthodox church and he is not comfortable with Patty's Catholicism, but he is willing to go along with it for his children. Many other couples have easily made this kind of compromise. Some couples, unlike these four, have widely divergent religious beliefs—for example, one partner is Catholic and the other is Jewish—but there is no wish to convert either partner. Or on the other hand, one partner is easily converted. When beliefs appear on the surface to be widely divergent (such as Catholic and Jewish), but they are relatively easily negotiated, I find that the underlying "religio" (serious concern) in the partners is similar. Their serious concerns and commitments are the same although their traditions have been different. Other couples struggle quite a lot about the rearing of children and the degree to which the children will be "trained" in a particular orientation. However, most couples who commit themselves to long-term relationships have some basis for a similar "religio" that allows them to sustain their differences and negotiate solutions to problems.

Where I find the greatest conflict in contemporary couples is in the area of spiritual "lifestyle." This includes issues of diet, ritual, leisure time, and reference groups. For example, Jonathon would like to keep a kosher household and celebrate Jewish holidays in a traditional manner. Karen belongs to a politically active, feminist-oriented Jewish group that is looser in its observances, but more serious about a number of political issues—for instance, peace in the Middle East. Here is a dialogue in which they are struggling to find compromises that suit both of them. (Jonathon still projects the Great Mother onto Karen from time to time.)

Jonathon: I guess I thought you'd want a kosher household for our children, since you came from a highly observant family, and that you'd want to do something to carry on traditions.

Jonathon (Double): I would enjoy *sharing* these family and religious traditions with you.

Karen: I never deceived you for a moment on these things. I told you how much I wanted to get away from the rigidity and sexism I grew up in. And in a way I feel that I keep a kosher household because I'm vegetarian; I'd like to raise our children as vegetarians too.

Jonathon: I guess you're saying that I should never have held out any hope that you and I could share these traditions (*Karen nods*) because you did tell me all of this. Somehow I just hoped that once we had children, things would change.

Karen: Well, we don't have children yet, but I doubt I will change on this issue.

Jonathon: I'm just sorry that we can't share certain kinds of rituals, because I know we agree on the bigger issues.

Karen: You're right. We do agree on the larger things, but I can't find a way to incorporate a lot of traditional Jewish beliefs that are sexist. I have to find some new slant on them.

Jonathon: I'm sympathetic to your feminism, but I would just like to put a word in for greater sharing.

This discussion led to Karen and Jonathon's talking more specifically about what they could do together. In the end, they both felt closer, and deeply touched by the search they would be making together for a form of spiritual practice that would suit both of them and connect them to the tradition that they both held to be central to their lives.

Some couples like Pamela and Charles have a long history of church attendance, but little sharing of spiritual beliefs. Once in a therapy session, Pamela asked Charles if he would talk about his spiritual beliefs, and he answered, "No." That concluded her foray into his beliefs. If couples can have effective dialogues about their spiritual beliefs, they usually discover an increased trust and intimacy.

Beliefs about dying and death are especially important for couples to share, respecting each other's views. If a couple stay together throughout most of the lifespan, they will likely encounter death together and can develop greater intimacy, respect, and understanding for each other in this encounter.

Sustaining a partner through the death of a parent can be a door opening to deepened appreciation of closeness, or a door closing on trust. Many women I have seen in individual psychotherapy have confessed particularly deep resentment and anger at their spouses for having neglected to be present or involved in the women's experiences with death, especially of a parent or sibling. In confronting a woman's projection of the Terrible Father or Hero (or the Lost Child, the flip side of the complex) onto her husband, I have noticed how strongly her defenses are organized to keep her seeing her partner only through a negative lens. "He should have *known* I needed his help when my mother was dying. I was with her constantly, and always exhausted. Why didn't he just help me out?" During a death crisis, many people anticipate that a partner will automatically perceive the dependence needs that the other feels. Often the other partner is also anxious and afraid—perhaps unfamiliar with death. It is very important that the person in need speak up and ask for what is needed. If a couple have not talked intimately about spiritual beliefs, and especially about death, then the crisis provides an opportunity to do so. If none of these issues has been opened, it may be difficult for a couple to come through the crisis and continue to trust their relationship. For this reason among many others, couples should attempt to have dialogues about their spiritual beliefs, especially in regard to death. What happens when one partner clams up, as Charles did with Pamela? Ideally the inquiring partner will go past these resistances by asking another question—such as "You don't seem to want to talk with me about these things—why?" If this reaches a dead end also, the next statement can be something like "I know this is an important issue for us and so I'd like to plan with you to set aside time to talk about it. When would you like do that?"

As I said above, I don't often hear major conflicts about religious beliefs in couple therapy. When I have heard serious, deep, and unresolvable conflicts (for example, between a partner who is an adamant rational atheist and another who has a new-age spiritual belief in the power of the goddess—a true case), an eventual separation has ensued. The few times we have met with couples who presented deep contradictory beliefs of a religious nature, those couples have eventually broken up. I am referring here to attitudes toward "religio" that are truly incompatible, not expressions of different religious traditions as I described above. It seems almost impossible for a couple to sustain highly contrasting beliefs about what is powerfully true and meaningful about human life. When partners are widely divergent in these beliefs, so many areas of life are laced with conflict, distrust, and opposing views of reality that they cannot bridge the gap.

Most couples have the same fundamental religious beliefs. Where there are differences in traditions, I have found that these differences are either benign or uncontested (the atheist and the Christian who don't try to convince each other, but share a common ground of humanism). The particular differences of spiritual beliefs are the ones that are often most important for couples to explore. Spiritual differences are similar to different preferences for leisure time: They need to be aired. As couples talk about the differences that connect them to preferences for diet, reference groups, charitable works, and beliefs about death, partners deepen their knowledge and intimate ties.

In some areas this involves taking back dream lover projections. For example, Jonathon will have to reconcile himself to the fact that Karen will not carry out his vision of the Great Mother in keeping a kosher home and traditional holiday celebrations. This may simply mean recognizing a sadness about it, or Jonathon may want to spend some holidays with his family of origin, inviting Karen to come along. If she chooses not to go, they will have to talk out thoroughly the reasons for being separate, as well as being quite reassuring about their love for each other.

Separate activities during leisure time, especially religious or spiritual ones, can threaten trust and stability. The overall sense of being friends or companions is the target to keep an eye on. When one partner begins to feel that the relationship does not provide enough "companionship" or friendship, both partners need to be alert to this symptom of possible dissatisfaction. As I've said several times throughout the chapter, marital satisfaction and stability are strongly linked to a sense of successful companionship for contemporary couples.

tolerable differences

The integration of dream lovers and the development of a relational self take place in an atmosphere of equality and trust. As we saw in the last chapter, equality may mean "equal influence" rather than equal income or sameness. Trust is a belief in the ability of both partners to sustain a shared horizon of meaning and honesty between them. Trust builds gradually through the process of handling conflicts without enacting dominance-submission and aggression. Trust is the product of airing differences and finding a way to work with them.

In the use of leisure time, how much difference can be tolerated without its being a threat to trust? I don't know a formula for determining this, but I believe the key issue is the capacity of each person to understand and accept the other's point of view. In other words, the partners do not have to agree or necessarily find a common ground, but they have to be able to understand and accept the other's view as valid for the other. For example, Larry does not like to attend church on Sundays with Louise. He and Louise have talked about this and she accepts the fact that Larry does not like organized religious ceremonies—and that he has private rituals of prayer and meditation that serve him better. For his part, Larry respects Louise in her desire to belong to a community of worship; he neither denigrates nor devalues Louise for this more traditional desire. Together Larry and Louise talk about their spiritual and religious beliefs. They enjoy hearing from each other the experiences and insights achieved through their different and separate means.

Although Patty and Joe go to church together, they spend a lot of weekend time separately. This is especially hard for Patty because she much prefers Joe's companionship to doing things alone or with her women friends. Patty enjoys attending workshops on self-improvement and various educational activities sponsored by community organizations. Joe prefers to watch sports on TV or outdoors. After Patty and Joe spend time separately, they plan ahead to have the evening or at least a couple of hours together. During this time they can trade stories and learn about each other's viewpoints. They can also share hugs and kisses that solidify their feelings of affection and appreciation for each other. This is important because they could become resentful of the differences in their preferred activities. As it is, they are able to deal with differences supportively, but if they had even fewer activities to share they would probably move over into the area of dissatisfaction. Going to church, to their children's school events, out to dinner, and to movies are the baseline that allows them to trust each other.

Karen and Jonathon spend almost all of their free time together. Because they have so many interests in common (tennis, movies, aerobic exercise, antique collecting), they can easily commit themselves to a lot of joint activities. Is there any problem with a couple spending most or even all of their leisure time together? From what I see in therapy and the research, I would say no. As long as the couple handle differences well, negotiating the particulars of an activity, it seems that spending leisure time together enhances feelings of closeness and trust. If partners attempt to fuse into each other and simply imagine that they are always enjoying exactly the same things (through projection), then there is a problem of avoiding differences. If partners are constantly competitive in their shared activities, then there is a problem with power struggle (and usually parental projections). But if partners simply have most preferences in common and spend time working out their individual differences, then a lot of sharing is a great blessing.

Differences in leisure preferences can be serious difficulties for any couple. Heterosexual couples, in particular, are at risk for being pulled apart by the kinds of gender-related differences that our survey described—debates about television watching, different conversational styles, different commitments to self-improvement. Early in a relationship, during the romance stage, partners are usually eager to accommodate to each other. During this time, preferences for shared leisure are usually high. Ideal dream lovers are fully projected, and both partners may believe they have found a soul mate. When the romance is over and disillusionment begins, partners begin to move away from shared activities as they project negative dream lovers and fear they have fallen into a wrong relationship. At this time, leisure preferences can interfere with trust. Angry and belligerent defenses around one's leisure preferences can disrupt conversations and prevent true dialogue. If she is annoyed by television watching and he refuses even to discuss the matter with her—and proceeds to watch the evening news during dinner each night—then there's going to be a lot of resentment and neglect associated with TV for her. If he is annoyed by "idle chatter" and she is unwilling even to find out what he means by the term, but indignantly goes on talking to him no matter what he requests, then he will probably resort to power moves. He'll ignore her and send her nonverbal signals (for example, looking away) when she tries to talk with him at times when he's distracted or too busy to listen.

Because they are a heterosexual couple, the partners might believe (as I discussed in Chapter 1) that togetherness should "just come naturally." When it doesn't and they are both feeling resentful about their differences, they are likely to decide that there are some deep dissatisfactions in this partnership. At this point, every preferred difference or disagreement can become a "sign" that something is "wrong." Rather than find out what is held in common that could form a bridge between them, partners caught in disillusionment will instead find every possible opportunity to project a negative dream lover (particularly a negative parental one) and "prove" that the other person is an unsatisfying, even wrong, partner. My clinical experience with disillusionment and negative projections fits well with the research findings on leisure time: that couples who spend a lot of leisure time apart (too much by some norm or evaluation) report being dissatisfied with their relationships. They feel resentful and neglected about the absence of the spouse.

In this chapter and elsewhere, I have tried to stress the importance of airing differences and negotiating solutions—either compromises or agreements to differ. The best possible outcome of disillusionment is a continuing ability to remain close friends and companions. The greater the agreement about leisure time, the better. When no agreement can be reached because of differences in preferences, circadian rhythms, work schedules, and the like, then differences must be made tolerable through understanding and reassurance. Most couples have some differences regarding the use of leisure time. They find those differences to be tolerable and even meaningful when they can make them an ongoing part of their shared meaning system. In the next chapter I will talk in more depth about this shared meaning system as a "fusion of horizons" between partners, as it permits differences within an atmosphere of trust.

chapter 8

healing the gender split

Before I even knew that I would write this book, the title for this chapter popped into my mind. My first reaction to it was to think, "How grandiose!" My second reaction was to consider seriously what might be cautiously hopeful about the possibility of the two sexes' trusting each other. For the first time in recorded history, I reminded myself, men and women are able to have a dialogue with each other, a conversation in which each speaker has a point of view (a legitimate voice) and is constrained to respect and understand the other. The recent wave of feminism has made this possible.

Feminism has made us all conscious of the meaning of gender. This new consciousness has awakened men as well as women. The effects of gender stereotypes are inhibiting and limiting for both sexes. The stories we tell ourselves about how men and women "should" be and behave have consequences for everyone's self-esteem, self-confidence, and satisfactions in life.

With increased consciousness of the negative effects of trivializing and silencing women, some men want to explore the conscious and unconscious implications of their dominance of others. The impulse to silence, trivialize, or resist female people is based not only on a desire for control or status but also on men's strange gender—their fantasies and fears about the opposite sex. Women also have erected barriers against understanding men, barriers that are made of female strange gender. Throughout this book I have emphasized the responsibility of both sexes for coming to terms with the implications of strange gender, for claiming and actively integrating the wishes, fears, ideals, and envy that are aspects of the Others within. Awareness and responsibility for strange gender can carry over into the larger world as well.

Some contemporary men's movements are consciousness-raising groups that look into the implications of male dominance. Men gather to reflect on dominance attitudes and unearned privileges that affect women and themselves in sometimes subtle, but always powerful ways. I heard recently from my friend and colleague, Jungian analyst Andrew Samuels, that a meeting of Men Against Sexism in England voted that men should not move into the newly established arena of gender studies until women have established themselves there. Although this specialty has been founded through women's efforts, it would be easy for men to become the "experts." Such conscious limitation of male privilege by men themselves is a direct alignment with the aim of equality between the sexes.

This kind of alignment often emerges from the benefits of equal influence in a heterosexual partnership. Male partners align themselves against unearned male privilege because they relish the joys, benefits, and erotic desires that emerge from heterosexual trust. Female partners align themselves against submission and silence (and for their own sovereignty) in relating to men because women also become alert to the fact that taking responsibility for their own lives leads to greater pleasure in relationships. Resentment, bitterness, and fear of each other dry up with the love for mature dependence. Women and men line up together with attitudes and possibilities for shared power between the sexes, in terms of decision making in sex, money, parenting, and leisure in private life, and shared influence in public life.

My own cautious optimism about heterosexual trust has been bred in dialogue therapy and through a growing awareness of our planetary crisis of overpopulation and depletion of resources. This crisis will force the end of dominance-submission or the end of our species, I would guess. Since we are a highly adaptive species, I believe that we will (even unintentionally) seek to establish new forms of relationship among ourselves and with the environment to preserve the species. The question is whether we can do so quickly enough to support our continuing psychological development—or whether we will be thrown back to more primitive survival standards through a massive crisis such as another major war or a disease epidemic (as AIDS already threatens to become).

Throughout the book I have alluded to a number of problems or barriers to heterosexual trust that make sexual equality a hard-to-imagine goal. I want to state them clearly here in summing up my perspective.

Barriers to Trust

1. The division of the human community into two exclusive groups (creating the sense of "opposites" both outside and within ourselves)
2. The differences of meaning, role, power, and privilege assigned by societies to each group
3. The resulting envy, idealization, and fear that fuel psychological complexes of dream lovers—complexes that mix stereotypes with archetypal image traces of our earliest dependent relationships
4. The projection of our dream lovers onto the opposite sex and the continuing stereotyping of them by ourselves and our same-sex peers
5. The resulting gender differences in interactive styles and power strategies that intensify stereotypes of "opposites" that are "naturally different" in human life

I believe we should neither silence nor dismiss gender differences (as if we could operate on a "no-differences" model), nor rigidify our categories by believing in "basic human differences" of biology or physical endowment in the two sexes.

Instead, let us describe and *examine* the differences we experience in our lives as female and male people, and try to understand how these differences arise: whether they come from projections of strange gender, socialization into a specific gender, or the sexual aspects of embodiment.

When women and men have joined together in conversations, dialogues, and studies of these lived differences, we may gradually come to sort out what the actual *limitations* might be for each sex, and what they might mean. Biological limitations of male and female bodies are "obvious" in terms of body functions and structures, but what these differences actually *mean* in terms of human character is not yet understood. We cannot understand the limitations of gender and sexuality without reclaiming dream lovers, our strange gender that has developed within our subjective experience. Strange gender completes each sex by expanding the categories that were originally called "self" and reclaiming identity that was originally named "other."

As a person who is committed to mutuality and reciprocity in human relationships, I have a strong commitment to sexual equality. By equality, I neither mean sameness nor fifty-fifty splits of resources and tasks. I mean equal influence and respect for everyone's sovereignty and rights. In some societies, like North American ones, these rights are individual and depend on individual responsibility. In other societies, these rights are more communal and shared. Whatever the design of the person, I endorse the equality of basic human rights and privileges (however these may be conceived in a particular society) among sexes and races.

In order for such a lofty goal to become practical, people would have to want it desperately. Sexual equality would fundamentally disrupt all of our current social and economic systems—and create chaotic transformations over a long period of time. In my view, the contemporary "unnatural" search for intimacy among heterosexual couples is a sign that people desire sexual equality in a new way, a way that may even be unconscious in any particular individual.

When I see that feminism has made this longing possible (in our society and others like it), I feel a surge of hope that our ongoing investments in human equality and shared relationships are bearing fruit even in my lifetime. As a feminist who is also a lover of men, and empathic with men, I have sometimes been challenged about my beliefs. Acknowledging injustices and oppression in the lives of women—recognizing a diversity of class and racial forms of suffering among women—I also ally myself with possibilities of development for both sexes. Both women and men have questioned me about this.

Where is my anger about inequality? Do I feel a conflict between my love for (and loyalty to) women and my love for men? When I say I am a feminist, am I saying something about blaming men? The fact is that I gave up blaming people even before I became a self-acknowledged feminist (before Shirley Chisholm ran for president in 1972, if you can remember that). I do not blame either sex for the social and political system we have inherited. I hold people responsible for what is under their control and dominion, not for what falls outside. In a fundamental way I hold all conscious adults to be responsible for their subjective states—emotions and actions. Some adults have self-awareness and can bring themselves under control through reflection. Others operate according to rules and traditions and bring themselves under control according to their traditions. (Even if I disagree with a particular tradition, I cannot blame an individual for carrying it out, especially if that person has no commitment to self-awareness.)

Naturally I try to spread "enlightenment" about sexual equality whenever I can, but not everyone is prepared to receive it—and I have no feelings of blame about that. Overall, I feel little inconsistency in being a feminist and a lover of men. In certain circumstances, as I describe below, I can be frustrated and irritated with men's prejudices and unconsciousness. I can feel the same way about women.

Dream lovers are projected by both sexes; stereotypes and prejudices are shared among us and are not the exclusive property of men. It is predictable that in every public lecture I give on feminism (no matter on what application, even one that is *equally* relevant to men), some women will "protect" men's feelings by implying that men are Lost

Children (unable to speak for themselves about issues of gender identity) or Great Fathers (only doing their jobs) or Heroes (the "new" wonders of caring fathers who want to share the housework). These are women's dream lovers, used as stereotypes about the "poor men" to mask whatever feeling a woman doesn't want to express (anger? fear?). I have never heard a man "protect" women's feelings in any lecture on masculinity or fathering that I've attended.

I've said many times throughout these chapters that people use dream lovers to reinforce stereotypes and also use stereotypes to reinforce dream lovers. We haven't yet reached a point at which we routinely and simply ask each other a question rather than assume that we know what is going on with a person of the opposite sex. When we do, many of our stereotypes will change as we discover that our dream lovers are inaccurate readings of others. In the meantime, I hold both sexes responsible for stereotypes, and I don't blame anyone for lack of self-awareness until that person is acquainted with gender meanings in a way that allows for reclaiming dream lovers.

Much of the time, I can sort through my own subjective states and see what is a dream lover (or stereotype) and what is an accurate reading of a male person (based on what that person has told me or, in some cases, how he has acted). Most of the time, I retain a cautious optimism about possibilities for heterosexual trust. Sometimes I lose it.

differences and common ground

Recently I was confronted with two different public situations that illustrate the range of my fears and hope. I present them here as examples of squelching and expanding my cautious optimism about partnerships between men and women. The first was a conference of executives from all over the world. In attendance were about forty-five top officials, heads of corporations, and administrators in government. Only three or four were women executives, although most of the men's wives were in attendance—for my presentation. I had been invited, among many other speakers, to present my thoughts and ideas about gender differences as part of a management development program. The people inviting me had encouraged me to speak about my current work and to anticipate friendly, informal conversation and discussion.

I presented a talk about "gender differences in relationships." For about an hour I held forth, giving definitions of gender and sex and talking about power, privilege, envy, and interactional styles as they affect our relating. I spoke briefly about dream lovers. I spoke at length about the differences in self-esteem between girls and boys in adolescence. I talked about the importance of changing institutions (in education, government, and elsewhere) so that our daughters, as well as our sons, can feel empowered to contribute to our future. Throughout the talk, I thought I was being reasonable, balanced, informative, and even occasionally funny and entertaining. I noticed that only a few women (and the people who had invited me) laughed at my jokes. When the time arrived for discussion, first a woman executive asked me a kind question about early development of gender and effects on self-esteem. After I answered her, a raft of men spoke out—mostly giving me mini-lectures, sometimes asking questions. Although they came from countries as diverse as Korea, the Netherlands, Japan, and the United States, they delivered a similar message: Women are pretty well off now; let the differences between the sexes stand and let's be happy about them; women are not serious about taking more responsibility; and who will take care of the children if everyone goes out to work?

These were responses I remembered from my first lectures about feminism to mixed groups of men and women in the mid-1970s. Now again, in the early 1990s, some men were hostile and accusatory (charging that I was "trying to turn women into men") while others were patronizing and relatively pleasant (lecturing me on the virtues of traditional differences). I spoke up and out in response to each man, and grew less popular as I did so. One man invited the "spouses to speak," but none of them did. One female executive, a beautiful dark woman from India, spoke out passionately about how cruel and difficult her life as a corporate leader (and a woman of color) had often been. She talked about the double bind of needing to be strong and tough in order to be a leader, and then being criticized as a "bitch" because she showed these qualities, and being overridden if she was more compliant and open. She spoke of her strong commitment to her own goals over the years, and her current fear that she might surrender everything that she had achieved to have greater peace of mind. I was grateful for and quite moved by her comments, but the men in the audience went on as though she had not spoken.

I had sat through almost an hour of this assault, with no real attention given to the information I had presented (no questions about it or desire to explore it), when one man spoke favorably about my opposition to biological explanations of gender. I thanked him and felt relieved that a man had spoken sympathetically, because I thought perhaps now other men would take seriously what I had presented. Instead, the attack continued with an Asian man alluding to "robots" taking care of our future children (because women would be out working), as though men and women together would be incapable of coming up with another solution for child care, and therefore sexual equality would doom us forever. Near the end a man asked the question, "If you emphasize differences and diversity so much, what is our common ground? Why can't we talk about how we are alike as human beings?" Because I was so exhausted, I just allowed an answer to roll off my tongue without much thought (what I see as my Underground Genius speaking up): "The common ground between us is our shared aim or goal—intimacy as a couple, cooperation on a project, or collaboration in work. Our common ground is what we honestly and openly share. We don't have to find our similarities in order to have a common ground." I felt relieved at this answer. It said something to me about what was happening: I had no common ground with most of the men present. They did not share my dreams of equality, nor did we have a project in common. Consequently they had used me as a target for their projections about "feminism" or about the uninformed, naïve Maiden Lover. The final questioner asked haughtily, "*What* do you envision as the future *relationship* between men and women?" When I answered simply "Partnership," he said (as if to inform me of my naïveté), "Do you think that *men* have *partnership* with each other?" and I responded, "No." I intended to convey that women might add something new to the equation of relationship, but I think my intention went unnoticed.

By the end of the talk I could feel the polarization in the room: Many of the "spouses" (all women) were in sympathy with me although they had said nothing, other women were openly sympathetic after the confrontation ended (rushing to the front of the room to congratulate me for my courage), and most of the men were hostile (with a few exceptions among the men who had invited me). Because of my ultimate goals of heterosexual trust and sexual equality, I deeply dislike polarizing a group along the gender split. I knew that this group was badly divided, but there was little I could do because we had no common ground, no dialogue, no give-and-take. Although I had been invited for my expertise on gender and relationship, most of the male audience did not want to consult with me. They preferred to project their dream lovers and teach me a thing or two. I was frustrated and angry. Why had I been invited and asked to prepare a presentation if no one would believe me? Why was my expertise so belittled?

While I was still pondering this, I had to present another paper—on "gender and individuation" at a conference on Jungian psychology two weeks later. This time I went in well defended, even armored, against what I anticipated might be attacks from the men in the audience. The audience (of about sixty people) was perhaps one-third male and I had no idea what their backgrounds might be. Surveying them briefly I could see that they were mostly middle aged and older, and I thought perhaps they had accompanied their wives for this day of presentations on the Jungian theory of individuation. I imagined they might find my commentary on gender irrelevant or irritating.

It turned out to be quite the contrary. What I encountered this time was support, encouragement, and empathy from every man who spoke, and the several men who surrounded me at lunch. When I talked about the importance of respecting differences, the men especially liked the idea that they would be respected and accepted in their own language and interactional styles. When I talked about self-esteem issues, they listened carefully and seemed to understand how internalized inferiority is a special problem for women, (not to dismiss the self-esteem problems of men, but simply to note that low self-esteem exists among a larger percentage of women than men). In my afternoon workshop and at lunch, what I discovered was that I shared a common ground with these men: They too wanted heterosexual equality and intimacy. They had themselves experienced belittlement and negative projections from their partners. Feelings of humiliation and distrust had been signals to them that their relationships could not work well if their female partners saw them as Lost Children (failed Heroes) or Terrible Fathers.

At this second conference, my expertise and information were used and discussed. I was received as a resource for ideas and information about heterosexual relating. My topic was specifically "individuation" through heterosexual intimacy in middle and later life, but most people seemed more interested in heterosexual intimacy than individuation. These people seemed already to know that intimacy leads to development. They wanted to know more about how to reach and sustain intimacy.

These two audiences were coming for very different purposes. The corporate executives had been sponsored by their corporations. The goal of the overall five-week program was "development," but I doubt that most of them had envisioned this as a process of psychological development—and certainly not development of gender consciousness. The participants at the Jungian conference were mostly nonclinicians, but they had come because they knew something about Jung's idea of individuation—the development of the "totality" of the personality. When I talked about reclaiming dream lovers and expanding one's sense of self through knowledge of one's unconscious wishes, fears, and motives, the audience was with me. We had a common ground in the goals of individuation and the method of dialogue. My advocacy of heterosexual intimacy and mature dependence was received with interest and curiosity. Men especially seemed to respect and understand it. Several of them asked what I thought about the idea of securing one's identity as an individual prior to forming an intimate relationship, as recommended in Sam Keen's recent book on masculinity.

I shared with them my belief that men and women have a radical new opportunity at this historical moment. It is an opportunity to do something that has never before been possible: to depend on each other for "mirroring transformations:" By this term I mean the reflections offered and the boundaries clarified of the self in intimate relationship. In my view, the dyadic relationship (two people in dialogue) is *the* relationship of human development, from early attachment bonds to dyads of student-teacher, client-therapist, and adult partners. Adult partners have the added advantage of commitment, history, and a lot of common ground. I believe that adults can accomplish their identity searches *within* intimate partnership, although any of us may need and benefit from psychotherapy, counseling, or other developmental resources along the way. Consciousness-raising groups can be helpful in aligning us with the goal of sexual equality, but they do not provide the necessary tools for intimacy with the opposite sex.

When people go off into same-sex groups, they are not confronted with the kind of tension and conflict that occurs between the sexes, especially between intimate partners. I know from my work with couples, and from research on gender identity, that being with the opposite sex is a different kind of encounter from being with one's own sex. It requires different skills and knowledge. As psychologist Eleanor Maccoby concluded after twenty-five years of research on gender differences, the two sexes behave differently when they are with each other and when they are among themselves. A person has many identities and many personalities. We practice different ones with different people.

Before beginning this book, I was much influenced by a German philosopher named Hans-Georg Gadamer in his conception of the "fusion of horizons," the ground of shared understanding. Gadamer's aim in his book on interpretation is to discover how a reader has access to the meaning of a text. Meaning is slightly different for each reader—and also different in various periods of time (and thus different from the author's original intention). How is a text understood by new readers or new interpreters when its meaning is always contextualized in immediate experience? Gadamer's interest in texts and their meanings attracted me as a way of seeing what might be taking place in a dialogue when people hold different views of the same issue (interpreting some "text" differently) but trust that somehow they will reach a new understanding, a new fusion of their horizons.

Gadamer claims that any particular interpretation can never be "the correct one" because the context (the assumptions, attitudes, and beliefs) in which a text is understood changes over time. Each new understanding corresponds to the context in which it occurs. A "fusion of horizons" is anyone's ability to reach a common ground between the text and a context so one finds a meaning that is relevant to the present moment. For example, contemporary critics continue to make new interpretations of ancient plays (Greek or Shakespearean usually) that add new meanings to our understanding of the plays. These are not "better" or "truer" interpretations. They simply link the play to our own context in some new way. And yet they are still interpretations of the same ancient play. The interpreter has discovered a new bridge that links the play (and all that it has traditionally meant) with the present.

In a dialogue we develop a fusion of horizons when we realize that no one particular view—yours or mine—is the "correct one" or the "true one." Each new statement, each viewpoint, is shaped by a speaker's current context and the shared aim of the dialogue. The outcome is surprise and discovery. We find a bridge that links our two interpretations and gives us new meaning. The speakers have discovered a meaning that neither could have anticipated alone. Witnessing this kind of fusion of horizons between a woman and a man (in one's own partnership) gradually opens the way to less defensiveness about the rightness of one's own view.

In an intimate relationship, partners come to trust the fusion of horizons over time. They trust the discovery of new meanings—new fusions—from engaging in dialogue, even in conflict. Dialogue itself becomes a common ground, an always-compelling emergent horizon between the speakers. Dialogue is especially useful for claiming and disclaiming projections of dream lovers, but it is also useful for all kinds of decision making and brainstorming.

In order for speakers to trust in a fusion, they must recognize that neither of them is "right" or has the final word. Together they will find an outcome that is unanticipated. In reclaiming dream lovers, dialogue between partners often leads to an expansion of the self, not simply new insight but a new compass of subjective possibilities.

cautious optimism

Throughout these chapters, I have traced the process of development through dialogue and reclaiming strange gender. In this chapter, I will put finishing touches on this process by looking with you at our four couples in the sixth session of dialogue therapy. As I explained in Chapter 1, the sixth of the two-hour sessions is the "completion session" for most couples who enter dialogue therapy. Because the sessions are about a month apart, couples have completed about six months of a transformation process, using dialogue to increase empathy and differentiation. A follow-up session occurs six months after the completion session. The follow-up gives the couple and the therapists an opportunity to check on the achievements of the therapy. Have they held up over time? If so, then the couple has completed the therapeutic process. If not, then another round of dialogue therapy (either three or six sessions) will be scheduled. Couples are also encouraged to return for consultation sessions if they need to do so, over the years.

When I talked about the steps from disillusionment to mature dependence back in Chapter 3, I noted that the second step, reclaiming dream lovers, was complex and involved a lot of development. I broke this step out into seven subparts as a way of clarifying what takes place within an individual. (Those seven steps are listed again below after the vignette of Patty and Joe.) Reclaiming aspects of the self that were originally (in infancy, childhood, or adolescence) discarded from conscious awareness because they were too overwhelming, or required extraordinary courage and responsibility, is a mighty feat. Dialogue therapy and dialogue in the relationship are a means of confronting oneself with hidden fears, ideals, wishes, and envy. Gradually one comes to know and accept strange gender in its diverse forms. After partners have reclaimed and understood their own dream lovers, then they are able to disclaim (resist) the projections of other dream lovers as not-self, saying either silently or aloud, "No thanks, that's not me." This discrimination between one's own dream lovers (always somewhat unconscious) and projections of another's dream lovers is a difficult judgment call. And yet each of us is responsible for making it after we have become self-aware. For myself, I certainly don't want to be the carrier of unwanted or underdeveloped aspects of my husband's personality if I can help it. He doesn't want mine either. Patty and Joe completed dialogue therapy with an acceptance of Patty's Terrible Father complex as an ongoing vulnerability in her personality—a tendency to make and expect aggressive attacks and harsh criticisms.

patty and joe

In this final session of dialogue therapy, Patty was a little weepy (her eyes a bit swollen) as she told Joe what she felt was the greatest change in herself as a result of their development together.

Patty: I know now what a really aggressive person I can be. It's not the way I want to be, but I can be cruel—and I have been in attacking and criticizing you for things that are really small. Although I have been afraid of you, afraid that you would hurt me like my father did, I have often been the one doing the hurting. I wonder if you can forgive me.

Joe: You want forgiveness for attacking me because you were acting like your father acted sometimes? (Patty nods.) Yeah, I really do forgive you because now I understand how terrifying it was when your dad went into rages at you. I know that you might never get over the damage he did. I can't say that I'm pleased about that, but I accept it as part of you.

Patty and Joe went on to talk about how Joe had put so much pressure on Patty to "be happy" when he saw her as his Maiden Lover. He had wanted her to have this "wonderful life" with him and to be grateful always for "all the things" he provided. Now he saw that he had to find that sense of joy inside of himself and not look to Patty to provide it.

Joe had begun to recognize that Patty was likely to be periodically somewhat depressed when she failed to reach her goals or when she felt in any way out of control. These would be occasions when her Terrible Father might attack internally and when she needed all of her psychic resources to control her own subjective states. Patty asked him just to accept these mood changes and to try to have an openness in hearing about her fears, because then her depressed feelings might change into gratitude, warmth, and appreciation. Joe agreed.

For his part, Joe had begun to feel himself to be more capable of taking the initiative to have fun and relax, especially with the family. Because Joe had had a tendency toward passive entertainment (watching TV or sports), he had often looked to the environment to make him "feel good." He had initially hoped that Patty would do that.

When she didn't and then criticized him, Joe would fight her as though she were his Terrible Mother—suffocating, demanding, overwhelming him with negativity. Even though Joe's mother had herself been quite a critic (mostly about cleanliness and household chores), Joe had had a secure attachment relationship with her and his father. Joe saw now that he had within him relational strengths (hopefulness, belief, and trust) that Patty had never had. Although this saddened him a little, Joe could see that he needed to take more of the initiative for relational pleasure and sharing fun times with Patty and his children.

Similarly Joe wanted to "let go" of his image of Patty as critic. He asked her simply to accept his way of talking and parenting and not to give him any more feedback unless he specifically asked for it.

Joe: I don't want to hear anything about how I talk or the words I use unless I ask your advice. Got that?

Patty: Yeah, it's pretty clear. I guess I thought I was already doing that because I try hard—

Patty (Double): How is it that I still seem to be giving you advice?

Joe: Sometimes you repeat what I've said to the kids and change some of the words to sound more like your words, you know what I mean?

Patty: (*Laughing*) You're right! I didn't even notice that because I guess I thought I knew the "right way" to discipline our kids. You're right, I'll let your words stand from now on. Is there anything else that bothers you about my feedback?

Joe: Just one other thing. You still don't thank me for my cooking. You don't have to compliment it, but I'd like you to say you appreciate it after you eat.

Patty: I apologize. I promise that I'll keep it in mind, but I wonder if you could just ask for a "thank you" if I forget.

At first Joe balked at this because he thought that his asking discredited the meaning of "thank you." My husband explained to him that Patty's resistant relational self and her negative parental dream lovers all mediate against her feelings of gratitude. Even though Patty wants to appreciate Joe, sometimes she will forget. Reminding her takes nothing away from her appreciation. It's just a reminder to become self-aware. She already has the motivation to feel grateful.

Patty also had opened up to her own Heroic strivings and her desire to "be somebody." She could see that she had ambition and motivation that Joe did not have and would never develop. When Patty felt anxious about her own achievements, she no longer criticized Joe for his "lack." Instead she asked for support from Joe when she was afraid.

Patty: You know that I'm studying for finals now?

Joe: No, actually I didn't. When do they start?

Patty: Not for two weeks, but I need a lot of time because I have to cope with my own anxiety that tends to operate by me having to do a lot of note cards and stuff. When I get all my cards done and in order, I feel a lot better. In the meantime, I'd really like your support, just by reassuring me that I'm smart enough and stuff.

Joe: I'm willing to do that if you don't just clam up every night and go to the library. I guess I need something back from you.

Patty: Like what?

Joe: Like a hug or a kiss, a little affection.

Patty: Okay. I can do that.

We were aware that Joe's envy of Patty's intelligence and ambition was still active. There's not much we can do about envy in couple therapy. Joe was not in individual psychotherapy and there was little opportunity for him to deal directly with his own more primitive emotions.

As I have said throughout, the best way to transform envy is through experiencing and acknowledging one's own resources. Joe was beginning to do this in his parenting and cooking skills, and now in his newfound initiative for planning fun times for the family. We hoped that eventually Joe might find a creative outlet for himself. It would need to be something that could make the link between his intelligence and his personal creative expression. In the meantime, Joe still felt good about his job at the food-processing plant. He was popular and effective and drew a lot of self-confidence from his co-workers' support.

By the sixth session, Joe and Patty were quite good at dialogue, even about difficult topics such as their lovemaking routines. They now had two nights a week set aside for lovemaking, and they had discovered a number of things that made these occasions pleasurable for Patty. Joe always enjoyed himself. Creating the "right mood" with candles and incense helped Patty, and she was more and more comfortable guiding Joe to help her achieve orgasm. Patty appeared to feel her own fears and vulnerabilities more directly now, and to ask Joe for support, instead of attacking him for his shortcomings.

Together they appreciated their children and were able to exchange points of view on parenting without a lot of distress. What marked them as a couple in this last session was the special attention and concern for Patty's vulnerabilities. Patty was facing dark feelings in herself, both her tendencies to attack others in moments of fear and her lack of trust in intimate bonds. Joe could see Patty more realistically now—in terms of her strengths of ambition, courage, and intelligence *and* her weaknesses of fears, aggression, and dread. He no longer looked forward to Patty's feeling "really happy" or even especially content. He realized that she would always be limited in her ability to feel trust and happiness within a close relationship. Patty also admired and appreciated Joe for his ability to reassure her, and to carry a secure sense of hope for their future when she felt despairing.

* * *

Mostly, I find that couples retain the changes they have made in dialogue therapy. Reclaiming dream lovers and suffering the expansion of oneself through recognition of fear, idealization, wishes, envy, and responsibility (which had previously been thought to belong to one's partner) means literally changing one's gender. One is no longer simply a woman or a man. Now one has expanded to include dream lovers and the possibilities and limitations these excluded Others bring. This results in a shift in subjectivity. One is more able to look through different lenses at experience and to see that one's own motives and meanings are difficult to track. With this recognition in hand, one has less of a tendency to try to bring another under control; it's difficult enough to keep track of oneself.

Before looking at the other three couples in their sixth session of dialogue therapy, I want to list again the specific steps in reclaiming dream lovers so that they can be kept clearly in mind as we listen to these couples for the last time.

Reclaiming Dream Lovers

- Seeing how early attachment patterns carry over to current relating: Am I secure, resistant, or avoidant when it comes to this or that relationship?
- Discovering one's major dream lovers by examining the fears, ideals, and wishes one feels for one's partner
- Knowing how one's dream lovers fit with parents' lived and unlived lives, hopes, and dreams
- Taking responsibility for one's subjective states: dream lovers and other complexes
- Claiming one's desires, ideals, wishes, fears, aggression, jealousy, and envy by actively changing to make them one's own
- Acknowledging the hurts one has caused in the past by projecting all of the above onto one's partner or others
- Putting into action one's strange gender in some way that keeps it a conscious part of oneself

It is through the process of effective dialogue that these steps are taken. Effective dialogue begins with the experience of a vulnerable self and the acceptance of an attachment relationship as the foundation of the self.

In dialogue therapy and my own life, I have come to believe that heterosexual intimacy is a goal that can be achieved. Men and women can learn to understand, respect, and sustain each other as maturely dependent, equal partners. Heterosexual intimacy does not solve the problem of inequality between the sexes, but it improves our overall ability to understand each other in all walks of life, and to find the means to cooperate on shared goals. For Patty and Joe, intimacy depends on their acceptance of each other and themselves, especially their weaknesses.

Does acceptance of another always depend on acceptance of oneself? In my view these two are intertwined in a spiraling interaction: When I witness my capacity to accept your weaknesses and failures, I am more open to accepting my own, and as I accept myself more fully, I am better able to accept yours. People and relationships change palpably through the reclaiming of dream lovers.

The particular change that is for me most moving is the shift in the way in which the gender story is told. Couples who trust in their fusion of horizons tell a hopeful story about the two sexes' relating. They describe themselves as "best friends" and say that their differences enhance their life together, even though they may be somewhat disruptive. They see themselves enlarged by each others' strengths and styles, and they can somehow imagine a future in which men and women would share in work and parenting in a way that brings equal privileges and equal power. In a sense they imagine a new world, one in which the sexes are equal.

larry and louise

When Larry and Louise walked through the door of the consulting room for their last session of dialogue therapy, we could hardly believe the sense of closeness they displayed. Larry opened the door for Louise and squeezed her hand a little before they sat down facing each other. When we asked them to talk about what they would like to accomplish in this last session, here is what they said:

Larry: I just want to thank you, Louise, for opening up to me emotionally and sexually. I know how hard it has been over the past months as you have remembered more and more of what happened with Uncle Rob, but I have never felt so close to you. Nor have I ever felt the respect that I now do. I just admire the work you've done in your own therapy and feel so hopeful about our life together. This almost makes me want to go into my own therapy.

Louise: Thank you too. I never thought I'd feel close to you again, and I guess I feel closer than ever.

Larry: Something that still bothers me, though, is how condescending I was for such a long time. I didn't believe that I was part of the problem between us. I tried to "fix" you because you reminded me of my depressed mother. I think I still may owe you an apology.

Louise: Yeah. I *was* tired of all your advice about my problems, but I can see that I played into it by complaining so much. When we were first married, I think I *wanted* you to fix me, but eventually I got out of that and then I just hated you every time you started preaching at me.

Larry: What can I say or do to apologize now?

Larry and Louise went on to a very useful dialogue about his desires to repair her and her anguish about wanting to be fixed or repaired. They spoke back and forth about their fears, wishes, and ideals for each other.

Louise's memory of incest with her uncle had revealed to all of us the reasons for her rigidity and defensiveness. Her tendency to appear as the "hag" to Larry's "hero" had faded entirely. In its place was a newfound courage and stability—an integration of her own Hero complex. She believed in herself in a new way, believed that she had the wherewithal to be more than she had been. She imagined a new career for herself and felt vitalized every time she shared the idea with Larry. Louise was thinking about going to graduate school in social work to become a psychotherapist.

Louise was comfortable now talking about how she had been critical and complaining in the past.

Louise: I realize now how much my father influenced me as a child. Because I put him on a pedestal and thought he was so intelligent and admirable I confused him with God. I always felt ashamed around my father as though I could never keep everything under control. When I complained about you in the past, I used the same contemptuous tone that he used with me. Do you know what I mean?

Larry: Sure I do. You sounded like you were my parent, like I was a stupid kid or something.

Louise: I'm afraid I felt that way too. Because you depended on me for a lot of domestic stuff—like laundry and meals—I imagined that you couldn't function without me organizing you. As though you needed a parent. I apologize for all of that. Now that I've backed out of the chores I resented, I see that you and the boys do fine without me.

Larry: I accept your apology.

Louise described how her feelings about Larry had shifted into the Lost Child side of the Hero complex when she began to feel helpless to control her own depression and bitterness. For years, she had managed her internal states by imagining that Larry was inferior to herself and her father. Although she didn't say so openly, she silently belittled any effort that Larry made to help her. (What did he know about the help she needed anyway? He wasn't able to do any of the things she needed help with and he wasn't the competent person her father had been—and so on) By belittling Larry and imagining him to be the Lost Child, she could cope better with her self-hatred and all of the rage and fear left from the incest trauma.

Now that Louise was conscious of this range of feelings connected to her past, she felt much better about being a homemaker and a wife. She commented on what fun it had been to plant their garden this spring, and how she now finds simple chores, like making the bed and doing the dishes, to be calming and relaxing. She was almost joyful in talking about how much more relaxed she feels with her sons. She no longer imagines they hate her.

Larry also felt better about himself as a father and homemaker. Letting go of his desire to fix his wife was quite liberating as he became more invested in being with his sons at home, and doing the chores that were part of everyday life. Even though Larry was now traveling a weekend per month in his new job, he felt more comfortable and happier with his home life. He recognized that when he and Louise began dialogue therapy, he had been unconsciously playing out the absent father role that his father had played. Now that he and Louise were able to relate fully on most issues in their lives, he found himself wanting more and more just to spend time with her and his sons at home.

Both Larry and Louise had come into marriage with resistant relational selves and so had not been able to feel direct security or ease in being dependent. Throughout the romance, Louise had played out the Maiden Lover to Larry's Great Father. They appeared to fit each other's ideal dream lovers. After they became parents and Larry competed with their sons for her attention, Louise changed her projection onto Larry, and imagined him either as the Lost Child (her failed Hero) or as the Terrible Father—critical and demanding that standards be met.

Larry still has not fully integrated his Maiden Lover, although he is beginning to feel a new vitality and creativity at home. He is contemplating a new hobby of stained-glass design. This kind of self-expression, in addition to the enthusiasm he now feels for his home life, might allow Larry to expand further his creative potential.

Since Louise remembered her abuse, it seems that Larry and Louise have gathered their forces in a mature dependence that is fostering new development in both of them. We believed that they had now provided a secure enough base in their relationship to develop selves that would be fully relational (secure relational selves). This is particularly fortunate because their teenage sons will soon be leaving home, and the parental couple will turn to their own attachment for the sense of continuity and pleasure that allows their family to go on.

Our culture is rife with unrealistic fantasies about romance in marriage. When these fantasies don't work out, some people believe that only an affair or divorce could alleviate the despair of disillusionment. Ideal dream lovers get projected onto a person outside. A good example of this attitude is found in journalist Dalma Heyn's book of interviews with American wives about their erotic lives, especially their extramarital affairs. Her reports, the stories told to her, are tales of passions squelched and identities lost through marriage. In her book about the "erotic silence" of American wives, Heyn offers no story in which the two sexes can be partners, friends, and lovers over time. Of course her aim is specifically to "expose" the underground erotic lives of American wives, but she fails to explain why she chose to locate eroticism exclusively in affairs. Her informants tell stories of "irresistible" and engrossing affairs with Mr. Underground Genius—the man who *appears* to be more erotic, passionate, inventive, and energetic than Mr. Nice Guy (read, failed Hero) at home. Unbeknownst to Heyn, the stories she encounters are tales of dream lovers, especially of the Genius, whom some married women imagine to be "out there" in the flesh (because the husband at home is stuck with the negative side of a dream lover complex, in some stage of disillusionment). In my view, it's a sad way to gain some version of sexual equality to have "equal affairs," as Heyn's book seems to advocate. Eroticism fares much better in an atmosphere of comfort and trust where both partners can learn about their pleasures. Comfort and trust are found in dialogue and mirroring transformations through which we claim our dream lovers as ourselves.

The stories we tell about gender and the meaning of the two sexes coupling are the containers into which we pour ourselves and our possibilities. Knowing about strange gender saves all of us from boredom. When we come to accept the complexity of our own gender identity and the range of possibilities in a partner, we discover that heterosexual intimacy can be *fascinating* throughout many decades of a committed relationship.

other implications of gender stories

Years ago I read a book of gender stories, researched and written by my friend and colleague, anthropologist Peggy Sanday. Her remarkable study of female power and male dominance reviews myths and cultural practices from over 150 tribal societies, looking for clues about the origins of sexual inequality. One of her main purposes was to show how gender images in creation stories ("In the beginning . . .") link up with the practices of parenting and decision making for men and women. She was interested in the ways in which our stories shape the actual practices by which we live. To this end, she reviewed and classified 112 creation stories as *feminine, masculine,* or *mixed,* based on categories of the sex of the creative agent, the place of origin, and the mode of creation.

For each of these classifications she found significant links to actual practices in the lives of men and women. The societies that had feminine creative origins were marked by egalitarianism and sharing between husband and wife. In describing one such tribal society, Sanday says:

> Childcare responsibilities are dispersed throughout the family group, whatever that group might be. Children are loved and cherished by all the adults. . . . perhaps because men do not band together for hunting or warfare, the . . . male is more involved with his family.

Images of the divine as female and nature as creative apparently provided the symbolic means by which males could readily and comfortably associate themselves with women, children, and the intimate development of the family.

In those societies (like our own) that had male or masculine creative origins, she found that "suspicion, competition, sexual antagonism, and rigid sexual segregation" were the norm. Perhaps most significant, it appeared that "disassociation of the father from children is in large part a disassociation from women." Stories that attributed ultimate power to male gods and masculine forces dictated "male rule" in a way that dissociated men from women.

According to Robert Bly, Sam Keen, and some other theorists of masculinity, the separation of the father from the family is a result of postindustrial nuclear family arrangements in which the father has been distanced because he works elsewhere. Sanday studied only tribal societies, no industrialized ones. In fifty-six of these tribal societies that had masculine creation stories, Sanday described father roles that sound remarkably like the prototype of the contemporary "distant father" about whom we hear so much: "Fathers in societies with exclusively masculine origin symbolism are distant, controlling figures who are inactive both in the care of infants and in the socialization of young children." In contrast to Bly, Sanday believes that the ways we symbolize sex and gender, and tell stories about who is powerful and why, are the overarching determinants of role expectations. Our symbolic expectations, the stories we are told by our peers and elders, cast us in roles that are difficult to change without self-awareness. When people tell stories about strong and courageous women whose welfare is essential to everyone's future, then men can fall into close association with women, readily joining them in the care of children. When people tell stories about distant, powerful, and vengeful male gods and heroes, men cannot find their identity in association with women, and indeed must dissociate from women (and children) in order to strengthen themselves.

It is the gender story and not the family form that comes first. We are all born into gender symbolism that is ongoing. Sanday claims that creation stories reveal the symbolic meaning and importance of male and female activities in the tribal societies she studied. It may be true that economic necessities and transformed labor laws resulted in the postindustrial breakup of the extended family in our own history, but it seems unlikely to me (based on Sanday's findings) that the preindustrial father in the Western world was ever *more* involved or nuturant with infants and children than fathers in tribal societies in which the masculine creator is dominant. The creator god in our society has been masculine throughout our recorded history. He is a god (whether in the form of Zeus, Yahweh, Allah, or God the Father) who rules from a distant place and cares little for the small necessities of nurturance, health, and sustenance. Even Jesus Christ, who is perhaps the most "nurturant" of the masculine gods, is rarely depicted in community with women and their affairs of child rearing and homemaking.

Sanday shows how creation stories are related to the dependence of people on the environment and forces beyond themselves. The ways in which people interact with and depend upon the land or other environments are symbolized in terms of what they idealize and fear. She says:

> If animals are in decline, the symbolism will surely be dressed in the sex of those who hunt. If the earth is the focus of dependence, then powers of the inner together with the fertilizing power of rain will be the subject of propitiation. If human rather than animal babies are wanted, then the gods will be humanized. From their dependence people select their symbolism.

Preindustrial Western societies (beginning with the Renaissance in Europe) were guided by much the same creation myths and symbolic narratives that guided industrial societies until the birth of modernism. Our masculine creation stories and tales of conquering heroes probably fit our ancestors' dependence on hunting, domestication of farm animals, the expansion of their families, and the domination of others who were native to the land.

Now that we no longer want to dominate and domesticate the earth for our survival, our gender stories are gradually and unintentionally changing to accommodate our new survival needs. When Sanday studied "mixed" creation stories in which both sexes are involved, she found little evidence of mixing of roles or sharing of activities between men and women. The stories depicted male and female gods as contributing differently to the beginning of life, and so she found that male and female people were performing different tasks in their daily lives: men providing for the "economic" stability and security of children (and expecting obedience in return), and women providing nurturance and training for infants and young children. It was a kind of "separate but equal" format, although clearly men had more power than women.

Mature dependence is a new story for the two sexes. It is a story that emphasizes dependence on each other's strengths and acceptance of each other's limitations. The particular plots and narratives that will characterize mature dependence in the future of heterosexual couples are emerging now among couples struggling to move beyond disillusionment.

karen and jonathon

In their final couple session, Jonathon walked confidently ahead of Karen and seemed prepared to make a statement. We were somewhat startled at Jonathon's greater presence because we had not noticed this change previously. Before we even invited them to speak, Jonathon began.

Jonathon: We're going to have a baby. It's amazing but true, and I know that it will change our lives enormously. But it's the one thing that I always hoped would happen for us.

Karen: I wish I could say that I'm thrilled, but I'm still kind of shocked. I wasn't really trying to get pregnant. You know, I just found out yesterday. I'm sort of scared about it.

Karen (Double): I'd like some help from you, Jonathon.

Jonathon: (*Reaching out to take her hand*) What can I do?

Karen: (*Sobbing*) You can say that I don't have to *have* this baby. I just want the freedom to decide instead of feeling stuck.

Jonathon: You feel stuck with having the baby?

Karen: Yeah. *I'm* pregnant and *you* want a baby so much. It just seems like a lot of responsibility that I'm really not sure I want. *You* want it, I know, but it will change my life a lot more than yours.

Jonathon: Yeah, I can see what you mean. But I can't agree to an abortion because it's my baby too.

This seemed like an inauspicious beginning for their final session. We encouraged Karen to say more about her experience to Jonathon.

She talked about her excitement with her work, and the sense of her developing her own Genius in some writing that she had begun to do for her office. More than any time before in her life, Karen felt proud and happy to be herself. She also spoke passionately and appreciatively about her intimate life with Jonathon. Ever since she and Jonathon had repaired their trust after her affair, and now that she knew more about the person that Jonathon actually was, she had felt wonderful about their sex life. Karen did not want to share Jonathon with another person yet. She felt there was a long future before them and she wanted to have "sort of a renewed honeymoon" with him now.

Jonathon did a lot of paraphrasing and supportive responding to Karen while she talked. He looked puzzled, and then he said, "It's your life and your body. You have to *want* any baby that we're going to have. If you really don't want to be pregnant now, I'll go along with an abortion. I'll be really sad about it though." With this response, Karen's face lit up and she rushed over to kiss Jonathon, saying how "perfect" his answer was.

Karen: I'm so happy that you can see that *my* body and my life will be changed by this. I guess I've been scared all along that I couldn't really be the kind of mother you wanted me to, or that *you* wanted to be or something. Now that you've actually *said* that you'd support an abortion, I really feel different about having a baby.

Jonathon: You do?

Karen: Yeah. It's not exactly a control thing, but it may be partly that. It's more like I felt kind of crowded out by your enthusiasm. I hadn't even wanted to get pregnant and now it seemed like you'd be running my life. Anyway, I'm not quite sure what I want to do.

Jonathon: You're saying that my enthusiasm was leaving you out? I guess I see what you mean. But mostly it came from feeling so good about our sex life and wanting to see the "concrete result" of our lovemaking. It's not just the baby that I'm wanting, it's the combination of *you with me*.

Jonathon and Karen spent most of the session acknowledging and talking about the hurts they had caused one another in the blindness of their earlier aggression—his passive aggression and her active aggression. Jonathon's withdrawals and shame, and Karen's attacks and affair, had been large hurdles to overcome.

In assessing their relationship, my husband and I emphasized the *differences* between them. More than the other couples, Karen and Jonathon had very different personality types. Karen was extraverted, active, worldly, political, and full of intelligent and erotic energy. Jonathon was introverted, more open and receptive, homegrown, and less ambitious but more relaxed. Karen's secure relational self and her dark, creative Genius lover were conscious and unconscious strengths. On the other hand, her projections of the Lost Child and Great Father onto Jonathon had not yet been integrated as her own vulnerability and provident capacities. Jonathon's resistant relational self and his Great Mother preoccupations had come across initially as less attractive conscious and unconscious features—seeking after admiration and approval, and the like. Jonathon had worked hard in the course of couple therapy to claim his own strengths as an intelligent and sensitive partner and human being. He had begun his own individual psychotherapy, and had come to see how entrapped he had been in his mother's dreams for him (her unlived life). He had also discovered that his father was a more courageous and admirable man than Jonathon had thought. Fearful about his angry and disappointed feelings about his father, Jonathon had been afraid to speak directly to him. In the course of his individual therapy, Jonathon had learned he could handle his conflicted feelings and speak with his father about Jonathon's perceptions of their relationship. He'd done so and felt relieved that his father could accept Jonathon's account of their past, although his father saw things somewhat differently. At his job, Jonathon was carefully building a solid clientele and a good public image as a responsible and involved young lawyer. Perhaps more than anything else, Jonathon had developed an ability to distinguish between anger and aggression. He could now become directly angry with those people he loved, without withdrawing or withholding (employing passive aggression). All of these new strengths had increased Jonathon's belief in himself as a full and competent partner to Karen.

As the two of them talked about the hurts they had caused each other, and as Karen especially began to feel her dependence on Jonathon's love, she gradually decided that she would have this baby. We, the therapists, were concerned at this major change of heart, because we had seen this kind of thing with Karen previously. We supported it, but advised them to come back for two more therapy sessions during the months of Karen's pregnancy—one about midway and one near the end.

We knew from working with other couples that pregnancy stirs feelings of envy (going both ways between the partners) and that Karen and Jonathon were still not solidly trusting each other in settling power disputes. She might envy his freedom from pregnancy and from the increased limitations of the body, and he might envy her reproductive capacities and greater intimacy with the baby (even prenatally). It seemed that Jonathon was moving toward having a secure relational self, but he was still somewhat afraid of Karen's more active claims for her viewpoint. Also Karen, though able to have a secure relational self, had some strong defenses against feeling her dependence needs and vulnerability. To some extent, we figured that the pregnancy might offer natural opportunities for both of them to break through into a secure attachment. Karen's vulnerability and needs would become more obvious during the distress of pregnancy, and Jonathon's nurturance and strength could be called forth in response. Without help, though, this pregnancy could also create more envy and barriers to trust between them. This couple appeared to be on the way to mature dependence, but not quite there yet.

Psychoanalyst Jacques Lacan is perhaps the most famous contemporary psychoanalytic voice speaking about the dichotomy of two genders as it divides the human community and the psyche. In Lacan's view, most of human society is organized by gendered themes through which our roles are "spoken" to us. Sanday has shown that creation myths are the organizing symbols for sex roles in tribal societies, in a way similar to Lacan's account of the everyday "symbolic order" that limits each of us by a particular gender assignment. One image that Lacan presents of this situation is a drawing of two doors side by side, marked "Ladies" and "Gentlemen." In public places, each of us marches through *one* of these doors in order to urinate and defecate. There is no third door for the discontent.

The stories that we tell about identity reverberate on all levels of culture and society, but the major organizing stories into which we are born can limit us forever. As Sanday says, "Origin myths establish 'who one is,' 'what is,' and 'why one behaves and acts in accordance with custom.' " When stories of masculinity emphasize aggression, dominance, and the critical importance of separating from women in order to find a masculine identity, perhaps we should expect that fathers will be distant from infants and young children. When stories of sex roles emphasize the different-but-equal themes of the "mixed" creation stories, we might expect that fathers and mothers will do different-but-equal kinds of things with their children. Mothers will nurture and fathers will provide material support. Only stories that honor reproductive processes themselves and give divine status to female creation seem to promise "natural" closeness of mothers and fathers with their infants and young children, with shared power between the sexes. Does this mean we should "return" to goddess-based cultures to discover sexual equality?

I don't think so. What we saw with Karen and Jonathon was the effect of dialogue as a new method leading to new stories. When Jonathon asked Karen what she wanted, and was able to listen while retaining his own viewpoint, he could see that Karen's sovereignty (her right to make a decision about a matter principally of *her* responsibility and *her* body) was paramount. Through the influence of feminism, Jonathon "knew" that Karen had the right to choose whether she would have a baby. When he acknowledged this right, Karen was able to make a choice that pleased him as well. Through a fusion of horizons they discovered an outcome that neither one could have anticipated. Karen wanted to have the baby!

As I alluded above, I see new possibilities for gender stories that go well beyond the two doors marked "Gentlemen" and "Ladies." The new stories evolve through fused horizons of dialogue between women and men. They are made possible by reclaiming dream lovers. Our inherited accounts of the gender dichotomy are rooted in projections of dream lovers. Stories of basic antagonism between the sexes—whether they depict women as demanding mothers and whores, or men as demons and lost children—are defensive projections of our own dream lovers. Stories of basic idealization of either sex—whether they depict men as great father-gods or women as great mother-goddesses—are defensive projections of our own ideals, and/or defensive dominance of the self over others.

Stories of dominance and antagonism between the sexes were used to organize men and women in social contexts very different from our present lives. Our survival no longer principally depends on men to fight, hunt, or domesticate animals. (We still depend too exclusively on men to lead our political institutions in North America. We lack stories of women presidents and senators.) Nor do we depend exclusively on women to nurture the young and the old, and provide all domestic care (although many women still fill these roles exclusively in their families).

Rather than needing male dominance or female nurturance, we (especially those of us in heavily industrialized countries who are well educated and resourceful) need to find solutions to overpopulation and environmental depletions. We need a new kind of story that focuses on the common ground of human survival on the planet. If male dominance was the story that got us into our current mess, then male dominance won't get us out. We need a story that emphasizes the *limitation* of power and the *cooperation* of people. That will be the story (with its many plots and narratives) that evolves between female and male speakers in dialogue about their conflicts and identities as sexual partners, parents, wage earners, and companionable friends. Limitation and cooperation are especially important themes for heterosexual couples in the last stage of the life cycle.

charles and pamela

Charles and Pamela were the couple who had initially seemed to us most stuck in the gender split, caught up in envy of each other's lives and resources. Of the four couples, they were the one that my husband and I had felt least hopeful about. Although Karen and Jonathon had had a break of trust in her betrayal, Charles and Pamela were fighting years of bitterness and envy, vastly unequal sex-role assignments, projective identification that had been rigidified, and the fact that their lives were coming to an end (so that failing health could disrupt pleasures). We were enormously pleased with the progress that they had made and actually rather astounded that Charles had begun individual psychotherapy and was enjoying it.

In their final session, they entered the room more timidly than the other couples had, giving me the impression that they were sad to see the process end and perhaps a little afraid that they would not do as well "on their own." My intuition was confirmed as Pamela began.

Pamela: I know we're doing a lot better, but I'm not sure how it all happened. I guess I'm afraid that when we're not coming here anymore, we'll get stuck in our old arguments. I know you're talking to me more directly now, but I don't know what I'm doing differently.

Charles: Are you afraid that you haven't changed sufficiently?

Pamela: Well that's part of it, but mostly I guess I'm still angry—now that I'm thinking of it—about all of the years when I carried the whole responsibility for our relationship. I was *always* the one who brought us to therapy *and* the one who brought up what's wrong. I'm still angry that I did so much more work than you did, and a little afraid that I'll still get stuck with bringing up problems.

Charles: Let's see if I understand: You're angry with me because you feel that only you cared about our relationship for so long, and that I didn't care. (*Pamela nods.*) Well, I disagree. All along I was in love with you and nobody else. I *wanted* to have sex and enjoy the closeness, but *you* didn't. I always felt that you preferred your father to me and that that was final. I had failed to take his place in your mind or heart.

Charles (Double): I'm afraid to help you with your feelings because I believe I'll fail, that you still prefer your father to me.

Pamela: Is that true? (*Charles nods.*) Well, I've never heard that before. I mean, I've never thought that my father was perfect or anything. He was—

Pamela (Double): I don't like to rely on your help because I'm still afraid of depending on you.

Pamela: That's very true, I'm *afraid* to depend on you because for so many years I couldn't or didn't (*weeping*), because I thought you weren't *attracted to me*. I see now how I brought all that on myself with my own self-hatred. Some of that is changing now. I like myself better and even sometimes *enjoy* my age, especially when I'm around the young kids at school. But I don't know if I can trust *you* to care about our relationship.

Charles: I care about it a lot. How can I prove that to you?

Pamela: By bringing up problems when you feel them, but you never seem to feel them. I don't know, maybe I'm more discontent than you are.

This exchange led into a dialogue about Pamela's aggression, the ways in which she replicated her father's disdainful and haughty attitudes in her criticisms of Charles.

Pamela was aware of how much she had envied Charles, and colluded with his feelings of invulnerability (false self). She had often belittled and trivialized his complaints about their marriage ("How could *you* possibly feel hurt when *you* have all the advantages around here?" and other aggressive attacks). Pamela's resistant relational self alternately identified with the Victim Child and the Terrible Father when she defended against her dependence on Charles. She had not yet worked her way out of this, nor had she really taken full responsibility for her own aggressive impulses. She lacked the vulnerable and somewhat saddened presentation of self (evident in Patty) that is often apparent in people who have integrated abusive parental dream lovers. Pamela had first idealized Charles, just as she had idealized her father, as a Great Father. After she became steeped in envy of Charles, she shifted to a Terrible Father projection. Because of her long-term financial dependence on Charles, it had been hard for her to feel fully adult in his presence—hence to feel anything other than the Victim Child (which enraged her). Although Pamela was moving toward mature dependence (returning to graduate school had helped her sense of competence in the world), she was still caught in a kind of quasi-independence in which she alternated between fear of her dependence and anxiety about her independence. This was a developmental transition that should have taken place in early adulthood, to dissolve her idealization of her father.

Charles will always be limited in his capacity for empathy, but he had resolved his projection onto Pamela of the Terrible Mother (bitch, witch, nag). In this session, my husband explained to Charles that Pamela was afraid that she would have to "give too much" in their relationship because she had experienced herself as "giving herself away" when she was an adolescent. She was only now feeling that she had possession of herself, and still afraid that she might somehow lose it. Although Charles was not to blame for the inequity of power and status in their marriage, Pamela had often felt envious of and angry at him. This had complicated the problem that she had in seeing herself as a worthwhile individual with rightful desires, wants, needs. Pamela had felt that she existed only to fulfill others' needs and to get their approval of her love (connected with her "gift" to Charles of a beautiful physical appearance, something she had doubted for the past fifteen years). Charles seemed to grasp all of this on a basic level, but he was unable to empathize with Pamela as he said, "I know that you're busy 'finding yourself' now and I can accept that, but I don't believe that I can do more. I'll continue to be supportive and to spend the time we've committed to each other, but I can't be the kind of man you're looking for."

I talked with Pamela about accepting Charles as someone who was limited in his ability to feel others' emotions. I suggested that she not expect Charles to know when there was a problem between them. Since she could feel that more keenly (Why? Because of her gender socialization, I would guess), then she could depend on herself to be the "signal" that something was wrong. I suggested that she mention such an observation to Charles and ask to have a dialogue about it. Charles would find some way to respond, I was sure, because he was now quite good at the skills of paraphrasing and asking exploratory questions. Pamela said she resented doing this. She did not want the responsibility for "feeling the feelings between us" because she believed this should "belong to both of us." Silently I noted to myself that her envy of Charles prevented her from feeling generous about her strengths. Openly I said to her that I thought she had greater consciousness in this area and thus a greater responsibility than Charles had. I suggested that she think of herself as courageous and powerful (Great Father and Hero) in mastering a task that Charles was afraid to do—afraid in an unconscious way, but afraid all the same.

Pamela reluctantly agreed that she would "be the bridge between us when something interferes with trust," and then she brought up an issue that she wanted to settle in this final session.

Pamela: I've been upset, angry I guess, that you left me out of your feelings about your sister's death. She died over a month ago and you haven't said anything to me about your feelings. I loved her too, and you haven't asked me about my grief.

Pamela (Double): I've felt a gap between us since your sister's death. I've wanted to be closer to you and to share our grief together.

Charles: (*With tears in his eyes*) I had no idea. I thought the services were touching, and that you'd cried enough. I guess I didn't want to burden you with more sadness.

Pamela: (*Weeping*) It's not a burden for me. It's a way of feeling closer, especially because her death means a loss for both of us. We've had so many wonderful times with her and Ted. I would like to know more about how you're doing. I know that you recently went through some of her things, her papers and things. What was that like?

The death of Charles's younger sister had awakened a new sense of vulnerability in Charles, something that Pamela had intuited but had not had the courage to ask about. Charles was not able to defend against his feelings of loss and grief for this much-cherished sibling. I could see that this loss might open up the possibility of unmasking his own needs and vulnerabilities—breaking down his false self. This loss was an opportunity for the two of them to feel more acutely their dependence on each other and the hopefulness of their own years ahead together.

We noted how well it had worked in the session for Pamela to "make the bridge" between them to grieve together. I reinforced to Pamela the idea that if she was willing to open the door between them when things were conflicted or disappointing, I believed that Charles would go through it. I believed that Charles would now take up the dialogue with her on an emotional level. Pamela seemed to trust that he would.

mutual respect and limitation

Dialogue therapy has helped me understand the role of mutual respect in the acceptance of limitation. As partners learn to respect each other's weaknesses (instead of attacking weaknesses), just as they respect each other's strengths, they often discover spontaneously the wisdom of limitation.

The Buddhist saying "All life is suffering" is an insight that is opaque for North Americans and Europeans, with our value of personal happiness. I believe that couples penetrate this insight when they learn to respect their own limitations. As I have come to understand it, the knowledge of death (recognized by us from about the age of three years on) is a reminder that our bonds with each other and our tasks in life are transitory. This knowledge is suffering. It is suffering because the attachments that we feel for each other, and for the earth itself, feel endless and eternal, and reach to the core of our very being. In order to love wholly we cannot bear to imagine the loss, the end, the separation from all to which we become attached—as it gradually becomes part of ourselves.

The dilemma of suffering and attachment is, it seems to me, the greatest lesson that life teaches us—repeatedly, whether or not we actually learn it. In order to engage the attachment, we must engage the suffering. Some of us feel this most keenly after we have children. Our attachment to our children puts us at risk for suffering every time a child has an accident, bad luck, is at risk. Isn't life simpler without the fear of loss? Some people—perhaps many, as I said earlier—have resistant relational selves, and so they only intermittently feel their dependence and attachment. They are defended against the suffering because they suffered too much too soon. Others, those few who cannot feel the attachment at all, have avoidant relational selves because they suffered far too much in their earliest attachments. Those people who have secure selves can feel deeply their dependence and attachment, and also the risk of anxiety, fear, and grief over loved ones.

In successful dialogue therapy, partners feel their attachment for each other as mature dependence. Then they face the limitation, the suffering, that the partner's failings bring—and ultimately the limitation of the self and the suffering that it brings. When I work in individual psychotherapy I find that the lesson of limitation is much harder to experience. Because the attachment bond between the client and me is built gradually and overlaps with feelings and fantasies of other attachments, the client's experience of losing me and being hurt by my failings comes only gradually (and sometimes not at all) to stand for the limitation of human love. Sometimes we miss this opportunity. What is especially gratifying about dialogue therapy is that this relatively brief encounter with a couple often brings such a fundamentally important human lesson into the foreground.

gender and splitting

Recently I read a poem that said something about the "social action of the poet." That line brought to mind my concern that I voice here, the "social action of the psychotherapist." My dedication to a human service profession includes a dedication to social change in the direction of greater consciousness and compassion. When I wrote *Female Authority: Empowering Women Through Psychotherapy* with Florence Wiedemann, I was adamant about stressing the social dimension of psychology and psychotherapy—and equally the psychological and therapeutic dimensions of society. In this last chapter I have wanted to convey the overlap I see between the capacity of heterosexual couples to be intimate and the possibilities for sexual equality in our future. In my view, heterosexual intimacy in a committed relationship would not have been possible for most of us (although the exceptional few are always with us) without the recent wave of feminism as a civil rights movement. Feminism has been therapeutic for our culture and society in creating the possibility of dialogue between women and men.

Concepts from depth psychology (Jung's psychology, object relations theory, and Freudian psychoanalysis) also provide possibilities for curing social ills, even as they may create others (such as parent blaming). Using a psychoanalytic concept, I want to add one more point to our discussion of healing the gender split. It involves the idea of "splitting" as a defense against ambivalence. Splitting means the separating of good and bad, right and wrong, white and black, masculine and feminine, in emotional moments when the conflict or tension between the two seems too much to bear. Splitting is a way of handling overwhelming tension or ambiguity that links back to our earliest perceptual experiences of other people.

When children are very young, from about eighteen months to three years old, they gradually learn to fuse their good (pleasurable) feelings with their bad (painful) feelings. The gradual construction or assemblage of a "whole" experience of another person out of many mixed experiences of faces, breasts, hands, voices, smells, and so on (the emotional image traces) includes the fusion of pleasure and pain as parts of one person—self or other. At first these two seem like opposites. If early development proceeds smoothly, however, we learn to feel ambivalent (good *and* bad) about others and ourselves. Some of us do not complete this development in our early years because the pleasures and pains seem impossibly separate, usually because the pain is overwhelming. By adulthood, though, most people can feel and express that "people are both good and bad"—and experience themselves in the same ambivalent soup.

In our earliest experiences of emotion, touch, and contact, we did not know that good and bad, pleasure and pain, were mixed together in people. These opposites seemed separated, into good people (Great Mother, Great Father) and bad people (Terrible Mother, Terrible Father). As adults we still sometimes sort the world out through "splitting"—making dichotomies—when we feel too overwhelmed to be ambivalent. This defense mechanism is used by all of us when we take sides in a fight: My side is good and virtuous; yours is bad and immoral. Most situations in human life are ambivalent (although there are exceptions when actions and people are, in fact, wrong and destructive—or right and good). Here I want to focus on one form of splitting that is common in regard to women and men.

This is the strong categorizing of "feminine" and "masculine" as two different and distinct natural qualities. Whether these two categories are called *yin* and *yang, dark* and *light, receptive* and *active,* or *related* and *autonomous,* they are indicative of a defensive splitting when they are used to sort out human beings, one from another. As psychoanalyst Jacques Lacan and French feminists after him have made so clear, the dichotomous split between the two genders is a division among and within people. Among people it creates two exclusive clubs in which membership is lifelong. Within people it creates a split between a conscious gender identity of self and an unconscious identity of Other. All human cultures sort people into two groups (with the possible exception of some tribal groups in which there is a "neuter" category), and the human psyche develops initially by noting opposites—inner and outer, self and other, dark and light. This is the first step in the development of consciousness. It is not the goal.

I cannot claim to know the goal of the development of human consciousness, either on the individual or the cultural level, but I do know (as so many contemporary scientists and theorists of consciousness are telling us) that human consciousness is a unity masking diversity. That is, we are individually composed of many parts, personalities, possible selves, and actual minds. We give ourselves the illusion of unity for practical purposes of getting around in one body-brain. Even the brain fools itself about knowing what's going on, as scientist Daniel Dennett has recently shown: We explain our behavior to ourselves in ways that give the impression that "I am in control," although the actual situation of the brain and its multiple needs and impulses belies that claim.

Using dichotomized gender typing to limit human consciousness in adulthood is a defensive maneuver. It is a way of confining the ambiguity and diversity of human possibilities and weaknesses. Every adult has available many talents, moods, attitudes, and needs that rarely conform to gendered expectations or social roles. We have witnessed this throughout the book in regard to the interaction between gender and strange gender, between the self and the Others within us. When we are anxious about our power, status, role, or privilege, we may want to split the world of gender into ourselves and others. When women get anxious about their lack of influence, decision-making authority, earning power, status, and personal sovereignty, they tend to claim their relational superiority. Then they sort people into "us" (relationally mature *women*) and "them" (developmentally disabled *men*). When men get anxious about their masculine identity, privileges, earning power, or personal worth, they may claim power and knowledge anxiously by sorting "us" (special and unique *men* with our special needs and skills) and "them" (*women* who can't understand us because they've never had the kind of responsibilities we've had). When the corporate executives argued that "differences between women and men are necessary," I think it was because they were defended against what they perceived as my encroachment on their special territory of being leaders and experts. I was trying to be an expert on gender and they believed they had already figured it all out, having been at the top where the view is panoramic.

Any situation in which a person becomes anxiously protective of self—because of either threat from the outside or anxiety from within—encourages splitting to some extent. We want to externalize what is perceived as bad (painful) and identify with what is perceived as good (desirable or pleasant). When we think about gender typing in most societies, we cannot ignore the fact that the dominant sex has generally functioned to protect the qualities that are desirable by describing the Other in terms of the less desirable qualities. At the conference with the executives, an Asian man spent a lot of time explaining to me the principles of yin and yang, and how the important thing was to accept them as equally powerful, although they are opposites. It was difficult to respond to his presentation because he had already decided that this opposition was right and true. I asked him to think about Confucianism and Taoism in terms of the *men* who taught these principles and practices. If women had been asked, would they have wanted to be included in the category of the receptive, the dark, and the natural (as opposed to the active, the light, and the cultural)? I believe that women, like men, would also want to be in the position of the active culture-maker in situations in which this is more obviously valued. The symbolic order into which most of us have been born is one that has been shaped over long periods of time by man-made symbols. Symbols of gender have served the function of protecting male dominance and providing social roles in which the sexes were unequal. It's not so hard to see why women and men have not been successful at valuing both sides of the gender dichotomy as equally worthwhile and powerful; it wasn't designed to be that way.

Back in the mid-1980s, a social psychologist named Jean Lipman-Blumen published a book that laid out an important premise about the issue of gender splitting. She showed through an analysis of dominance hierarchies of many types—racism, ethnocentrism, ageism, and the like—that gender roles are a *blueprint* for other forms of dominance-submission. Her thesis was that sex differences are primary. We live within the implications of our gender assignment—now even before birth for some infants—before we learn about other differences of human life (racial and ethnic differences are not apparent until we interact with those outside of the family of origin). We learn about dominance-submission through the blueprint of gender assignment. The labeling of difference, and the belief that one group is better or more important than another, can be traced back to the primacy of gender categories. This primary division of the human community is not a "different-but-equal" division. It is a power-over division that encourages us to see other differences in the same way.

Sexual and racial equality is a lofty goal, as I said earlier. Not because it is wholly beyond us, in our ability to imagine such a world, but because it would mean a radical change in our whole way of life. If at this moment, for instance, women all over the world were suddenly compensated with equal pay for the work they do (at home and in the marketplace), all major economic systems would collapse. That is because these systems are founded on unpaid and underpaid labor performed largely by women.

So how can I believe, as I do, that we may live in sexual equality within the next hundred years? In my view we are at a turning point in human history in regard to our own self-awareness. In the past, only the exceptional few—the sages or the poets or the mystics—were able to invest themselves in developing self-awareness. Now this possibility is available to the masses, at least to those people for whom the mythopoetic way of life no longer works, those of us who grope for meaning outside of clear traditions and rules. Increasingly we have the capacity to understand our own motives and to move beyond the simple unconscious defenses that promote a self-protective view of the world and others.

As I work with myself and other people on the expansion of self-awareness through greater consciousness and compassion, I am deeply moved by the emergence of mature dependence leading to a transcendence of the self. The practice of dialogue returns our strange genders to ourselves, and opens our curiousity about our partners. We come "to stand on common ground, here and there gritty with pebbles," as poet Denise Levertov puts it. This common ground is the shared horizon of meaning between a man and a woman. It inspires hope to witness this development even on a small scale, among couples and individuals I have known and treated. The search for intimacy between the sexes and the practice of dialogue are the signs I read as hope for the future. Taking the chance of mature dependence—especially with a partner of the opposite sex—is charting a new frontier. It is a chance worth taking to heal the gender split, as the healing between women and men may ease unfairness, inequality, and dominance everywhere.

acknowledgments

This book has been years in the making. For the past decade, my husband and I have been seeing couples in dialogue therapy. The contributions of these unnamed people have been essential to my understanding of how partners develop and change in an intimate relationship. More times than I can remember, these people astounded me with their courage, commitment, persistence, and continuing transformations. Betrayal, years of estrangement, the mixed loyalties of a stepfamily, illness, traumatic abuse in childhood, financial losses, entrenched aggression, and even the death of a child are the barriers that have been overcome by renewed trust. Ed Epstein has been my companion through all this. As my best friend and partner he has made contributions exceeding my ability to acknowledge them. He is my support and sounding board. I look forward to many more decades of our life and work together.

In an immediate way, my agent and my editor have been the next most important people on this project. My agent, Beth Vesel, is all that I could wish for: smart, funny, feminist, ambitious, kind, empathic, organized, insistent, and protective of my interests. She and her fiancé, Frazier Moore, have become my dear friends. Their marriage and partnership will be filled with mirroring transformations as these two talented people care for each other over the years. My editor, Maria Guarnaschelli, is a jewel. Far exceeding my expectations of an editor, Maria has been keenly attuned to all levels of this project. Her skill, intelligence, warmth, generosity, humor, and enthusiasm have filled me with motivation to succeed at bringing my ideas to a wider audience. Maria is a personal inspiration, as well. In her meetings with my husband and children, she has been one of the most generous and authentic human beings I have ever encountered. Her husband, John Guarnaschelli, has contributed his sharp insights and clear questions. His commitment to human development through understanding gender identity is evident in any meeting with him. He too is funny, generous, and warm.

Other people have helped a great deal too. Each week I teach in a seminar at the Institute of Pennsylvania Hospital in Philadelphia. It's called the Seminar on Epistemology, Development, and Psychotherapy, designed to stimulate new interests in the psychiatric residents and to satisfy basic intellectual needs of the faculty. For the past five years, I have engaged in loving debate and friendship with the other faculty members: Harvey Horowitz, Ellio Frattaroli, Bill Overton, Maggie Baker, and Howard Baker. As faculty and staff at the institute, we have struggled to be innovators in teaching and practice. Many ideas in this book are direct products of the seminar. I am deeply grateful to my colleagues and to the many students who have contributed to our discussions.

My dearest friend and colleague, Demaris Wehr, carefully read the manuscript and offered suggestions. As always, she contributed to my life on many levels. She and her husband, David Hart, have spent many hours with Ed and me over the past decade, refining the groundwork for equality in a heterosexual partnership. We love them very much.

Another close friend, Stan Perelman, read the manuscript and offered much support. He and his wife, Nancy, have been dear friends and companions over more than a decade. Stan and I trained together to be Jungian analysts and are still "partners in crime," as we challenge our colleagues to find new directions for the development of Jung's psychology. Stan is the best kind of revolutionary—thoughtful and provocative, but not aggressive.

Sociologist and friend Valeria Freysinger assisted me with the chapter on leisure time from its conception through its realization. She worked with her students at Miami University in Ohio to collect the survey data and to score it. It has been a great pleasure to know her. Psychologist Kathe Kirkman has been the "scholar in residence" for this book as she checked references in the library, sought obscure articles in journals, and wrote many of the notes. Without her expertise and help, I could not have amassed the rich notes and bibliography this book makes available.

Anthropologist and friend Peggy Reeves Sanday has contributed her intelligent analysis of gender and power. Not only through her books and articles, but especially through our ongoing dialogues, Peggy has changed my mind many times. Over the years Peggy, her children, and her husband have become our close friends. Peggy's courage has been especially inspirational as she faced down authorities with evidence of sexual violence against women, especially on college campuses.

My greatest teacher, Jane Loevinger, has to be mentioned because of her lifetime effect on my work. She never oversimplified her approach to the human mind to make it fit some external agenda. Rather, her work has been both scientific and complex in its sensitive account of human development. It has been a model for me in all I do.

I would also like to thank my colleagues and dear friends at Clinical Associates West in Radnor, Pennsylvania. Phillip Bennett, Bob Schoenholtz, Ilene Wasserman, and Harvey Horowitz have been supportive and engaged with this project throughout. Joy and Lew Mills have a special role as our other team of dialogue therapists. Their enduring and vital marital partnership, attuned skills as therapists, and willingness to help out at any level are an inspiration. I am very grateful to them for many things, but especially for their involvement in dialogue therapy. My administrative assistant, Ricki Gero, is wonderful. Well organized, quick, sympathetic, and endearing, Ricki sprinkles all of her communications with a good dose of humor. She keeps my life running a lot more smoothly and happily than it would without her. She has been especially helpful on the preparations for publication. I appreciate her in every way.

My children, Amber, Colin, Noah, and Arne, are the best. I have almost run out of adjectives to describe the richness of my relationships, but these four people are bright, unique, confrontive of my flaws, funny, challenging, and impressive as human beings. Young adults, they are truly individuals—different from each other and courageous in charting new territory. Most of all, I respect their values and integrity. I could not have been more blessed in my relationships. Without this matrix, this book could not have been born.

leisure questionnaire

Please use the following scale to indicate the extent to which the statement describes you. There are no right or wrong, better or worse answers. Circle the number that gives the answer most like you for each of the statements.

Not at all — Most of the time

1----2----3----4----5----6----7----8----9----10

1. When I am talking in ordinary conversations with friends or family (not work related) . . .
   a. I am mostly trying to make a point.

      1----2----3----4----5----6----7----8----9----10

   b. I want to express my personal feelings.

      1----2----3----4----5----6----7----8----9----10

c. I am eager to understand the other person's feelings.

1----2----3----4----5----6----7----8----9----10

d. I am eager to understand the other person's viewpoint.

1----2----3----4----5----6----7----8----9----10

e. I am trying to solve the problem at hand.

1----2----3----4----5----6----7----8----9----10

f. I see ways that I am similar to the other person.

1----2----3----4----5----6----7----8----9----10

2. When my spouse and I travel by car on a pleasure trip . . .

a. I prefer the major highways (faster route).

1----2----3----4----5----6----7----8----9----10

b. I prefer the scenic route even if it's less direct.

1----2----3----4----5----6----7----8----9----10

c. I prefer to listen more than talk.

1----2----3----4----5----6----7----8----9----10

d. I prefer to talk more than listen.

1----2----3----4----5----6----7----8----9----10

3. Ideally I think that couples should . . .

a. Learn to talk out their differences.

1----2----3----4----5----6----7----8----9----10

b. Accept differences without talking them out.

1----2----3----4----5----6----7----8----9----10

c. Find a way to change their differences to be more similar.

1----2----3----4----5----6----7----8----9----10

d. Learn about each other's points of view.

1----2----3----4----5----6----7----8----9----10

4. At the end of a busy day . . .

a. I like to engage in good conversation with my spouse.

1----2----3----4----5----6----7----8----9----10

b. I like to watch television to relax.

1----2----3----4----5----6----7----8----9----10

c. I want to sit quietly (with snack or drink) and not be disturbed.

1----2----3----4----5----6----7----8----9----10

d. I am annoyed when my spouse wants to talk.

1----2----3----4----5----6----7----8----9----10

e. I am annoyed when my spouse wants to watch TV.

1----2----3----4----5----6----7----8----9----10

5. When I look forward to leisure time I imagine . . .

a. Myself learning or reading.

1----2----3----4----5----6----7----8----9----10

b. Active play (e.g., tennis) or exercise.

1----2----3----4----5----6----7----8----9----10

c. Myself napping or passively enjoying life.

1----2----3----4----5----6----7----8----9----10

d. My spouse will direct our activities.

1----2----3----4----5----6----7----8----9----10

6. Over the weekend with my spouse, I am annoyed by . . .

a. Idle chatter.

1----2----3----4----5----6----7----8----9----10

b. Criticisms of my activities.

1----2----3----4----5----6----7----8----9----10

c. Television watching.

1----2----3----4----5----6----7----8----9----10

d. Serious conversations.

1----2----3----4----5----6----7----8----9----10

e. Interruptions of my chosen activities.

1----2----3----4----5----6----7----8----9----10

f. Unnecessary expenditure of money.

1----2----3----4----5----6----7----8----9----10

Please answer the last few questions, which will allow for a description of study respondents. Check or write in the correct response:

7. Number of years together as a couple: ______

Number of years *married* to current spouse: ______

8. Previously married? ______ Yes ______ No (go to #9)

How many years? ______

9. Sex: ______ Male ______ Female

10. Age: ______

11. Level of education:

    ______ Less than twelve years ______ High school graduate
    ______ Some college ______ Associate degree
    ______ Baccalaureate degree ______ Master's degree
    ______ Advanced graduate work (Ph.D., Ed.D., M.D., etc.)

12. Race: ______ Caucasian ______ African-American
    ______ Hispanic ______ Asian
    ______ Other: ______________________________

13. Occupation: ______________________________

14. How many hours per week do you work (i.e., spend on your paid employment)? ______

15. What is your annual family income (before taxes, etc.)?

    ______ Less than $15,000 ______ $15,001–$25,000
    ______ $25,001–$35,000 ______ $35,001–$45,000
    ______ $45,001–$55,000 ______ $55,001–$65,000
    ______ $65,001–$75,000 ______ More than $75,000

THANK YOU VERY MUCH FOR YOUR PARTICIPATION!

notes

introduction

Page

11 Sullivan: See H. S. Sullivan, *The Collected Works of Harry Stack Sullivan, M.D.,* ed. H. S. Perry and M. L. Gawel (New York: W. W. Norton, 1956); H. S. Sullivan, *The Interpersonal Theory of Psychiatry* (New York: W. W. Norton, 1953).

12 Fairbairn: See W. R. Fairbairn, *Psychoanalytic Studies of the Personality* (Boston: Routledge & Kegan Paul, 1952); W. R. Fairbairn, *An Object Relations Theory of the Personality* (New York: Basic Books, 1954).

12 "a discipline of thought": P. Young-Eisendrath, "Rethinking Feminism, the Animus and the Feminine," in C. Zweig (ed.), *To Be a Woman* (Los Angeles: Tarcher, 1990), p. 160.

16 "(the corpus callosum) of the female brain is thicker": For an interesting discussion of this sex difference, see C. Tavris, *The Mismeasure of Woman* (New York: Simon & Schuster, 1992), pp. 43–56.

17 Money: See J. Money, *Sexual Signatures: On Being a Man or a Woman* (Boston: Little, Brown, 1975).

17 "To invoke": J. Bruner, *Acts of Meaning* (Cambridge, MA: Harvard University Press, 1990), p. 23.

17 Hare-Mustin and Marecek: See R. T. Hare-Mustin and J. Marecek, "The Meaning of Difference: Gender Theory, Postmodernism, and Psychology," *The American Psychologist* 43, No. 6 (1988): 455–464.

17 "different languages": See C. Gilligan, *In a Different Voice: Psychological Theory and Women's Development* (Cambridge, MA: Harvard University Press, 1982).

17 Jung: See C. G. Jung, *The Collected Works of C. G. Jung: Aion,* 2nd ed., trans. R.F.C. Hull (Princeton, NJ: Princeton University Press, 1959).

17 Freud: See S. Freud, *The Psychopathology of Everyday Life,* 2nd ed., J. Strachey (ed.), *The Standard Edition of the Complete Psychological Works of Sigmund Freud,* Vol. 6 (London: Hogarth Press, 1960).

18 Hare-Mustin and Marecek, "The Meaning of Difference."

chapter 1

Page

23 "strange gender": This term, of my invention, is related intimately to Carl Jung's idea of "contrasexuality," although my premises are very different from his. Jung's notion that everyone has a biologically based, opposite-sex personality, derived from genetic traces of the other sex (hormonal, morphological, and so on), is "essentialist." It assumes that personality characteristics are founded on biology: They have essential roots outside of any social influences. In my view, both gender and its Otherness (the opposite within) are cultural constructs of enormous significance for personality and development.

The divergence between my view and Jung's is enormous in regard to the role of culture, stereotypes, role expectations—the "stories of gender" into which we are born. Whereas Jung believed that gender differences are destined through biological determination, I believe that gender (in all of its ramifications) is flexible and dependent on context.

On the other hand, Jung's theory of contrasexuality, as the development of an opposite-sex personality in the second half of life, was the origin of my thinking about Otherness, strange gender, and dream lovers. Jung's belief that all of us are somehow faced with our Otherness through confronting our own unconsciousness, especially through our projections, has been my starting point.

For more information about Jung's theory on the subject of contrasexuality and development, see C. G. Jung, *The Collected Works of C. G. Jung: Aion,* 2nd ed., Vol. 9, Part II, Chapter III, trans. R.F.C. Hull (Princeton, NJ: Princeton University Press, 1959), pp. 11–22. For a discussion of stages of life, see Chapter VI of the *Collected Works,* Vol. 8, pp. 387–403.

24 "dream lovers": This is my term that relates closely to Jung's terms *anima* for men's feminine nature and *animus* for women's masculine nature. Again, although I drew my inspiration from Jung's theory of a biologically based opposite-sex personality, I emphasize the cultural construction of gender, the category of "opposite," and projection in my theory of dream lovers.

In my treatment of Otherness, I have been influenced both by Jung and by Jacques Lacan. For Jung's definitions of *anima* and *animus,* see his *Collected Works,* Vol. 6, pp. 467–470. For information on Lacan's treatment of gender and Otherness, see especially his *Feminine Sexuality,* ed. J. Mitchell, trans. and ed. J. Rose (New York: W. W. Norton, 1982); J. Smith and W. Kerrigan (eds.), *Interpreting Lacan: Psychiatry and the Humanities,* Vol. 6 (New Haven, CT: Yale University Press, 1983). For my own approach to animus/anima as psychological complexes (rather than as archetypes of biological difference), see especially Chapter 4 of P. Young-Eisendrath and F. Wiedemann, *Female Authority: Empowering Women Through Psychotherapy* (New York: Guilford Press, 1987), and P. Young-Eisendrath, "Gender, Animus, and Related Topics," in N. Schwart-Salant and M. Stein (eds.), *Gender and Soul in Psychotherapy* (Wilmette, IL: Chiron, 1991).

To quote myself from the latter: "The division into two genders, inscribed by culture with different power and status meanings, marks each of us from birth onward, leaving us always as outsiders to the others. The nature of gender difference, arising in culture and designated through a form of embodiment, marks us with a culturally inscribed meaning and makes the contrasexual other a perpetual outsider, an unconscious complex of not-I" (p. 151).

25 "Most kids at four": Two-year-olds can identify the sex of people in pictures, and three-year-olds normally refer to themselves as either boys or girls. It is not until approximately age six or seven, however, that most children understand that gender is an enduring feature of another person and of themselves (gender constancy). See L. Kohlberg, "A Cognitive-Developmental Analysis of Children's Sex-Role Concepts and Attitudes," in E. E. Maccoby (ed.), *The Development of Sex Differences* (Stanford, CA: Stanford University Press, 1966); J. Money, "Differentiation of Gender Identity," *JSAS Catalog of Selected Documents in Psychology* 6, No. 4 (1976); D. Ruble, "Sex-Role Development," in M. H. Bornstein and M. E. Lamb (eds.), *Development Psychology: An Advanced Textbook* (Hillsdale, NJ: Lawrence Erlbaum, 1983).

26 "Same-sex love relationships": For literature discussing the intimate relationships of gay men and lesbians, see L. A. Peplau and S. L. Gordon, "The Intimate Relationships of Lesbians and Gay Men," in E. R. Allgeier and N. B. McCormick (eds.), *Gender Roles and Sexual Behavior* (Palo Alto, CA: Mayfield, 1982); J. Harry, "Gay Male and Lesbian Family Relationships," in E. Macklin (ed.), *Contemporary Families and Alternate Lifestyles: Handbook on Research and Theory* (Beverly Hills, CA: Sage, 1983); M. Caldwell and L. A. Peplau, "Balance of Power in Lesbian Relationships," *Sex Roles* 10, No. 1 (1984): 587–599; J. DeCecco, *Gay Relationships* (New York: Harrington Park Press, 1988).

27 "my appearance was the only access to power I had": For a discussion of feminine narcissism and the social context that condones appearance as a source of power for women, see Young-Eisendrath and Wiedemann, *Female Authority,* pp. 19–22.

27 "commitment phobia": Dr. Connell Cowan and Dr. Melvyn Kinder suggest in their highly successful *Smart Women/Foolish Choices* (New York: Clarkson N. Potter, 1985) that men who avoid commitment in relationships don't fully trust their own autonomy—they fear "becoming healthily dependent on a woman" (pp. 96–97).

28 "something from our earliest family relationships": See E. S. Person, *Dreams of Love and Fateful Encounters: The Power of Romantic Passion* (New York: W. W. Norton, 1988).

28 "disillusionment": For discussion of disillusionment and heterosexual intimacy, see D. Reiss, *The Family's Construction of Reality* (Cambridge, MA: Harvard University Press, 1981); L. C. Wynne (ed.), *The State of the Art in Family Therapy Research: Controversies and Recommendations* (New York: Family Process Press, 1988).

29 "dialogue therapy": P. Young-Eisendrath, *Hags and Heroes: A Feminist Approach to Jungian Psychotherapy with Couples* (Toronto: Inner City Books, 1984).

31 "Looking into hearts of men": Cowan and Kinder report in *Smart Women/Foolish Choices* on a "rising tide of utter frustration" (p. 5) and disappointment in men by women, but they see the problem as centered in the distorted expectations of women and not in the attitudes or behaviors of men.

31 "men feel depreciated in the modern couple": See Chapter 16 in D. Gottlieb, *Family Matters: Healing in the Heart of the Family* (New York: Dutton, 1991).

32 "speak from her feelings": Discussions about gender differences in empathy and the desire and ability to relate to others are common in the popular press. The assumption that women are more empathic and relationally oriented than men is based, to some extent, on research findings. In 1983, Nancy Eisenberg reviewed over one hundred studies of gender differences in empathy and concluded that there is a "huge sex difference in self-report of empathy [women reported themselves more empathic] as measured with questionnaires. . . ." However, when heart rates or videotaped facial reactions were analyzed, no consistent differences in empathy between men and women were found. These findings suggest that women are more likely to report themselves as empathic, and that men may experience similar empathy but express it less overtly. N. Eisenberg and R. Lennon, "Sex Differences in Empathy and Related Capacities," *Psychological Bulletin* 94 (1983): 100–131.

33 "eyeball-to-eyeball . . . shoulder-to-shoulder": In *You Just Don't Understand: Women and Men in Conversation* (New York: William Morrow, 1990, p. 246), Deborah Tannen describes videotapes used in a research project to analyze gender differences in physical alignment during conversations: "At every age, the girls and women sit closer to each other and look at each other directly. At every age, the boys and men sit at angles to each other—in one case, almost parallel—and never look directly into each other's faces."

33 "shamefully out of step": The experience of shame detracts from the potential of positive relationships because it cannot coexist with self-esteem or self-confidence. See G. Kaufman and L. Raphael, *Dynamics of Power: Fighting Shame and Building Self-esteem,* 2nd ed. (Rochester, VT: Schenkman Books, 1991); S. M. Retzinger, *Violent Emotions: Shame and Rage in Marital Quarrels* (Newbury Park, CA: Sage, 1991); D. L. Nathanson (ed.), *The Many Faces of Shame* (New York: Guilford Press, 1987); J. V. Jordan, *Relational Development: Therapeutic Implications of Empathy and Shame* (Wellesley, MA: Stone Center, Wellesley College, 1989).

33 "obsessed with self-improvement": Recently, Valeria Freisinger and I conducted a study concerning the leisure preferences of men and women (see Chapter 7 for discussion of the study results). Twenty-one percent of the women and only 6.4 percent of the men indicated that learning and reading are leisure activities that they look forward to most of the time (indicated by a high rating). A statistically significant difference between the mean response ratings of men and women on this issue of "self-improvement" was found in this study.

34 "Many men envy": Frank Conroy summarized "What Men Envy About Women" (*Glamour,* March 1990, pp. 252–253) as follows: "Women tend to share with each other, to pool their knowledge and experience into a kind of bank of feminine wisdom"; they have a "kind of baseline empathy . . . alert to what they have in common more than what they don't"; "women seem closer to their bodies . . . more accepting of the idea of a spiritual and physical unity"; and women have the "ability to bear children."

34 "The emotional rewards of oppression": See C. Epstein, *Deceptive Distinctions: Sex, Gender, and the Social Order* (New Haven, CT: Yale University Press, 1988).

35 " 'hidden heroism' of female lives": This hidden heroism can be seen, in part, in the disproportionate hours worked by women in the home and in wage disparity on the job. Shelley Coverman reports that, throughout the 1980s, domestic labor provided by men averaged eleven hours per week, while women not employed outside the home put in more than fifty hours per week and working wives between twenty-six and thirty-three hours per week at home. Overall, wives provided between 70 and 92 percent of domestic labor. See S. Coverman, "Women's Work Is Never Done: The Division of Domestic Labor," in J. Freeman (ed.), *Women: A Feminist Perspective* (Mountain View, CA: Mayfield, 1989). Census Bureau figures for 1990 (cited by Karen Pennar in "Women Are Still Paid the Wages of Discrimination," *Business Week,* October 28, 1991, p. 35) indicate that year-round, full-time women workers (across all occupations) earn 71 percent of men's income. The averages by job classifications include 57 percent for sales, 64 percent for managerial jobs, and 66 percent for service jobs (in which women averaged an annual income of $12,136). This apparent increase in women's wages over the past three years, according to Pennar, reflects "declining men's earnings after adjustment for inflation." Interestingly, Barnet Wagman and Nancy Folbre reported that the percentage of women who earn more than $30,000 a year increased to 10.3 percent in 1986 (compared with a decline to 37 percent for men) and the percentage of women who earned under $10,000 increased to 19.1 percent in 1986 (compared with a stable 10 percent for men). See B. Wagman and N. Folbre, "The Feminization of Inequality: Some New Patterns," *Challenge* 31, No. 6 (1988): 56–59.

35 "Women surprise themselves . . . in midlife": In midlife, women are often freed from their responsibilities to others and find in themselves great strength and satisfaction. For many, high accomplishments begin only after this freedom is obtained. See C. Heilbrun, *Hamlet's Mother and Other Women* (New York: Columbia University Press, 1990).

35 "women may expect men to be the heroes": R. M. Eisler and J. A. Blalock suggest that "rigid commitment to masculine schemata for appraisal and coping with life's problems may both produce stress and result in dysfunctional coping patterns in men," such as "the inhibition of emotional expressiveness, reliance on aggression, power, and control, and obsession with achievement and success." R. M. Eisler and J. A. Blalock, "Masculine Gender Role Stress: Implications for the Assessment of Men," *Clinical Psychology Review* 11 (1991): 45.

36 "competitions prepare young men": For a discussion of competition and its consequences, see A. Kohn, *No Contest: The Case Against Competition* (Boston: Houghton Mifflin, 1986).

36 " 'powerful' gender club": Joseph Pleck writes: "In addition to hierarchy over women, men create hierarchies and rankings among themselves according to criteria of 'masculinity.' " He continues: "Our society uses the male heterosexual-homosexual dichotomy as a central symbol for *all* the rankings of masculinity. . . . Any kind of powerlessness or refusal to compete becomes imbued with the imagery of homosexuality." J. H. Pleck, "Men's Power with Women, Other Men, and Society: A Men's Movement Analysis," in R. A. Lewis (ed.), *Men in Difficult Times: Masculinity Today and Tomorrow* (Englewood Cliffs, NJ: Prentice Hall, 1981), p. 239.

37 "dreams of youth": D. J. Levinson, C. N. Darrow, E. B. Klein, M. H. Levinson, and B. McKee, *The Seasons of a Man's Life* (New York: Knopf, 1978). Levinson describes the importance of "the Dream" for men as a "vision of a life" and the "imagined possibility that generates excitement and vitality" (p. 91). Inability to capture "the Dream" leads a man to lose "his sense of aliveness and purpose." For a comparison of "the Dream" in the lives of women, see P. Daniels, "Dream vs. Drift in Women's Careers: The Question of Generativity," in B. Goldman and B. Forisha (eds.), *Outside on the Inside: Women and Organizations* (Englewood Cliffs, NJ: Prentice Hall, 1981).

37 "Midlife men are often sadly disappointed": Levinson et al. (*The Seasons of a Man's Life*) suggest that some men, because of "irreparable defeats in pre-adulthood or early adulthood . . . lack the inner and outer resources for creating a minimally adequate life structure in middle adulthood. They face a middle age of constriction and decline" (p. 243). This feeling of "male grief" is often the reference point for masculine identity search, such as that described by Robert Bly, but it may refer more to male idealism and subsequent disillusion than to loss of fathers. See R. Bly, *Iron John: A Book About Men* (Reading, MA: Addison-Wesley, 1990).

38 "[the male's] greater earning power": As of 1988, a woman with a college degree was still earning only 59 cents to the dollar earned by a male of the same or considerably less education. For a review of the relevant statistics and research, see S. Faludi, *Backlash: The Undeclared War Against American Women* (New York: Crown, 1991), Chapter 13.

38 "Cultural stereotypes": These abound in popular media presentations of men and women. As Susan Faludi points out in Chapter 4 of *Backlash,* these media representations, especially of women, present images of characteristics desired rather than a reflection of existing reality. Most often, men are presented as powerful and capable engineers of outcomes, and women are depicted as either supporters or detractors to men's endeavors.

39 "Emotional image traces": Current research findings suggest strongly that the preverbal experiences of infants and young children are sorted into emotionally based cognitive categories. See D. Stern, *The Interpersonal World of the Infant* (New York: Basic Books, 1985); M. Mahler, "On Human Symbiosis and the Vicissitudes of Individuation," *Journal of the American Psychoanalytic Association* 15, (1967): 740–763; M. Mahler, F. Pine, and A. Bergman, *The Psychological Birth of the Human Infant: Symbiosis and Individuation* (New York: Basic Books, 1975); P. Lichtenberg and D. G. Norton, *Cognitive and Mental Development in the First Five Years of Life: A Review of Recent Research* (Chevy Chase, MD: National Institute of Mental Health, 1970); J. D. Lichtenberg, *Psychoanalysis and Infant Research* (Hillsdale, NJ: Analytic Press, 1983).

39 "psychological complexes": For a review of Jung's theory of psychological complexes, see the *Collected Works,* Vol. 8, pp. 92–104.

Jung's later theory of complexes included the idea that *every* complex is characterized by an emotional state that emanates from a core archetypal image. The complex itself is a collection of associated bits of experience (e.g., ideas, habits, sensations) that cohere through a common emotional state or meaning. An archetype is a universal tendency to form a particular coherent image (e.g., the Great Mother) in a particular emotional state (e.g., contentment or satisfaction). A complex becomes a subpersonality of the unconscious when it is enacted or experienced repeatedly. A complex originally cohered in a situation of emotional arousal (i.e., a set of stimuli), and re-experiencing either that situation or the archetypal image traces (in sights, sounds, smells, etc.) may evoke the complex.

39 "stem from the gut": See the literature listed in the fourth note to p. 72 in relation to preverbal cognitive categorization of emotional experience.

40 "stereotypes of 'us' and 'them' ": For an overview of the psychological, cultural, and societal determinants and consequences of stereotyping and dominance hierarchies, see R. Brown, *Social Psychology,* 2nd. ed. (New York: Free Press, 1986). See also S. Gilman, *Difference and Pathology: Stereotypes of Sexuality, Race, and Madness* (Ithaca, NY: Cornell University Press, 1985).

41 "negatively powerful images of Mother and Father . . . early helpless dependence": These issues are explored in the following works: M. Klein, *"Love, Guilt and Reparation" and Other Works* (New York: Dell, 1975); M. Klein, *The Psychoanalysis of Children,* trans. A. Strachey (New York: Humanities Press, 1969); M. Klein, P. Heimann, and R. E. Money-Kyrle (eds.), *New Directions in Psychoanalysis: The Significance of Infant Conflict in the Pattern of Adult Behavior* (London: Tavistock, 1955); M. Lewis and L. M. Michalson (eds.), *Children's Emotions and Moods: Developmental Theory and Measurement* (New York: Plenum Press, 1983); M. Lewis and C. Saarni (eds.), *The Socialization of Emotion* (New York: Plenum Press, 1985); M. Lewis and L. A. Rosenblum (eds.), *The Uncommon Child* (New York: Plenum Press, 1981); M. Lewis and L. A. Rosenblum (eds.), *The Child and Its Family* (New York: Plenum Press, 1979).

41 childhood abuse: A 1985 *Los Angeles Times* poll surveying 2,627 men and women over the age of sixteen found that 27 percent of the women and 15 percent of the men claimed to be victims of childhood sexual abuse. After interviewing the 416 female and 169 male respondents who reported in that poll that they had been abused, M. Gordon summarized his findings about the victims' experiences:
84 percent of the males and 98 percent of the females had been abused by males; 16 percent of the males and 30 percent of the females had been abused at home; 56 percent of the males and 28 percent of the females (abused by family members) had been abused by a cousin or sibling; and 43 percent of the males and 72 percent of the females (abused by family members) had been abused by a parent, grandparent, stepparent, aunt, or uncle. From the data it can be inferred that 16 percent of the males and 2 percent of the females had been abused by females; persons outside the

immediate family are more likely to abuse boys than girls; relatives who abuse boys are likely to be closer to them in age than relatives who abuse girls. For a complete report of the findings, see M. Gordon, "Males and Females as Victims of Childhood Sexual Abuse: An Examination of the Gender Effect," *Journal of Family Violence* 5, No. 4 (1990): 321–332. Additional statistics on childhood abuse are found in Chapter 5 of this book.

42 "magical belief": See J. Piaget, *The Language and Thought of the Child,* trans. M. Warden, (New York: Harcourt, Brace, 1926); J. Piaget, *The Moral Judgment of the Child* (New York: Free Press, 1932); L. Zusne and W. H. Jones, *Anomalistic Psychology: A Study of Magical Thinking,* 2nd ed., (Hillsdale, NJ: Lawrence Erlbaum, 1989).

42 "projections": For Jung's definition of projection, see his *Collected Works,* Vol. 6, p. 457. See also G. E. Vaillant, *Adaptation to Life* (Boston: Little, Brown, 1977).

43 "projective identification": See J. Sandler, *Projection, Identification, Projective Identification* (Madison, CT: International Universities Press, 1987); T. H. Ogden, *The Matrix of the Mind: Object Relations and Psychoanalytic Dialogue* (Northvale, NJ: J. Aronson, 1986).

46 "children feel intrinsically responsible": According to Alice Miller, a child often feels responsible for his or her parents' moods, and that responsibility can have negative long-range outcomes for the child. See, for example, A. Miller, *Thou Shalt Not Be Aware: Society's Betrayal of the Child,* trans. H. Hannum and H. Hannum (New York: Farrar, Straus & Giroux, 1984); A. Miller, *For Your Own Good: Hidden Cruelty in Child-rearing and the Roots of Violence,* trans. H. Hannum and H. Hannum (New York: Farrar, Straus & Giroux, 1983); A. Miller, *Prisoners of Childhood,* trans. R. Ward (New York: Basic Books, 1981).

47 "midlife couples ... blaming each other": Lillian Rubin suggests that some of the confusion and disillusionment midlife couples face is based on the fact that, unlike earlier concerns about employment and child rearing, the problems of midlife are less defined, outside the realm of personal experience, and there are few models of successful mutual accommodation in the media. She states: "Both women and men [are] stuck in a painful bind, each blaming the other for failures to meet cultural fantasies.... She isn't the dependent, helpless, frivolous child-woman.... He isn't the independent, masterful, all-powerful provider." L. B. Rubin, *Worlds of Pain: Life in the Working-Class Family* (New York: Basic Books, 1976), p. 178.

49 "passive aggressive": Individuals with a passive-aggressive personality disorder never confront a problem situation directly. They express their hostility in indirect and nonviolent ways, such as pouting, being stubborn, procrastinating, or "forgetting." They resent authority and manage not to comply with the demands others make of them through their passive-aggressive acts. For a discussion of passive aggression as a defense mechanism, see Vaillant, *Adaptation to Life.*

50 "separation threat": The threat of separation is explored in the works of Robert Weiss. See especially R. S. Weiss and D. Burlage, *The Family: A Review of Current Research Issues* (Cambridge, MA: American Institutes for Research, 1976); R. S. Weiss,

Marital Separation (New York: Basic Books, 1975); R. S. Weiss, *Loneliness: The Experience of Emotional and Social Isolation* (Cambridge, MA: MIT Press, 1973). See also J. Bowlby, *Attachment and Loss,* Vol. 1 (London: Hogarth Press, 1969).

53 "I'll do anything for you": See Person, *Dreams of Love and Fateful Encounters.*

59 "gender role specializations": According to Betty Friedan in *The Feminine Mystique* (New York: Dell, 1963, p. 13), the role expectation for middle-class white women before the 1970s was "housewife and mother," consumer, and status symbol (based on beauty, health, education, and concern for her family).

59 "gender assignments based on powerful assumptions": Research indicates that the descriptions given by many trained clinicians of a "healthy adult male" and a "healthy adult, sex unspecified," were identical. These descriptions included strength, objectivity, competence, and independence. When asked to describe the "healthy adult female," the same respondents suggested greater weakness, less competence, more emotional expression, and greater subjectivity than was expected from either a "healthy man" or a "healthy adult." This revealing finding clearly shows that if women behave like healthy adults, they are seen as unwomanly; but if they behave as a woman is expected to behave, they are seen as less than "healthy adults." See I. K. Broverman, D. M. Broverman, F. E. Clarkson, P. S. Rosenkrantz, and S. R. Vogel, "Sex-Role Stereotypes and Clinical Judgments of Mental Health," *Journal of Consulting and Clinical Psychology* 34 (1970): 1–7; I. K. Broverman, S. R. Vogel, D. M. Broverman, F. E. Clarkson, and P. S. Rosenkrantz, "Sex-Role Stereotypes: A Current Appraisal," *Journal of Social Issues* 28 (1972): 59–78. See also G. Baruch and R. Barnett, "Role Quality, Multiple Role Involvement, and Psychological Well-being in Midlife Women," *Journal of Personality and Social Psychology* 51 (1986): 578–585.

59 "staying at home": In a study of three hundred American women, aged thirty-five to fifty-five, Grace Baruch, Rosalind Barnett, and Carolyn Rivers found that challenging paid work, accompanied by supportive egalitarian relationships with men, contributes to the sense of well-being for adult women. The role of "stay-at-home childbearing," according to these authors, is seen as one of today's "high-risk" occupations. See G. Baruch, R. Barnett, and C. Rivers, *Life Prints: New Patterns of Love and Work for Today's Woman* (New York: McGraw-Hill, 1983).

60 "[men's] overestimation of themselves, women's . . . underestimation": In their book on women and competence, Rosalind Barnett and Grace Baruch review some of the research on this interesting gender difference. For example, they cite one large-scale study of senior college students in which the male students with C+ averages believed themselves competent to earn Ph.D.'s. The women in this study with B+ or better averages did not see themselves as competent for this advanced degree. See R. C. Barnett and G. K. Baruch, *The Competent Woman: Perspectives on Development* (New York: Irvington Publishers, 1978).

60 "Vicarious authority or creativity": For examples of women fostering creativity in their children, spouses, and lovers, see P. Phillips and F. Rozendal, "Giving Birth to a Child or Idea: The Feminine Dilemma," *Social Behavior and Personality* 11, No. 1

(1983): 56–64. They comment, "Historically, women have been forced to create vicariously by supporting another person who creates (e.g., a child). More direct creativity of music, painting, or ideas has been reserved for men" (p. 56).

61 "Envy": See especially M. Klein, *"Envy and Gratitude" and Other Works.* (New York: Delacorte Press, 1975).

62 "biological differences": Several researchers have presented evidence that the brain pathways that determine behavior differ from males to females in some ways because chromosomal differences cause differences in the hormones produced in each sex. See A. A. Ehrhardt and H.F.L. Meyer-Bahlburg, "Effects of Prenatal Sex Hormones on Gender-Related Behavior," *Science* 211 (1981): 1312–1318; N. J. MacLusky and F. Naftolin, "Sexual Differentiation of the Central Nervous System," *Science* 211 (1981): 1294–1303. However, Jerome Bruner presents a compelling argument that while biological structure may impose "constraints on action . . . it is culture, not biology, that shapes human life and the human mind. . . ." J. Bruner, *Acts of Meaning* (Cambridge, MA: Harvard University Press, 1990), p. 34.

62 "we cannot escape our embodiment": It is interesting to note, however, that in a study of 121 male transsexuals who had received sex-reassignment surgery, over 90 percent reported satisfactory outcomes. See I. B. Pauly, "The Current Status of the Change of Sex Operation," *Journal of Nervous Mental Disorders* 147, No. 5 (1968): 460–471. However, Robert Stoller warns that the term *sex-change operation* is actually a misnomer. See R. J. Stoller, *Presentations of Gender* (New Haven, CT: Yale University Press, 1985).

62 "When sex is anomalous": J. Money and A. A. Ehrhardt, in *Man and Woman, Boy and Girl: The Differentiation and Dimorphism of Gender Identity from Conception to Maturity* (Baltimore: Johns Hopkins University Press, 1972), conclude from their research with babies whose gender was reassigned postnatally due to structural abnormalities that gender identity, for the most part, occurs after birth. Money, in "Differentiation of Gender Identity," suggests that hormones establish "thresholds that facilitate or hinder the emergence and manifestations of given forms of behavior" (p. 20), but that "socialization" is the primary influence on gender differences in behaviors. See also J. Money, *Sexual Signatures: On Being a Man or a Woman* (Boston: Little, Brown, 1975); J. Money, *Sex Errors of the Body: Dilemmas, Education, Counseling* (Baltimore: Johns Hopkins University Press, 1968).

62 "men are expected to be more nurturant": See P. Sanday, *Female Power and Male Dominance: On the Origins of Sexual Inequality* (Cambridge, England: Cambridge University Press, 1981).

62 "women have less power than men": See Epstein, *Deceptive Distinctions.*

65 "mature dependence": See W. R. Fairbairn, *Psychoanalytic Studies of the Personality* (Boston: Routledge & Kegan Paul, 1952); W. R. Fairbairn, *An Object Relations Theory of the Personality* (New York: Basic Books, 1954).

65 "committed love relationship": See C. G. Jung, "Marriage as a Psychological Relationship," in the *Collected Works,* 2nd ed., Vol. 9, Part II.

chapter 2

Page

67 "De Anima": In H. Nemerov, *A Howard Nemerov Reader* (Columbia, MO: University of Missouri Press, 1991), p. 25. (Poem originally published 1962.)

69 "Dreaming allows us to review ourselves": For reviews on dreams and dream interpretation, see J. A. Hall, *Jungian Dream Interpretation: A Handbook of Theory and Practice* (Toronto: Inner City Books, 1983); J. A. Hall, *Clinical Uses of Dreams: Jungian Interpretation and Enactments* (New York: Grune & Stratton, 1977); E. C. Whitmont, *The Symbolic Quest: Basic Concepts of Analytic Psychology* (New York: Putnam, 1969); E. Whitmont and S. B. Perera, *Dreams, a Portal to the Source* (New York: Routledge, 1989).

70 "taking seriously . . . only things said by men": See C. Heilbrun, *Writing a Woman's Life* (New York: W. W. Norton, 1988).

70 Freud's Oedipus complex: See S. Freud, "Some Psychical Consequences of the Anatomical Distinction Between the Sexes," in J. Strachey (ed.), *The Standard Edition of the Complete Psychological Works of Sigmund Freud,* Vol. 19 (London: Hogarth Press, 1961). (Original work published 1925.)

70 "anima": Jung offered many definitions of *anima* throughout his work and still others have been added by James Hillman and his followers.

Perhaps the most frequent (and perplexing) use made by Jung of the term is "soul"—its meaning in Latin. Indeed poet Nemerov also uses anima to mean soul, but he no doubt alludes also to Jung's meaning in the poem because Nemerov (private communication) was quite familiar with Jungian psychology. Although Jung defines anima as soul, he also limits its use to mean the unconscious sub-personality of a man, the man's Otherness projected onto woman, earth, and nature. This implies, of course, that a woman might not have a soul.

In one of Jung's definitions of *anima*, he draws attention to the complementary relationship of the anima and a man's conscious attitude, saying, "The anima usually contains all those common human qualities which the conscious attitude lacks. The tyrant tormented by bad dreams, gloomy forebodings, and inner fears is a typical figure. . . . Thus his anima contains all those fallible human qualities his persona lacks. If the persona is intellectual, the anima will quite certainly be sentimental." From C. G. Jung, *The Collected Works of C. G. Jung: Aion*, 2nd ed., Vol. 6, trans. R.F.C. Hull (Princeton, NJ: Princeton University Press, 1959), p. 468.

70 "Marriage as a Psychological Relationship": In Jung, *Collected Works,* Vol. 9, Part II.

71 "differentiation and boundary setting": See M. Bowen, "The Use of Family Theory in Clinical Practice," *Comprehensive Psychiatry* 7 (1966): 345–374.

72 *"femme inspiratrice":* The "muse" is rarely a wife, as writer Carolyn Heilbrun puts it in *Hamlet's Mother and Other Women* (New York: Columbia University Press, 1990, p. 153): ". . . poems begin in passion, an emotion hard to retain for him who wears the socks one darns. In any case, passion of this sort does not belong to marriage, which is quite a different state, however fervent its sexual life. Muses are never husbands, and rarely wives."

72 "women and men are not equals": The power differential between men and women stands as a roadblock to total understanding. See C. F. Epstein, *Deceptive Distinctions: Sex, Gender, and the Social Order* (New Haven, CT: Yale University Press, 1988).

72 "psychological complex": See second note for p. 39.

72 "image traces": *RIG* (representations of interactions that have been generalized) is the term used by Daniel Stern to describe a composite of images, feelings, perceptions, and actions that evoke memories of significant caregiver interactions. Stern also uses the term *evoked companion* to describe an accumulation of feelings about previously lived experiences that are evoked in the place of presently experienced reality. See D. Stern, *The Interpersonal World of the Infant* (New York: Basic Books, 1985). See also G. Bower, "Mood and Memory," *American Psychologist* 36 (1981): 129–148.

75 "Primary emotions are wired in": See C. Trevarthen, "Emotions in Infancy: Regulators of Contact and Relationships with Persons," in K. R. Scherer and P. Ekman (eds.), *Approaches to Emotions* (Hillsdale, NJ: Lawrence Erlbaum, 1984).

75 "self-conscious emotion": For example, pride, shame, guilt, or envy. Michael Lewis and his associates use the term *secondary emotions* for emotions such as pride or embarrassment that are self-conscious and self-evaluative. These emotions emerge at approximately the age of two and a half. See M. Lewis, M. W. Sullivan, C. Stanger, and M. Weiss, "Self-development and Self-conscious Emotions," *Child Development* 60 (1989): 146–156; M. Lewis, *Shame: The Exposed Self* (New York: Free Press, 1991).

75 "cues and scripts": See R. S. Lazarus, "Progress on a Cognitive-Motivational-Relational Theory of Emotion," *American Psychologist* 46, No. 8 (1991): 819–834.

77 "archetypes": For a full treatment of the evolution of the term *archetype* in Jung's work, see P. Young-Eisendrath and J. Hall, *Jung's Self Psychology: A Constructivist Perspective*. (New York: Guilford Press, 1991). My definition of *archetype* fits exclusively with Jung's work on the concept after 1945. He changes what was initially an essentialist (Kantian) concept of "mental image" to something akin to an "innate releasing mechanism" in evolutionary biology. Jung's later definition refers to a predisposition to the *coherence* of specific images in emotionally aroused states. Human beings are "prewired" to form images of the Great Mother and Terrible Mother universally, no matter the culture, for example. These images cohere in states of powerful affect during powerless infancy. They continue to arouse us in predictable ways later in life.

78 Sand: See Heilbrun, *Writing a Woman's Life*, pp. 33–37.

79 "A mature state of self-reflection": Jane Loevinger's model of ego development reflects the development of cognitive complexity and self in relation with others by differentiating nine levels or stages. At the Self-aware level (the norm among American women), an individual experiences increasing self-awareness and the emergence of introspective capacities. At the Conscientious stage (more differentiated and cognitively complex than Self-aware), an individual becomes more aware of the broader social context and of other people's points of view, and develops a richer inner life and mutuality in interpersonal relations. See J. Loevinger, *Ego Development* (San Francisco: Jossey-Bass, 1976); J. Loevinger and R. Wessler, *Measuring Ego Development I: Construction and Use of a Sentence Completion Test* (San Francisco: Jossey-Bass, 1970).

79 Beck: See C. J. Beck, *Everyday Zen* (New York: HarperCollins, 1989).

79 "capacity for reflective thought": Formal thought operations are described in D. Elkind, *Child Development and Education: A Piagetian Perspective* (New York: Oxford University Press, 1976); D. Elkind, *The Child and Society: Essays in Applied Child Development* (New York: Oxford University Press, 1979); D. Elkind, "Egocentrism in Adolescence," *Child Development* 38 (1967): 1025–1034.

80 "adults are capable of reflecting": See W. F. Overton, (ed.), *The Relationship Between Social and Cognitive Development* (Hillsdale, NJ: Lawrence Erlbaum, 1983); W. F. Overton, *Reasoning, Necessity, and Logic: Developmental Perspectives* (Hillsdale, NJ: Lawrence Erlbaum, 1990); W. Overton, "Piaget: The Logic of Creativity and the Creativity of Logic," *Contemporary Psychology* 34, No. 7 (1989): 629–631; W. Overton, "The Structure of Developmental Theory," in P. van Geert and L. P. Moss (eds.), *Annals of Theoretical Psychology* (New York: Plenum Press, 1990); W. F. Overton, S. L. Ward, I. Noveck, J. Black, and D. P. Obrein, "Form and Content in the Development of Deductive Reasoning," *Developmental Psychology* 23 (1987): 22–30.

80 " 'mythopoetic' way of life": Current-day versions of the mythopoetic lifestyle can be seen in "reclaiming manhood retreats" of the modern men's movement and cults of goddess worship. See R. Bly, *Iron John: A Book About Men* (Reading, MA: Addison-Wesley, 1990); M. Adler, *Drawing Down the Moon: Witches, Druids, Goddess-worshipers, and Other Pagans in America Today* (Boston: Beacon Press, 1986); J. Campbell, *The Power of Myth* (New York: Doubleday, 1988).

82 "Most of us fall apart": See the literature on the "divided self," especially R. D. Laing, *The Divided Self* (New York: Pantheon Books, 1969); R. D. Laing, *Sanity, Madness and the Family,* 2nd ed. (Baltimore: Penguin Books, 1969); R. D. Laing, *Self and Others,* 2nd ed. (New York: Pantheon Books, 1969).

82 "medieval folktale": See P. Young-Eisendrath, *Hags and Heroes: A Feminist Approach to Jungian Psychotherapy with Couples* (Toronto: Inner City Books, 1984).

83 Greek myths: See P. Young-Eisendrath and F. Wiedemann, *Female Authority: Empowering Women Through Psychotherapy* (New York: Guilford Press, 1987); C. Kerenyi, *The Gods of the Greeks* (London: Thames & Hudson, 1974).

83 "Myths and folktales": Greek and Roman mythology represent the dominant mythological framework for Western culture. These stories were traditionally used to instruct and entertain, but they also contribute to our understanding of functioning in human groups over the lifespan. For descriptions of the use of mythology in a therapeutic context, see Young-Eisendrath and Wiedemann, *Female Authority*.

84 "Terrible Mother": For discussion of the Terrible Mother as a barrier to intimacy and opposition to the power of a female caregiver, see especially N. Chodorow, *The Reproduction of Mothering: Psychoanalysis and the Sociology of Gender* (Berkeley, CA: University of California Press, 1976); D. Dinnerstein, *The Mermaid and the Minotaur: Sexual Arrangements and Human Malaise* (New York: Harper & Row, 1976).

85 "Woody Allen's portrayals": See, for example, "Oedipus Wrecks" in the film *New York Stories* (1989).

85 "sexual abuse or stimulation": Although sexual abuse perpetrated by women is much less common than that by men, according to one large survey 16 percent of sexually abused males reported that they had been abused by females. See M. Gordon, "Males and Females as Victims of Childhood Sexual Abuse: An Examination of the Gender Effect," *Journal of Family Violence* 5, No. 4 (1990): 321–332.

85 "Great Mother is Aphrodite": See Young-Eisendrath and Wiedemann, *Female Authority,* pp. 115–119.

86 Lacan: See E. A. Grosz, *Jacques Lacan: A Feminist Introduction* (London: Routledge, 1990); J. H. Smith and W. Kerrigan (eds.), *Interpreting Lacan* (New Haven, CT: Yale University Press, 1983); B. Benvenuto, *The Works of Jacques Lacan: An Introduction* (New York: St. Martin's Press, 1986).

86 "The Mother enshrined": Susan Faludi's *Backlash: The Undeclared War Against American Women* (Chapter 4) details a call for the return to motherhood in the popular press—often at the pens of women authors. Philip Wylie coined the term *momism* to describe two psychological "types" ("destroying mothers" and "seductive mothers") and presented a very negative view of "moms" that has continued in the popular press. See P. Wylie, *Sons and Daughters of Mom* (Garden City, NY: Doubleday, 1971). See also A. Dally, *Inventing Motherhood: The Consequences of an Ideal* (New York: Schocken Books, 1982).

87 Aphrodite and Circe: See Kerenyi, *The Gods of the Greeks.*

87 Pandora: See Young-Eisendrath and Wiedemann, *Female Authority* (pp. 94–97 and 205–211), for a presentation of the use of the Pandora myth in a therapeutic intervention.

87 Eve: See K. Chernin, *Reinventing Eve: The Search for a Feminine Culture* (New York: Random House, 1987).

87 "objectification of women": The objectification of women through art, literature, and media presentations has been indicted by various researchers in connection with such negative outcomes for women as anorexia nervosa, bulimia, and male violence toward women. See D. G. Linz, E. Donnerstein, and S. Penrod, "Effects of Long-Term Exposure to Violent and Sexually Degrading Depictions of Women," *Journal of Personality and Social Psychology* 55, No. 5 (1988): 758–768; P. A. McLong, and D. E.

Taub, "Anorexia Nervosa and Bulimia: The Development of Deviant Identities," *Deviant Behavior* 8, No. 2 (1987): 177–189.

88 "Sexual crimes against women": In a recent survey of 6,159 college students, 27.5 percent of the women had experienced an act that met the legal definition of rape and 7.7 percent of the men admitted having perpetrated such an act. See M. P. Koss, C. A. Gidycz, and N. Wisniewski, "The Scope of Rape: Incidence and Prevalence of Sexual Aggression and Victimization in a National Sample of Higher Education Students," *Journal of Consulting and Clinical Psychology* 55, No. 2 (1987): 162–170. Another group of researchers has coined the term *rape prone* to describe men who commit rape even when they have access to willing sexual partners. A subgroup of these rape-prone men use rape as their most preferred sexual activity. See K. Freund, H. Scher, I. G. Racansky, K. Campbell, and G. Heasman, "Males Disposed to Commit Rape," *Archives of Sexual Behavior* 15, No. 1 (1986): 23–35. See also T. Beneke, *Men on Rape* (New York: St. Martin's Press, 1982), pp. 1–2.

88 Irigaray: See L. Irigaray, *Speculum of the Other Woman,* trans. G. C. Gill (Ithaca, NY: Cornell University Press, 1985); L. Irigaray, *This Sex Which Is Not One*, trans. C. Porter and C. Burke (Ithaca, NY: Cornell University Press, 1985).

89 "Amazons and virgin goddess": See, for example, W. B. Tyrrell, *Amazons, a Study in Athenian Mythmaking* (Baltimore: Johns Hopkins University Press, 1984); D. J. Sobol, *The Amazons of Greek Mythology* (South Brunswick, NJ: A. S. Barnes, 1972); Kerenyi, *The Gods of the Greeks.*

89 "theories of gender and sex differences": Nancy Chodorow, for one, has argued that men, "because they are mothered by women," do not grow up with relational capacities and needs, or the basis for "empathy" that women develop through primary identification with the mother. See Chodorow, *The Reproduction of Mothering*, p. 260. For a review of theories of gender, see R. T. Hare-Mustin, and J. Marecek, "The Meaning of Difference: Gender Theory, Postmodernism, and Psychology," *The American Psychologist* 43, No. 6 (1988): 455–464.

90 "childhood sexual abuse": See G. T Hotaling, D. Finkelhor, J. T. Kirkpatrick, and M. A. Straus (eds.), *Family Abuse and Its Consequences: New Directions in Research* (Newbury Park, CA: Sage, 1988); V. V. Wolfe and D. A. Wolfe, "The Sexually Abused Child," in E. J. Mash and L. G. Terdal (eds.), *Behavioral Assessment of Childhood Disorders*, 2nd ed. (New York: Guilford Press, 1988); L. E. A. Walker (ed.), *Handbook on Sexual Abuse of Children: Assessment and Treatment Issues* (New York: Springer, 1988).

91 "never recover even a rudimentary trust": See L. Davis, *The Courage to Heal Workbook: For Women and Men Survivors of Child Sexual Abuse* (New York: Harper & Row, 1990).

93 "language and achievement": For a description of a nationwide poll assessing self-esteem, educational experiences, interest in math and science, and career aspirations of girls and boys aged nine to fifteen, see American Association of University Women, *Shortchanging Girls, Shortchanging America* (Washington, DC: Greenberg-Lake, 1991).

93 "dissociated state": For discussions on dissociative disorders and multiple personality, see especially E. R. Hilgard, *Divided Consciousness: Multiple Controls in Human Thought and Action* (New York: Wiley, 1986); F. W. Putnam, *Diagnosis and Treatment of Multiple Personality Disorder* (New York: Guilford Press, 1989); P. McKeller, *Mindsplit: The Psychology of Multiple Personality and the Dissociated Self* (London: Dent, 1979).

93 "self-mutilation, starvation": See A. R. Favazza, *Bodies Under Siege: Self-mutilation in Culture and Psychiatry* (Baltimore: Johns Hopkins University Press, 1987); K. Chernin, *The Hungry Self: Women, Eating and Identity* (New York: Times Books, 1985).

96 Hephaestus: See Young-Eisendrath and Wiedemann, *Female Authority* (pp. 92–93, 173–196), for a presentation on Hephaestus.

96 "women artists projected their Genius": See, for example, R. M. Paris, *Camille: The Life of Camille Claudel, Rodin's Muse and Mistress,* trans. L. E. Tuck (New York: Seaver Books, 1988). For stories about the women in Jung's life, see C. Douglas, *Woman in the Mirror: Analytical Psychology and the Feminine* (Boston: Sigo Press, 1989). See also E. Young-Bruehl, *Anna Freud: A Biography* (New York: Summit Books, 1988).

97 "boys' games and ideas are more important": See B. Sutton-Smith, *The Psychology of Play* (Salem, NH: Ayer, 1976).

97 Gawain: The story of Sir Gawain and Lady Ragnell provides the context for an exploration of human relationships, especially relationships between men and women. Gawain, the heroic nephew of King Arthur, is also well known through the story of his adventure with the Green Knight, a symbol of the declining reign of nature deities. See Young-Eisendrath, *Hags and Heroes*, for elaboration and interpretation.

99 "universal principles of Masculine and Feminine": Many Jungian analysts presume healthy sex differences reflect universal principles. For a discussion of this issue in depth, see Douglas, *Woman in the Mirror*.

100 "gender as a cultural division": See, for example, E. E. Maccoby, "Gender as a Social Category, *Developmental Psychology* 24, No. 6 (1988): 755–765. See also J. Lacan, *Feminine Sexuality*, ed. J. Mitchell, ed. and trans. J. Rose (New York: W. W. Norton, 1982).

100 "intimate relating": For example, see J. V. Jordan, *Courage in Connection: Conflict, Compassion, Creativity* (Wellesley, MA: Stone Center, Wellesley College, 1990); I. P. Stiver, *The Meanings of "Dependency" in Female-Male Relationships* (Wellesley, MA: Stone Center, Wellesley College, 1984); L. B. Rubin, *Intimate Strangers: Men and Women Together* (New York: Harper & Row, 1983).

100 "In men, Eros": Jung, *Collected Works*, Vol. 9, Part I, p. 14.

100 "men . . . cannot relate adequately": Many theorists of masculinity believe that men are unable to express their feelings and are emotionally distant because of the absence of a caregiver of the same sex in the early years, a father who would allow for intimate relating and secure gender identity. See Dinnerstein, *The Mermaid and* *the Minotaur;* Rubin, *Intimate Strangers*; L. Rubin, *Just Friends: The Role of Friendship in Our Lives* (New York: Harper & Row, 1985).

101 " 'dichotomy' of gender differences": See J. B. Miller, *Toward a New Psychology of Women* (Boston: Beacon Press, 1976); Chodorow, *The Reproduction of Mothering;* Dinnerstein, *The Mermaid and the Minotaur*.

101 Chodorow: See *The Reproduction of Mothering*.

101 Rubin and Woodman: See M. Woodman, *Leaving My Father's House: A Journey to Conscious Femininity* (Boston: Shambhala, 1992); M. Woodman, *The Owl Was a Baker's Daughter: Obesity, Anorexia Nervosa and the Repressed Feminine—A Psychological Study* (Toronto: Inner City Books, 1980); Rubin, *Intimate Strangers;* Rubin, *Just Friends.*

101 "I fused feminist theories": See Young-Eisendrath, *Hags and Heroes* (especially Chapter 2).

101 "claims against this dichotomy": See E. V. Spelman, *The Inessential Woman: Problems of Exclusion in Feminist Thought* (Boston: Beacon Press, 1988); Hare-Mustin and Marecek, "The Meaning of Difference"; Epstein, *Deceptive Distinctions.*

102 "The boy child": Rubin, *Just Friends*, pp. 98–99.

103 "women were furious": See J. Shapiro, *Men: A Translation for Women* (New York: NAL/Dutton, 1992).

104 "Women do not trust": C. Olivier, *Jocasta's Children: The Imprint of the Mother,* trans. G. Craig (London: Routledge, 1989), p. 48.

104 "is never satisfied": Ibid., p. 44.

104 "paradise lost": Ibid., p. 39.

104 "the man emerges": Ibid., p. 42.

105 Maccoby: See E. E. Maccoby, "Gender and Relationships: A Developmental Account," *American Psychologist* 45, No. 4 (1990): 513–520.

105 "This no doubt": Ibid., 513.

106 "She explicitly rejects": D. Tannen, *You Just Don't Understand: Women and Men in Conversation* (New York: William Morrow, 1990), pp. 14–16.

chapter 3

Page

108 "codependence": See J. A. Kitchens, *Understanding and Treating Codependence* (Englewood Cliffs, NJ: Prentice Hall, 1991); A. W. Schaef, *Co-dependence: Misunderstood—Mistreated* (Cambridge, MA: Harper & Row, 1986); C. L. Whitfield,

Healing the Child Within: Discovery and Recovery for Adult Children of Dysfunctional Families (Pompano Beach, FL: Health Communications, 1987).

109 "therapeutic cults": For a discussion of the similarities between cults or new religious movements (e.g., the Unification Church), lay organizations that employ peer assistance (e.g., Alcoholics Anonymous), and professionally directed self-help programs (e.g., certain drug-rehabilitation programs), and an explanation of the impact of these "charismatic groups" on clinical practice, see M. Galater, "Cults and Zealous Self-help Movements: A Psychiatric Perspective," *The American Journal of Psychiatry* 147, No. 5 (1990): 543–551. Sexual abuse in religious groups is discussed in L. Friedman, *Meetings with Remarkable Women: Buddhist Teachers in America* (Boston: Shambhala, 1987).

109 Fairbairn: See W. R. Fairbairn, *Psychoanalytic Studies of the Personality* (Boston: Routledge & Kegan Paul, 1952); W. R. Fairbairn, *An Object Relations Theory of Personality* (New York: Basic Books, 1954).

112 Macmurray: See J. Macmurray, *Self in Action*, Vol. I of *The Forms of the Personal* (London: Faber & Faber, 1961); J. Macmurray, *Persons in Relation*, Vol. II of *The Forms of the Personal* (Atlantic Highlands, NJ: Humanities Press, 1961).

113 Macmurray, *Persons in Relation*, p. 48.

113 "Children who are able to trust": See J. Bowlby, *Child Care and the Growth of Love*, 2nd ed. (Baltimore: Penguin Books, 1965); M.D.S. Ainsworth, *Patterns of Attachment: A Psychological Study of the Strange Situation* (Hillsdale, NJ: Lawrence Erlbaum, 1978); J. Bowlby, *A Secure Base: Parent-Child Attachment and Healthy Human Development* (New York: Basic Books, 1988); J. Bowlby, *Attachment and Loss*, Vol. 1 (London: Hogarth Press, 1969).

113 Winnicott: See D. W. Winnicott, *Mother and Child: A Primer of First Relationships* (New York: Basic Books, 1957); D. W. Winnicott, *Home Is Where We Start From*, 1st ed., compiled and ed. C. Winnicott, R. Sheperd, and M. Davis (New York: W. W. Norton, 1986); D. W. Winnicott, *The Family and Individual Development* (New York: Basic Books, 1965); D. W. Winnicott, *The Maturational Process and the Facilitating Environment* (New York: International University Press, 1965).

115 "Children are driven": C. G. Jung, "Marriage as a Psychological Relationship," in *The Collected Works of C. G. Jung: Aion,* 2nd ed., Vol. 9, Part II, trans. R.F.C. Hull (Princeton, NJ: Princeton University Press, 1959), p. 191. (Original work published 1925).

115 "Self is the story we tell": See C. Taylor, *Sources of the Self: The Making of the Modern Identity* (Cambridge, MA: Harvard University Press, 1989); R. Harré, *Personal Being: A Theory for Individual Psychology* (Cambridge, MA: Harvard University Press, 1984); R. Harré, "The 'self' as a Theoretical Concept," in M. Krausz (ed.), *Relativism: Interpretation and Confrontation* (Notre Dame, IN: University of Notre Dame Press, 1989); R. Schafer, *Aspects of Internalization* (New York: International Universities Press, 1968); R. Schafer, *A New Language of Psychoanalysis* (New Haven, CT; Yale University Press, 1976).

116 "explained by others . . . explain ourselves": See especially Macmurray, *Persons in Relation*, and Harré, "The 'Self' as a Theoretical Concept."

117 "relational self": See especially H. S. Sullivan, *The Interpersonal Theory of Psychiatry* (New York: W. W. Norton, 1953). See also M. Klein, *The Psycho-analysis of Children*, trans. A. Strachey (London: Hogarth Press, 1969); H. S. Sullivan, *The Collected Works of Harry Stack Sullivan, M.D.*, ed. H. S. Perry and M. L. Gawel (New York: W. W. Norton, 1956); Fairbairn, *Psychoanalytic Studies of the Personality;* H. Kohut, *The Restoration of the Self* (New York: International Universities Press, 1977); H. Kohut, *The Search for the Self: Selected Writings of Heinz Kohut, 1950–1978*, ed. P. H. Ornstein (New York: International Universities Press, 1978); D. Stern, *The Interpersonal World of the Infant* (New York: Basic Books, 1985).

117 "The basic elements": J. V. Jordan, A. Kaplan, J. B. Miller, I. Stiver, and J. Surrey, *Women's Growth in Connection: Writings from the Stone Center* (New York: Guilford Press, 1991), p. 59. See also J. V. Jordan, "Empathy and the Mother-Daughter Relationship," *Work in Progress* 2 (1983): 2–5; A. G. Kaplan, *The "Self-in-relation": Implications for Depression in Women* (Wellesley, MA: Stone Center, Wellesley College, 1984); J. B. Miller, *Toward a New Psychology of Women* (Boston: Beacon Press, 1976); I. Stiver, "Work Inhibitions in Women: Clinical Considerations," *Stone Center Work in Progress Papers* 82 (1983): 1–11; J. L. Surrey, *Self-in-relation: A Theory of Women's Development* (Wellesley, MA: Stone Center, Wellesley College, 1985).

118 "defined by relationships": See, for example, C. Gilligan, *In a Different Voice: Psychological Theory and Women's Development* (Cambridge, MA: Harvard University Press, 1982); M. F. Belenky, B. M. Clinchy, N. R. Goldberger, and J. M. Tarule, *Women's Ways of Knowing: The Development of Self, Voice, and Mind* (New York: Basic Books, 1986); Jordan et al., *Women's Growth in Connection*.

119 "In order to be conscious of myself": Jung, "Marriage as a Psychological Relationship," p. 190.

119 "One is a self": Taylor, *Sources of the Self*, p. 35.

119 Harré: See Harré, *Personal Being*.

120 "caregivers who completely abandon a child": See especially A. J. Sameroff and R. N. Emde (eds.), *Relationship Disturbances in Early Childhood: A Developmental Approach* (New York: Basic Books, 1989).

120 "false self": This defensive presentation of self results from an inadequate parental environment, according to some theorists. See, for example, D. W. Winnicott, *Playing and Reality* (London: Tavistock, 1971); Winnicott, *The Maturational Process and the Facilitating Environment*; H. Kohut, *The Analysis of Self* (New York: International Universities Press, 1971); B. F. Kernberg, *Object-Relations Theory and Clinical Psychoanalysis* (Northvale, NJ: Jason Aronson, 1976); J. F. Masterson, *The Search for the Real Self* (New York: Free Press/Macmillan, 1988).

122 "Bowlby and his followers": See M.D.S. Ainsworth, M. C. Blehar, E. Walters, and S. Wall, *Patterns of Attachment* (Hillsdale, NJ: Lawrence Erlbaum, 1978); M. Main,

"Exploration, Play, and Cognitive Functioning Related to Infant-Mother Attachment," *Infant Behavior and Development* 6, No. 2 (1983): 167–174.

126 "Prior to full maturity": Jane Loevinger's theory of ego development delineates stages through which an individual passes toward mature cognitive complexity and differentiation. The Conscientious stage represents a point at which formal thought operations and a sense of personal identity permit empathic relating. Prior to this stage, depth in relationships is limited by impulsive, self-protective, conformist, and approval-seeking behaviors. See J. Loevinger, *Ego Development* (San Francisco: Jossey-Bass, 1976); J. Loevinger and R. Wessler, *Measuring Ego Development I: Construction and Use of a Sentence Completion Test* (San Francisco: Jossey-Bass, 1970).

129 "What I give should be given back": This statement echoes what has been called the "universal norm of reciprocity"—that a benefit received requires an equivalent benefit in return. For a review of reciprocity from ancient to modern times, see A. W. Gouldner, "The Norm of Reciprocity: A Preliminary Statement," *American Sociological Review* 25 (1960): 161–178.

130 "men feel free to interrupt women": For a review of current research on interrupting behavior and gender styles of communicating, see D. Tannen, *You Just Don't Understand: Women and Men in Conversation* (New York: William Morrow, 1990), pp. 188–215.

chapter 4

Page

136 "In this country": C. Tavris, *Anger: The Misunderstood Emotion,* 2nd ed. (New York: Simon & Schuster/Touchstone, 1989), p. 69. (Originally published 1982.)

137 "thought-reading": For a description of the "Mind-Reading Delusion," see C. Tavris, *The Mismeasure of Woman* (New York: Simon & Schuster, 1992), p. 267.

138 "mean repetitive exchange": For a discussion of the differences between men's and women's styles of conflict, see D. Tannen, *You Just Don't Understand: Women and Men in Conversation* (New York: William Morrow, 1990), p. 149–187.

140 "person who makes the most money": See M. Millman, *Warm Hearts, Cold Cash: The Intimate Dynamics of Families and Money* (New York: Free Press, 1991).

141 "Terrible Parent": See first note for p. 41.

141 "creation myths": For examples of female creators, see Tavris, *The Mismeasure of Woman*, p. 74. See also R. T. Eisler, *The Chalice and the Blade: Our History, Our Future* (Cambridge, MA: Harper & Row, 1987); E. Neumann, *The Great Mother: An Analysis of the Archetype,* trans. R. Manheim (Princeton, NJ: Princeton University Press, 1964).

142 "A Bigger Context": See J. Beck, *Everyday Zen* (New York: HarperCollins, 1989).

143 Darwin: See C. Darwin, *The Expression of the Emotions in Man and Animals* (London: John Murray, 1872).

144 Bowlby: See J. Bowlby, *Attachment and Loss,* Vol. 1 (London: Hogarth Press, 1969); J. Bowlby, *Attachment and Loss: Separation,* Vol. 2 (New York: Basic Books, 1973).

145 "Apathy . . . final product of being separated": This sense of apathy is derived in part from the lack of perceived control over the individual's outcomes. For a discussion of the effects of "learned helplessness," see H. Selye, *The Stress of Life,* 2nd ed. (New York: McGraw-Hill, 1976). See also Bowlby, *Attachment and Loss: Separation,* Vol. 2; R. A. Spitz, *The First Year of Life: A Psychoanalytic Study of Normal and Deviant Development of Object Relations* (New York: International Universities Press, 1965).

145 Ainsworth and Main: See M.D.S. Ainsworth, M. C. Blehar, E. Waters, and S. Wall, *Patterns of Attachment* (Hillsdale, NJ: Lawrence Erlbaum, 1978); M. Main, "Exploration, Play, and Cognitive Functioning Related to Infant-Mother Attachment," *Infant Behavior and Development* 6, No. 2 (1983): 167–174.

145 "normal grief": The stages of normal grief have been summarized as follows: (1) numbness, shock, disbelief (which might include denial, anger, and/or despair); (2) yearning and protest (intense preoccupation with the deceased, self-reproach, guilt about minor omissions, anger toward the deceased for leaving); (3) despair (apathy and depression, withdrawal, inability to concentrate); and (4) recovery and restitution (accepting the changes in self and the situation, returning to initiative and independence). According to W. Stroebe and M. S. Stroebe, these four stages are normal to the grieving process, but the time for passage to the next stage and the intensity of experience in each stage vary considerably from individual to individual. See W. Stroebe and M. S. Stroebe, *Bereavement and Health: The Psychological and Physical Consequences of Partner Loss* (New York: Cambridge University Press, 1987). See also V. Kast, *A Time to Mourn: Growing Through the Grief Process* (Lower Lake, CA: Great Tradition, 1988).

146 "trial separations": According to the U.S. Bureau of the Census, in 1983, 2.4 percent of the population were separated from their spouses because of relational discord. A survey by B. L. Bloom and associates of 2,940 ever-married (married at least once) adults found that 17 percent had experienced marital separation at least once, and of those individuals, 77 percent got divorced, 11 percent remained separated but married, and 12 percent reconciled. Another survey, by G. C. Kitson, concluded that one couple in six is likely to separate at some point in the relationship, and that approximately 25 percent either remained separated or reconciled, and the remainder got divorced. See U.S. Bureau of the Census, "Marital Status and Living Arrangements," March 1983 Current Population Reports, Series P-20, No. 389. (Washington, DC: Government Printing Office, 1984); B. L. Bloom, W. F. Hodges, R. A. Caldwell, L. Systra, and A. R. Cedrone, "Marital Separation: A Community Survey," *Journal of Divorce* 1

(1977): 7–19; G. C. Kitson, "Marital Discord and Marital Separation: A County Survey," *Journal of Marriage and the Family* 47, No. 3 (1985): 693–700.

146 "live together": Some couples live together to test their compatibility prior to marriage, which suggests a plan of commitment. Other cohabitants live together with no explicit long-term promises to each other; however, anecdotal evidence suggests that at least one of the cohabiting partners usually assumes that a commitment exists. Unfortunately, little research is available about cohabiting couples (with or without a commitment) who dissolve the partnership prior to marriage.

Research findings do suggest, however, that cohabitation does not enhance marital stability, and that men may benefit more than women from this arrangement.

For example, in a follow-up study of a subsample of 12,841 participants in a national longitudinal study, researchers found that 20.7 percent of the women and 22.9 percent of the men had lived with their eventual spouses at least one month prior to marriage. Although couples who had cohabited remained married for shorter periods of time than noncohabitants, when total years of living together were considered, there was no difference. The authors of this study suggest that cohabitation does not indicate less commitment to marriage, nor does it enhance marital stability. See J. D. Teachman and K. A. Polonko, "Cohabitation and Marital Stability in the United States," *Social Forces* 69, No. 1 (1990): 207–220. In another study, 59 percent of the couples prepared for remarriage (after divorce from another person) by living together. In this study, husbands who had not cohabited reported more disagreements and more marital problems, and indicated less affection from their spouses. For the wives who had cohabited, only frequency of disagreements was significantly higher than for noncohabiting wives. According to the authors, cohabitation "seems to be more effective ... for men than for women." See L. H. Ganong and M. Coleman, "Preparing for Remarriage: Anticipating the Issues, Seeking Solutions," *Family Relations* 38 (1989): 28–33.

147 "strong relational needs": For a good discussion of the differences between love and attachment, see R. S. Weiss, *Marital Separation* (New York: Basic Books, 1975), pp. 36–46.

147 Bowlby: See *Attachment and Loss*, both vols.

148 "periodic long separations": In today's society, in part because of women's rise in the professions, "commuter marriages" are becoming fairly common. Some of the negative effects of these arrangements include limitation of everyday talk, inability to share planned leisure activities, and loss of shared "nonactivities" (just being together). See N. Gerstel and H. E. Gross, "Commuter Marriages: A Review," *Marriage and Family Review* 5, No. 2 (1982): 71–93. See also J. Schor, *The Overworked American: The Unexpected Decline of Leisure* (New York: Basic Books, 1991).

150 "identification with the aggressor": Anna Freud suggested that "by impersonating the aggressor, assuming his [*sic*] attributes, or imitating his aggression, the child [or adult] has transformed himself [*sic*] from the person threatened into the person who makes threats." A. Freud, "Comments on Trauma," in S. Furst (ed.), *Psychic Trauma* (New York: Basic Books, 1967), p. 113. Identification with the aggressor has also been strongly implicated in research on the transmission of violence from generation to generation. See especially A. H. Green, "Generational Transmission of Violence in Child Abuse," *International Journal of Family Psychiatry* 6, No. 4 (1985): 389–403; M. Sugar, "Sexual Abuse of Children and Adolescents," *Adolescent Psychiatry* 11 (1983): 199–211.

150 Freud: See A. Freud, *The Ego and the Mechanisms of Defense* (New York: International Universities Press, 1946). (Original work published 1936).

152 Klein: See M. Klein, *"Love, Guilt and Reparation" and Other Works* (New York: Dell, 1975).

153 "a perceived unfairness or injustice": The concept of "procedural injustice" (the unfairness of the procedures by which an individual is unable to attain an expected positive outcome) has been the basis of numerous studies in social psychology. The four expected responses to procedural injustice are: anger, lower achievement striving, devaluation of the object or outcome, and self-depreciation. See, for example, M. M. Mark, "Expectations, Procedural Justice, and Alternative Reactions to Being Deprived of a Desired Outcome," *Journal of Experimental Social Psychology* 21, No. 2 (1985): 114–137.

153 "Human anger is": Tavris, *Anger,* p. 38.

155 "Most of the time": Ibid., p. 159.

156 "self-statement": The "I" statement is a fundamental aspect of most training in assertive communications. For a description of the use of self statements, see T. Gordon and N. Burch, *T.E.T.: Teacher Effectiveness Training* (New York: Peter Wyden, 1974).

162 "parent-child relational configuration": Object relations theory states that every psychological complex has an "object" and a "subject" pole. This point is made repeatedly by Thomas Ogden in *The Matrix of the Mind: Object Relations and the Psychoanalytic Dialogue* (Northvale, NJ: Jason Aronson, 1986) and *The Primitive Edge of Experience* (Northvale, NJ: Jason Aronson, 1989). In Jung's theory of the "mother complex," he implied that both "mother" and "child" images were evoked by the complex, but he did not clarify, as Ogden has, that the "paranoid-schizoid split" is a complex that always results in a self-other configuration.

Transactional analysis also utilizes the concepts of child and parent configurations, as well as the concept of "adult," to describe relational communications patterns. Development of the concept of transactional analysis is usually credited to Eric Berne and was later popularized by Thomas A. Harris. See E. Berne, *Games People Play* (New York: Ballantine Books, 1985), and T. A. Harris, *I'm O.K., You're O.K.* (New York: Avon, 1976).

See also J. F. Masterson's theory of "rewarding" and "withholding" object-relational units, in *The Real Self: A Developmental, Self, and Object Relations Approach* (New York: Brunner-Mazel, 1985).

163 Hart: Jungian psychoanalyst and psychologist David Hart has written several papers on the psychology of the passive-aggressive man that have been delivered in public lectures, but not published. He is compiling them into a book (personal communication).

163 "Tavris summarizes": Tavris, *Anger,* pp. 179–202.

164 "sexes differ . . . in expressing fear and sadness": Extensive research on inexpressiveness by males has generally found that women express sadness, love, and happiness more than men. In one study of 100 male and 125 female college students, self-rated expression of fear and sadness, and the level of confidence in the ability to express these emotions, were significantly higher for women than for men. See J. O. Balswick, *The Inexpressive Male* (Lexington, MA: Lexington Books, 1988); M. J. Blier and L. A. Blier-Wilson, "Gender Differences in Self-Rated Emotional Expressiveness," *Sex Roles* 2, Nos. 3/4 (1989): 287–295.

164 "more women than men said they were likely to cry": W. D. Frost and J. R. Averill, *Sex Differences in the Everyday Expression of Anger* (paper presented to the Eastern Psychological Association, Washington, D.C., 1978).

165 "expressing your feelings is good": In the 1970s, a number of popular therapy movements seemed to advocate "letting it all hang out." It has become clear since then that impulsive expression of feelings is not a sign of health, but may be a sign of certain ethnic orientations. For an account of ethnic differences in feeling expression, see M. McGoldrick, J. K. Pearce, and T. Giordana (eds.), *Ethnicity and Family Therapy* (New York: Guilford Press, 1982).

167 "a real problem-solver": According to Deborah Tannen, "Many men see themselves as problem solvers," so "a complaint or a trouble is a challenge to their ability to think of a solution . . ." Often, however, when women discuss a problem of concern, they are looking for comfort, sympathy, or understanding and not a solution. See Tannen, *You Just Don't Understand,* p. 52.

169 "men disclaim the force or power": See T. Beneke, *Men on Rape* (New York: St. Martin's Press, 1982).

chapter 5

Page

172 "sex in order to feel intimate": For example, see C. Tavris, *The Mismeasure of Woman* (New York: Simon & Schuster, 1982), p. 244.

173 Hite: See S. Hite, *The Hite Report* (New York: Macmillan, 1976).

173 Kaplan: See H. S. Kaplan, *The New Sex Therapy* (New York: Brunner/Mazel, 1974).

173 "1983 survey of 1,453 married women": D. Grosskopf, *Sex and the Married Woman* (New York: Simon & Schuster, 1983).

173 *Redbook Magazine:* "Who, What, Where and How Do You Love?," *Redbook Magazine,* Oct. 1989, p. 134.

173 *Kinsey Institute:* J. M. Reinisch, *The Kinsey Institute New Report on Sex* (New York: St. Martin's Press, 1990).

174 "Heterosexual love": N. Wolf, *The Beauty Myth: How Images of Beauty Are Used Against Women* (New York: William Morrow, 1991), p. 142.

174 "in the dark": For illustrations, see D. Heyn, *The Erotic Silence of the American Wife* (New York: Random House, 1992).

174 "orgasm rates": Reinisch, *The Kinsey Institute New Report on Sex.*

176 "What little girls learn": Wolf, *The Beauty Myth,* p. 157.

177 G spot: The G spot (or Grafenberg spot) was named for the German gynecologist who first described it. For a discussion, see Tavris, *The Mismeasure of Woman,* pp. 232–245.

177 "To date": Ibid., p. 235.

178 "boys are initiated": See P. R. Sanday, *Fraternity Gang Rape: Sex, Brotherhood and Privilege on Campus* (New York: New York University Press, 1990).

178 "when girls say no": Peggy Reeves Sanday describes in "Working a Yes Out" that for some men "no" is meaningless, because if they keep trying (even against physical resistance) or get a girl drunk, she may give in. So, in the minds of many, "no" only means "maybe." See especially Chapter 5 in Sanday, *Fraternity Gang Rape.*

179 "shame can then inhibit a man's sexual desire": See M. Lewis, *Shame: The Exposed Self* (New York: Free Press, 1991).

180 "lack of female sexual desire": According to a recent article by Esther Davidowitz, Dr. Ira Reiss says that ISD (inhibited sexual desire) is the number one sexual dysfunction in the country today. See E. Davidowitz, "Double Income, No Sex," *Redbook Magazine,* May 1992, pp. 90ff.

182 "sexual violence against women": According to a recent article in *The New York Times,* "Each year an estimated six million women are beaten by the men they live with, and 30 percent of women who become homicide victims die at the hands of men with whom they have a 'family' relationship." J. E. Brody, "Personal Health," *New York Times,* March 18, 1992.

184 "incest and sexual abuse": A vast majority of adults who report being the victims of childhood sexual abuse acknowledge that the perpetrator was an adult male. In a review of the research on childhood sexual abuse, David Finkelhor summarized that of the adults who reported being abused as children, 7 to 8 percent had been abused by fathers or stepfathers, 16 to 42 percent had been abused by other family members (usually uncles or older brothers), and 32 to 60 percent had been abused by nonrelatives. See D. Finkelhor, "The Sexual Abuse of Children: Current Research Reviewed," *Psychiatric Annals: The Journal of Continuing Psychiatric Education* 17, No. 4 (1987): 233–241.

184 "her uncle threatened": For a discussion of how threats are used in child abuse, see L. Berliner and J. R. Conte, "The Process of Victimization: The Victim's Perspective," *Child Abuse and Neglect* 14, No. 1 (1990): 29–40.

186 Davis: See L. Davis, *Allies in Healing: When the Person You Love Was Sexually Abused as a Child—A Support Book for Partners* (New York: HarperCollins, 1991); L. Davis, *The Courage to Heal Workbook: For Men and Women Survivors of Child Sexual Abuse* (New York: HarperCollins, 1990).

187 "Almost one in three": The difficulty of determining accurate estimates of sexual abuse is based in part on various research methods and survey questions. After an extensive review of the existing data from various studies, David Finkelhor suggested that at least 5 percent of adults report some type of sexual abuse in childhood, with survey results ranging between 6 and 62 percent for women and between 3 and 31 percent for men. Diana Russell reported in *The Secret Trauma: Incest in the Lives of Girls and Women* (New York: Basic Books, 1987) that more than 38 percent of the 933 women she surveyed reported being victims of sexual abuse (16 percent of the abuse had been by family members) prior to age eighteen. A *Los Angeles Times* poll (August 25, 1985) of two thousand adults found sexual abuse among 27 percent of the women and 16 percent of the men. See Finkelhor, "The Sexual Abuse of Children."

187 "so early in life": The American Humane Association reported in a 1988 study titled "National Incidence and Prevalence of Child Abuse and Neglect" that, while sexual abuse of children can and does occur at very young ages, the incidence rate tends to be higher among older children, reaching a peak between ages twelve and fourteen.

187 "Sexual deadness . . . sexual drivenness": Often a sexually abused child discovers that sex can be a way of manipulating others, and that sexual favors can be exchanged for affection, privileges, and attention—hence, a sort of sex-drivenness. On the other hand, victims of childhood sexual abuse often experience less satisfaction with adult sexual relationships, in part because of depression, loss of self-esteem, or lack of trust. See especially A. Browne and D. Finkelhor, "The Impact of Child Sexual Abuse: A Review of the Research," *Psychological Bulletin* 99, No. 1 (1986): 66–77.

188 "fatherly figure has physically attacked a young girl": Fatherly figures (fathers, stepfathers, uncles, etc.) are the most common source of sexual abuse committed against young girls. One recent study highlighted an important correlate of father-daughter abuse: In a comparison of fifty-six fathers who had abused their daughters and fifty-four fathers who had not, one major difference between the two groups was that the abusing fathers had participated in the care of their daughters significantly less during the first three years of life than nonabusing fathers. See H. Parker and S. Parker, "Father-Daughter Sexual Child Abuse: An Emerging Perspective," *American Journal of Orthopsychiatry* 56, No. 4 (1986): 531–549.

188 "violence of male partners against their lovers": According to 1985 statistics, 113 out of 1,000 husbands inflict some type of violence on their wives, and 30 inflict what would be considered severe wife beating. The same study by M. A. Straus and R. J. Gelles also indicated that wife-to-husband violence is slightly higher (121 out of 1,000 women use some violence against their husbands, and 44 inflict what would be considered severe violence). These researchers emphasized that a great deal of the violence by wives against husbands is retaliation or self-defense, and that the same type of act (for example, a punch) is more likely to inflict pain and injury when carried out by a man than a woman. Straus and K. R. Williams also report that while 17.1 percent of male homicide victims are killed by family members, 41.9 percent of women victims are killed by family members. Between 1980 and 1984, 6,408 men and 10,521 women were killed by their partners. See M. A. Straus and R. J. Gelles, "Societal Change and Change in Family Violence from 1975 to 1985 as Revealed by Two National Surveys," *Journal of Marriage and the Family* 48, No. 3 (1986): 465–479; M. A. Straus and K. R. Williams, *Homicide Victimization and Offense Rates by Age, Gender, Race, Relation of Victim to Offender, Weapon Used, and Circumstances, for the United States, 1976–79 and 1980–84* (Durham, NH: University of New Hampshire Family Research Laboratory, 1988).

188 Walker: See L. E. Walker, "Psychology and Violence Against Women," *American Psychologist* 44 (1989): 695–702. See also L. E. Walker, *The Battered Woman* (New York: HarperCollins, 1980); L. E. Walker, *The Battered Woman Syndrome* (New York: Springer, 1984); L. E. Walker, *Terrifying Love: Why Battered Women Kill and How Society Responds* (New York: HarperCollins, 1989).

188 "to contact a shelter or domestic abuse project": The National Domestic Violence Hotline phone number is (800) 333-SAFE (7233); (800) 873-6363 for the hearing impaired.

189 "one in four or five couples": See second note for p. 188.

190 "the most common crime worldwide": In the early 1970s, for example, an estimated four hundred thousand Bangladeshi women were raped by Pakistani soldiers during a nine-month conflict. See S. Brownmiller, *Against Our Will* (New York: Simon & Schuster, 1975), pp. 78–86.

192 Bly and Keen: See R. Bly, *Iron John: A Book About Men* (Reading, MA: Addison-Wesley, 1990); S. Keen, *Fire in the Belly* (New York: Bantam Books, 1991); G. Corneau, *Absent Fathers, Lost Sons: The Search for Masculine Identity*, trans. L. Shouldice (Boston: Shambhala, 1991).

193 "from the nightly news to MTV": One study analyzed a sample of sixty-two music videos and found frequent occurrences of sex, violence, and crime. The sexual and violent content was characterized by innuendo and suggestiveness, according to the researchers, perhaps reflecting the adolescent audience appeal. R. L. Baxter, C. deRiemer, A. Landini, and L. Leslie, "A Content Analysis of Music Videos," *Journal of Broadcasting and Electronic Media* 29, No. 3 (1985): 333–340. See also Chapter 6 of Susan Faludi's *Backlash: The Undeclared War Against American Women* (New York: Crown, 1991).

194 "associate masturbation with shame": June Reinisch reports that letters to the Kinsey Institute indicate that guilt and anxiety are among the main problems associated with masturbation. See Reinisch, *The Kinsey Institute New Report on Sex*.

198 "darkness of female sexual pleasure": See C. Heilbrun, *Hamlet's Mother and Other Women* (New York: Ballantine Books, 1990).

198 "An appreciation of male diversity": Tavris, *The Mismeasure of Woman,* p. 243.

199 "fatigue and anxiety": See A. Dally, *Inventing Motherhood: Consequences of an Ideal* (New York: Schocken Books, 1982).

200 "Physical battering": Dr. Murray Straus, one of the leading researchers in the area of family violence, suggests that there is not much difference between socioeconomic groups or races in regard to moderate violence between spouses (shoving, pushing, etc.), but serious types of violence are more prevalent in lower socioeconomic groups. Straus and his colleague Craig Allen further state that the greater the husband's resources, the less likely he is to use physical violence, and the more a wife's resources exceed her husband's, the more likely the husband is to use physical force. See M. Straus, *Battered Women and the New Hampshire Justice System* (Durham, NH: University of New Hampshire Family Research Laboratory, 1980); M. A. Straus and C. M. Allen, "Resources, Power, and Husband-Wife Violence," in M. A. Straus and G. T. Hotaling (eds.), *The Social Causes of Husband-Wife Violence* (Minneapolis: University of Minnesota Press, 1980); M. A. Straus and R. J. Gelles, *Physical Violence in American Families: Risk Factors and Adaptations to Violence in 8,145 Families* (New Brunswick, NJ: Transaction Publications, Rutgers University, 1989).

201 "between 25 percent and 45 percent": One recent study estimated that between 10 and 14 percent of all married women have actually been raped by their husbands. This study classified marital rapes into three categories: battering rapes (about 45 percent), force-only rapes (more "middle class," more restrained, and motivated by power, control, or showing who is boss—approximately 45 percent), and obsessive rape (unusual sexual practices—approximately 10 percent). D. Finkelhor and K. Yllo, *License to Rape: Sexual Abuse of Wives* (New York: Free Press, 1985).

201 "Rape signs": See T. Beneke, *Men on Rape* (New York: St. Martin's Press, 1982), pp. 6–10.

202 "In all of the sexual fantasies": Ibid., p. 30.

202 Sanday: Quoted in ibid., p. 10.

203 "Rape is a *man's* problem": Ibid., p. 172.

203 "Let's say I see": Ibid., p. 44 (italics in original).

204 "I tried to get her": Ibid., pp. 11–23.

205 "sexual harassment": In a recent study of 214 women faculty members and 276 women graduate students, 75.1 percent of the faculty and 63.8 percent of the students reported suffering some degree of sexual harassment. Of those reporting harassment, 38.3 percent of the faculty and 20.7 percent of the students reported seduction (propositions, innuendos, etc.), 3.7 percent of the faculty and 3.6 percent of the students reported bribery (offers of payment for sex), 5.6 percent of the faculty and 2.8 percent of the students reported sexual imposition (touching, fondling, etc.), and 0.9 percent of the faculty and 1.1 percent of the students reported threats. See L. Brooks and A. R. Perot, "Reporting Sexual Harassment," *Psychology of Women Quarterly* 15 (1991): 31–47.

206 "confused their appearance with sexiness": See especially Wolf, *The Beauty Myth.*

220 "An honorable human relationship": A. Rich, *Women and Honor: Some Notes on Lying* (Pittsburgh: Cleis Press, 1990), p. 3.

chapter 6

Page

223 "Freud stressed . . . love and work": See S. Freud, *The Psychopathology of Everyday Life,*, 2nd ed., J. Strachey (ed.), *The Standard Edition of the Complete Psychological Works of Sigmund Freud,* Vol. 6 (London: Hogarth Press, 1960).

223 Baruch and Barnett: See G. Baruch and R. Barnett, "Role Quality, Multiple Role Involvement, and Psychological Well-being in Midlife Women," *Journal of Personality and Social Psychology* 51 (1986): 578–585.

224 "paid work enhances health": In their study of 389 midlife women and 293 midlife men, Lerita Coleman, Toni Antonucci, and Pamela Adelmann found that "the work role . . . decreased the likelihood that one suffered from poor health." L. M. Coleman, T. C. Antonucci, and P. K. Adelmann, "Role Involvement, Gender, and Well-being," in F. J. Crosby (ed.), *Spouse, Parent, Worker: On Gender and Multiple Roles* (New Haven, CT: Yale University Press, 1987), p. 144.

225 "Being financially dependent": M. Millman, *Warm Hearts and Cold Cash: The Intimate Dynamics of Families and Money* (New York: Free Press, 1991), p. 94.

225 "take on something new": For a discussion of women who have made midlife transitions and a guide for successful transitioning, see J. H. Lennox and J. H. Shapiro, *Lifechanges: How Women Can Make Courageous Choices* (New York: Crown, 1990).

227 "But there come times": A. Rich, *The Dream of a Common Language* (New York: W. W. Norton, 1978), p. 74.

228 "Far from complaining": Millman, *Warm Hearts and Cold Cash,* p. 82.

230 "stay-at-home child rearing": See Baruch and Barnett, "Role Quality"; C. Rivers, R. Barnett, and G. Baruch, *Beyond Sugar and Spice: How Women Grow, Learn, and Thrive* (New York: Putnam, 1979); G. Baruch, R. Barnett, and C. Rivers, *Life Prints: New Patterns of Love and Work for Today's Woman* (New York: McGraw-Hill, 1983).

230 Bernard: See J. Bernard, *The Future of Marriage* (New York: World, 1972).

230 "[men] vulnerable to financial dependence": In times of recession, such as we have recently experienced in America, men as well as women experience financial limitation and dependence. Harvey Brenner presents a comprehensive study of the relationship between economic instability and mental hospital admissions rates from the Civil War to the present. In his book, Brenner presents strong evidence that economic changes may explain the majority of all trend movements toward increasing psychiatric admissions. He notes, "We have observed a marked tendency for male admissions to react far more sensitively to the economic downturn than female admissions." M. H. Brenner, *Mental Illness and the Economy* (Cambridge, MA: Harvard University Press, 1973), p. 170.

231 Hochschild: See A. Hochschild and A. Machung, *The Second Shift: Working Parents and the Revolution at Home* (New York: Viking, 1989).

232 "One woman": Millman, *Warm Hearts and Cold Cash,* p. 135.

232 Blumstein and Schwartz: See P. Blumstein and P. Schwartz, *American Couples* (New York: William Morrow, 1983).

235 Thorne: See especially B. Thorne, C. Kramarae, and N. Henley (eds.), *Language, Gender, and Society* (Rowley, MA: Newbury House, 1983); B. Thorne and N. Henley (eds.), *Language and Sex: Difference and Dominance* (Rowley, MA: Newbury House, 1975).

235 "when a woman returns to the work force": Juliet Schor suggests that, while some statistics indicate an increase in the number of hours of domestic labor by men, this increase reflects the fact that more men are out of the paid labor force and at home more of the time. Joseph Pleck counters that men do not actually increase their domestic labor when their wives work outside the home, but because the wives are doing less housework, the husbands do proportionally (but not actually) more work than before their wives began working. But, as Robert Weiss has suggested, men are more likely to accept lower standards of housekeeping than to increase their contributions. In another study (Pederson, Cain, Zaslow, and Anderson), fathers in dual-earner families interacted less with their infants than those in father-breadwinner families. To some extent this reduction in paternal child care was a result of the working mother's spending more evening time with her child. See J. Schor, *The Overworked American: The Unexpected Decline of Leisure* (New York: Basic Books, 1991), p. 38; J. H. Pleck, "Husbands' Paid Work and Family Roles: Current Research Issues," in H. Lopata and J. H. Pleck (eds.), *Research in the Interweave of Social Roles: Families and Jobs,* Vol. 3 (Greenwich, CT: JAI Press, 1983); R. S. Weiss, "Men and Their Wives' Work," in F. J. Crosby (ed.), *Spouse, Parent, Worker: On Gender and Multiple Roles* (New Haven, CT: Yale University Press, 1989); F. A. Pederson, R. L. Cain, M. J. Zaslow, and B. J. Anderson, "Variation in Infant Experience Associated with Alternative Family Roles," in L. Laosa and I. Sigel (eds.), *Families as Learning Environments for Children* (New York: Plenum Press, 1982).

236 "Slowly, I began": G. Steinem, *Revolution from Within: A Book of Self-esteem* (Boston: Little, Brown, 1992), p. 266. Italics in original.

240 "the most common definition": In a 1989 survey for *The Yankelovich Monitor* (1989 edition), 37 percent of the men (and 32 percent of the women) defined masculinity as being a good family provider.

241 "Pooling": Millman, *Warm Hearts and Cold Cash,* p. 170.

242 "It's often joked": Ibid., p. 52.

243 Woolf: See V. Woolf, *A Room of One's Own* (San Diego: Harcourt Brace Jovanovich, 1989). (Original work published 1929.)

243 Rubin: See L. B. Rubin, *Women of a Certain Age: The Midlife Search for Self* (New York: Harper & Row, 1979).

246 "prenuptial financial agreements": The estimated use of prenuptial agreements in the United States increased threefold between 1978 and 1988. These agreements are made to protect the more affluent spouse—usually the husband. See B. Q. Quint, "Prenuptial Agreements: When Do They Make Sense and for Whom?," *Glamour,* November 1989, pp. 132–134.

248 Rich: A. Rich, *Of Woman Born* (New York: W. W. Norton, 1976).

248 Dally: A. Dally, *Inventing Motherhood: The Consequences of an Ideal* (New York: Schocken Books, 1982).

248 "[parents] held accountable . . . for our children's actions": For a discussion of "Mother's guilt," see Dally, *Inventing Motherhood.*

249 "Mothers bear the burden": Ibid., p. 18.

250 Dally: *Inventing Motherhood.*

256 "Divine Child": Jung's archetypal image of the perfect blending of masculine and feminine elements is exhibited in a child who comes to be known as a god, as in the case of the Christ Child. Another example is the traditional ceremony for finding the successor to the Dalai Lama by searching for a child who recognizes the identifying signs. This same "divine child" symbolism is sometimes activated at the birth of a first child (or a long-awaited child), when the parents feel as though they've given birth to a very special child—a divinity. The parents must learn gradually to take back the projection of uniqueness in order for the child to develop as an ordinary youngster. See E. Neumann, *The Child* (Boston: Shambhala, 1990).

258 "aggressive conflict between parents": In their study of sixty families who had experienced divorce, Judith Wallerstein and Joan Kelly found that the "greatest disruptions in the children's lives were those that stemmed from pervasive changes in parental mood. . . . explosive interactions were, for most of the youngsters, the hallmark of the divorce experience." J. S. Wallerstein and J. B. Kelly, *Surviving the Breakup: How Children and Parents Cope with Divorce* (New York: Basic Books, 1990), p. 26. See also D. Gottlieb, *Family Matters: Healing in the Heart of the Family* (New York: NAL/Dutton, 1991).

259 "mixed loyalty": See the following works by E. B. Visher and J. Visher: *Old Loyalties, New Ties: Therapeutic Strategies with Stepfamilies* (New York: Brunner-Mazel, 1988); *Stepfamilies: Myths and Realities* (New York: Carol Publishing Group, 1980); *Stepfamilies: A Guide to Working with Stepparents and Stepchildren* (New York: Brunner-Mazel, 1979).

260 "the terrible stepmother": Although many popular folk and fairytales center around an evil stepmother (e.g., Cinderella, Snow White and the Seven Dwarves), rarely is an evil stepfather the villain.

261 Visher: See note for p. 259.

261 "studies of adult children of divorce": Wallerstein and Kelly, *Surviving the Breakup.*

263 "equality of influence": The terms *equity* and *equality* are popularly used interchangeably; however, there are distinctions between the two concepts that should be pointed out. For example, *equality* basically suggests that rewards should be equally distributed regardless of contributions. *Equity,* on the other hand, suggests that "all things are *not* equal" and that rewards should be allocated based on contributions (or investments). It is interesting to note that most research studies of expectation of future reward show that most people expect equality (equal distribution) rather than equity as a principle for reward. See, for example, W. Austin, "Friendship and Fairness: Effects of Type of Relationship and Task Performance on Choice of Distribution Rules," *Personality and Social Psychology Bulletin* 6 (1980): 402–407; E. G. Shapiro, "Effects of Expectation of Future Interaction on Reward Allocation in Dyads: Equity or Equality," *Journal of Personality and Social Psychology* 31 (1975): 873–880.

chapter 7

Page

265 "recent popular movie": *Fried Green Tomatoes* (1992).

265 "husband obviously watches too much TV": In a recent study of 107 working adults, television viewing accounted for 6.6 percent of waking life—or 40 percent of all leisure time—with men spending only slightly more viewing time than women. Sixty percent of this viewing time occurred with other family members (71 percent for married subjects). See R. Kubey and M. Csikszentmihalyi, *Television and the Quality of Life: How Viewing Shapes Everyday Experience* (Hillsdale, NJ: Lawrence Erlbaum, 1990).

267 Schor: See J. Schor, *The Overworked American: The Unexpected Decline of Leisure* (New York: Basic Books, 1991).

268 "leisure time at home": Home-based leisure is especially prominent in the lives of families with young children. The percentage of leisure time spent in the home by all age groups has increased over recent years. For a review of the research, see S. A. Glyptis and D. A. Chambers, "No Place like Home," *Leisure Studies* 1 (1982): 247–262.

271 "women's search for self-improvement": See third note for p. 33.

271 "1982 national study of adults": United Media Enterprises Report on Leisure in America, *Where Does the Time Go?* (New York: United Media Enterprises, 1982).

271 "importance of leisure to marital satisfaction": For a review, see D. K. Orthner and J. A. Mancini, "Leisure Impacts on Family Interaction and Cohesion," *Journal of Leisure Research* 22, No. 3 (1990): 125–137; D. K. Orthner, "Patterns of Leisure and Marital Interaction," *Journal of Leisure Research* 8 (1976): 98–111.

271 "1987 national survey": Decision Research, *Leisure Study* (Lexington, MA: Decision Research Corporation, 1987).

271 "husbands and wives who share leisure . . . more satisfied": Dennis Orthner and Jay Mancini summarize: "So pervasive is this relationship that there does not appear to be any recent study that fails to find an association between joint activities and marital satisfaction." Orthner and Mancini, "Leisure Impacts on Family Interaction and Cohesion," p. 127. Other researchers suggest that shared leisure has a greater impact on the marital satisfaction of women than men. See G. T. Smith, D. K. Snyder, T. J. Trull, and B. R. Monsma, "Predicting Relationship Satisfaction from Couples' Use of Leisure Time," *American Journal of Family Therapy* 16, No.1 (1988): 3–13.

271 "independent, individual leisure activities": Dennis Orthner and Jay Mancini report: "All of the studies reviewed found that spending time alone was associated with lower levels of marital satisfaction. This finding is consistently more true for wives than husbands, suggesting that women may be more likely to interpret their larger amount of individual activity time as rejection or lack of concern by their marital partner." Orthner and Mancini, "Leisure Impacts on Family Interaction and Cohesion," pp. 127–128.

273 "parallel activities": See D. K. Orthner, "Leisure Activity Patterns and Marital Satisfaction over the Marital Career," *Journal of Marriage and the Family* 37 (1975): 91–102; B. J. Palisi, "Marriage Companionship and Marriage Well-being: A Comparison of Metropolitan Areas in Three Countries," *Journal of Comparative Family Studies* 15 (1984): 43–57.

273 "1988 study . . . of parallel leisure": T. B. Holman and M. Jacquart, "Leisure Activity Patterns and Marital Satisfaction: A Further Test," *Journal of Marriage and the Family* 50 (1988): 69–78.

273 "television watching 'anesthetizes' people": See Orthner, "Leisure Activity Patterns and Marital Satisfaction over the Marital Career."

273 "1976 study of American families": P. C. Rosenblatt and M. R. Cunningham, "Television Watching and Family Tensions," *Journal of Marriage and the Family* 38, No. 1 (1976): 105–111.

274 "Preschool children": D. K. Orthner and L. J. Axelson, "The Effects of Wife Employment on Marital Sociability," *Journal of Comparative Family Studies* 11 (1980): 531–543; M. S. Hill, "Marital Stability and Spouses' Shared Time: A Multidisciplinary Hypothesis," *Journal of Family Issues* 9 (1988): 427–451.

276 Tannen: See D. Tannen, *You Just Don't Understand: Women and Men in Conversation* (New York: William Morrow, 1990), pp. 74–95.

283 "1989 study": L. L. Hoopes and J. W. Lounsbury, "An Investigation of Life Satisfaction Following a Vacation: A Domain-Specific Approach," *Journal of Community Psychology* 17, No. 2 (1989): 129–140.

287 "1980 national survey of American families": See M. Straus, R. Gelles, and S. Steinmetz, *Behind Closed Doors* (New York: Doubleday, 1980).

288 "worldwide study of military families in 1980": D. K. Orthner, *Families in the Blue: A Study of the U.S. Air Force Married and Single Parent Families* (Washington, DC: Department of the Air Force, 1980).

288 Orthner: See D. K. Orthner, "Leisure and Conflict in Families," in B. G. Gunter, J. Stanley, and R. St. Clair (eds.), *Transitions to Leisure: Conflict and Leisure in Families* (New York: University Press, 1985).

289 "Early in marriage": See D. K. Orthner, "Conflict and Leisure Interaction in Families," in B. G. Gunter, J. Stanley, and R. St. Clair (eds.), *Transitions to Leisure: Conceptual and Human Issues* (Lanham, MD: University Press of America, 1985).

289 "gap between their preferences and actual activities": In a discussion titled "The Quality of Leisure," Lillian Rubin notes that most of the husbands and wives she studied often expressed a "deep longing" for freedom and fun associated with leisure, but, "in general, their leisure hours are more often spent together in the rigidly, sex-segregated activities of earlier generations" (p. 202). See especially Chapter 10 in L. B. Rubin, *Worlds of Pain: Life in the Working-Class Family* (New York: Basic Books, 1976).

289 "fourth area of conflict": Orthner, "Leisure and Conflict in Families."

291 "Religion appears to me": C. G. Jung, *Psychology and Religion* (New Haven, CT: Yale University Press, 1938), p. 5.

291 "Contemporary spiritual movements": For discussions of "The New Christians" (the Children of God, the Jesus People, the charismatic revival movement, and the Unification Church), "The Eastern Religions" (the Divine Light Mission, Transcendental Meditation, Hare Krishna, and Subud), and "The Occult" (witchcraft, Satanism, and The Process/The Foundation), see D. Cohen, *The New Believers: Young Religion in America* (New York: M. Evans, 1975).

294 "During a death crisis": See P. R. Silverman, *Helping Women Cope with Grief* (Beverly Hills, CA: Sage, 1981); S. Stephans, *When Death Comes Home* (New York: Morehouse-Barlow, 1973); S. B. Troop and W. A. Green (eds.), *The Patient, Death and the Family* (New York: Scribner's, 1974).

chapter 8

Page

302 AIDS: The national incidence of reported cases of acquired immunodeficiency syndrome surpassed 69,000 by late 1988 and more than 39,000 patients had died. At least 450,000 Americans will be diagnosed with AIDS by the end of 1993, based on government research projections. Estimates by the U.S. Public Health Service suggest that more than one million Americans are currently infected by the human immunodeficiency virus (HIV), which leads to AIDS. See E. K. Nichols, *Mobilizing Against AIDS* (Cambridge, MA: Harvard University Press, 1989).

310 Maccoby: See E. E. Maccoby, "Gender as a Social Category," *Developmental Psychology* 24 (1988): 755–765; E. E. Maccoby, "Gender and Relationships: A Developmental Account," *American Psychologist* 45 (1990): 513–520.

310 Gadamer: See H.-G. Gadamer, *Truth and Method* (New York: Crossroad, 1985).

322 Heyn: See D. Heyn, *Erotic Silence of the American Wife* (New York: Random House, 1992).

322 "book of gender stories": P. Sanday, *Female Power and Male Dominance: On the Origins of Sexual Inequality* (Cambridge, England: Cambridge University Press, 1981).

323 "Childcare responsibilities": Ibid., p. 62.

323 "disassociation of the father": Ibid., p. 63.

323 Bly and Keen: See note for p. 192.

324 "Fathers in societies": Sanday, *Female Power and Male Dominance,* p. 63.

325 "If animals are in decline": Ibid., p. 72.

329 Lacan: See J. Lacan, *Feminine Sexuality*, ed. J. Mitchell, ed. and trans. J. Rose (New York: W. W. Norton, 1982).

330 "Origin myths": Sanday, *Female Power and Male Dominance*, p. 74.

339 "Split between the two genders": See Lacan, *Feminine Sexuality.*

340 Dennett: See D. C. Dennett, *Consciousness Explained* (Boston: Little, Brown, 1991); D. C. Dennett, *Brainstorms: Philosophical Essays on Mind and Psychology* (Cambridge, MA: MIT Press, 1991); D. C. Dennett, *The Intentional Stance* (Cambridge, MA: MIT Press/Bradford Books, 1987).

341 Lipman-Blumen: See J. Lipman-Blumen, *Gender Roles and Power* (Atlantic Highlands, NJ: Humanities Press, 1983).

342 "to stand on common ground": D. Levertov, *The Jacob's Ladder* (New York: New Directions, 1958), p. 1.

bibliography

Adler, M. *Drawing Down the Moon: Witches, Druids, Goddess-worshippers and Other Pagans in America Today*. Boston: Beacon Press, 1987.

Ainsworth, M.D.S. *Patterns of Attachment: A Psychological Study of the Strange Situation*. Hillsdale, NJ: Lawrence Erlbaum, 1978.

Ainsworth, M.D.S.; Blehar, M. C.; Waters, E.; and Wall, S. *Patterns of Attachment*. Hillsdale, NJ: Lawrence Erlbaum, 1978.

American Association of University Women. *Shortchanging Girls, Shortchanging America*. Washington, DC: Greenberg-Lake, 1991.

Austin, W. "Friendship and Fairness: Effects of Type of Relationship and Task Performance on Choice of Distribution Rules." *Personality and Social Psychology Bulletin* 6 (1980): 402–407.

Balswick, J. O. *The Inexpressive Male*. Lexington, MA: Lexington Books, 1988.

Barnett, R. C., and Baruch, G. K. *The Competent Woman: Perspectives on Development*. New York: Irvington Publishers, 1978.

Baruch, G., and Barnett, R. "Role Quality, Multiple Role Involvement, and Psychological Well-being in Midlife Women." *Journal of Personality and Social Psychology* 51 (1986): 578–585.

Baruch, G.; Barnett, R.; and Rivers, C. *Life Prints: New Patterns of Love and Work for Today's Woman*. New York: McGraw-Hill, 1983.

Baxter, R. L.; deRiemer, C.; Landini, A.; and Leslie, L. "A Content Analysis of Music Videos." *Journal of Broadcasting and Electronic Media* 29, No. 3 (1985): 333–340.

Beck, J. *Everyday Zen*. New York: HarperCollins, 1989.

Belenky, M. F.; Clinchy, B. M.; Goldberger, N. R.; and Tarule, J. M. *Women's Ways of Knowing: The Development of Self, Voice, and Mind*. New York: Basic Books, 1986.

Beneke, T. *Men on Rape*. New York: St. Martin's Press, 1982.

Benvenuto, B. *The Works of Jacques Lacan: An Introduction*. New York: St. Martin's Press, 1986.

Berliner, L., and Conte, J. R. "The Process of Victimization: The Victim's Perspective." *Child Abuse and Neglect* 14, No. 1 (1990): 29–40.

Bernard, J. *The Future of Marriage*. New York: World, 1972.

Berne, E. *Games People Play*. New York: Ballantine Books, 1985.

Blier, M. J., and Blier-Wilson, L. A. "Gender Differences in Self-rated Emotional Expressiveness." *Sex Roles* 2, Nos. 3/4 (1989): 287–295.

Bloom, B. L.; Hodges, W. F.; Caldwell, R. A.; Systra, L.; and Cedrone, A. R. "Marital Separation: A Community Survey." *Journal of Divorce* 1 (1977): 7–19.

Blumstein, P., and Schwartz, P. *American Couples*. New York: William Morrow, 1983.

Bly, R. *Iron John: A Book About Men*. Reading, MA: Addison-Wesley, 1990.

Bowen, M. "The Use of Family Theory in Clinical Practice." *Comprehensive Psychiatry* 7 (1966): 345–374.

Bower, G. "Mood and Memory." *American Psychologist* 36 (1981): 129–148.

Bowlby, J. *Child Care and the Growth of Love*. 2nd ed. Baltimore: Penguin Books, 1965.

———. *Attachment and Loss*, Vol. 1. London: Hogarth Press, 1969.

———. *Attachment and Loss: Separation*, Vol. 2. New York: Basic Books, 1973.

———. *A Secure Base: Parent-Child Attachment and Healthy Human Development*. New York: Basic Books, 1988.

Brenner, M. H. *Mental Illness and the Economy*. Cambridge, MA: Harvard University Press, 1973.

Brooks, L., and Perot, A. R. "Reporting Sexual Harassment." *Psychology of Women Quarterly* 15 (1991): 31–47.

Broverman, I. K.; Broverman, D. M.; Clarkson, F. E.; Rosenkrantz, P. S.; and Vogel, S. R. "Sex-Role Stereotypes and Clinical Judgments of Mental Health." *Journal of Consulting and Clinical Psychology* 34 (1970): 1–7.

Broverman, I. K.; Vogel, S. R.; Broverman, D. M.; Clarkson, F. E.; and Rosenkrantz, P. S. "Sex-Role Stereotypes: A Current Appraisal." *Journal of Social Issues* 28 (1972): 59–78.

Brown, R. *Social Psychology*. 2nd ed. New York: Free Press, 1986.

Browne, A., and Finkelhor, D. "The Impact of Child Sexual Abuse: A Review of the Research." *Psychological Bulletin* 99, No. 1 (1986): 66–77.

Brownmiller, S. *Against Our Will*. New York: Simon & Schuster, 1975.

Bruner, J. *Acts of Meaning*. Cambridge, MA: Harvard University Press, 1990.

Caldwell, M., and Peplau, L. A. "Balance of Power in Lesbian Relationships." *Sex Roles* 10, No. 1 (1984): 587–599.

Campbell, J. *The Power of Myth*. New York: Doubleday, 1988.

Chernin, K. *The Hungry Self: Women, Eating and Identity*. New York: Times Books, 1985.

———. *Reinventing Eve: The Search for a Feminine Culture*. New York: Random House, 1987.

Chodorow, N. *The Reproduction of Mothering: Psychoanalysis and the Sociology of Gender*. Berkeley, CA: University of California Press, 1978.

Cohen, D. *The New Believers: Young Religion in America*. New York: M. Evans, 1975.

Coleman, L. M.; Antonucci, T. C.; and Adelmann, P. K. "Role Involvement, Gender, and Well-being." In F. J. Crosby (ed.) *Spouse, Parent, Worker: On Gender and Multiple Roles*. New Haven, CT: Yale University Press, 1987.

Corneau, G. *Absent Fathers, Lost Sons: The Search for Masculine Identity*. Trans. L. Shouldice. Boston: Shambhala, 1991.

Coverman, S. "Women's Work Is Never Done: The Division of Domestic Labor." In J. Freeman (ed.), *Women: A Feminist Perspective*. Mountain View, CA: Mayfield, 1989.

Cowan, C., and Kinder, M. *Smart Women/Foolish Choices*. New York: Clarkson N. Potter, 1985.

Dally, A. *Inventing Motherhood: The Consequences of an Ideal*. New York: Schocken Books, 1982.

Daniels, P. "Dream vs. Drift in Women's Careers: The Question of Generativity." In B. Goldman and B. Forisha (eds.) *Outside on the Inside: Women and Organizations*. Englewood Cliffs, NJ: Prentice Hall, 1981.

Darwin, C. *The Expression of the Emotions in Man and Animals*. London: John Murray, 1872.

Davis, L. *The Courage to Heal Workbook: For Men and Women Survivors of Child Sexual Abuse*. New York: HarperCollins, 1990.

———. *Allies in Healing: When the Person You Love Was Sexually Abused as a Child—A Support Book for Partners*. New York: HarperCollins, 1991.

DeCecco, J. *Gay Relationships*. New York: Harrington Park Press, 1988.

Decision Research. *Leisure Study*. Lexington, MA: Decision Research Corporation, 1987.

Dennett, D. C. *Brainstorms: Philosophical Essays on Mind and Psychology*. Cambridge, MA: MIT Press, 1978.

———. *The Intentional Stance*. Cambridge, MA: MIT Press/Bradford Books, 1987.

———. *Consciousness Explained*. Boston: Little, Brown, 1991.

Dinnerstein, D. *The Mermaid and the Minotaur: Sexual Arrangements and Human Malaise*. New York: Harper & Row, 1976.

Douglas, C. *Woman in the Mirror: Analytical Psychology and the Feminine*. Boston: Sigo, 1989.

Ehrhardt, A. A., and Meyer-Bahlburg, H.F.L."Effects of Prenatal Sex Hormones on Gender-Related Behavior." *Science* 211 (1981): 1312–1318.

Eisenberg, N., and Lennon, R. "Sex Differences in Empathy and Related Capacities." *Psychological Bulletin* 94 (1983): 100–131.

Eisler, R. M., and Blalock, J. A. "Masculine Gender Role Stress: Implications for the Assessment of Men." *Clinical Psychology Review* 11 (1991): 45–60.

Eisler, R. T. *The Chalice and the Blade: Our History, Our Future*. Cambridge, MA: Harper & Row, 1987.

Elkind, D. "Egocentrism in Adolescence." *Child Development* 38 (1967): 1025–1034.

———. *Child Development and Education: A Piagetian Perspective*. New York: Oxford University Press, 1976.

———. *The Child and Society; Essays in Applied Child Development*. New York: Oxford University Press, 1979.

Epstein, C. *Deceptive Distinctions: Sex, Gender, and the Social Order*. New Haven, CT: Yale University Press, 1988.

Fairbairn, W. R. *Psychoanalytic Studies of the Personality*. Boston: Routledge & Kegan Paul, 1952.

———. *An Object Relations Theory of the Personality*. New York: Basic Books, 1954.

Faludi, S. *Backlash: The Undeclared War Against American Women*. New York: Crown, 1991.

Favazza, A. R. *Bodies Under Siege: Self-mutilation in Culture and Psychiatry*. Baltimore: Johns Hopkins University Press, 1987.

Finkelhor, D. "The Sexual Abuse of Children: Current Research Reviewed." *Psychiatric Annals: The Journal of Continuing Psychiatric Education* 17, No. 4 (1987): 233–241.

Finkelhor, D., and Yllo, K. *License to Rape: Sexual Abuse of Wives*. New York: Free Press, 1985.

Franz, M. L. *Projection and Re-collection in Jungian Psychology: Reflections of the Soul*. Trans. W. H. Kennedy. LaSalle, IL: Open Court, 1980.

Freud, A. *The Ego and the Mechanisms of Defense*. New York: International Universities Press, 1946. (Original work published 1936.)

———. "Comments on Trauma." In S. Furst (ed.), *Psychic Trauma*. New York: Basic Books, 1967.

Freud, S. *The Psychopathology of Everyday Life*. 2nd ed. J. Strachey (ed.), *The Standard Edition of the Complete Psychological Works of Sigmund Freud,* Vol. 6. London: Hogarth Press, 1960.

———. "Some Psychical Consequences of the Anatomical Distinction Between the Sexes." In J. Strachey (ed.), *The Standard Edition of the Complete Psychological Works of Sigmund Freud*, Vol. 19. London: Hogarth Press, 1961.

Freund, K.; Scher, H.; Racansky, I. G.; Campbell, K.; and Heasman, G. "Males Disposed to Commit Rape." *Archives of Sexual Behavior* 15, No. 1 (1986): 23–35.

Friedan, B. *The Feminine Mystique*. New York: Dell, 1963.

Friedman, L. *Meetings with Remarkable Women: Buddhist Teachers in America*. Boston: Shambhala, 1987.

Frost, W. D., and Averil, J. R. *Sex Differences in Everyday Expression*. Paper presented to the Eastern Psychological Association, Washington, DC, 1978.

Gadamer, H.-G. *Truth and Method*. New York: Crossroad, 1985.

Galater, M. "Cults and Zealous Self-help Movements: A Psychiatric Perspective." *The American Journal of Psychiatry* 147, No. 5 (1990): 543–551.

Ganong, L. H., and Coleman, M. "Preparing for Remarriage: Anticipating the Issues, Seeking Solutions." *Family Relations* 38 (1989): 28–33.

Gerstel, N., and Gross, H. E. "Commuter Marriages: A Review." *Marriage and Family Review* 5, No. 2 (1982): 71–93.

Gilligan, C. *In a Different Voice: Psychological Theory and Women's Development*. Cambridge, MA: Harvard University Press, 1982.

Gilman, S. *Difference and Pathology: Stereotypes of Sexuality, Race, and Madness*. Ithaca, NY: Cornell University Press, 1985.

Glyptis, S. A., and Chambers, D. A. "No Place like Home." *Leisure Studies* 1 (1982): 247–262.

Gordon, M. "Males and Females as Victims of Childhood Sexual Abuse: An Examination of the Gender Effect." *Journal of Family Violence* 5, No. 4 (1990): 321–332.

Gordon, T. and Burch, N. *T.E.T.: Teacher Effectiveness Training*. New York: Peter Wyden, 1974.

Gottlieb, D. *Family Matters: Healing in the Heart of the Family*. New York: NAL/Dutton, 1991.

Gouldner, A. W. "The Norm of Reciprocity: A Preliminary Statement." *American Sociological Review* 25 (1960): 161–178.

Green, A. H. "Generational Transmission of Violence in Child Abuse." *International Journal of Family Psychiatry* 6, No. 4 (1985): 389–403.

Grosskopf, D. *Sex and the Married Woman*. New York: Simon & Schuster, 1983.

Grosz, E. A. *Jacques Lacan: A Feminist Introduction*. London: Routledge, 1990.

Hall, J. A. *Clinical Uses of Dreams: Jungian Interpretation and Enactments*. New York: Grune & Stratton, 1977.

———. *Jungian Dream Interpretation: A Handbook of Theory and Practice*. Toronto: Inner City Books, 1983.

Hare-Mustin, R. T., and Marecek, J. "The Meaning of Difference: Gender Theory, Postmodernism, and Psychology." *The American Psychologist* 43, No. 6 (1988): 455–464.

Harré, R. *Personal Being: A Theory for Individual Psychology*. Cambridge, MA: Harvard University Press, 1984.

———. "The 'Self' as a Theoretical Concept." In M. Krausz (ed.), *Relativism: Interpretation and Confrontation*. Notre Dame, IN: University of Notre Dame Press, 1989.

Harris, T. A. *I'm O.K., You're O.K.* New York: Avon, 1976.

Harry, J. "Gay Male and Lesbian Family Relationships." In E. Macklin (ed.), *Contemporary Families and Alternate Lifestyles: Handbook on Research and Theory*. Beverly Hills, CA: Sage, 1983.

Heilbrun, C. *Writing a Woman's Life*. New York: W. W. Norton, 1988.

———. *Hamlet's Mother and Other Women*. New York: Ballantine Books, 1990.

Heyn, D. *The Erotic Silence of the American Wife*. New York: Random House, 1992.

Hilgard, E. R. *Divided Consciousness: Multiple Controls in Human Thought and Action*. New York: Wiley, 1986.

Hill, M. S. "Marital Stability and Spouses' Shared Time: A Multidisciplinary Hypothesis." *Journal of Family Issues* 9 (1988): 427–451.

Hite, S. *The Hite Report*. New York: Macmillan, 1976.

Hochschild, A., and Machung, A. *The Second Shift: Working Parents and the Revolution at Home*. New York: Viking, 1989.

Holman, T. B., and Jacquart, M. "Leisure Activity Patterns and Marital Satisfaction: A Further Test." *Journal of Marriage and the Family* 50 (1988): 69–78.

Hoopes, L. L., and Lounsbury, J. W. "An Investigation of Life Satisfaction Following a Vacation: A Domain-Specific Approach." *Journal of Community Psychology* 17, No. 2 (1989): 129–140.

Hotaling, G. T.; Finkelhor, D.; Kirkpatrick, J. T.; and Straus, M. A. (eds.). *Family Abuse and Its Consequences: New Directions in Research*. Newbury Park, CA: Sage, 1988.

Irigaray, L. *Speculum of the Other Woman*. Trans. G. C. Gill. Ithaca, NY: Cornell University Press, 1985.

———. *This Sex Which Is Not One*. Trans. C. Porter and C. Burke. Ithaca, NY: Cornell University Press, 1985.

Jordan, J. V. "Empathy and the Mother-Daughter Relationship." *Stone Center Work in Progress Papers* 2 (1983): 2–5.

———. *Relational Development: Therapeutic Implications of Empathy and Shame*. Wellesley, MA: Stone Center, Wellesley College, 1989.

———. *Courage in Connection: Conflict, Compassion, Creativity*. Wellesley, MA: Stone Center, Wellesley College, 1990.

Jordan, J. V.; Kaplan, A.; Miller, J. B.; Stiver, I.; and Surrey, J. *Women's Growth in Connection: Writings from the Stone Center*. New York: Guilford Press, 1991.

Jung, C. G. *Psychology and Religion*. New Haven, CT: Yale University Press, 1938.

———. *The Collected Works of C. G. Jung: Aion*. 2nd ed. Trans. R.F.C. Hull. Princeton, NJ: Princeton University Press, 1959.

Kaplan, A. G. *The "Self-in-relation": Implications for Depression in Women*. Wellesley, MA: Stone Center, Wellesley College, 1984.

Kaplan, H. S. *The New Sex Therapy*. New York: Brunner/Mazel, 1974.

Kast, V. *A Time to Mourn: Growing Through the Grief Process*. Lower Lake, CA: Great Tradition, 1988.

Kaufman, G., and Raphael, L. *Dynamics of Power: Fighting Shame and Building Self Esteem*. 2nd ed. Rochester, VT: Schenkman, 1991.

Keen, S. *Fire in the Belly*. New York: Bantam Books, 1991.

Kerenyi, C. *The Gods of the Greeks*. London: Thames & Hudson, 1974.

Kernberg, O. F. *Object-Relations Theory and Clinical Psychoanalysis*. Northvale, NJ: Jason Aronson, 1976.

Kitchens, J. A. *Understanding and Treating Codependence*. Englewood Cliffs, NJ: Prentice Hall, 1991.

Kitson, G. C. "Marital Discord and Marital Separation: A County Survey." *Journal of Marriage and the Family* 47, No. 3 (1985): 693–700.

Klein, M. *The Psychoanalysis of Children*. Trans. A. Strachey. New York: Humanities Press, 1969.

———. *"Envy and Gratitude" and Other Works*. New York: Delacorte, 1975.

———. *"Love, Guilt and Reparation" and Other Works*. New York: Dell, 1975.

Klein, M.; Heimann, P.; and Money-Kyrle, R. E. (eds.). *New Directions in Psychoanalysis: The Significance of Infant Conflict in the Pattern of Adult Behavior*. London: Tavistock, 1955.

Kohlberg, L. "A Cognitive-Developmental Analysis of Children's Sex-Role Concepts and Attitudes." In E. E. Maccoby (ed.), *The Development of Sex Differences*. Stanford, CA: Stanford University Press, 1966.

Kohn, A. *No Contest: The Case Against Competition*. Boston: Houghton Mifflin, 1986.

Kohut, H. *The Analysis of Self*. New York: International Universities Press, 1971.

———. *The Restoration of the Self*. New York: International Universities Press, 1977.

———. *The Search for the Self: Selected Writings of Heinz Kohut, 1950–1978*. Ed. P. H. Ornstein. New York: International Universities Press, 1978.

Koss, M. P.; Gidycz, C. A.; and Wisniewski, N. "The Scope of Rape: Incidence and Prevalence of Sexual Aggression and Victimization in a National Sample of Higher Education Students." *Journal of Consulting and Clinical Psychology* 55, No. 2 (1987): 162–170.

Kubey, R., and Csikszentmihalyi, M. *Television and the Quality of Life: How Viewing Shapes Everyday Experience*. Hillsdale, NJ: Lawrence Erlbaum, 1990.

Lacan, J. *Feminine Sexuality*. Ed. J. Mitchell, ed. and trans. J. Rose. New York: W. W. Norton, 1982.

Laing, R. D. *The Divided Self*. New York: Pantheon Books, 1969.

———. *Sanity, Madness and the Family*. 2nd ed. Baltimore: Penguin Books, 1969.

———. *Self and Others*. 2nd ed., New York: Pantheon Books, 1969.

Lazarus, R. S. "Progress on a Cognitive-Motivational-Relational Theory of Emotion." *American Psychologist* 46, No. 8 (1991): 819–834.

Lennox, J. H., and Shapiro, J. H. *Lifechanges: How Women Can Make Courageous Choices*. New York: Crown, 1990.

Levertov, D. *The Jacob's Ladder*. New York: New Directions, 1958.

Levinson, D. J.; Darrow, C. N.; Klein, E. B.; Levinson, M. H.; and McKee, B. *The Seasons of a Man's Life*. New York: Knopf, 1978.

Lewis, M. *Shame: The Exposed Self*. New York: Free Press, 1991.

Lewis, M., and Michalson, L. M. (eds.). *Children's Emotions and Moods: Developmental Theory and Measurement*. New York: Plenum Press, 1983.

Lewis, M., and Rosenblum, L. A. (eds.). *The Child and Its Family*. New York: Plenum Press, 1979.

———. *The Uncommon Child*. New York: Plenum Press, 1981.

Lewis, M., and Saarni, C. (eds.). *The Socialization of Emotion*. New York: Plenum Press, 1985.

Lewis, M.; Sullivan, M. W.; Stanger, C.; and Weiss, M. "Self-development and Self-conscious Emotions." *Child Development* 60 (1989): 146–156.

Lichtenberg, J. D. *Psychoanalysis and Infant Research*. Hillsdale, NJ: Analytic Press, 1983.

Lichtenberg, P., and Norton, D. G. *Cognitive and Mental Development in the First Five Years of Life: A Review of Recent Research*. Chevy Chase, MD: National Institute of Mental Health, 1970.

Linz, D. G.; Donnerstein, E.; and Penrod, S. "Effects of Long-Term Exposure to Violent and Sexually Degrading Depictions of Women." *Journal of Personality and Social Psychology* 55, No. 5 (1988): 758–768.

Lipman-Blumen, J. *Gender Roles and Power*. Atlantic Highlands, NJ: Humanities Press, 1983.

Loevinger, J. *Ego Development*. San Francisco: Jossey-Bass, 1976.

Loevinger, J., and Wessler, R. *Measuring Ego Development I: Construction and Use of a Sentence Completion Test*. San Francisco: Jossey-Bass, 1970.

Maccoby, E. E. "Gender as a Social Category." *Developmental Psychology* 24, No. 6 (1988): 755–765.

———. "Gender and Relationships: A Developmental Account." *American Psychologist* 45, No. 4 (1990): 513–520.

MacLusky, N. J., and Naftolin, F. "Sexual Differentiation of the Central Nervous System." *Science* 211 (1981): 1294–1303.

Macmurray, J. *The Forms of the Personal: Self in Action,* Vol. 1. London: Faber & Faber, 1961.

———. *The Forms of the Personal: Persons in Relation,* Vol. 2. Atlantic Highlands, NJ: Humanities Press, 1961.

Mahler, M. "On Human Symbiosis and the Vicissitudes of Individuation." *Journal of the American Psychoanalytic Association* 15 (1967): 740–763.

Mahler, M.; Pine, F.; and Bergman, A. *The Psychological Birth of the Human Infant: Symbiosis and Individuation*. New York: Basic Books, 1975.

Main, M. "Exploration, Play, and Cognitive Functioning Related to Infant-Mother Attachment." *Infant Behavior and Development* 6, No. 2 (1983): 167–174.

Mark, M. M. "Expectations, Procedural Justice, and Alternative Reactions to Being Deprived of a Desired Outcome." *Journal of Experimental Social Psychology* 21, No. 2 (1985): 114–137.

Masterson, J. F. *The Real Self: A Developmental, Self, and Object Relations Approach*. New York: Brunner-Mazel, 1985.

———. *The Search for the Real Self*. New York: Free Press/Macmillan, 1988.

Masterson, J. F., and Klein, R. (eds.). *Psychotherapy of the Disorders of the Self: The Masterson Approach*. New York: Brunner-Mazel, 1988.

McGoldrick, M.; Pearce, J. K.; and Giordana, T. (eds.). *Ethnicity and Family Therapy*. New York: Guilford Press, 1982.

McKeller, P. *Mindsplit: The Psychology of Multiple Personality and the Dissociated Self*. London: Dent, 1979.

McLong, P. A., and Taub, D. E. "Anorexia Nervosa and Bulimia: The Development of Deviant Identities." *Deviant Behavior* 8, No. 2 (1987): 177–189.

Miller, A. *Prisoners of Childhood*. Trans. R. Ward. New York: Basic Books, 1981.

———. *For Your Own Good: Hidden Cruelty in Child-rearing and the Roots of Violence*. Trans. H. Hannum and H. Hannum. New York: Farrar, Straus & Giroux, 1983.

———. *Thou Shalt Not Be Aware: Society's Betrayal of the Child*. Trans. H. Hannum and H. Hannum. New York: Farrar, Straus & Giroux, 1984.

Miller, J. B. *Toward a New Psychology of Women*. Boston: Beacon Press, 1976.

Millman, M. *Warm Hearts and Cold Cash: The Intimate Dynamics of Families and Money*. New York: Free Press, 1991.

Mitchell, J., and Rose, J. (eds.). *Feminine Sexuality: Jacques Lacan and the Ecole Freudienne*. Trans. J. Rose. New York: W. W. Norton, 1985.

Money, J. *Sex Errors of the Body: Dilemmas, Education, Counseling*. Baltimore: Johns Hopkins University Press, 1968.

———. *Sexual Signatures: On Being a Man or a Woman*. Boston: Little, Brown, 1975.

———. "Differentiation of Gender Identity." *JSAS Catalog of Selected Documents in Psychology* 6, No. 4 (1976).

Money, J., and Ehrhardt, A. A. *Man and Woman, Boy and Girl: The Differentiation and Dimorphism of Gender Identity from Conception to Maturity*. Baltimore, MD: Johns Hopkins University Press, 1972.

Nathanson, D. L. (ed.). *The Many Faces of Shame*. New York: Guilford Press, 1987.

Nemerov, H. *A Howard Nemerov Reader*. Columbia, MO: University of Missouri Press, 1991.

Neumann, E. *The Great Mother: An Analysis of the Archetype*. Trans. R. Manheim. Princeton, NJ: Princeton University Press, 1964.

———. *The Child*. Boston: Shambhala, 1990.

Nichols, E. K. *Mobilizing Against AIDS*. Cambridge, MA: Harvard University Press, 1989.

Ogden, T. H. *The Matrix of the Mind: Object Relations and the Psychoanalytic Dialogue*. Northvale, NJ: Jason Aronson, 1986.

———. *The Primitive Edge of Experience*. Northvale, NJ: Jason Aronson, 1989.

Olivier, C. *Jocasta's Children: The Imprint of the Mother*. Trans. G. Craig. London: Routledge, 1989.

Orthner, D. K. "Leisure Activity Patterns and Marital Satisfaction over the Marital Career." *Journal of Marriage and the Family* 37 (1975): 91–102.

———. "Patterns of Leisure and Marital Interaction." *Journal of Leisure Research* 8 (1976): 98–111.

———. *Families in the Blue: A Study of the U.S. Air Force Married and Single Parent Families*. Washington, DC: Department of the Air Force, 1980.

———. "Conflict and Leisure Interaction in Families." In B. G. Gunter, J. Stanley, and R. St. Clair (eds.), *Transitions to Leisure: Conceptual and Human Issues*. Lanham, MD: University Press of America, 1985.

———. "Leisure and Conflict in Families." In B. G. Gunter, J. Stanley, and R. St. Clair (eds.), *Transitions to Leisure: Conflict and Leisure in Families*. New York: New York University Press, 1985.

Orthner, D. K., and Axelson, L. J. "The Effects of Wife Employment on Marital Sociability." *Journal of Comparative Family Studies* 11 (1980): 531–543.

Orthner, D. K., and Mancini, J. A. "Leisure Impacts on Family Interaction and Cohesion." *Journal of Leisure Research* 22, No. 3 (1990): 125–137.

Overton, W. F. (ed.). *The Relationship Between Social and Cognitive Development*. Hillsdale, NJ: Lawrence Erlbaum, 1983.

———. "Piaget: The Logic of Creativity and the Creativity of Logic." *Contemporary Psychology* 34, No. 7 (1989): 629–631.

———. *Reasoning, Necessity, and Logic: Developmental Perspectives*. Hillsdale, NJ: Lawrence Erlbaum, 1990.

———. "The Structure of Developmental Theory." In P. van Geert and L. P. Moss (eds.), *Annals of Theoretical Psychology*. New York: Plenum Press, 1990.

Overton, W. F.; Ward, S. L.; Noveck, I.; Black, J.; and Obrein, D. P. "Form and Content in the Development of Deductive Reasoning." *Developmental Psychology* 23 (1987): 22–30.

Palisi, B. J. "Marriage Companionship and Marriage Well-being: A Comparison of Metropolitan Areas in Three Countries." *Journal of Comparative Family Studies* 15 (1984): 43–57.

Paris, R. M. *Camille: The Life of Camille Claudel, Rodin's Muse and Mistress*. Trans. L. E. Tuck. New York: Seaver Books, 1988.

Parker, H., and Parker, S. "Father-Daughter Sexual Child Abuse: An Emerging Perspective." *American Journal of Orthopsychiatry* 56, No. 4 (1986): 531–549.

Pauly, I. B. "The Current Status of the Change of Sex Operation." *Journal of Nervous Mental Disorders* 147, No. 5 (1968): 460–471.

Pederson, F. A.; Cain, R. L.; Zaslow, M. J.; and Anderson, B. J. "Variation in Infant Experience Associated with Alternative Family Roles." In L. Laosa and I. Sigel (eds.), *Families as Learning Environments for Children*. New York: Plenum Press, 1982.

Peplau, L. A., and Gordon, S. L. "The Intimate Relationships of Lesbians and Gay Men." In E. R. Allgeier and N. B. McCormick (eds.), *Gender and Roles and Sexual Behavior*. Palo Alto, CA: Mayfield, 1982.

Person, E. S. *Dreams of Love and Fateful Encounters: The Power of Romantic Passion*. New York: W. W. Norton, 1988.

Phillips, P., and Rozendal, F. "Giving Birth to a Child or Idea: The Feminine Dilemma." *Social Behavior and Personality* 11, No. 1 (1983): 56–64.

Piaget, J. *The Language and Thought of the Child*. Trans. M. Warden. New York: Harcourt, Brace, 1926.

———. *The Moral Judgment of the Child*. New York: Free Press, 1932.

Pleck, J. H. "Men's Power with Women, Other Men, and Society: A Men's Movement Analysis." In R. A. Lewis (ed.), *Men in Difficult Times: Masculinity Today and Tomorrow*. Englewood Cliffs, NJ: Prentice Hall, 1981.

———. "Husband's Paid Work and Family Roles: Current Research Issues." In H. Lopata and J. H. Pleck (eds.), *Research in the Interweave of Social Roles: Families and Jobs*, Vol. 3. Greenwich, CT: JAI Press, 1983.

Putnam, F. W. *Diagnosis and Treatment of Multiple Personality Disorder*. New York: Guilford Press, 1989.

Reinisch, J. M. *The Kinsey Institute New Report on Sex*. New York: St. Martin's Press, 1990.

Reiss, D. *The Family's Construction of Reality*. Cambridge, MA: Harvard University Press, 1981.

Retzinger, S. M. *Violent Emotions: Shame and Rage in Marital Quarrels*. Newbury Park, CA: Sage, 1991.

Rich, A. *Of Woman Born*. New York: W. W. Norton, 1976.

———. *The Dream of a Common Language*. New York: W. W. Norton, 1978.

———. *Women and Honor: Some Notes on Lying*. Pittsburgh: Cleis Press, 1990.

Rivers, C.; Barnett, R.; and Baruch, G. *Beyond Sugar and Spice: How Women Grow, Learn, and Thrive*. New York: Putnam, 1979.

Rosenblatt, P. C., and Cunningham, M. R. "Television Watching and Family Tensions." *Journal of Marriage and the Family* 38, No. 1 (1976): 105–111.

Rubin, L. B. *Worlds of Pain: Life in the Working-Class Family*. New York: Basic Books, 1976.

———. *Women of a Certain Age: The Midlife Search for Self*. New York: Harper & Row, 1979.

———. *Intimate Strangers: Men and Women Together*. New York: Harper & Row, 1983.

———. *Just Friends: The Role of Friendship in Our Lives*. New York: Harper & Row, 1985.

Ruble, D. "Sex-Role Development." In M. H. Bornstein and M. E. Lamb (eds.), *Developmental Psychology: An Advanced Textbook*. Hillsdale, NJ: Lawrence Erlbaum, 1983.

Russell, D. *The Secret Trauma: Incest in the Lives of Girls and Women*. New York: Basic Books, 1987.

Sameroff, A. J., and Emde, R. N. (eds.). *Relationship Disturbances in Early Childhood: A Developmental Approach*. New York: Basic Books, 1989.

Sanday, P. R. *Female Power and Male Dominance: On the Origins of Sexual Inequality*. Cambridge, England: Cambridge University Press, 1981.

———. *Fraternity Gang Rape: Sex, Brotherhood and Privilege on Campus*. New York: New York University Press, 1990.

Sandler, J. *Projection, Identification, Projective Identification*. Madison, CT: International Universities Press, 1987.

Schaef, A. W. *Co-dependence: Misunderstood—Mistreated*. Cambridge, MA: Harper & Row, 1986.

Schafer, R. *Aspects of Internalization*. New York: International Universities Press, 1968.

———. *A New Language for Psychoanalysis*. New Haven, CT: Yale University Press, 1976.

Schor, J. *The Overworked American: The Unexpected Decline of Leisure*. New York: Basic Books, 1991.

Selye, H. *The Stress of Life*. 2nd ed. New York: McGraw-Hill, 1976.

Shapiro, E. G. "Effects of Expectation of Future Interaction on Reward Allocation in Dyads: Equity or Equality." *Journal of Personality and Social Psychology* 31 (1975): 873–880.

Shapiro, J. *Men: A Translation for Women*. New York: NAL/Dutton, 1992.

Silverman, P. R. *Helping Women Cope with Grief*. Beverly Hills, CA: Sage, 1981.

Smith, G. T.; Snyder, D. K.; Trull, T. J.; and Monsma, B. R. "Predicting Relationship Satisfaction from Couples' Use of Leisure Time." *American Journal of Family Therapy* 16, No. 1 (1988): 3–13.

Smith, J. H., and Kerrigan, W. (eds.). *Interpreting Lacan: Psychiatry and the Humanities*, Vol. 6. New Haven, CT: Yale University Press, 1983.

Sobol, D. J. *The Amazons of Greek Mythology*. South Brunswick, NJ: A. S. Barnes, 1972.

Spelman, E. V. *The Inessential Women: Problems of Exclusion in Feminist Thought*. Boston: Beacon Press, 1988.

Spitz, R. A. *The First Year of Life: A Psychoanalytic Study of Normal and Deviant Development of Object Relations*. New York: International Universities Press, 1965.

Steinem, G. *Revolution from Within: A Book of Self-esteem*. Boston: Little, Brown, 1992.

Stephans, S. *When Death Comes Home*. New York: Morehouse-Barlow, 1973.

Stern, D. *The Interpersonal World of the Infant*. New York: Basic Books, 1985.

Stiver, I. P. "Work Inhibitions in Women: Clinical Considerations." *Stone Center Work in Progress Papers* 82 (1983): 1–11.

———. *The Meanings of "Dependency" in Female-Male Relationships*. Wellesley, MA: Stone Center, Wellesley College, 1984.

Stoller, R. J. *Presentations of Gender*. New Haven, CT: Yale University Press, 1985.

Stone, M. *When God Was A Woman*. San Diego: Harcourt Brace Jovanovich, 1978.

Straus, M. A. *Battered Women and the New Hampshire Justice System*. Durham, NH: University of New Hampshire Family Research Laboratory, 1980.

Straus, M. A., and Allen, C. M. "Resources, Power, and Husband-Wife Violence." In M. A. Straus and G. T. Hotaling (eds.), *The Social Causes of Husband-Wife Violence*. Minneapolis: University of Minnesota Press, 1980.

Straus, M. A., and Gelles, R. J. "Societal Change and Change in Family Violence from 1975 to 1985 as Revealed by Two National Surveys." *Journal of Marriage and the Family* 48, No. 3 (1986): 465–479.

———. *Physical Violence in American Families: Risk Factors and Adaptations to Violence in 8,145 Families*. New Brunswick, NJ: Transaction Publications, Rutgers University, 1989.

Straus, M. A.; Gelles, R. J.; and Steinmetz, S. *Behind Closed Doors*. New York: Doubleday, 1980.

Straus, M. A., and Williams, K. R. *Homicide Victimization and Offense Rates by Age, Gender, Race, Relation of Victim to Offender, Weapon Used, and Circumstances, for the United States, 1976–79 and 1980–84*. Durham, NH: University of New Hampshire Family Research Laboratory, 1988.

Stroebe, W., and Stroebe, M. S. *Bereavement and Health: The Psychological and Physical Consequences of Partner Loss*. New York: Cambridge University Press, 1987.

Sugar, M. "Sexual Abuse of Children and Adolescents." *Adolescent Psychiatry* 11 (1983): 199–211.

Sullivan, H. S. *The Interpersonal Theory of Psychiatry*. New York: W. W. Norton, 1953.

———. *The Collected Works of Harry Stack Sullivan, M. D.* Ed. H. S. Perry and M. L. Gawel. New York: W. W. Norton, 1956.

Surrey, J. L. *Self-in-relation: A Theory of Women's Development*. Wellesley, MA: Stone Center, Wellesley College, 1985.

Sutton-Smith, B. *The Psychology of Play*. Salem, NH: Ayer, 1976.

Tannen, D. *You Just Don't Understand: Women and Men in Conversation*. New York: William Morrow, 1990.

Tavris, C. *Anger: The Misunderstood Emotion*. New York: Simon & Schuster/Touchstone, 1989. (Original work published 1982.)

———. *The Mismeasure of Woman*. New York: Simon & Schuster, 1992.

Taylor, C. *Sources of the Self: The Making of the Modern Identity*. Cambridge, MA: Harvard University Press, 1989.

Teachman, J. D., and Polonko, K. A. "Cohabitation and Marital Stability in the United States." *Social Forces* 69, No. 1 (1990): 207–220.

Thorne, B., and Henley, N. (eds.) *Language and Sex: Difference and Dominance*. Rowley, MA: Newbury House, 1975.

Thorne, B.; Kramarae, C.; and Henley, N. (eds.). *Language, Gender, and Society*. Rowley, MA: Newbury House, 1983.

Trevarthen, C. "Emotions in Infancy: Regulators of Contact and Relationships with Persons." In K. R. Scherer and P. Ekman (eds.), *Approaches to Emotions*. Hillsdale, NJ: Lawrence Erlbaum, 1984.

Troop, S. B., and Green, W. A. (eds.). *The Patient, Death and the Family*. New York: Scribner's, 1974.

Tyrrell, W. B. *Amazons, a Study in Athenian Mythmaking*. Baltimore: Johns Hopkins University Press, 1984.

United Media Enterprises Report on Leisure in America. *Where Does the Time Go?* New York: United Media Enterprises, 1982.

U.S. Bureau of the Census. "Marital Status and Living Arrangements." March 1983 Current Population Reports, Series P-20, No. 389. Washington, DC: Government Printing Office, 1984.

Vaillant, G. E. *Adaptation to Life*. Boston: Little, Brown, 1977.

Visher, E. B., and Visher, J. *Stepfamilies: A Guide to Working with Stepparents and Stepchildren*. New York: Brunner-Mazel, 1979.

———. *Stepfamilies: Myths and Realities*. New York: Carol Publishing Group, 1980.

———. *Old Loyalties, New Ties: Therapeutic Strategies with Stepfamilies*. New York: Brunner-Mazel, 1988.

Wagman, B., and Folbre, N. "The Feminization of Inequality: Some New Patterns." *Challenge* 31, No. 6 (1988): 56–59.

Walker, L. E. *The Battered Woman*. New York: HarperCollins, 1980.

———. *The Battered Woman Syndrome*. New York: Springer, 1984.

———. "Psychology and Violence Against Women." *American Psychologist* 44 (1989): 695–702.

———. *Terrifying Love: Why Battered Women Kill and How Society Responds*. New York: HarperCollins, 1989.

———. *Handbook on Sexual Abuse of Children: Assessment and Treatment Issues*. New York: Springer, 1988.

Wallerstein, J. S., and Kelly, J. B. *Surviving the Breakup: How Children and Parents Cope with Divorce*. New York: Basic Books, 1990.

Weiss, R. S. *Loneliness: The Experience of Emotional and Social Isolation*. Cambridge, MA: MIT Press, 1973.

———. *Marital Separation*. New York: Basic Books, 1975.

———. "Men and Their Wives' Work." In F. J. Crosby (ed.), *Spouse, Parent, Worker: On Gender and Multiple Roles*. New Haven, CT: Yale University Press, 1989.

Weiss, R. S., and Burlage, D. *The Family: A Review of Current Research Issues*. Cambridge, MA: American Institutes for Research, 1976.

Whitfield, C. L. *Healing the Child Within: Discovery and Recovery for Adult Children of Dysfunctional Families*. Pompano Beach, FL: Health Communications, 1987.

Whitmont, E. C. *The Symbolic Quest: Basic Concepts of Analytic Psychology*. New York: Putnam, 1969.

Whitmont, E. C., and Perera, S. B. *Dreams, a Portal to the Source*. New York: Routledge, 1989.

Winnicott, D. W. *Mother and Child: A Primer of First Relationships*. New York: Basic Books, 1957.

———. *The Family and Individual Development*. New York: Basic Books, 1965.

———. *The Maturational Process and the Facilitating Environment*. New York: International University Press, 1965.

———. *Playing and Reality*. London: Tavistock, 1971.

———. *Home Is Where We Start From*. Compiled and ed. C. Winnicott, R. Sheperd, and M. Davis. New York: W. W. Norton, 1986.

Wolf, N. *The Beauty Myth: How Images of Beauty Are Used Against Women*. New York: William Morrow, 1991.

Wolfe, V. V., and Wolfe, D. A. "The Sexually Abused Child." In E. J. Mash and L. G. Terdal (eds.), *Behavior Assessment of Childhood Disorders*, 2nd ed. New York: Guilford Press, 1988.

Woodman, M. *The Owl Was a Baker's Daughter: Obesity, Anorexia Nervosa and the Repressed Feminine: A Psychological Study*. Toronto: Inner City Books, 1980.

———. *Leaving My Father's House: A Journey to Conscious Femininity*. Boston: Shambhala, 1992.

Woolf, V. *A Room of One's Own*. San Diego: Harcourt Brace Jovanovich, 1989. (Original work published 1929.)

Wylie, P. *Sons and Daughters of Mom*. Garden City, NY: Doubleday, 1971.

Wynne, L. C. (ed.). *The State of the Art in Family Therapy Research: Controversies and Recommendations*. New York: Family Process Press, 1988.

Young-Bruehl, E. *Anna Freud: A Biography*. New York: Summit Books, 1988.

Young-Eisendrath, P. *Hags and Heroes: A Feminist Approach to Jungian Psychotherapy with Couples.* Toronto: Inner City Books, 1984.

———. "Rethinking Feminism, the Animus and the Feminine." In C. Zweig (ed.), *To Be a Woman*. Los Angeles: Tarcher, 1990.

———. "Gender, Animus, and Related Topics." In N. Schwart-Salant and M. Stein (eds.), *Gender and Soul in Psychotherapy,* Chiron Clinical Series. Wilmette, IL: Chiron, 1991.

Young-Eisendrath, P., and Hall, J. *Jung's Self Psychology: A Constructivist Perspective*. New York: Guilford Press, 1991.

Young-Eisendrath, P., and Wiedemann, F. *Female Authority: Empowering Women Through Psychotherapy*. New York: Guilford Press, 1987.

Zusne, L., and Jones, W. H. *Anomalistic Psychology: A Study of Magical Thinking*. 2nd ed. Hillsdale, NJ: Lawrence Erlbaum, 1989.

INDEX

index